Student's name: ______________________ Assignment date: __

Primary Grades Math Test Review Assessment

低年级数学 測試複習考核

Frank Ho Amanda Ho

何数棋谜 培训

Ho Math Chess Learning Centre

Student's name: ____________________ Assignment date: ________________

Table of contents

Student's name: ____________________ Assignment date: ________________

Student's name: ____________________ Assignment date: ______________

Student's name: ____________________ Assignment date: ________________

Student's name: ____________________ Assignment date: ________________

Student's name: ____________________ Assignment date: ________________

Student's name: ____________________ Assignment date: ________________

Student's name: ____________________ Assignment date: ________________

Student's name: ____________________ Assignment date: ________________

Student's name: ____________________ Assignment date: ________________

Preface

We have seen that many students did their homework but still could not get A mark consistently. One of the problems is that even though they did their homework or assignments, but the problems given in quizzes or tests by their day school teachers are different from what they did in their homework. Some students also need more practice or tests, and there are not enough test problems in their textbooks. Often it because some students could use a quick review to boost their marks.

This workbook was not written just for reviewing, testing, or assessing purposes. Students can also use it to learn new concepts and get ahead.

It is challenging to produce a workbook to be used worldwide by instructors all over the world. This workbook can be used worldwide to meet the needs of students with advanced abilities in many countries. How did we produce such a workbook? We have combed through many math books produced by many countries and areas, including China, the USA, Canada, Hong Kong, Taiwan, Singapore etc., to compare their contents and studied their exam papers. We also studied many math problems in the IB program, SSAT math part, and regional and international math assessments. Doing these researches allows us to produce some problems that have a very high standard and some average problems for beginner's level.

All drawings in this workbook may not represent the exact scales.

This workbook can be used for lower and middle grades.

Frank Ho
Amanda Ho

December 22, 2015

Please email your comments or suggestions about this workbook to fho1928@gmail.com.

Ho Math Chess Primary Grades Math

Test Review assesssment 何数棋謎低年级数学测试複習考核

Student's name: ____________________ Assignment date: ________________

***** Part 1 Whole numbers operations *****

Results of additions or subtractions less than or equal to 20

3 + 7 =	9 + 7 =	11– 3 =	13 – 4 =
13 + 7 =	3 + 6 =	8 + 6 =	11 – 5 =
18 – 9 =	8 + 6 =	9 + 5 =	7 + 6 =
3 + 7 =	14 – 5 =	11 – 5 =	8 + 3 =
11 + 7 =	17 – 3 =	12 – 7 =	12 + 6 =
5 + 7 =	17 – 5 =	14 + 6 =	5 + 9 =
15 – 2 =	4 + 6 =	6 + 7 =	14 – 5 =
11 + 6 =	13 – 4 =	9 + 6 =	7 + 4 =
6+ 8 =	15 – 6 =	5 + 16 =	5 + 6 =
17 – 3 =	12 + 6 =	17 – 6 =	12 + 6 =
13 – 4 =	4 + 12 =	13 + 5 =	5 + 14 =
7 + 6 =	11 – 6 =	5 + 13 =	15 – 8 =
5 + 6 =	19 – 7 =	14 + 6 =	14 + 6 =
18 – 5 =	12 – 5 =	5 + 14 =	5 + 15 =
16 – 7 =	14 + 6 =	12 – 7 =	9 + 7 =
14 + 6 =	6+ 13 =	13– 4 =	5 + 6 =
15 + 4 =	16 – 2 =	11 + 6 =	13 – 5 =
10 – 4 =	6 + 6 =	5 + 6 =	12 – 5 =
17 – 2 =	5 + 6 =	12 + 6 =	17 – 4 =
13 + 6 =	18– 9 =	5 + 12 =	11 + 8=
5 + 8 =	12– 5 =	20 – 4 =	5 + 6 =
12– 5 + 2 =	6 + 9 – 3 =	11 + 7 – 6 =	12– 5 + 5 =
3 + 13 – 2 =	14 – 9 + 2 =	12 + 4 – 2 =	5 + 9 – 7 =
17 – 8 + 1 =	10 + 9 – 6 =	13– 4 + 5 =	1 +19 – 2 =
1 + 9 – 2 = 8	18 – 5 + 3 =	1 + 9 – 2 =	11– 5 + 5 =

Ho Math Chess Primary Grades Math

Test Review assesssment 何数棋謎低年级数学测试複習考核

Student's name: ____________________ Assignment date: ________________

3-digit addition or subtraction with borrowing from or carrying over

587 − 497	210 − 199	301 − 198	507 − 368	255 − 146	371 − 183
202 − 106 96	821 −738	542 −453	345 − 254	222 − 133	344 − 255 89
204 −115	221 −216	369 −298	333 − 287	567 − 476	345 −298
911 − 799	412 − 234	587 + 497	210 +199	301 + 198	345 +254
911 +799	507 +368	255 +146	371 +183	202 +106	821 +738
542 + 453	222 + 133	344 + 255	204 + 115	221 +216	369 + 298
333 + 287	567 + 476	345 +298	487 + 234	534 + 287	321 +478
487 − 234	534 − 287	521 − 478	471 − 289	505 − 386	431 − 278

Student's name: ____________________ Assignment date: ________________

Repeated addition, multiplication

Problems	Skip counting from n	m groups of n circles each	Repeated additions	Arrays (row × column)
3 × 5	Skip counting from 5 5, 10, 15	3 groups of 5 circles each (○○○○○) (○○○○○) (○○○○○)	3 repeated additions of 5 5 + 5 + 5 = 15	3 rows by 5 columns ○○○○○ ○○○○○ ○○○○○
5 × 3				
				○○○○○○ ○○○○○○ ○○○○○○
				○○○ ○○○ ○○○ ○○○ ○○○ ○○○
	5, 10, 15, 20			○○○○○ ○○○○○ ○○○○○ ○○○○○

Student's name: ____________________ Assignment date: ________________

Repeated subtraction and division

Problems	Skip counting from n	m groups of n equal number of items (circles) in each group	Repeated subtractions
Divide 24 pies into a group of 4 each. How many groups?	Skip counting from 4 4, 8, 12, 16, 20, 24 6 groups	24 items with 4 in each group ○○○○ ○○○○ ○○○○ ○○○○ ○○○○ ○○○○	Repeated subtractions of 4 24 – 4 – 4 – 4 – 4 – 4 – 4 = 0
Share 12 oranges by 3 persons. How many oranges does each person get?			
21 cookies with 3 in each group. How many groups are there?			
Divide 20 balls into 5 groups with an equal number of balls in each group.			

Student's name: ____________________ Assignment date: ________________

Multiplication

4 × 7	10 × 9	21 × 8	87 × 4	45 × 8
69 × 8	21 × 6	55 × 6	45 × 9	7 × 68
497 × 9	301 × 5	12 × 11	71 × 83	21 × 38
42 × 53	45 × 54	33 × 87	67 × 76	799 × 54
202 × 106	222 × 133	344 × 255	204 × 115	471 × 289
505 × 386	431 × 278	709 × 806	507 × 497	890 × 608

Student's name: ____________________ Assignment date: ________________

Divisions with 0 in the quotient

2 ⟌ 42	21 ⟌ 42	21 ⟌ 42042
3 ⟌ 420	12 ⟌ 420	12 ⟌ 4204200
3 ⟌ 36036	12 ⟌ 36036	12 ⟌ 36003600
4 ⟌ 4800408	3 ⟌ 4800408	24 ⟌ 4800408
5 ⟌ 5055015	3 ⟌ 5055015	15 ⟌ 555015
37 ⟌ 16761	29 ⟌ 11223	19 ⟌ 11153

Ho Math Chess Primary Grades Math

Test Review assesssment 何数棋謎低年级数学测试複習考核

Student's name: ____________________ Assignment date: ________________

Mixed operations

4 × 3 =	18 ÷ 3 =	26 − 9 =	43 + 8 =
3 + 9 =	17 − 9 =	24 × 5 =	16 ÷ 2 =
15 − 4 =	12 × 9 =	23 + 8 =	12 ÷ 4 =
25 ÷ 5 =	26 − 9 =	24 × 3 =	21 + 3 =
4 × 4 =	45 ÷ 9 =	18 + 7 =	19 − 8 =
14 × 5 =	18 + 7 =	15 − 7 =	25 + 9 =
16 + 5 =	14 − 9 =	17 × 4 =	21 ÷ 3 =
23 + 8 =	23 − 9 =	14 × 6 =	48 ÷ 6 =
14 × 7 =	16 ÷ 8 =	23 − 7 =	17 + 8 =
14 ÷ 7 =	23 − 9 =	18 × 3 =	23 + 5 =
26 × 3 =	24 + 8 =	23 − 9 =	28 ÷ 4 =
12 ÷ 6 =	15− 9 =	17 × 3 =	77 + 8 =
4 × 9 =	25 ÷ 5 =	14 − 8 =	55 + 8 =
13 − 4 =	24 × 8 =	23 + 8 =	27 ÷ 3 =
4 × 3 =	36 ÷ 6 =	27 − 9 =	29 + 8 =
18 − 9 =	14 × 7 =	33 + 7 =	21 ÷ 3 =
24 × 3 =	15 ÷ 5 =	24 − 9 =	23 + 8 =
23 + 8 =	13− 9 =	23 − 6 =	49 ÷ 7 =
40 ÷ 8 =	24 × 5 =	31 − 9 =	34 + 5 =
24 × 5 =	13 + 8 =	27 − 8 =	54 ÷ 9 =
15 − 9 =	36 ÷ 9 =	24 × 5 =	29 + 8 =

Student's name: ____________________ Assignment date: ________________

Test of mixed operations

14 × 3 =	12 ÷ 3 =	96 – 9 =	13 + 8 =
32 + 9 =	12 – 9 =	44 × 5 =	36 ÷ 2 =
55 – 4 =	14 × 9 =	13 + 8 =	12 ÷ 4 =
55 ÷ 5 =	21 – 9 =	14 × 3 =	69 + 3 =
24 × 4 =	27 ÷ 9 =	18 + 8 =	19 – 8 =
34 × 5 =	17 + 7 =	23 – 7 =	15 + 9 =
56 + 5 =	91 – 9 =	15 × 4 =	69 ÷ 3 =
43 + 8 =	41 – 9 =	34 × 6 =	72 ÷ 6 =
14 × 7 =	24 ÷ 8 =	21 – 7 =	37 + 8 =
84 ÷ 7 =	33 – 9 =	14 × 3 =	53 + 5 =
16 × 3 =	74 + 8 =	26 – 9 =	72 ÷ 4 =
72 ÷ 6 =	21 – 9 =	14 × 3 =	78 + 8 =
14 × 9 =	75 ÷ 5 =	16 – 8 =	85 + 8 =
47 – 4 =	24 × 8 =	33 + 8 =	24 ÷ 3 =
24 × 3 =	96 ÷ 6 =	77 – 9 =	23 + 8 =
28 – 9 =	14 × 5 =	73 + 7 =	81 ÷ 3 =
84 × 3 =	25 ÷ 5 =	24 – 9 =	93 + 8 =
93 + 8 =	23 – 9 =	33 – 6 =	42 ÷ 7 =
40 ÷ 8 =	34 × 5 =	81 – 9 =	64 + 5 =
34 × 5 =	93 + 8 =	77 – 8 =	54 ÷ 9 =
35 – 9 =	36 ÷ 9 =	34 × 5 =	39 + 8 =

Ho Math Chess Primary Grades Math

Test Review assesssment 何数棋謎低年级数学测试複習考核

Student's name: ____________________ Assignment date: ________________

Mixed operations

24 × 3 =	39 ÷ 3 =	42 − 9 =	53 + 8 =
33 + 9 =	12− 7 =	34 × 5 =	36 ÷ 4 =
53 − 6 =	24 × 9 =	23 + 8 =	54 ÷ 6 =
45 ÷ 5 =	12 − 9 =	24 × 3 =	59 + 4 =
14 × 4 =	36÷ 9 =	28 + 8 =	91 − 8 =
33 × 5 =	27 + 7 =	13 − 7 =	35 + 9 =
57 + 5 =	92 − 9 =	16 × 4 =	96 ÷ 3 =
25 + 8 =	43 − 9 =	32 × 6 =	36 ÷ 6 =
13 × 7 =	40 ÷ 8 =	23 − 7 =	39 + 8 =
63 ÷ 7 =	23 − 9 =	41 × 3 =	57 + 5 =
18 × 3 =	75 + 8 =	27 − 9 =	32 ÷ 4 =
84 ÷ 6 =	28 − 9 =	17 × 3 =	77 + 8 =
17 × 9 =	85 ÷ 5 =	17 − 8 =	85 + 8 =
20 − 4 =	16 × 8 =	34 + 8 =	21 ÷ 3 =
23 × 3 =	84 ÷ 6 =	75 − 9 =	24 + 8 =
28 − 9 =	14 × 5 =	73 + 7 =	84 ÷ 3 =
83 × 3 =	75 ÷ 5 =	31 − 9 =	95 + 8 =
92 + 8 =	28− 9 =	21 − 9 =	49 ÷ 7 =
48 ÷ 8 =	35 × 5 =	83 − 9 =	63 + 5 =
32 × 5 =	99 + 8 =	71 − 8 =	45 ÷ 9 =
23 − 9 =	45 ÷ 9 =	30 × 5 =	33 + 8 =

Student's name: ____________________ Assignment date: ________________

Number representations

Number in one, ten, hundred, and thousand representing by number blocks

A number can be expressed by using graphics representation, and it is called number blocks.

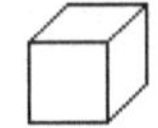

1 or 1 unit

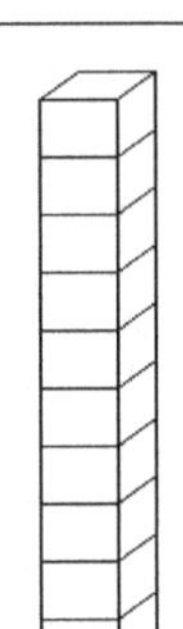

1 ten

or 10 units

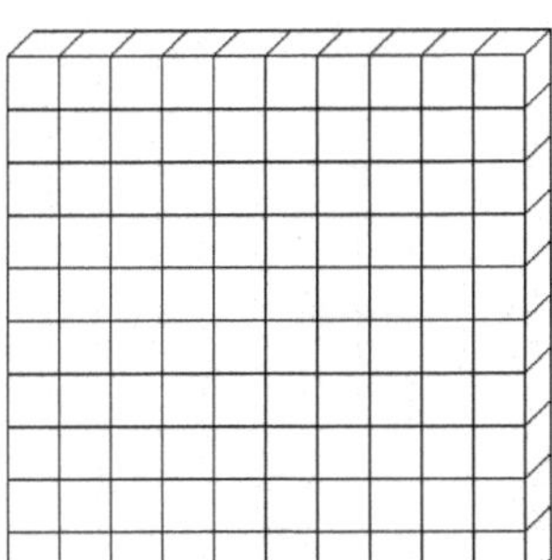

1 hundred
or _______ units

or _______ tens

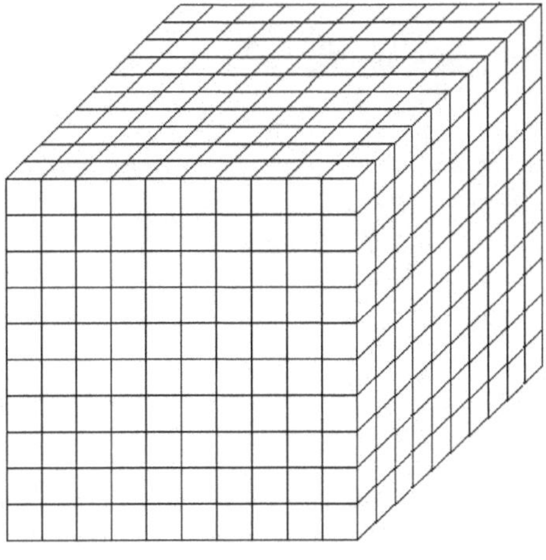

1 _______

or 1000 units

or _______ tens

or _______ hundreds

Student's name: ____________________ Assignment date: ________________

Convert number blocks to the standard number representing by digits.

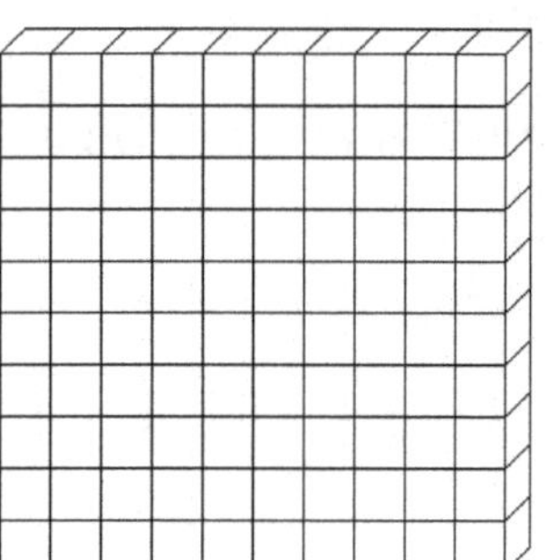
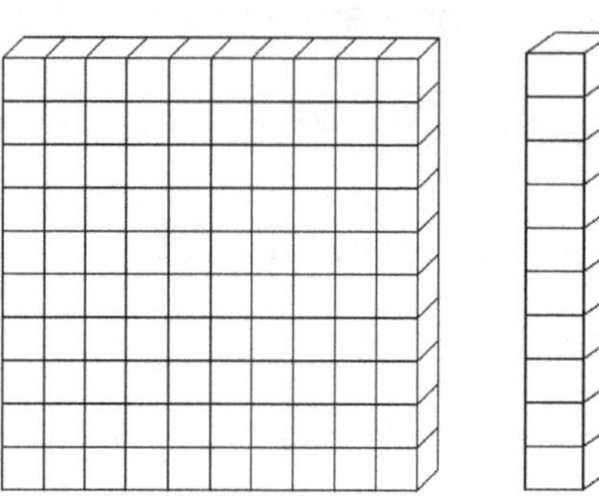
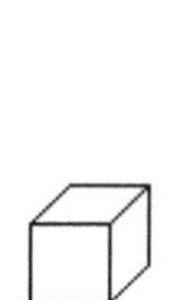

____

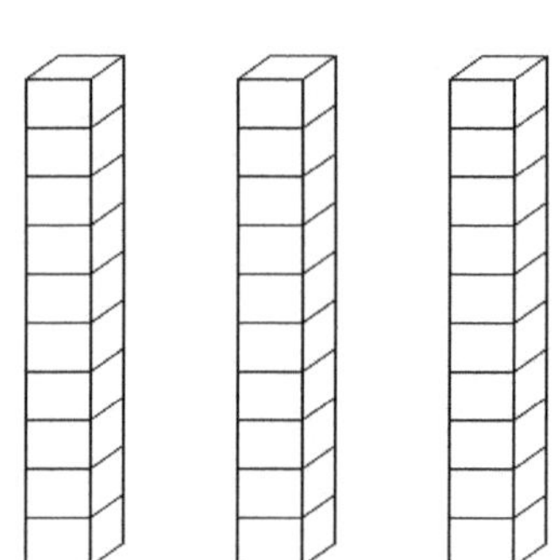
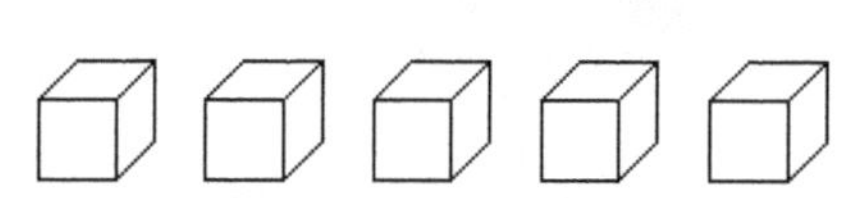

____

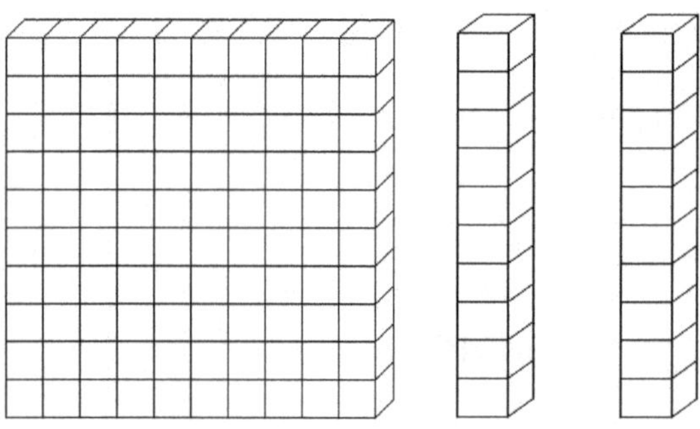
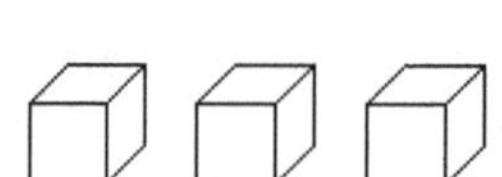

____

Student's name: ____________________ Assignment date: ________________

Convert number blocks to the standard number representing by digits.

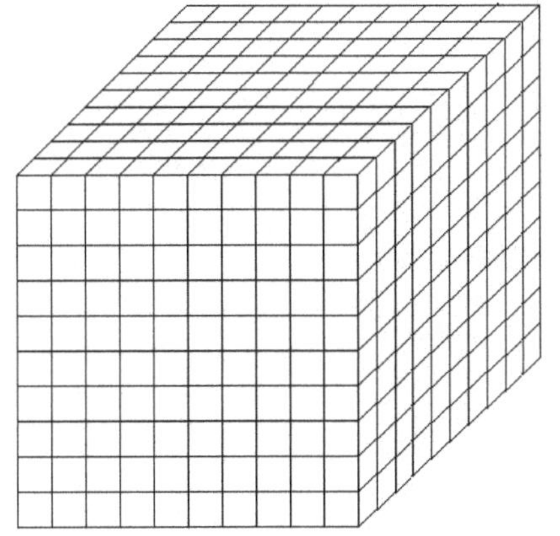
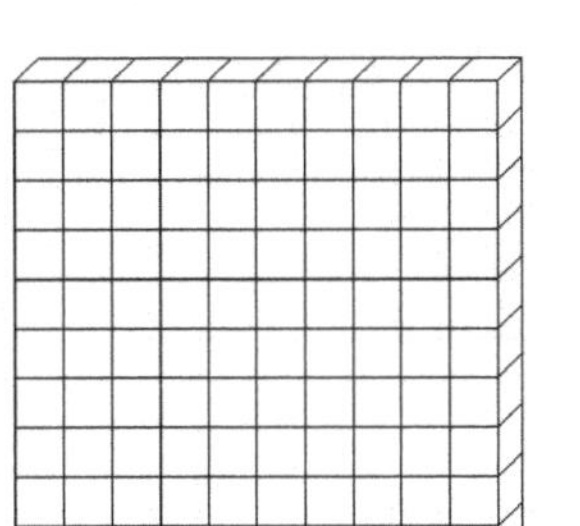
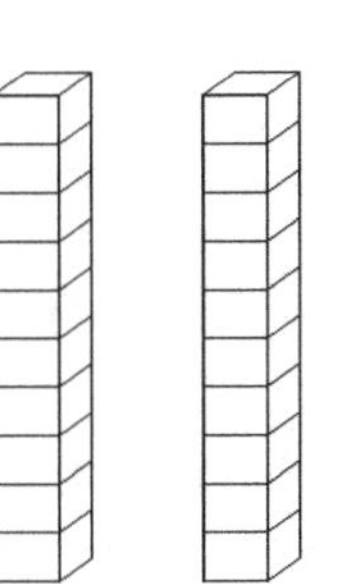
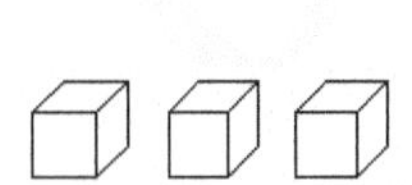

____

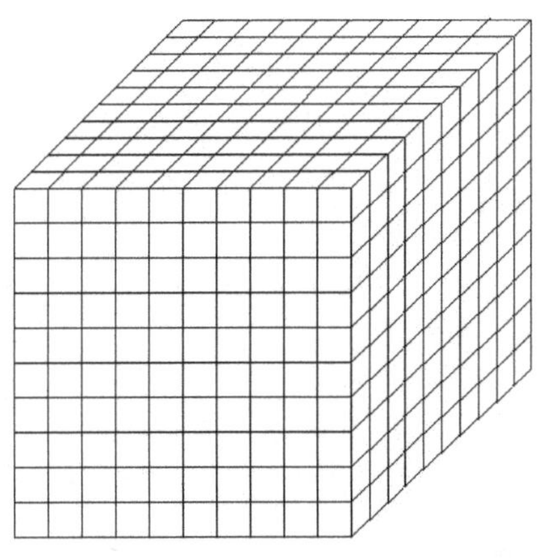
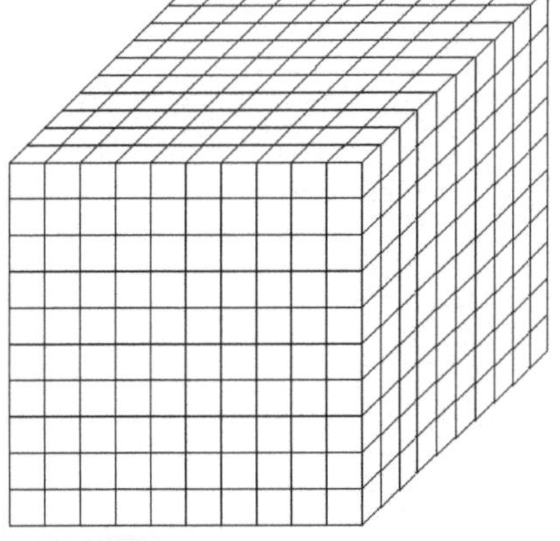
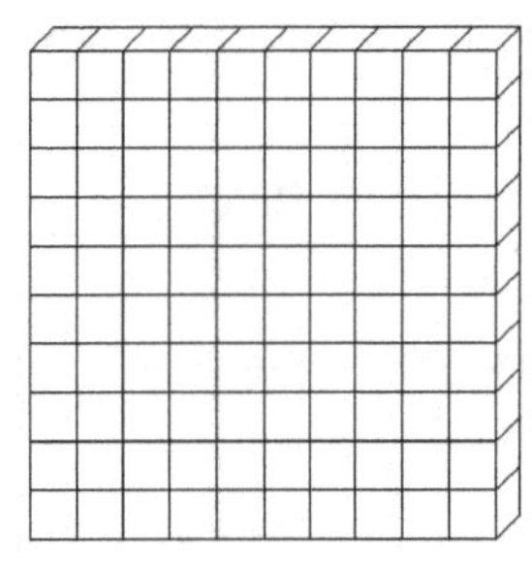

____

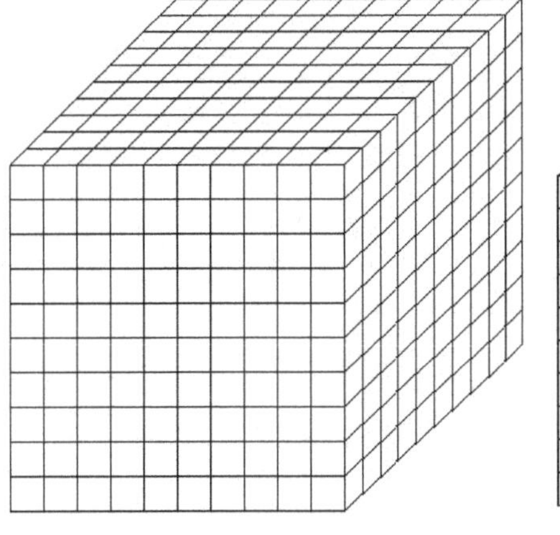
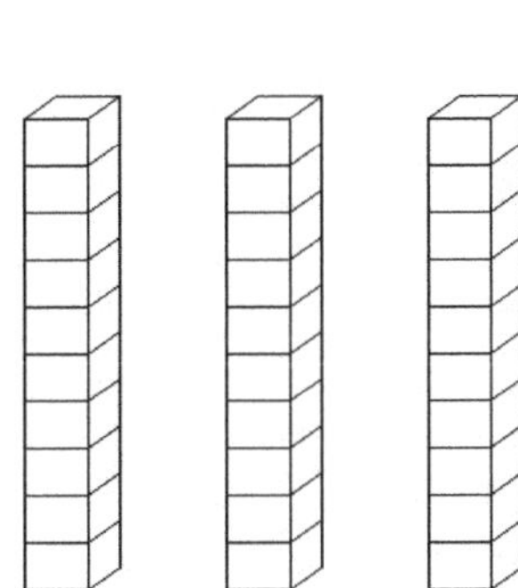
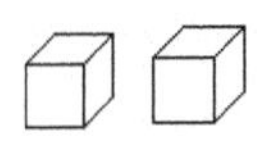

____

Student's name: ____________________ Assignment date: ________________

Convert words to standard numbers.

1. four thousand two hundred seventy-three __________.

2. six thousand eight hundred thirty-one __________.

3. one thousand ninety-five __________.

4. two thousand two hundred three __________.

5. five thousand six hundred ten __________.

6. four thousand five hundred nine __________.

7. eleven thousand two hundred thirty-four __________.

8. three hundred seventeen __________.

9. thirteen hundred fifty-three __________.

10. eight thousand two __________.

11. four thousand twelve __________.

12. six thousand three hundred three __________.

13. nine thousand eighty-five __________.

14. three thousand one hundred six __________.

15. six thousand nine __________.

Student's name: ____________________ Assignment date: ______________

Convert the standard number to English words.

1. 3000 ____.

2. 2574 ____.

3. 743 ____.

4. 2500 ____.

5. 2308 ____.

6. 3089 ____.

7. 6800 ____.

8. 5614 ____.

9. 8009 ____.

10. 60 ____.

11. 7800 ____.

12. 0 ____.

13. 3604 ____.

14. 5740 ____.

15. 6396 ____.

16. 7009 ____.

Student's name: ____________________ Assignment date: ________________

Whole number place value

A number may have one or more digits written from left to right, and each digit has a value depending on where it is placed. Understanding the concept of place value allows us to be able to read a number.
The names for place values are called differently when the same digit is placed at different locations.

Example

1234.4321

The above number is read as four thousand two hundred thirty-four and four thousand three hundred twenty-one thousandths

The names of place values for the whole numbers part and decimals part can be read as follows:

The ones place is also called the units' place.

If there are no place values, then how do you say the following number?

11111.1111

It would be awkward to say one one one one one point one one one one.

Student's name: ____________________ Assignment date: ________________

Choose the correct *place value* of 6 in each of the following numbers.

1.	1356	a. ones	b. tens	c. hundreds	d. thousands
2.	2657	a. ones	b. tens	c. hundreds	d. thousands
3.	6732	a. ones	b. tens	c. hundreds	d. thousands
4.	3651	a. ones	b. tens	c. hundreds	d. thousands
5.	7896	a. ones	b. tens	c. hundreds	d. thousands
6.	6312	a. ones	b. tens	c. hundreds	d. thousands
7.	2561	a. ones	b. tens	c. hundreds	d. thousands
8.	7463	a. ones	b. tens	c. hundreds	d. thousands

Student's name: ____________________ Assignment date: ________________

Choose the correct face *value* of 6 (The value at each place value representing by each digit.) in each of the following numbers.

1356	a. 6 ones	b. 6 tens	c. 6 hundreds	d. 6 thousands
2657	a. 6 ones	b. 6 tens	c. 6 hundreds	d. 6 thousands
6732	a. 6 ones	b. 6 tens	c. 6 hundreds	d. 6 thousands
3651	a. 6 ones	b. 6 tens	c. 6 hundreds	d. 6 thousands
7896	a. 6 ones	b. 6 tens	c. 6 hundreds	d. 6 thousands
6312	a. 6 ones	b. 6 tens	c. 6 hundreds	d. 6 thousands
2561	a. 6 ones	b. 6 tens	c. 6 hundreds	d. 6 thousands
7463	a. 6 ones	b. 6 tens	c. 6 hundreds	d. 6 thousands

Student's name: ____________________ Assignment date: ________________

Expanded forms of standard whole numbers

A standard number can be rewritten by the sum of its digits. This representation is called expanded from.

Example

Standard form: 3618 (English Words: three thousand six hundred twenty-eight)

Expanded form in *face value* of each digit:
3000 + 600 + 20 + 8

Expanded form in *place value* of each digit using English words:
3 thousands + 6 hundreds + 2 tens + 8 ones

Write the following number in expanded from using face value.

1. 6358 = 6000 + 300 + 50 + 8
2. 7420 = ____________________
3. 5837 = ____________________
4. 7256 = ____________________
5. 1943 = ____________________
6. 9162 = ____________________
7. 7903 = ____________________
8. 6820 = ____________________

Circle the number which is the greatest in the following.

- $3 \times 1000 + 4 \times 100 + 2 \times 10 + 5 \times 1$
- $3 \times 1000 + 5 \times 100 + 1 \times 10 + 5 \times 1$
- 3 thousands + 5 hundreds + 5 tens + 4 ones
- 3505
- 3560

Student's name: ____________________ Assignment date: ________________

Write each number in expanded form using English words.

1. 7042 = 7 thousands + 4 tens + 2 ones

2. 3805 = ____

3. 1237 = ____

4. 3065 = ____

5. 4200 = ____

6. 3080 = ____

7. 5003 = ____

8. 4251 = ____

Student's name: ____________________ Assignment date: ________________

Convert expanded form to standard form.

1. 6000 + 200 + 50 + 3 = 6253
2. 2000 + 500 + 30 + 8 = __________
3. 4000 + 600 + 10 + 2 = __________
4. 7000 + 200 + 9 = __________
5. 3000 + 400 + 8 = __________
6. 9000 + 200 + 50 = __________
7. 1000 + 7 = __________
8. 2000 + 80 + 6 = __________
9. 8000 + 100 + 5 = __________
10. 6 thousands + 5 hundreds + 2 tens + 9 ones = __________
11. 8 thousands + 3 hundreds + 1 ten + 7 ones = __________
12. 6 thousands + 2 hundreds + 4 tens + 5 ones = __________
13. 3 thousands + 8 hundreds + 5 ones = __________
14. 2 thousands + 4 hundreds + 3 tens + 9 ones = __________
15. 7 thousands + 7 tens + 6 ones = __________
16. 5 thousands + 3 hundreds + 8 tens = __________
17. 1 thousand + 8 tens + 1 one = __________

Student's name: ____________________ Assignment date: ________________

Write each number in all English words.

1. 21 tens ________two hundred ten__________
2. 32 tens ____________________________
3. 470 tens ____________________________
4. 36 hundreds ____________________________
5. 67 hundreds ____________________________
6. 18 hundreds ____________________________
7. 371 hundreds ____________________________
8. 4562 ones ____________________________
9. 35 hundreds ____________________________
10. 720 tens ____________________________
11. 29 hundreds ____________________________
12. 75 tens ____________________________
13. 10 hundreds ____________________________
14. 20 tens ____________________________
15. 305 tens ____________________________
16. 50 hundreds ____________________________
17. 1009 ones ____________________________
18. 107 tens ____________________________

Student's name: ____________________ Assignment date: ________________

Find as many ways as you can to show the following numbers.

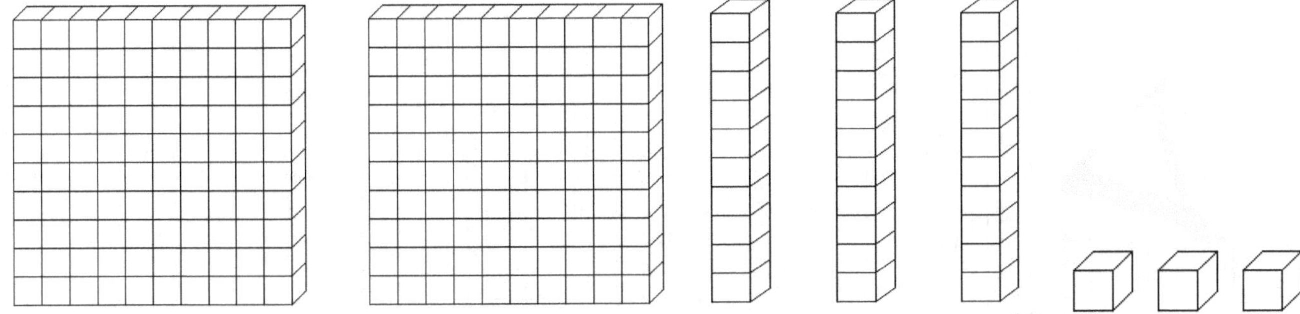

1.	Hundreds	Tens	Ones
2.	2	3	3
3.	2	2	13
4.			
5.			
6.			
7.			
8.			
9.			
10.			
11.			
12.			
13.			
14.			
15.			

Student's name: ____________________ Assignment date: ________________

Find as many ways as you can to show the following numbers.

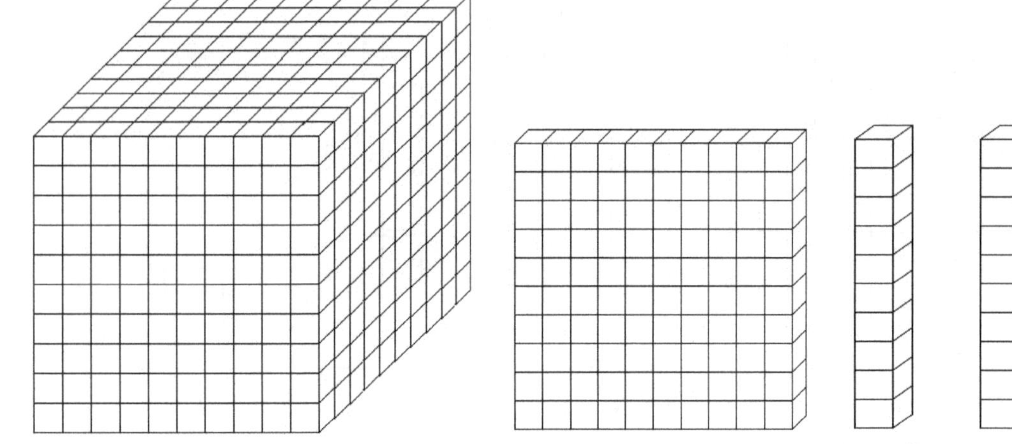

	Thousands	Hundreds	Tens	Ones
1.	1	1	2	3
2.	1	1	1	13
3.				
4.				
5.				
6.				
7.				
8.				
9.				
10.				
11.				
12.				
13.				
14.				

Student's name: ____________________ Assignment date: ________________

Circle the number that is closest to the leftmost number.

1.	560	a. 660	b. 521	c. 570	d. 568
2.	374	a. 384	b. 375	c. 743	d. 4374
3.	2560	a. 5236	b. 600	c. 3560	d. 2568
4.	3646	a. 364	b. 4578	c. 3656	d. 6613
5.	6894	a. 7012	b. 894	c. 8964	d. 9864
6.	2573	a. 2563	b. 2571	c. 2671	d. 2753
7.	8649	a. 9864	b. 8650	c. 8641	d. 4689
8.	2000	a. 999	b. 2111	c. 2005	d. 1999
9.	50	a. 25	b. 35	c. 45	d. 65
10.	4673	a. 4670	b. 4637	c. 4736	d. 7463
11.	6830	a. 6803	b. 6930	c. 6840	d. 6831
12.	6009	a. 9006	b. 6090	c. 9060	d. 6900
13.	2584	a. 2588	b. 2594	c. 2684	d. 3584
14.	2895	a. 1895	b. 2995	c. 2589	d. 2890
15.	6825	a. 7000	b. 6000	c. 6500	d. 5682
16.	4792	a. 7294	b. 4800	c. 4700	d. 4900

Student's name: ____________________ Assignment date: ________________

Count up or count down.

Example: Start at 10 and count up by 2's. 10 , 12 , 14 , 16 , 18 .

Start at 100 and count c by 5's. 100 , 95 , 90 , 85 , 80 .

1. Start at 45 and count up by 10's. ______ , ______ , ______ , ______ , ______.

2. Start at 29 and count up by 5's. ______ , ______ , ______ , ______ , ______.

3. Start at 300 and count up by 100's. ______ , ______ , ______ , ______ , ______.

4. Start at 10 and count up by 100's. ______ , ______ , ______ , ______ , ______.

5. Start at 4 and count up by 5's. ______ , ______ , ______ , ______ , ______.

6. Start at 19 and count down by 3's. ______ , ______ , ______ , ______ , ______.

7. Start at 102 and count v by 5's. ______ , ______ , ______ , ______ , ______.

8. Start at 115 and count down by 10's. ______ , ______ , ______ , ______ , ______.

9. Start at 925 and count back by 100's.______ , ______ , ______ , ______ , ______.

10. Start at 95 and count back by 3's. ______ , ______ , ______ , ______ , ______.

11. Start at 197 and count up by 25's. ______ , ______ , ______ , ______ , ______.

Student's name: ____________________ Assignment date: ________________

12. Start at 256 and count up by 50's. ______ , ______ , ______ , ______ , ______.

13. Start at 720 and count up by 200's. ______ , ______ , ______ , ______ , ______.

14. Start at 528 and count down by 20's. ______ , ______ , ______ , ______ , ______.

15. Start at 239 and count down by 10's. ______ , ______ , ______ , ______ , ______.

16. Start at 137 and count up by 50's. ______ , ______ , ______ , ______ , ______.

Student's name: ____________________ Assignment date: ________________

Greater than, more than, less than, between

Fill in each blank.

1. 10 greater than 4000 ____________________.
2. 300 less than 1000 ____________________.
3. 3 more than 200 ____________________.
4. 200 more than 5000 ____________________.
5. between 199 and 201 ____________________.
6. 1 less than 400 ____________________.
7. 40 more than 1060 ____________________.
8. between 6832 and 6834 ____________________.
9. 2 more than 998 ____________________.
10. 5 less than 2001 ____________________.

Student's name: ____________________ Assignment date: ________________

What number am I given place values (word problems of place values)?

I am a 3-digit number and have twice as many hundreds as tens, three times as many tens as ones. What am I?
I have half as many tens as hundreds, half as many hundreds as ones. I am over four-hundred. What am I?
I have 8 thousands, twice as many ones as thousands, half as many hundreds as ones and 3 more tens than ones. What am I?
I have a consecutive 4-digit number with the thousands place value as the largest digit. My ones of this number is calculated as follows: $4 - 2 \div 2$. What am I?
I have 15 hundreds, 9 tens, and 17 ones. What am I?
I am a 4-digit consecutive number and my ones digit is 1. What am I?

Ho Math Chess Primary Grades Math

Test Review assesssment 何数棋謎低年级数学测试複習考核

Student's name: ____________________ Assignment date: ________________

Place value word problems

1. There is a 2-digit number. The last digit is five. The number is between thirty and forty. What can that number be?

2. There are two zeros in a number and the number is less than two hundred. What can that number be?

3. There is a 3-digit number. The sum of its digits is three and there are no zeros in it. What can that number be?

are

4. The tens digit is twice as much as the ones digit. What could be the sum of the tens digit and the ones digit?

   Circle the correct answer.

   4, 5, 7, 8, 9

5. The left most digit 1 of the number 1234.4221 is how many times of the right-most 1?

6. I am a 4-digit number and my ones is 3 more than 2. My tens is 3 more than 1. My hundreds is 2 less than 10. My thousands is the result of splitting my hundreds equally. What am I?

Student's name: ____________________ Assignment date: ________________

The greatest and the least number

	digits	the greatest number	the least number with no leading 0's. No leading zeros.
1.	2, 4, 6, 8	8642	2468
2.	2, 3, 5, 8		
3.	4, 0, 7, 3		
4.	5, 1, 4, 7		
5.	3, 0, 2, 5		
6.	7, 4, 8, 3		
7.	5, 7, 2, 1		
8.	3, 9, 0, 2		
9.	2, 5, 5, 7		
10.	6, 1, 1, 8		
11.	2, 0, 0, 5		
12.	3, 6, 4, 5		
13.	6, 7, 5, 5		
14.	6, 0, 0, 6		

Student's name: ____________________ Assignment date: ________________

Compare the following numbers using > (greater than) or < (less than).

1.	6324	__	4879	2.	7303	__	4898
3.	5463	__	5364	4.	12685	__	12856
5.	120	__	1200	6.	999	__	1000
7.	2231	__	2241	8.	4478	__	4487
9.	5655	__	6555	10.	7538	__	7601
11.	3250	__	4103	12.	96	__	120

Circle the number that is greater than the number on the left most

1.	3518	a. 5138	b. 1468	c. 8351	d. 3185
2.	6484	a. 3684	b. 6548	c. 8446	d. 6348
3.	7951	a. 3758	b. 7953	c. 7591	d. 8001
4.	6083	a. 3806	b. 3386	c. 6088	d. 6830
5.	2753	a. 5237	b. 3572	c. 2537	d. 2235
6.	9732	a. 9741	b. 7933	c. 9823	d. 9703
7.	2063	a.3000	b.2300	c.2100	d.2000
8.	1650	a.1500	b.1600	c.1560	d.1056

Student's name: ____________________ Assignment date: ________________

Order each set of numbers from least to greatest.

1. 1643, 789, 6732, 5673

____.

2. 4573, 4628, 6274, 2890

____.

3. 55365, 56365, 55465, 55366

____.

4. 4731, 4745, 4754, 5474

____.

5. 5720, 3792, 7558, 5721

____.

Order each set of numbers from greatest to least.

1. 6743, 7643, 4673, 4763

____.

2. 5304, 4998, 8994, 4899

____.

3. 1000, 9999, 1002, 2001

____.

4. 85735, 85635, 85935, 76895,

____.

5. 5782, 4628, 5728, 6482

____.

Student's name: ____________________ Assignment date: ________________

Test of number representation and place value

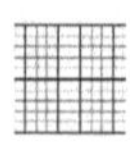

Solve the following number riddle. I have 13 tens, 7 ones, 3 hundreds. What am I?
I am 237 and I have 1 hundred and 9 ones. How many tens do I need to make up to 237?

Number written in standard form	Whole number written in English words	Number written in expanded form	Written in number and words using place values	Represented by Base Ten blocks	Value of the underlined digit
$46\underline{3}$					
$2\underline{5}9$					
$\underline{3}10$					
$\underline{4}302$					

Student's name: ____________________ Assignment date: ________________

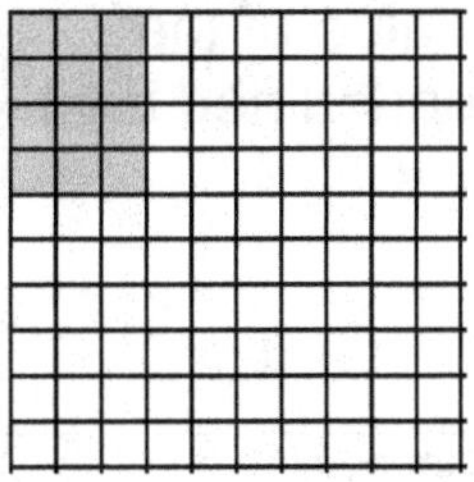

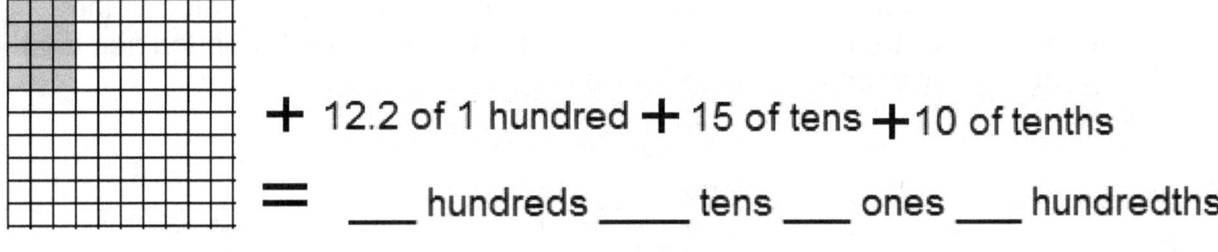

+ 12.2 of 1 hundred + 15 of tens + 10 of tenths

= ___ hundreds ____ tens ___ ones ___ hundredths

120 + 15 +  = ?

Find A and B.

$$\begin{array}{r} BA \\ -\ 74 \\ \hline 16 \end{array} \qquad \begin{array}{r} 6A \\ -\ B5 \\ \hline 18 \end{array}$$

Standard numbers	English words of place values of the underlined digit.	Face values	Rounding
$\underline{3}75,231,872.2134$			Round at 1,000,000.
$375,231,872.21\underline{3}5$			Round at 100th.

Student's name: ____________________ Assignment date: ________________

Number written in standard form	Number written in English words	Number written in expanded form	Written in number and words using place values	Represented by Base Ten blocks	Value of the underlined digit
			3 hundreds + 5 tens + 2 ones		Not available
96					Not available

Represented the following base ten blocks by fewer blocks

Standard number is?

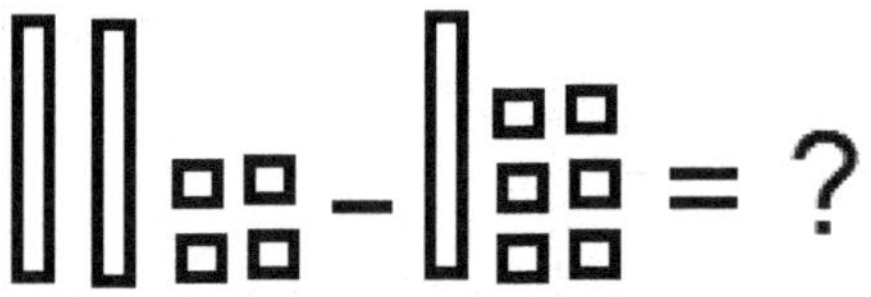

= ?

Student's name: ____________________ Assignment date: ________________

Use only digits 0 1 4 5 9 to create numbers and each digit cannot be repeated in each number.

Problems	Answers
What is the largest 4-digit number?	
What is the largest 3-digit number?	
What is the largest 4-digit even number?	
What is the largest 4-digit odd number?	
What is the largest 4-digit number with 4 in the hundreds place?	
What is the largest 4-digit number with 8 in the thousands place?	
What is the largest 4-digit number that is divisible by 4?	
What is the largest 3-digit odd number that is divisible by 3?	
What is the largest 3-digit even number that is divisible by 4?	

4213 – 2918 = 10 × ____ + 100 × ____ + 1000 × __+ 1 × ____

Student's name: ____________________ Assignment date: ________________

***** Part 2 Number Theory *****

Factor and primes

A natural number can always be expressed as a product of two other natural numbers. These two natural numbers are called factors. If a natural number can only be a product of the other two numbers, then this number is a prime number. If the factor is a prime, then it is called a prime factor.

The "Repeated Division`` method is used to find factors or prime factors.

What is the greatest odd factor of 48?
How many primes are there from 10 to 30?
The number x is a prime factor of 9, then what is the prime factor x + 3 =?
The greatest odd factor of 60 is ___________. 15

Student's name: ____________________ Assignment date: ________________

Multiplier

A number can be multiplied by 1, 2, 3, …etc.. These products are also called multiples. A number has infinite multiples. The results in the times table from 1×1 to 1×9 are multiples of 1.

I am a multiple of 5 between 0 and 39 and am also an odd number. What numbers could I be?
I am a multiple of 5 between 0 and 39 and am also an even number. What numbers could I be?
I am a multiple of 5 greater than 39 and less than 58 and am an even number. What numbers could I be?
I am a multiple of 5 greater than 39 and less than 58 and am an odd number. What numbers could I be?
I am a multiple of both 3 and 5 between 0 and 39 and am also an odd number. What numbers could I be?
I am a multiple of both 4 and 5 between 29 and 59. What numbers could I be?
I am a multiple of both 4 and 7 and am less than 100. What numbers could I be?

Ho Math Chess Primary Grades Math

Test Review assesssment 何数棋謎低年级数学测试複習考核

Student's name: ____________________ Assignment date: ________________

Odd and even numbers

Many students will answer that even numbers are 2, 4, 6, 8,… etc., but what happens to 1212? Is it even or odd? To understand that if the last digit (the rightmost one) of a number is 0, 2, 4, 6, 8, then it is an even number is important. In contrast, if the last digit (the rightmost one) of a number is 1, 3, 5, 7, 9, then it is an odd number.

.

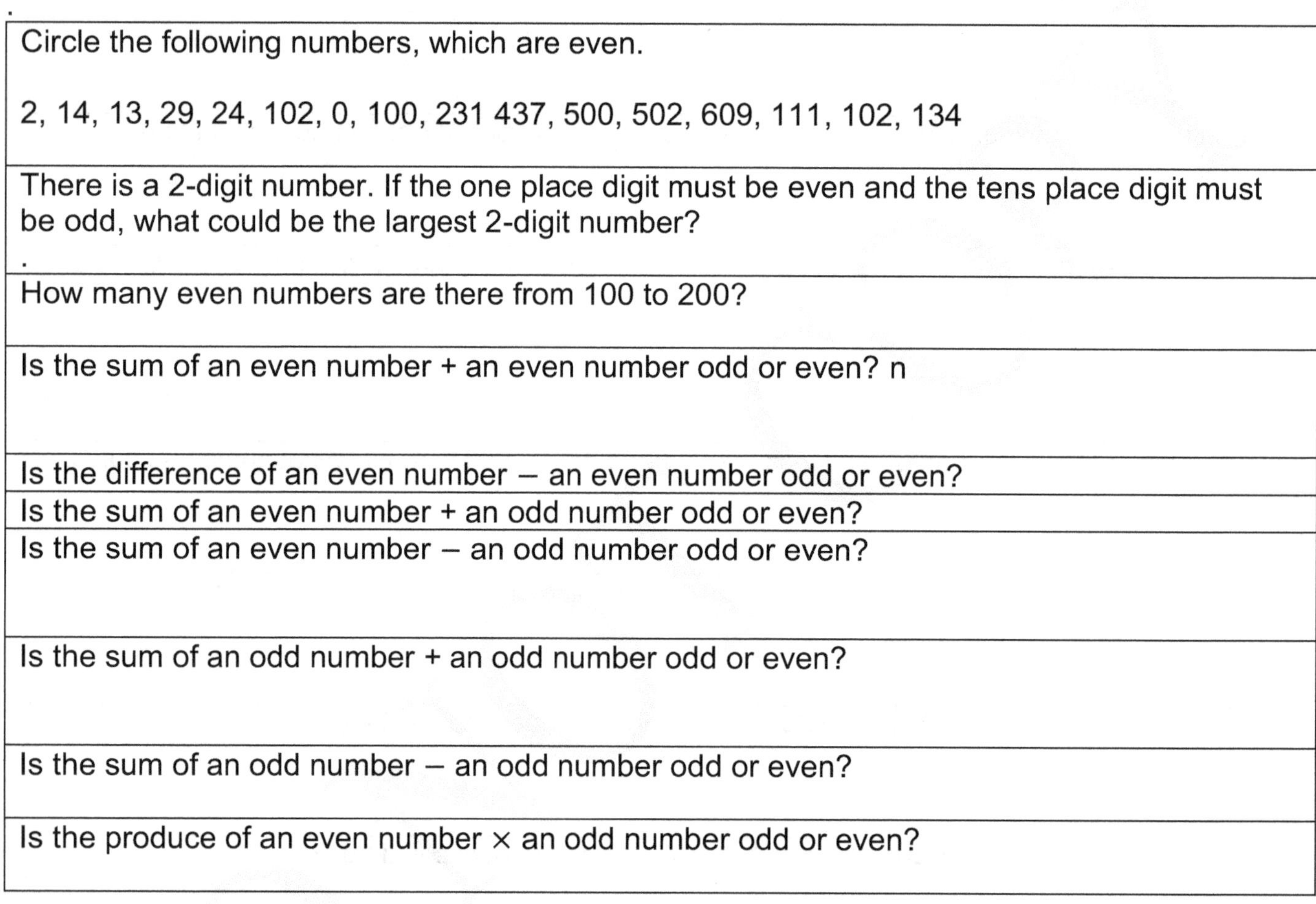

Circle the following numbers, which are even. 2, 14, 13, 29, 24, 102, 0, 100, 231 437, 500, 502, 609, 111, 102, 134
There is a 2-digit number. If the one place digit must be even and the tens place digit must be odd, what could be the largest 2-digit number? .
How many even numbers are there from 100 to 200?
Is the sum of an even number + an even number odd or even? n
Is the difference of an even number – an even number odd or even?
Is the sum of an even number + an odd number odd or even?
Is the sum of an even number – an odd number odd or even?
Is the sum of an odd number + an odd number odd or even?
Is the sum of an odd number – an odd number odd or even?
Is the produce of an even number × an odd number odd or even?

Student's name: ____________________ Assignment date: ________________

Divisibility Rules

Divisor	Numbers Divisible	Example	Reason
2	The last digit is even	8336	the last digit is even
3	The sum of digits is divisible by 3	411	4 + 1 + 1 = 6, 6 is divisible by 3
4	The last two digits are '00' or exactly divisible by 4	2132	32 ÷ 4 = 8
5	The last digit is '5' or '0'	3265	The unit digit is '5'
6	Any even number divisible by 3	1248	Is even and 1+2+4+8 = 15 is divisible by 3.
8	The last three digits are '00' or exactly divisible by 8	4624	624 ÷ 8 = 78
9	Sum of digits is divisible by 9	3141	3+1+4+1= 9 is divisible by 9.
10	The last digit is '0'	3620	unit digit is '0'

Student's name: ____________________ Assignment date: ________________

Divisibility rules word problems

Circle the following numbers which are divisible by 2 or 5. 10, 25, 50, 15, 30, 14, 16, 20, 55, 56, 100, 90
The ratio of the number of even numbers divisible by 4 between 17 to 29 to the number of odd numbers divisible by 3 between 24 and 36 is ________.
When a number is divided by 13 the quotient is 3 and the remainder is 2. What is the remainder of the same number is divided by 5?
What numbers between 111 and 279 are divisible by both 3 and 5?
There are three consecutive numbers and each of them is less than 100.The smallest is divisible by 3, the middle number is divisible by 2, and the largest is divisible by 5. What are these three numbers?
How many numbers less than 200 are divisible by either 2 or 5 but not both?

Student's name: ____________________ Assignment date: ________________

2, 3, and 5 are used to make a three-digit number $\overline{abc}$. The three digit number $\overline{abc}$ is divisible by 2. $\overline{ab}$ is divisible by 5. What is $\overline{abc}$?
Find the sum of all counting numbers less than 20, which are not divisible by 2 or 3.
The number 2325 is divisible by 3 and also 5. What is the next larger number which is divisible 3 and 5?
What is the smallest number that is divisible by 3, 5, and 7, but not divisible by 4, 6, or 8?

Student's name: ____________________ Assignment date: ________________

Mark "√" if the number is divisible by the following.

	36	29	72	45	51	70
By 2						
By 3						
By 5						
By 10						

Mark "√" if the number is divisible by the following.

	310	512	341	524	136	372
By 2						
By 4						
By 8						

Mark "√" if the number is divisible by the following.

	258	441	639	139	204	342
By 3						
By 6						
By 9						

1. Write the largest 3- digit number that is divisible by 2.
2. Write the largest 3- digit number that is divisible by 3.
3. Write the largest 3- digit number that is divisible by 6.

Student's name: ____________________ Assignment date: ________________

***** Part 3 Order of operations *****

When finding the value for an expression (called evaluating), the way to do it is from left to right and use the rule of BEDMAS (bracket, exponent, division, multiplication, addition, subtraction). It means:

Do the bracket first.
Do the exponents second
Then do division or multiplication, depending on whichever comes first.
Finally, do addition or subtraction depending on whichever comes first.

For example, $3 + 2 - 4 + (2 + 3) \div 5 \times 2 - 1 + 2^2$
$= 5 - 4 + 5 \div 5 \times 2 - 1 + 4$
$= 1 + 1 \times 2 - 1 + 4$
($5 \div 5$ must be done before multiplication and been added to others)
$= 1 + 2 - 1 + 4$
$= 3 - 1 + 4$
$= 2 + 4$
$= 6$

If there are addition, subtraction, multiplication, and division in the expression, do multiplication and division first, then do addition and subtraction. The order is usually from left to right.

Evaluate the following expressions.

Expressions	Value	Comments
$7 - 2 \times 3$		
$7 - (2 \times 3)$		Are the brackets necessary? ______
$(7 - 2) \times 3$		
$2 \times 7 - 3$		
$(2 \times 7) - 3$		Are the brackets necessary? _____
$2 \times (7 - 3)$		
$4 \times 5 + 6 \times 7$		

Student's name: ____________________ Assignment date: ________________

Test of evaluating the following expressions

Expressions	Value	Comments
$4 \times (5 + 6) \times 7$		
$4 \times (5 + 6 \times 7)$		
$(4 \times 5 + 6) \times 7$		
$45 \div 5 + 9 \div 3$		
$(45 \div 5) + (9 \div 3)$		Are brackets necessary? ________
$42 \div (5 + 9) \div 3$		
$48 \div (5 + 9 \div 3)$		
$(45 \div 5 + 9) \div 3$		
$1 + 2 + 3 \div 3 - 2 - 1$		
$(1 + 2 + 3) \div (3 - 2) - 1$		
$1 + 2 + 3 \div (3 - 2) - 1$		
$1 + 2 + 3 \div 3 \times 2 - 1$		
$1 + 2 + 3 \div 3 \times (2 - 1)$		
$\frac{2 + 4 \div 2}{8 + 6 \times 2} = ?$		

Student's name: ____________________ Assignment date: ________________

Evaluate mixed operations by using the order of operations.

$7 \times 4 + 3 \times 8$
$= 28 + 24$
$= 52$

$7 \times 9 - 16 \div 2$
$= 63 - 8$
$= 55$

1. $6 \times 5 + 9 \times 4$

2. $8 \div 2 - 9 \div 3$

3. $5 \times 7 - 6 \div 2$

4. $5 \times 9 + 3 \times 6$

5. $8 \div 4 - 7 \div 7$

6. $5 \times 7 + 8 \div 4$

7. $6 \div 3 + 9 \times 6$

8. $8 \div 2 + 4 \times 7$

9. $9 \times 2 + 3 \times 7$

10. $8 \times 3 + 6 \div 2$

Student's name: ____________________ Assignment date: ________________

Evaluate mixed operations by using the order of operations.

$8 + 2 \times 7 + 6$
$= 8 + 14 + 6$
$= 28$

$5 + 9 \div 3 - 2$
$= 5 + 3 - 2$
$= 6$

1. $5 + 7 \times 8 + 3$

2. $5 + 8 \div 2 + 6$

3. $4 + 16 \div 2 - 5$

4. $7 + 3 \times 7 - 9$

5. $8 + 6 \div 2 + 7$

6. $8 + 4 \times 6 + 5$

7. $7 + 12 \div 3 - 5$

8. $9 - 15 \div 3 + 8$

9. $7 + 24 \div 6 + 8$

10. $9 + 21 \div 3 - 7$

Student's name: ____________________ Assignment date: ________________

***** Part 4 Shortcuts for number computation *****

Some shortcuts can be used to do computation mentally. These shortcuts allow students to do computation more efficiently and improve their computation skills.

Student's name: ____________________ Assignment date: ________________

Multiplied by 5.

Try to find a matching 2 so that $2 \times 5 = 10$.

Example

$5 \times 16 = \underline{5 \times 2} \times 8 = 10 \times 8 = 80$

$124 \times 5 = 62 \times \underline{2 \times 5} = 62 \times 10 = 620$

1. $5 \times 46 =$
2. $5 \times 58 =$
3. $64 \times 5 =$
4. $78 \times 5 =$
5. $102 \times 5 =$
6. $372 \times 5 =$
7. $5 \times 612 =$
8. $5 \times 406 =$
9. $306 \times 5 =$
10. $1004 \times 5 =$

11 $92 \times 5 =$

12. $5 \times 3040=$

Student's name: ____________________ Assignment date: ________________

Multiplied by 25

Try to find a matching 4 so that $4 \times 25 = 100$

Example:

$25 \times 8 = \underline{25 \times 4} \times 2 = 100 \times 2 = 200$
$132 \times 25 = 33 \times \underline{4 \times 25} = 33 \times 100 = 3300$

1. $28 \times 25 =$
2. $44 \times 25 =$
3. $25 \times 36 =$
4. $25 \times 72 =$
5. $25 \times 124 =$
6. $84 \times 25 =$
7. $172 \times 25 =$
8. $452 \times 25 =$
9. $208 \times 25 =$
10. $356 \times 25 =$

11 $25 \times 332 =$

12. $704 \times 25 =$

Student's name: ____________________ Assignment date: ________________

Multiplied by 125

Try to find a matching 8 so that 8 × 125 = 1000

Example

125 × 48 = 125 × 8 × 6 = 1000 × 6 = 6000
168 × 125 = 21 × 8 × 125 = 21 × 1000 = 21000

1. 125 × 16 =
2. 125 × 48 =
3. 88 × 125 =
4. 72 × 125 =
5. 96 × 125 =
6. 125 × 56 =
7. 125 × 24 =
8. 64 × 125 =
9. 80 × 125 =
10. 125 × 160 =
11 32 × 125 =
12. 125 × 720 =

Student's name: ____________________ Assignment date: ________________

Multiplied an even number by a number ending with 5.

Example

26 × 35 = 13 × 2 × 35 = 13 × 70 = 910
45 × 38 = 45 × 2 × 19 = 90 × 19 = 1710

1. 15 × 28 =
2. 35 × 74 =
3. 15 × 34 =
4. 25 × 52 =
5. 36 × 45 =
6. 66 × 35 =
7. 128 × 35 =
8. 14 × 85 =
9. 75 × 12 =
10. 135 × 16 =
11 325 × 6 =
12. 715 × 4 =

Student's name: ____________________ Assignment date: ________________

Numbers ending in 5 multiply by the number itself

Example

15 × 15 = 1 × (1+1) 25 = 225
35 × 35 = 3 × (3+1) 25 = 1225

1. 25 × 25 =

2. 45 × 45 =

3. 35 × 35 =

4. 95 × 95 =

5. 55 × 55 =

6. 65 × 65 =

7. 85 × 85 =

8. 75 × 75 =

9. 15 × 15 =

10. 195 × 195 =

11 105 × 105 =

12. 205 × 205 =

Student's name: ____________________ Assignment date: ________________

Multiplied by 11

Example

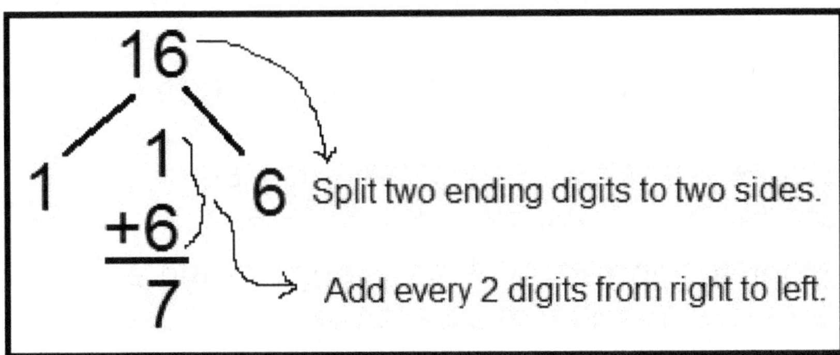

16 × 11 = 1(1 + 6) 6 = 176

11 × 37 = 3 (3 + 7) 7 = 3 (10) 7 = 407

1. 24 × 11 =

2. 11 × 18 =

3. 32 × 11 =

4. 11 × 27 =

5. 61 × 11 =

6. 11 × 81 =

7. 56 × 11 =

8. 78 × 11 =

9. 11 × 77 =

10. 11 × 84 =

11. 11 × 123 =

12. 458 × 11 =

Student's name: ____________________ Assignment date: ________________

Shortcut for adding numbers ending with 0's

This shortcut can also be used for subtraction.

Thousands adding thousands

1. 4000 + 9000 = 1300	2. 5000 + 9000 =	3. 5000 + 3000 =
4. 7000 + 4000 =	5. 3000 + 2000 =	6. 6000 + 800 =
7. 8000 + 5000 =	8. 7000 + 3000 =	9. 7000 + 7000 =
10. 6000 + 3000 =	11. 5000 + 4000 =	12. 3000 + 7000 =
13. 8000 + 4000 =	14. 9000 + 7000 =	15. 9000 + 8000 =

Fill in each blank to add up to thousands or ten thousand.

1. 5000 + ______ = 10000	2. 3000 + ______ = 10000
3. 6700 + ______ = 10000	4. 5200 + ______ = 10000
5. 7420 + ______ = 10000	6. 3810 + ______ = 10000
7. 8409 + ______ = 10000	8. 3617 + ______ = 10000
9. 2509 + ______ = 5000	10. 2175 + ______ = 3000
11. 3096 + ______ = 7000	12. 3289 + ______ = 6000
13. 2078 + ______ = 4000	14. 2843 + ______ = 5000
15. 1745 + ______ = 8000	16. 2004 + ______ = 7000

Student's name: ____________________ Assignment date: ________________

The following does subtraction to get nice numbers ending with 0 first.

$25 + \underline{36 - 16}$
$= 25 + 20$
$= 45$

$31 - 17 + 47$
$= 31 + \underline{47 - 17}$
$= 31 + 30$
$= 61$

1. 42 + 37 – 17

2. 23 – 16 + 36

3. 41 – 28 + 38

4. 63 – 35 + 45

5. 72 – 38 + 58

6. 57 + 21 – 47

7. 53 – 24 + 44

8. 56 + 33 – 46

9. 39 + 41 – 29

10. 37 – 29 + 49

Student's name: ____________________ Assignment date: ________________

multiplied or divided by 10, 100, or 1000

Multiplied by the power of multiples of 10 Add the sum of ending zeros two factors to the end of the non-zero product. 2 × 5 = 10 4 × 25 = 100, 5 × 20 = 100 8× 125 = 1000	Divided by the power of multiples of 10 Cross out the same number of ending zeros of both dividend and divisor. 3120000 ÷ 300 = 10400
10 × 10 =	10 ÷ 10 =
100 × 10 =	100 ÷ 10 =
200 × 2 × 5 = 1000	200 ÷ 2 ÷ 50 =
7200 × 900 =	7200 ÷ 900 =
300 × 570000 =	570000 ÷ 300 =
40000 ×1560000 =	1560000 ÷ 40000 =
8005 ×76000 =	576000 ÷ 800 =
6500 × 4 × 25 =	6500 ÷ 8÷ 125 =
105000× 700 =	105000÷ 700 =
472000 × 400 =	472000 ÷ 400 =
50000 × 2000 =	50000 ÷ 2000 =
640000 × 40010 =	640000 ÷ 40010 =
10 × 8 × 125 =	100 ÷ 10 =
100 × 4 × 25 =	1000 ÷ 4÷ 25 =
200 × 5 × 20 =	2000 ÷ 10 =
7200 × 9000 =	72000 ÷ 900 =
570000 × 3000 =	5700000 ÷ 300 =
1560000 ×400000 =	15600000 ÷ 40000 =
576000 × 8000 =	5760000 ÷ 800 =
6500 × 500 =	65000 ÷ 50 =
105000× 7000 =	1050000÷ 700 =
472000 × 4000 =	4720000 ÷ 400 =
50000 × 20000 =	500000 ÷ 2000 =

,

Student's name: ____________________ Assignment date: ________________

Shortcuts for mixed operation

The following expressions can be thought of as vertical formats so that the top and the bottom number can be reduced by a common factor first.

$28 \times \underline{36 \div 9}$

$= 28 \times 4$

$= 112$

$57 \div 3 \times 6$

$= 57 \times \underline{6 \div 3}$

$= 57 \times 2$

$= 114$

1. $56 \times 12 \div 4$

2. $64 \div 4 \times 8$

3. $81 \div 3 \times 9$

4. $51 \times 26 \div 13$

5. $84 \div 7 \times 21$

6. $75 \times 15 \div 5$

7. $53 \times 36 \div 12$

8. $84 \div 6 \times 48$

9. $68 \div 4 \times 24$

10. $35 \times 66 \div 11$

Student's name: ____________________ Assignment date: ________________

***** Part 5 Different methods of computing and number models *****

Other than the traditional method of computing from right to left, there are other computing methods.
For the exploratory study, these methods are often mentioned in math textbooks.

Student's name: ____________________ Assignment date: ________________

Front end Addition

Front end computation is a good way to do mental math, and this technique can also be used for estimating.

Example 1

Vertical format

```
  24
+ 35
----
  54 ⇦ Add the leftmost digit digits (tens place) first,
+  5 ⇦ then add the digits (ones place) next to the right.
----
  59
```

Horizontal format

24 + 35 = 24 + 30 + 5 = 54 + 5 = 59

Example 2

Vertical format

```
   37
+  87
-----
  117 ⇦ Add the leftmost digits (tens place) first,
+   7 ⇦ then add the digits (ones place) next to the right.
-----
  124
```

Horizontal format

37 + 87 = 37 + 80 + 7 = 117 + 7 = 124

Student's name: ____________________ Assignment date: ________________

Example 3

Vertical format

$$
\begin{array}{r}
498 \\
+\ 789 \\
\hline
1198 \\
80 \\
+\quad 9 \\
\hline
1278 \\
+\quad 9 \\
\hline
1287
\end{array}
$$

1198 ⇦ Add the leftmost digit (hundreds place) first.
80 ⇦ Add the tens place.
9 ⇦ Add the ones place.

Horizontal format

498 + 789 = 498 + 700 + 80 + 9 = 1198 + 80 + 9 = 1278 + 9 = 1287

Student's name: ____________________ Assignment date: ________________

Test of front end addition

Calculate the following in horizontal format.

48 + 59
63 + 89
892 + 587
893 + 758
398 + 929

Student's name: ____________________ Assignment date: ________________

Front end subtraction

Example 1

Vertical format

$$\begin{array}{r} 98 \\ -\ 86 \\ \hline 18 \\ -\ 6 \\ \hline 12 \end{array}$$

18 ⇦ Subtract the leftmost digit (tens place) first. (98 - 80 = 18).

6 ⇦ Subtract the next right digit (ones place).

12 ⇦ Add the 2 differences.

Horizontal format

98- 86 = 98 – 80 – 6 = 18 – 6 = 12

Example 2

Vertical format

$$\begin{array}{r} 87 \\ -\ 39 \\ \hline 57 \\ -\ 9 \\ \hline 48 \end{array}$$

57 ⇦ Subtract the leftmost digit (tens place) first.

9 ⇦ Subtract the next right digit (ones place).

48 ⇦ Subtract

Horizontal format

87 – 39 = 87 – 30 -9 = 57 – 9 = 48

Student's name: ____________________ Assignment date: ________________

Example 3

Vertical format

```
  762
- 685
-----
  162   ⇦ Subtract the leftmost digit (hundreds place) first. (762 - 600 = 162)
-  85   ⇦ Subtract the next right digit (tens place).
-----
   82
-   5   ⇦ Subtract the next right digit (ones place).
-----
   77
```

Horizontal format

762 – 685 = 762 -600 – 80 – 5 = 162 – 80 – 5 = 82 – 5 = 78

Student's name: ____________________ Assignment date: ________________

Test of front end subtraction

Calculate the following in horizontal format.

59 – 48
89 – 63 26
892 – 587
893 – 758
328 – 229

Student's name: ____________________ Assignment date: ________________

Different subtraction methods

The following methods could be used to master subtraction skills.

Strategies	Procedure	Comments
Intuitive	Some students have done enough computations to the extent they just Know the answers.	Requires the student's willingness to learn and memorize.
Borrowing 10	1 1 – 7 1 ten is borrowed to minus 7 (to get 3) and then add 1 to get the answer 4.	A universal method can be used to subtract all facts.
Making ten (adding the bottom to 10)	1 1 – 7 3 added to 7 is 10, so 3 plus 1 is 4. This method is similar to the above borrowing 10	A universal method can be used to subtract all facts.
Counting back	1 1→1 0→ 9 – 2 Subtract 1 from 11 to make 10, and then subtract 1 again to make 9.	A universal method but still doing the counting and using less reasoning and logic.
Adding the bottom to 10	1 1 →1 3 – 8 → – 1 0	Making the bottom number to be 10 by addition. A universal approach for all subtraction facts but requires multiple operators.
Subtracting top to 10	1 2 →1 0 – 3 → – 1	A reverse method similar to the above idea but by subtracting the top number down to 10.
Turn subtraction into addition	13 + 4 6 +3 = 9	A universal method and also fast in getting answers.

Student's name: ____________________ Assignment date: ________________

A different method of subtraction by subtracting a nice number ending with 0 first

Example: 65 – 28 = $65 \overset{+2}{-} 28 \overset{+2}{=} 67 - 30 = 37$

Evaluate using shortcut where applicable.

71 – 19

85 – 57

63 – 29

75 – 38

61 – 27

83 – 48

73 – 59

82 – 37

85 – 49

72 – 28

Student's name: ____________________ Assignment date: ________________

Addition or subtraction word problems

1. At Kitchener Elementary school, there are 230 boys and 250 girls. How many children are there in the school altogether?

2. Ms. Munson's kindergarten class painted 18 pictures on Wednesday and 20 pictures on Thursday. How many more pictures did they paint on Thursday?

3. For Show & Tell, twins Lenny and Lonny each brought 24 rocks to school. How many rocks did they bring in all?

4. Mr. Singh started with 150 pieces of chalk. By the end of the week, he had broken 86 of them. How many pieces of chalk does Mr. Singh have left?

Student's name: ____________________ Assignment date: ________________

5. Gina Gardener spots 24 spotted butterflies and 14 plain butterflies in her flower garden. What is the sum number of butterflies in her garden?

6. Erin Entomologist finds 89 red ants, 38 brown ants and 84 black ants marching back to their anthill in her yard. How many more black ants than brown ants are there? How many more red ants than black ants are there? What is the total number of ants of any colour in her yard?

7. In the morning, Professor Chris counted 23 neutrinos in the mine. In the afternoon, his grad student counted 17 neutrinos. How many neutrinos did they count that day?

Student's name: ____________________ Assignment date: ________________

Mixed Word Problems

8. Al has a collection of 111 books. He donated 16 books last year and 21 books this year. How many books does he have left?

9. Michelle loves collecting small plastic animals. She has 35 cats and 30 ducks. How many animals does she have in her collection?

10. A school has three dining halls. Each dining hall has 22 tables. If there are four children at each table, how many children can stay for lunch?

11. Chris made thirty-two statements in class. Mark said that eleven of them were wrong. How many correct statements did Chris make?

Student's name: ____________________ Assignment date: ________________

12. There are 23 doves and 419 crows in Harlandale Woods. How many birds are there in total in Harlandale Woods?

13. It takes 4 minutes to make a glass of pineapple juice. How many glasses of juice can be made in 3 hours and 4 minutes?

14. Last month, John worked for 186 hours, Gord worked for 134 hours, and Alexei worked 32 hours more than John. How many hours did they work altogether?

15. There are 80 hens and 25 sheep on a farm. How many animals are there on the farm?

Student's name: ____________________ Assignment date: ________________

16. Invitations were sent to 106 relatives for a family get-together. Only 93 relatives came. How many relatives did not come?

17. A zoo has 59 brown monkeys and 34 black monkeys. How many monkeys are there in the zoo?

18. Mr. Bloomburg will be 72 next year. His son is 34 years younger than he is. How old is his son right now?

19. There are 30 ice cream cakes in Dairy King. If each cake is cut into 8 pieces and then each part is further cut into 2 pieces, how many pieces of cake are there in all?

Student's name: ____________________ Assignment date: ________________

20. There are 66 vans and 54 buses in the parking lot. How many vehicles are there in the parking lot?

21. A jungle has 784 deer, of which 523 are spotted. How many deer do not have spots?

22. There are 69 men and 30 women in a Boeing 737 jet airplane. How many passengers are there altogether?

23. Mr. Lee drove his new car 31 kilometres on Tuesday and 85 kilometres on Wednesday. How many kilometres did he drive over these two days?

Student's name: ____________________ Assignment date: ________________

24. Clara-Anne has 18 teddy bears. She gives away 5 of them to her best friend. How many teddy bears does she have now?

25. Regina is a mechanic. She repaired 39 cabs and 28 cars last month. How many vehicles did she repair all together?

26. There are five members of Ronaldo's family. The family's total weight is 284 kg, and Ronaldo weighs 40 kg. How many kilograms do the other four members weigh?

27. Mr. Mandela used 93 litres of fuel last month. He used 56 litres this month. How many litres of fuel were consumed in the two months?

Student's name: ____________________ Assignment date: ________________

28. The sum of two numbers is 31, and their product is 240. What are these two numbers?

29. When divided by 5 leaves a remainder of 3. It is a two-digit number less than 50. The two digits are equal.

30. The product of three children's ages is 36. The sum of their ages is 11. How old are they?

31. When divided by 5 leaves a remainder of 4. It is a two-digit number less than 50. The two digits are equal.

32. Arthur bought a computer paper package for $15 and 3 pens at $2 each. He got a $5 change back after he paid. How much did he pay?

Student's name: ____________________ Assignment date: ________________

33. Eileen divided her paper clips equally into 17 boxes, with five clips in each box with 4 clips left over. How many paper clips did she have at the beginning?

34. It is now 7:20 p.m. In 2 hours 45 minutes, Marylou will go to a concert. At what time will she go to a concert?

35. Julie can finish her 20 practice questions in half an hour. At this speed, how many practice questions can he finish in 3 and a half hours?

Student's name: ____________________ Assignment date: ________________

4 basic operations word problems with the wording as or x times as many (As …as)

Kumar has $309. Pauline has twice as much as Kumar. How much does Pauline have?
Kumar has $44. Pauline has half as much as Kumar. How much does Pauline have?
Kumar has 212 marbles. Pauline has 3 less than half as many as Kumar. How many does Pauline have?
Kumar has $214. Pauline has $15 more than half as much as Kumar. How much does Pauline have?
Kumar has $129. Pauline has 3 times as much as Kumar. How much does Pauline have?
After Pauline gave $3 to Kumar, then Kumar had $214. Kumar had $4 less than twice as much as Pauline had. How much did Pauline have at the beginning?
Joanne told her mother. "If I had done twice as correct as I answered in the test, I would have 6 more points than I have now".. How many points did Joanne actually get on the test?

Student's name: ____________________ Assignment date: ________________

Brent rode 15 km to a park, and on the way home, he rode three times as far to his uncle's home. How far did he ride to his uncle's house from the park?
Brent sold 219 raffle tickets. Pauline sold 9 times as many. How many tickets did Pauline sell?
Pauline and her 4 friends like to share 705 candies equally. How many candies would each person get?
Pauline memorizes 23 vocabularies per day. How many vocabularies will she memorize in 25 days?
Brent buys lunch meat at $0.99 per 100 g. How much will it cost him if he buys 1.2 kg?
Brent makes half as much as Pauline per hour. Pauline makes $75 per 5 hours. How much will Brent make in 5 hours?
Pauline finishes reading a book in 10 days. At half of the reading speed, how long will it take Pauline to finish reading the same book?
Brent runs 15 km per day. At the same rate, how many days would Brent have run if his total distance is 225 km?

Student's name: ____________________ Assignment date: ________________

Test of advanced word problems

Bob has 149 more stamps than Adam. Cathy has 229 more stamps than Bob. Altogether they have 767 stamps. How many stamps does each one of them have? Hint: Use the Line Segment Diagram to solve.
9119 people were in the sports stadium last night. 3557 of them were women, and there were 879 fewer women than men. The rest were children. How many children were in the sports stadium last night?
Vera wants to give two cans of fruit juice to each of her 13 friends invited to her birthday party. How many 6-pack of juice cans must she buy?

Student's name: ____________________ Assignment date: ________________

***** Part 6 Decimal *****

Division models

The division is a reverse operation or works backwards of multiplication, such as the following multiplication equation.

The number of groups (sets, factor 1) × objects shared in each group (object 2) = total number of objects (product).

To find the number of groups (sets) when a number of objects and the number of objects shared (divided) by each group are given, we have to find *the number of groups* model.

To find the number of objects shared (divided, averaged) by each group when several objects and the number of groups (sets) are given, then we have the *finding the number of objects shared (divided, averaged) by each group* (set) model.

.

Model 1 Finding the number of groups (sets)

English Word Problems	How to solve it? Method 1 - Draw a model. This method is slow, so it is only used for teaching division concept purposes. Draw loops around the counters to show the numbers in each group (set). Each object is represented by a circle (counter).	Method 2 – Use work backwards of the multiplication method This method is used for all computations. Complete the division mathematical equation sentence.	Objects are what has been shared or divided. Set is the number of groups. The average is the number of things or objects being divided in each set (group).
Frank bought 12 cat cans. He wants to place 3 cans in a bag. How many bags does he need?	Step 1. Draw 12 circles to represent 12 real cans. Step 2. Loop every 3 cans. Step 3. Count the number of loops, and the total number of loops is the number of bags (groups, sets) needed. ○○○○○○ ○○○○○○	_____ ÷ _____ = _____	What has been divided into sets? _____ How many sets are there? _____ How many are in each set? _____

Student's name: ____________________ Assignment date: ________________

Frank bought 20 cat cans. He wants to place 5 cans in a bag. How many bags does he need?	○○○○○ ○○○○○ ○○○○○○ ○○○○○○	___ ÷ __ = __	What has been divided into sets? _____ How many sets are there? ____ How many are in each set? ____
Frank bought 15 cat cans. He wants to place 3 cans in a bag. How many bags does he need?	Draw the counters (circles) yourself.	___ ÷ __ = __	What has been divided into sets? _____ How many sets are there? ____ How many are in each set? ____
Pauline earned 6 stamps for each hour of work. She earned 27 stamps in total. How many hours did she work?		__ ÷ __ = __	What has been divided into sets? _____ How many sets are there? ____ How many are in each set? ____

Student's name: ____________________ Assignment date: ________________

Model 2 Finding the number of objects shared (divided) in each group (set)

Problems	Draw loops around the counters to show the numbers shared by each group. Each object is represented by a circle (counter).	Complete the division sentence.	What has been divided into sets? _____ How many sets are there? ____ How many are in each set? ____
Frank bought 12 pencils to have them shared by 4 classes equally. How many pencils does each class get?	○○○○○○ ○○○○○○	__ ÷ __ = __	What has been divided into sets? _____ How many sets are there? ____ How many are in each set? ____
Frank bought 20 pencils to have them shared by 5 classes equally. How many pencils does each class get?	○○○○○ ○○○○○ ○○○○○ ○○○○○	__ ÷ __ = __	What has been divided into sets? _____ How many sets are there? ____ How many are in each set? ____
Frank bought 16 pencils to have them shared by 4 classes equally. How many pencils does each class get?	Draw the counters yourself.	__ ÷ __ = __	What has been divided into sets? _____ How many sets are there? ____ How many are in each set? ____
Pauline earned 30 stamps for her work. She worked for 5 hours. How many stamps did she earn each hour? Assume she earned the same number of stamps for each hour.		__ ÷ __ = __	What has been divided into sets? _____ How many sets are there? ____ How many are in each set? ____

Student's name: ____________________ Assignment date: ________________

Multiplication and division models

model	Write multiplication equations or division equations
	$4 \times 5 = 20$ 4 repeated 5 times. $5 \times 4 = 20$ 5 repeated 4 times.
	$20 \div 5 = 4$ 20 divided into groups of 5. There are 4 in each group. $20 \div 4 = 5$ 20 divided into 4 each group. There are 5 groups.

Model	Mathematical sentence (equation)
= +	
	In the multiplication model In the division model
+ + +	In multiplication equation
– – –	In division equation

Student's name: ____________________ Assignment date: ________________

○○○○○ ○○○○○ ○○○○○ ○○○○○	The left model shows 4 × 4 = 16. Draw to show how it can also show 2 × 8 = 16 ○○○○○ ○○○○○ ○○○○○ ○○○○○ Draw to show how it can also show 20 ÷ 3 has the quotient of 6 with the remainder 1 ○○○○○ ○○○○○ ○○○○○ ○○○○○

Student's name: ____________________ Assignment date: ________________

Decimals

A number can be a whole number such as 0, 1, 2, 3, etc. What happens if we want to show just part of a whole? For example, one chocolate bar is cut into 10 smaller pieces, then how to say each smaller part in math?

We can say it in fraction as $\frac{1}{10}$.

The notation of $\frac{1}{10}$ can be explained in the following ways:

1. Read it from the bottom-up. There are 10 parts and only one part I is taken.
2. Reading it from top to down, we say one-tenth.
3. Divide without leaving any remainder if it is divisible. To stop division when used up all digits of dividend and leave the quotient with the remainder is a fraction.

decimal	fraction
$10 \div 3 = ?$ Hint: To think 1 as 1.0000 so you can drop down as many zeros as you want when there are no more digits in dividend. Place a decimal point once you start to drop down 0. 3.33 3) 10 9 10 9 10 9 1	When dividing, leave the answer in remainder format. For example, $10 \div 3 = 3\frac{1}{3}$ 3 3) 10 9 1

In the above case 3, since 1 = 1.00000, we produce a division quotient 0.1 and this format of the number is called decimal number or just called it decimal.

Student's name: ____________________ Assignment date: ________________

Why we need decimals when we already have fractions?

It is because we found in some cases, the use of fractions are awkward in our verbal communications, for example, a 3-digit fraction $\frac{129}{419}$ is a mouthful to say, but it is easier to say using its equivalent value when converting to decimal as *******. In our monetary system, it is also easier to use $25.13 instead of $\$25\frac{13}{100}$.

Student's name: ____________________ Assignment date: ________________

A decimal number = whole number + fraction (including a decimal point in tenths, hundredths, thousandths, etc.)

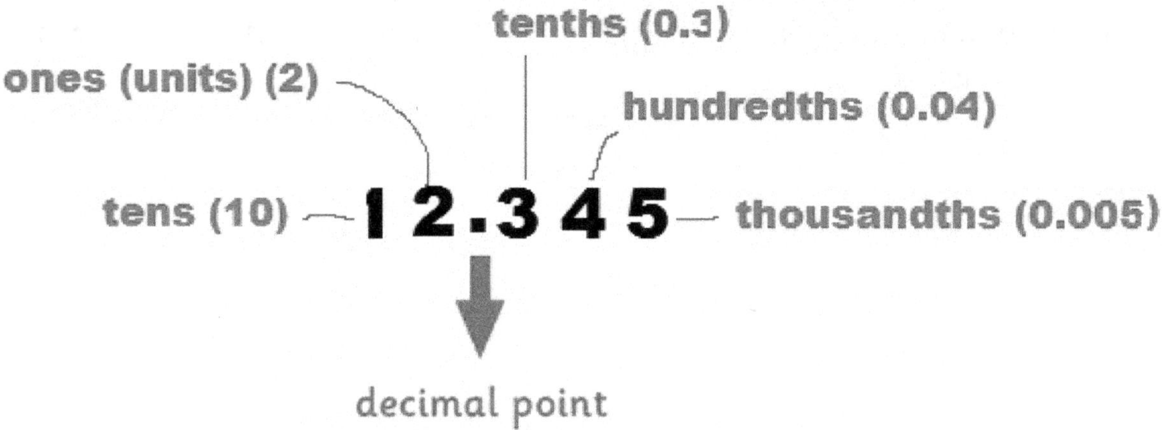

十位,个位点,十分位, 百分位,千分位

As we can see from the above place value diagram, the decimal point is only to separate the whole number from the fraction. Each number from left to right is scaled down 10 times, Ten times smaller than ones place will be tenth ($\frac{1}{10}$), that is why there is no "oneth" in the fraction part of a decimal number.

Decimal representations

Since decimals can be converted into fractions and also the other way around, so the graphic representation of both numbers is identical. We can use block tens or number lines to illustrate decimals, just as in fractions.

In primary schools, we normally learn tenths (one decimal place), hundredths (2-decimal place), or even thousandths (3-decimal place).

Student's name: ____________________ Assignment date: ________________

Division to decimal to fraction

problem	Decimal division	fraction
1 ÷ 10 =	10) 1 □ ; quotient □□ ; □□	
1 ÷ 100 =	100) 1 □□ ; quotient □□□ ; □□□	
2 ÷ 100 =	100) 2 □□ ; quotient □□□ ; □□□	
22 ÷ 220 =	220) 2 2 □ ; quotient □□□ ; □□□	

Student's name: ____________________ Assignment date: ________________

Tenths

Students could be introduced to the money system of dollars and cents to get to know the decimals. Students also should have the concept of the place value so they could understand the decimals much better. For example, the 1's in the following number mean very differently due to its place value.

1111.11

Students should study the place value to understand the tenth, hundredth, or thousandths and higher place values.

Each digit in a number has its own place value. The following is an example.

millions
hundred thousands
ten thousands
thousands
hundreds
tens
ones
and
tenths
hundredths
thousandths
ten thousandths

2222222.2222

Ho Math Chess Primary Grades Math

Test Review assesssment 何数棋謎低年级数学测试複習考核

Student's name: ____________________ Assignment date: ________________

Tenths

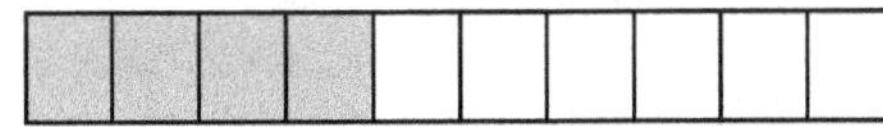

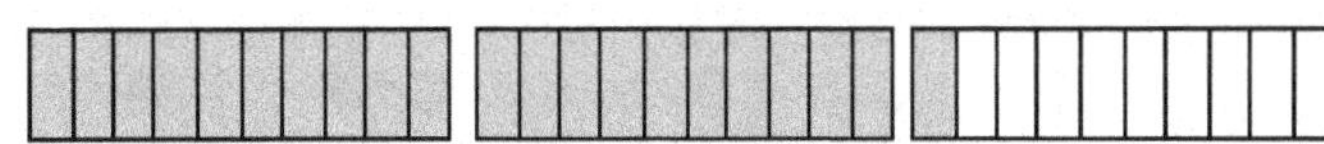

$0.4 = \frac{4}{10}$ It is read as four-tenths.

$2.1 = 2\frac{1}{10}$ It is read as two and one-tenth.

Ones	Decimal point	Tenths
0	•	4

Ones	Decimal point	Tenths
2	•	1

1. Express the shaded part in fractions and decimals.

1. 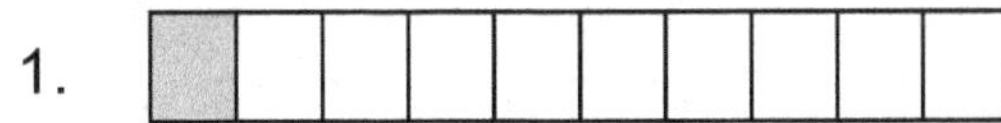 $\frac{1}{10}$ 0.1

2. ______ ______

3. ______ ______

4. ______ ______

5. ______ ______

6. ______ ______

7. ______ ______

8. 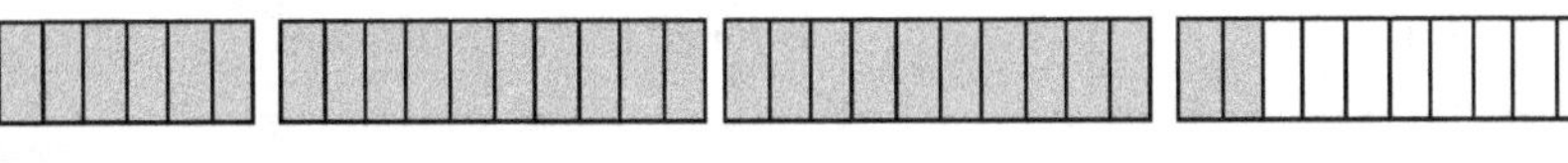 ______ ______

Student's name: ____________________ Assignment date: ________________

2. Write the value of each point as a decimal.

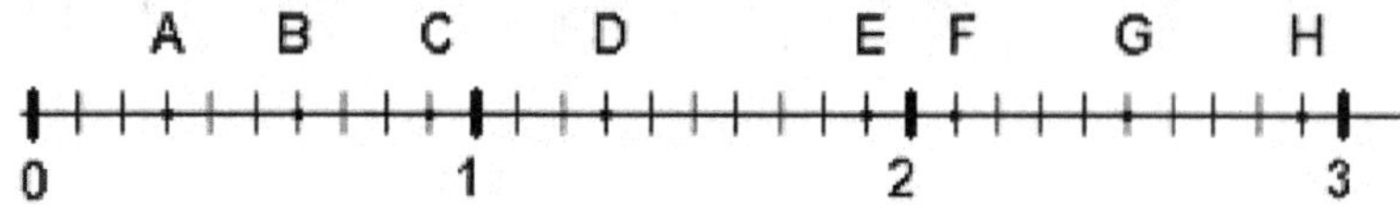

A:______ B:______ C:______ D:______ E:______ F:______ G:______ H:______

3. Draw the length of AB.

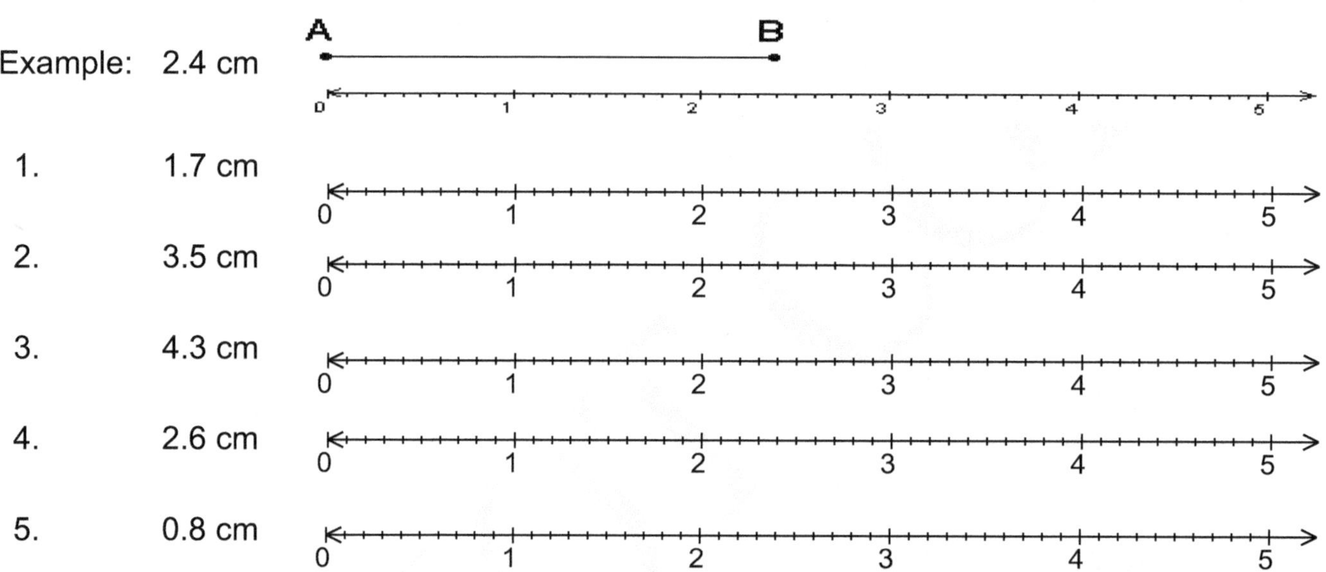

4. Complete the following chart.

	Fraction	Decimal	Words
1.	$2\frac{8}{10}$		
2.		1.5	
3.			two and five-tenths
4.	$6\frac{4}{10}$		
5.			four and three tenths

Student's name: ____________________ Assignment date: ________________

Hundredths (% = per hundredth)

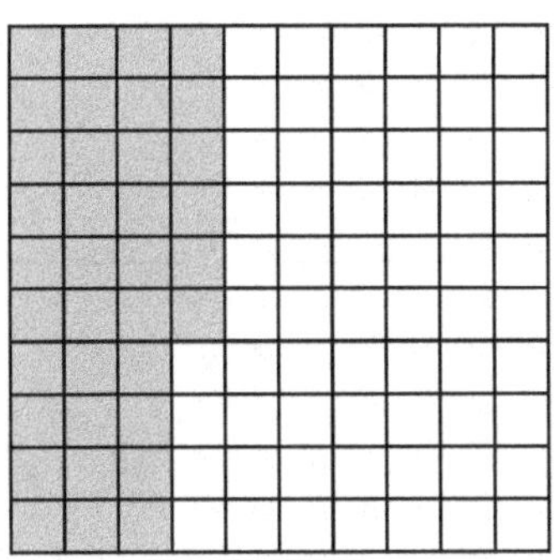

$0.36 = \frac{36}{100}$ It is read as thirty-six hundredths.

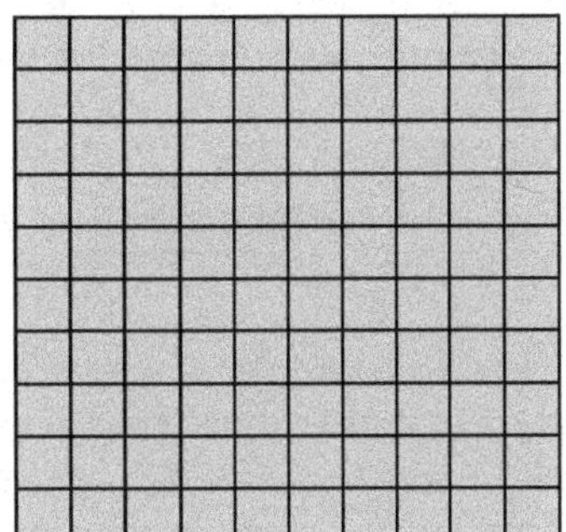
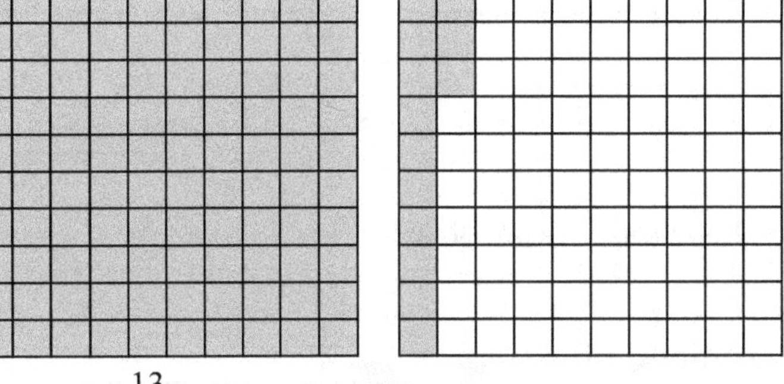

$1.13 = 1\frac{13}{100}$ It is read as one and thirteen hundredths.

Ones	Decimal point	Tenths	Hundredths
0	•	3	6

Ones	Decimal point	Tenths	Hundredths
1	•	1	3

1. Express the shaded part in fractions and decimals.

1. 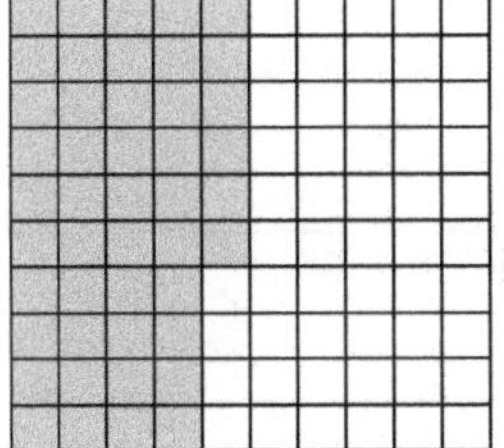

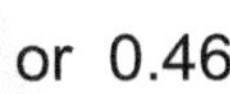
$\frac{46}{100}$ or 0.46

2. 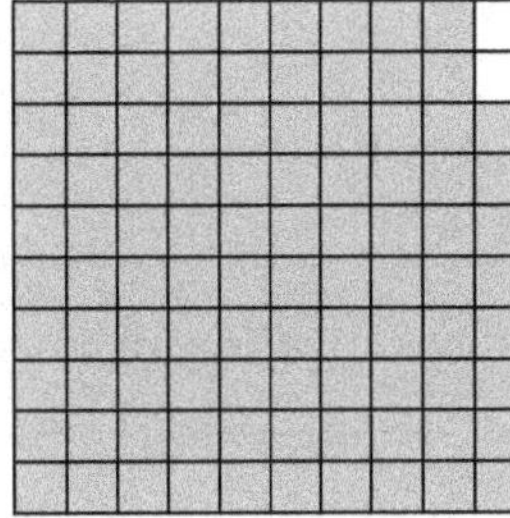

__________ or __________

3. 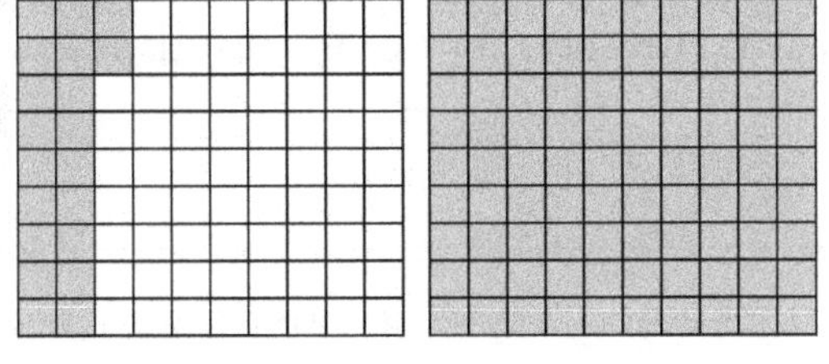

__________ or __________

4. 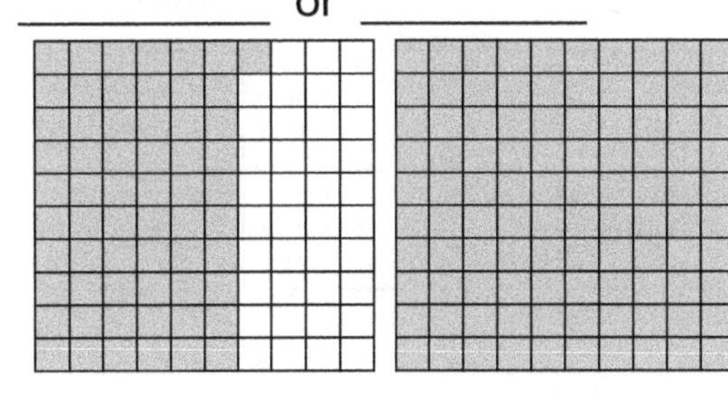

__________ or __________

Student's name: ____________________ Assignment date: ________________

2. Write the value of each point as a decimal.

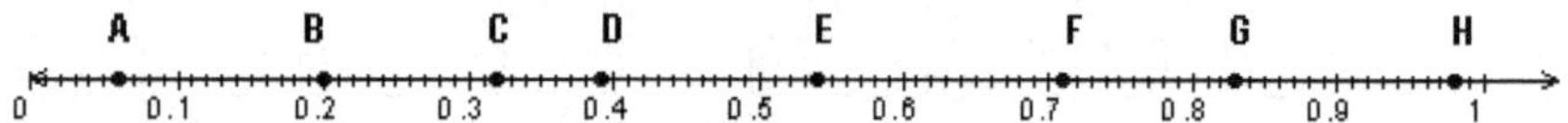

A:______ B:______ C:______ D:______ E:______ F:______ G:______ H:______

3. Draw the length of AB.

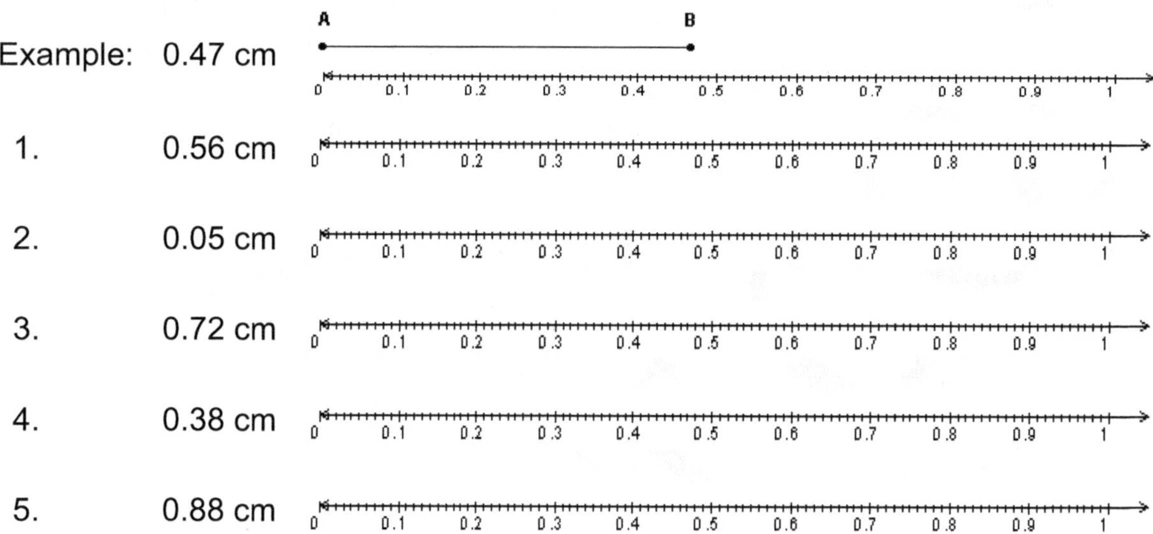

4. Complete the following chart.

	Fraction	Decimal	Words
1.	$5\frac{23}{100}$		
2.		8.09	
3.			two and twenty-seven hundredths
4.	$4\frac{31}{100}$		
5.			three and fifty-nine hundredths

Student's name: ____________________ Assignment date: ________________

Compare decimals.

1. 0.53 [>] 0.27

2. 0.24 ☐ 0.79

3. 0.36 ☐ 0.81

4. 0.18 ☐ 0.05

5. 0.71 ☐ 0.52

6. 0.53 ☐ 0.06

7. 0.84 ☐ 4.57

8. 5.09 ☐ 0.37

9. 2.05 ☐ 0.72

10. 0.74 ☐ 1.85

11. 5.07 ☐ 0.59

12. 3.90 ☐ 0.78

13. 0.35 ☐ 2.13

14. 0.47 ☐ 3.18

15. 7.90 ☐ 7.09

16. 3.75 ☐ 3.71

17. 3.36 ☐ 3.47

18. 6.09 ☐ 6.03

19. 1.95 ☐ 1.92

20. 2.67 ☐ 2.63

21. 7.04 ☐ 0.74

22. 8.52 ☐ 8.51

23. 1.52 ☐ 7.43

24. 2.49 ☐ 3.74

25. 5.03 ☐ 5.30

26. 2.87 ☐ 3.52

Student's name: ____________________ Assignment date: ________________

Order the following decimals from least to greatest.

1. 0.26, 0.62, 2.06

____

2. 9.52, 5.43, 7.86

____

3. 2.78, 2.74, 2.79

____

4. 4.74, 4.61, 4.83

____

5. 5.09, 5.73, 3.17

____

6. 9.07, 1.75, 4.68

____

Order the following decimals from greatest to least.

1. 6.30, 0.68, 2.96

____

2. 5.04, 0.45, 4.05

____

3. 0.36, 0.06, 0.63

____

4. 3.16, 3.18, 3.11

____

5. 8.45, 4.58, 4.85

____

6. 5.14, 0.14, 8.14

____

Student's name: ____________________ Assignment date: ________________

Decimal computations for advanced students

The whole number divided by the whole number	Decimal divided by whole	Whole divided by decimal	Decimal divided by decimal	Operated by the power of 10
1 ÷ 3	12.12 ÷ 3	300 ÷ 0.3 $=\frac{300}{0.3}=$	3.9 ÷ 0.3	3.9 ÷ 10
1 ÷ 5	10.05 ÷ 5	1515 ÷ 0.03	15.15 ÷ 0.03	15.15 ÷ 10000
1 ÷ 7	21.021 ÷ 7	1414 ÷ 0.7	14.14 ÷ 0.3	14.14 ÷ 0.1
21 ÷ 5	0.002525 ÷ 5	25251414 ÷ 0.5	252514.14 ÷ 0.5	252514.14 ÷ 0.001
31 ÷ 4	2829.028 ÷ 4	2829028 ÷ 0.04	28.29028 ÷ 0.04	28.29028 × 0.01
205 ÷ 25	0.502625 ÷ 5	502625 ÷ 0.05	5026.25 ÷ 0.05	5026.25 × 10000
125 ÷ 8	125.125 ÷ 25	125125 ÷ 2.5	1251.25 ÷ 2.5	1251.25 ÷ 10
18 ÷ 15	30.015 ÷ 15	30015 ÷ 1.5	300.15 ÷ 1.5	30015 ÷ 100

Student's name: ____________________ Assignment date: ________________

Adding and subtracting decimal by lining up decimal point using models

+ = _______ + _______ = ______

– 

= _______ – _______ = ______

4 + 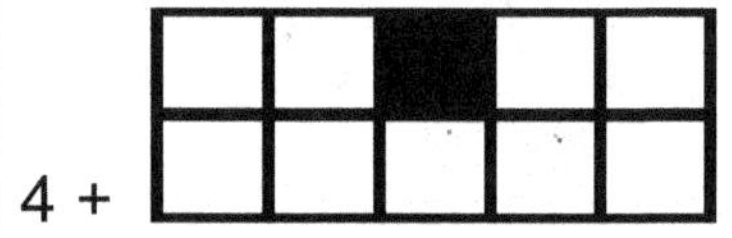 –1 –  = 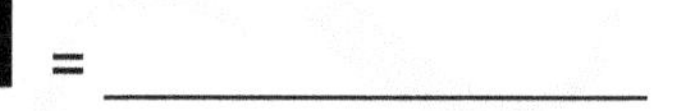

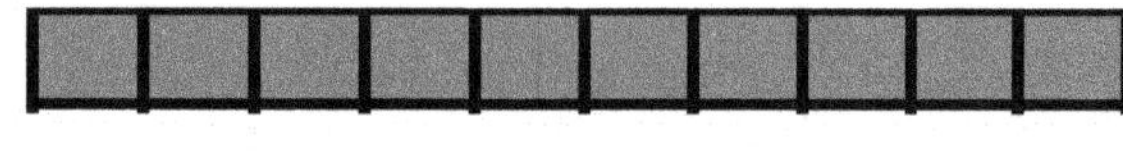 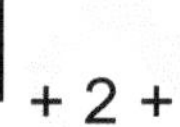 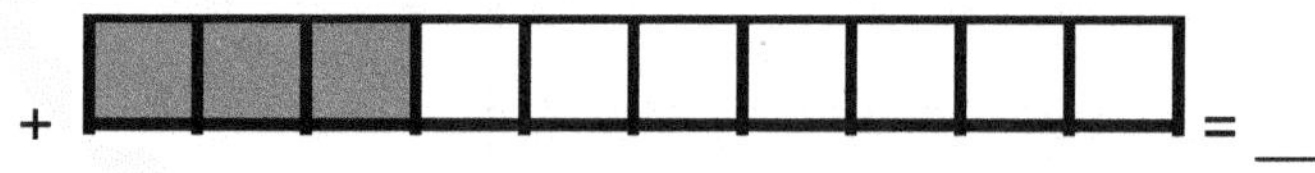 = ______

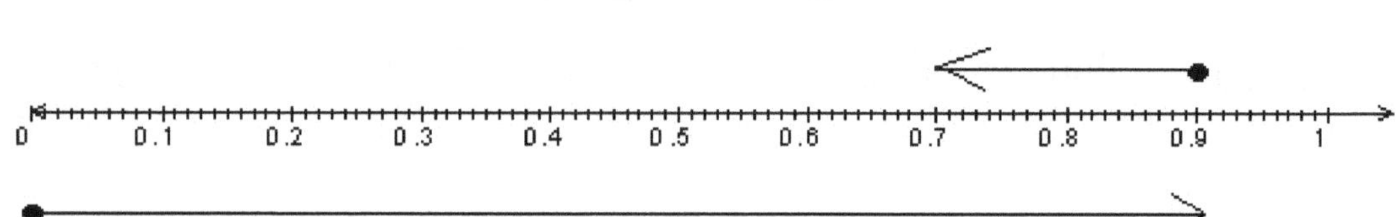

Circle the correct answer for the above number line operation.

0.9 + 0.2 = 1.1
0.9 – 0.2 = 0.7
0.9 – 0.7 = 0.2
0.9 + 0.7 = 1.6

Student's name: ____________________ Assignment date: ________________

Adding and subtracting decimal hundredths using grid or plot

Does the right-hand side 100 grid show what decimal addition by using two colours? ____________ + _________ = ______	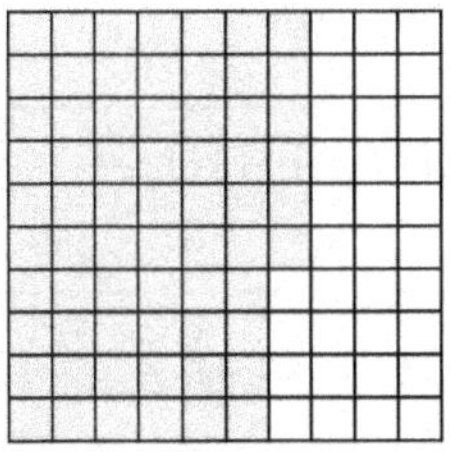
The right-hand side 100 grid shows decimal subtraction by using crossed-out squares for subtracting numbers. ____________ – _________ = ______ –	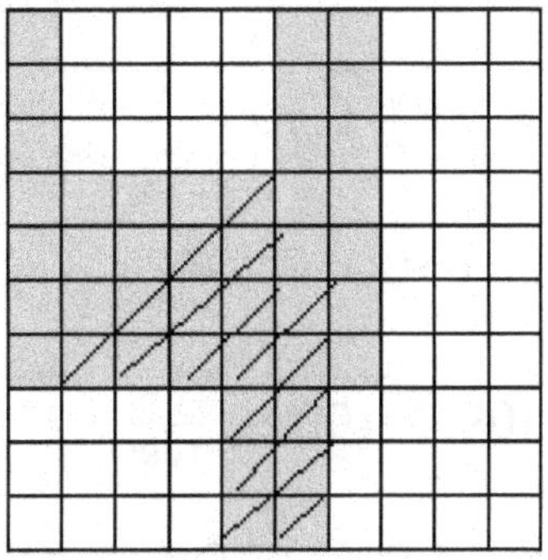
What decimal is the shaded area on the right figure?	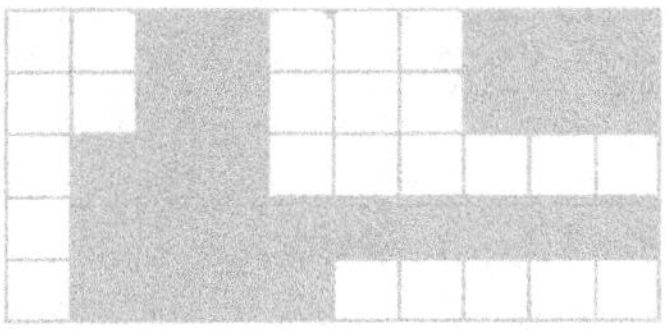
What decimal is the shaded area on the right figure?	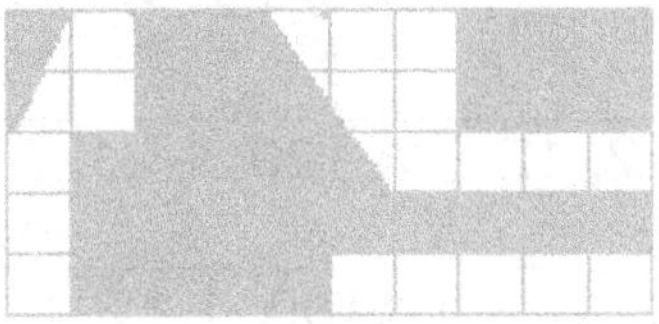
What decimal is the shaded area on the right figure?	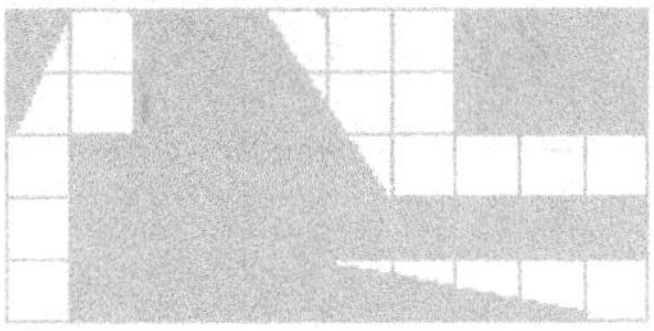

Student's name: ____________________ Assignment date: ________________

Circle the following equivalent decimals on the right side to the farthest left side decimal.

0.01	0.010, $\frac{1}{10}$, $\frac{1}{100}$, $\frac{2}{200}$, 0.001
0.91	0.9100, 0.091, 0.910, $\frac{91}{10}$, $\frac{91}{100}$, 91%
0.333…	$\frac{1}{3}$, $\frac{3}{9}$, $\frac{3}{10}$, 0.3, 0.33, $0.\overline{3}$
1.90	1.9, 1.900, 1.09, $1\frac{90}{100}$, $1\frac{9}{10}$
2.1 – 1.91	0.19, 0.91, 0.190, $\frac{19}{10}$, $\frac{19}{100}$
2.31 – 2.3	0.1, 0.010, 0.01, $\frac{1}{100}$
2.109	2.0109, 2.1090, $2\frac{109}{1000}$, $2 + 109$, $2 + 0.109$
2 – 1.091	1.099, 1.009, 1.909, 1.9090
11.11 + 1.11	12.22, 12.022, 12.220, $12\frac{22}{100}$
1.98 × 2	1.98+1.9, 1.98× 2 ÷ 2
1.98 ÷ 2	0.99, $\frac{99}{100}$, 0.990, 0.099, 0.999
1.212 × 1000	1212, 121, 12120, 1.212000
10 × 1.11 × 10	111, 121, 1.1100, 1.110× 10
2.213 × 10	212.3, 2.213, 2.1230, 21.23

Student's name: ____________________ Assignment date: ________________

Answers

Circle the following equivalent decimals on the right side to the farthest left side decimal.

Student's name: ____________________ Assignment date: ________________

Decimals Addition

When do decimal addition, we should line the decimal points up.

$$\begin{array}{r} 2.3 \\ +\ 5.8 \\ \hline 8.1 \end{array}$$

1. $\begin{array}{r} 1.5 \\ +\ 6.3 \\ \hline \end{array}$	7. $\begin{array}{r} 4.1 \\ +\ 2.5 \\ \hline \end{array}$	13. $\begin{array}{r} 5.4 \\ +\ 9.3 \\ \hline \end{array}$
2. $\begin{array}{r} 3.4 \\ +\ 4.6 \\ \hline \end{array}$	8. $\begin{array}{r} 2.5 \\ +\ 0.7 \\ \hline \end{array}$	14. $\begin{array}{r} 2.3 \\ +\ 8.7 \\ \hline \end{array}$
3. $\begin{array}{r} 3.7 \\ +\ 6.3 \\ \hline \end{array}$	9. $\begin{array}{r} 4.8 \\ +\ 3.2 \\ \hline \end{array}$	15. $\begin{array}{r} 4.4 \\ +\ 8.9 \\ \hline \end{array}$
4. $\begin{array}{r} 5.8 \\ +\ 2.6 \\ \hline \end{array}$	10. $\begin{array}{r} 2.4 \\ +\ 6.7 \\ \hline \end{array}$	16. $\begin{array}{r} 3.1 \\ +\ 0.9 \\ \hline \end{array}$
5. $\begin{array}{r} 4.6 \\ +\ 0.3 \\ \hline \end{array}$	11. $\begin{array}{r} 5.5 \\ +\ 2.5 \\ \hline \end{array}$	17. $\begin{array}{r} 0.8 \\ +\ 0.3 \\ \hline \end{array}$
6. $\begin{array}{r} 6.3 \\ +\ 3.6 \\ \hline \end{array}$	12. $\begin{array}{r} 0.2 \\ +\ 9.4 \\ \hline \end{array}$	18. $\begin{array}{r} 4.5 \\ +\ 7.8 \\ \hline \end{array}$

Student's name: ____________________ Assignment date: ________________

Decimals Addition

Example:

$$\begin{array}{r} 1.62 \\ +\ 5.24 \\ \hline 6.86 \end{array}$$

1. $\begin{array}{r} 2.52 \\ +\ 7.13 \\ \hline \end{array}$

2. $\begin{array}{r} 2.52 \\ +\ 5.18 \\ \hline \end{array}$

3. $\begin{array}{r} 2.72 \\ +\ 5.49 \\ \hline \end{array}$

4. $\begin{array}{r} 8.95 \\ +\ 1\ \ 05 \\ \hline \end{array}$

5. $\begin{array}{r} 7.35 \\ +\ 4.79 \\ \hline \end{array}$

6. $\begin{array}{r} 7.48 \\ +\ 4.37 \\ \hline \end{array}$

7. $\begin{array}{r} 3.25 \\ +\ 2.43 \\ \hline \end{array}$

8. $\begin{array}{r} 3.63 \\ +\ 5.45 \\ \hline \end{array}$

9. $\begin{array}{r} 3.62 \\ +\ 7.48 \\ \hline \end{array}$

10. $\begin{array}{r} 4.36 \\ +\ 7.57 \\ \hline \end{array}$

11. $\begin{array}{r} 5.89 \\ +\ 7.25 \\ \hline \end{array}$

12. $\begin{array}{r} 5.35 \\ +\ 9.28 \\ \hline \end{array}$

13. $\begin{array}{r} 2.37 \\ +\ 6.41 \\ \hline \end{array}$

14. $\begin{array}{r} 1.37 \\ +\ 5.25 \\ \hline \end{array}$

15. $\begin{array}{r} 2.19 \\ +\ 6.67 \\ \hline \end{array}$

16. $\begin{array}{r} 3.43 \\ +\ 8.89 \\ \hline \end{array}$

17. $\begin{array}{r} 3.57 \\ +\ 8.89 \\ \hline \end{array}$

18. $\begin{array}{r} 4.38 \\ +\ 7.76 \\ \hline \end{array}$

Student's name: ____________________ Assignment date: ________________

Across Addition

1) 4.6 + 3.3 = ____	2) 6.2 + 2.5 = ____	3) 2.8 + 3.1 = ____
4) 0.7 + 3.8 = ___	5) 0.9 + 0.2 = ___	6) 9.6 + 2.2 = _____
7) 6.3 + 7.5 = ____	8) 8.1 + 3.6 = ___	9) 7.7 + 4.6 = _____
10)5.2 + 3.8 = _____	11)6.4 + 0.6 = ____	12)9.4 + 1.7 = ____
13)9.3 + 0.8 = ____	14)8.2 + 2.8 = ____	15)5.0 + 6.3 = _____

Student's name: ____________________ Assignment date: ________________

horizontal Addition

1) 4.72 + 3.25 = ____	2) 4.15 + 3.43 = ____	3) 4.72 + 3.11 = ____
4) 4.72 + 0.46 = ___	5) 4.25 + 7.09 = ___	6) 5.13 + 7.34 = _____
7) 4.62 + 0.28 = ____	8) 4.52 + 0.37 = ___	9) 0.56 + 7.35 = _____
10) 6.48 + 3.09 = ____	11) 5.73 + 1.64 = ____	12) 4.72 + 5.76 = ____
13) 0.09 + 2.65 = ____	14) 6.42 + 5.78 = ____	15) 4.27 + 8.09 = ____

Student's name: ____________________ Assignment date: ________________

Decimal Subtraction

The same as addition, always line the decimals up.

$$\begin{array}{r} 5.6 \\ -\ 2.1 \\ \hline 3.5 \end{array}$$

1. $\begin{array}{r} 6.8 \\ -\ 2.5 \\ \hline \end{array}$

2. $\begin{array}{r} 6.4 \\ -\ 3.6 \\ \hline \end{array}$

3. $\begin{array}{r} 7.5 \\ -\ 6.9 \\ \hline \end{array}$

4. $\begin{array}{r} 6.0 \\ -\ 4.7 \\ \hline \end{array}$

5. $\begin{array}{r} 7.6 \\ -\ 5.7 \\ \hline \end{array}$

6. $\begin{array}{r} 16.1 \\ -\ 9.3 \\ \hline \end{array}$

7. $\begin{array}{r} 5.9 \\ -\ 1.8 \\ \hline \end{array}$

8. $\begin{array}{r} 5.3 \\ -\ 1.8 \\ \hline \end{array}$

9. $\begin{array}{r} 8.5 \\ -\ 7.6 \\ \hline \end{array}$

10. $\begin{array}{r} 3.5 \\ -\ 0.7 \\ \hline \end{array}$

11. $\begin{array}{r} 8.2 \\ -\ 1.9 \\ \hline \end{array}$

12. $\begin{array}{r} 25.7 \\ -\ 13.2 \\ \hline \end{array}$

13. $\begin{array}{r} 7.8 \\ -\ 4.4 \\ \hline \end{array}$

14. $\begin{array}{r} 5.5 \\ -\ 4.7 \\ \hline \end{array}$

15. $\begin{array}{r} 3.7 \\ -\ 3.3 \\ \hline \end{array}$

16. $\begin{array}{r} 0.9 \\ -\ 0.3 \\ \hline \end{array}$

17. $\begin{array}{r} 19.1 \\ -\ 6.9 \\ \hline \end{array}$

18. $\begin{array}{r} 14.7 \\ -\ 8.1 \\ \hline \end{array}$

Student's name: ____________________ Assignment date: ________________

Decimal Subtraction

$$\begin{array}{r} 7.59 \\ -\ 2.43 \\ \hline 5.16 \end{array}$$

1. $\begin{array}{r} 5.67 \\ -\ 1.43 \\ \hline \end{array}$

2. $\begin{array}{r} 6.79 \\ -\ 0.33 \\ \hline \end{array}$

3. $\begin{array}{r} 5.58 \\ -\ 0.07 \\ \hline \end{array}$

4. $\begin{array}{r} 10.73 \\ -\ 3.66 \\ \hline \end{array}$

5. $\begin{array}{r} 26.00 \\ -\ 21.05 \\ \hline \end{array}$

6. $\begin{array}{r} 35.19 \\ -\ 7.04 \\ \hline \end{array}$

7. $\begin{array}{r} 6.78 \\ -\ 3.41 \\ \hline \end{array}$

8. $\begin{array}{r} 4.17 \\ -\ 3.64 \\ \hline \end{array}$

9. $\begin{array}{r} 2.73 \\ -\ 0.18 \\ \hline \end{array}$

10. $\begin{array}{r} 12.07 \\ -\ 8.28 \\ \hline \end{array}$

11. $\begin{array}{r} 35.63 \\ -\ 11.68 \\ \hline \end{array}$

12. $\begin{array}{r} 63.43 \\ -\ 33.68 \\ \hline \end{array}$

13. $\begin{array}{r} 7.89 \\ -\ 3.75 \\ \hline \end{array}$

14. $\begin{array}{r} 6.16 \\ -\ 2.64 \\ \hline \end{array}$

15. $\begin{array}{r} 2.15 \\ -\ 1.07 \\ \hline \end{array}$

16. $\begin{array}{r} 17.01 \\ -\ 14.85 \\ \hline \end{array}$

17. $\begin{array}{r} 17.20 \\ -\ 16.48 \\ \hline \end{array}$

18. $\begin{array}{r} 27.72 \\ -\ 2.69 \\ \hline \end{array}$

Student's name: ____________________ Assignment date: ________________

Horizontal Subtraction

1) 6.7 – 3.28 = ____	2) 4.8 – 1.05 =____	3) 3.8 – 2.29 = _____
4) 6.3 – 3.812 = ______	5) 8.31 – 4.79 = ______	6) 6.41 – 5.919 = ____
7) 9.1 – 0.63 = ______	8) 4.8 – 0.92 = ______	9) 7.3 – 0.24 = ____
10)5.03 – 3.1 = _____	11)8.04 – 6.2 = ______	12)4.09 – 1.9 = ____
13)11.6 – 7.5 = _____	14)12.7 – 8.8 = ______	15)13.2 – 4.5 = _____

Student's name: ____________________ Assignment date: ________________

1)5.703 – 3.124 = ____	2)6.407 – 2.353 =____	3)5.407 – 1.254 = _____
4)6.306 – 6.2723 = ______	5)7.605 – 3.5887 = ______	6)3.517 – 0.6334 = ____
7)5.4 – 1.57 = ______	8)8.0 – 0.07 = ______	9)5.7 – 1.86 = ____
10) 12.64 – 6.07 = _____	11) 37.58 – 3.19 = _____	12) 16.48 – 6.03 = ____
13) 52.71 – 23.49 = ____	14) 25.43 – 18.20 = ____	15) 10.01 – 4.13 = _____

Student's name: ____________________ Assignment date: ________________

Place value computation including decimals and fractions including decimals and fractions

Do not ask students to work on this page until they understand the decimal place values.

2 hundreds and 2 thousands + 4 hundreds and 15 hundredths = ___________
213 thousandths + 49 hundredths = -______________
Fifty and 50 hundredths – twenty-nine and 39 thousandths = ____________
one hundred twenty-three times 9 + $\frac{97}{100}$ = ____________________
two hundred thirty-three – $9\frac{7}{100}$ = ____________________
If [grid] + $\frac{7}{100}$ + $\frac{?}{100}$ = 1, what is the value of "?"?

Decimal and fraction conversion

Decimal	fraction
0.21	?
0.212	? $\frac{53}{250}$
?	
?	$\frac{5}{20}$
?	$1\frac{1}{5}$
$\frac{52}{25}+1.02$	?
$\frac{2}{0.25}$	?

Student's name: ____________________ Assignment date: ________________

Estimating Sums by rounding to ones

5.6 →	6		5.6 is close to 6
+ 2.3 →	+ 2		2.3 is close to 2
.	8		6 + 2 = 8. So 5.6 + 2.3 is about 8.

1.	4.2 → + 7.5 →	+	2.	5.2 → + 1.6 →	+
3.	2.4 → + 5.1 →	+	4.	7.3 → + 0.6 →	+
5.	5.9 → + 3.7 →	+	6.	4.5 → + 7.7 →	+
7.	4.2 → + 3.6 →	+	8.	4.7 → + 7.1 →	+
9.	5.6 → + 8.2 →	+	10.	5.4 → + 3.2 →	+
11	6.9 → + 2.4 →	+	12.	4.5 → + 7.3 →	+

Student's name: ____________________ Assignment date: ________________

Estimating differences

$$\begin{array}{r} 8.7 \\ -\ 3.2 \\ \hline . \end{array} \rightarrow \begin{array}{r} 9 \\ -\ 3 \\ \hline 6 \end{array}$$

8.7 is close to 9
3.2 is close to 3
9 – 3 = 6 . So 8.7 – 3.2 is close to 6.

1. $\begin{array}{r} 5.3 \\ -\ 1.6 \\ \hline \end{array} \rightarrow -$ ______

2. $\begin{array}{r} 7.5 \\ -\ 3.8 \\ \hline \end{array} \rightarrow -$ ______

3. $\begin{array}{r} 7.2 \\ -\ 5.3 \\ \hline \end{array} \rightarrow -$ ______

4. $\begin{array}{r} 6.6 \\ -\ 1.8 \\ \hline \end{array} \rightarrow -$ ______

5. $\begin{array}{r} 7.2 \\ -\ 0.3 \\ \hline \end{array} \rightarrow -$ ______

6. $\begin{array}{r} 5.2 \\ -\ 4.5 \\ \hline \end{array} \rightarrow -$ ______

7. $\begin{array}{r} 5.1 \\ -\ 3.6 \\ \hline \end{array} \rightarrow -$ ______

8. $\begin{array}{r} 8.1 \\ -\ 3.6 \\ \hline \end{array} \rightarrow -$ ______

9. $\begin{array}{r} 7.7 \\ -\ 1.3 \\ \hline \end{array} \rightarrow -$ ______

10. $\begin{array}{r} 3.4 \\ -\ 0.7 \\ \hline \end{array} \rightarrow -$ ______

11 $\begin{array}{r} 8.2 \\ -\ 5.6 \\ \hline \end{array} \rightarrow -$ ______

12. $\begin{array}{r} 3.4 \\ -\ 2.8 \\ \hline \end{array} \rightarrow -$ ______

Student's name: ____________________ Assignment date: ________________

Relating decimals to measuring length

Metric measurement ladder diagram

The Metric system uses the same prefix words to memorize all three weight, length, and capacity measurements.

As you move the list of prefixes, the next unit is 10 times the current one. As you move down the list, the next unit is the 10th of the current one.

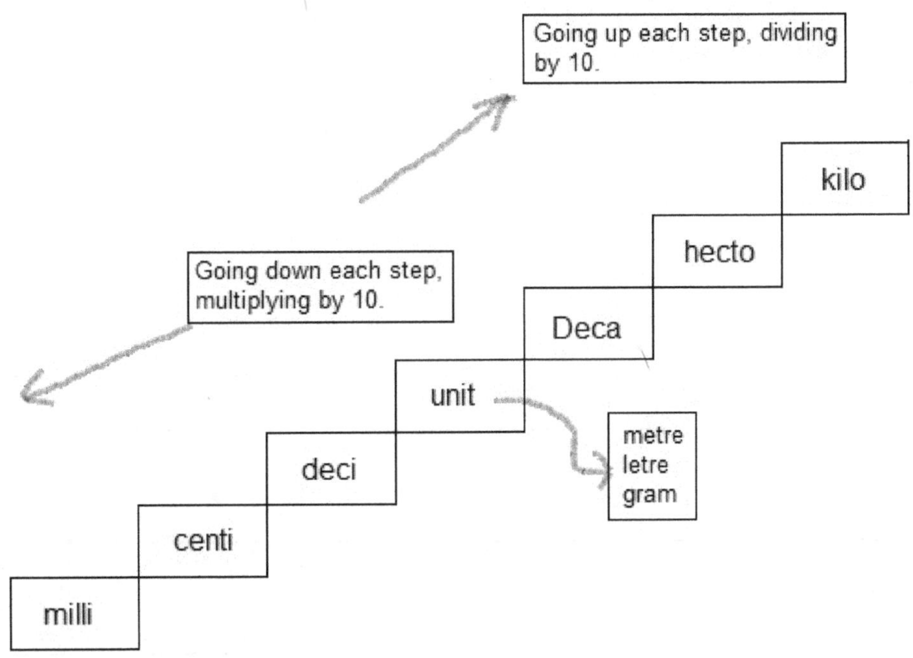

1 m = 10 dm = 100 cm, 1 dm =0.1 m
1 dm = 10 cm, 1 cm = 0.1 dm
1 cm = 10 mm, 1 mm = 0.1 cm

Ho Math Chess Primary Grades Math

Test Review assesssment 何数棋謎低年级数学测试複習考核

Student's name: ____________________ Assignment date: ________________

4 m 8 dm = 4 m + _____ m = _____m
2 cm 6 mm = 2 cm + ______ cm = _____ cm
4 km 4 m = 4 km + _____ km = _____ km
4.5 m 3 cm = ____ 4.5 m + ______m = _______ m
31 mm = ______ cm _____ mm
2500 cm = ______ km ______m = _______ km
45 cm = _____ dm _____cm = _______ dm = ______m
1100 mm = ______ cm = _______ dm = ______ m = ________ km
1100 mm – 99 cm = ____ cm
12.1m = ______ cm = ______ mm
34.55 mm +1.3 cm = _________ cm
1345 mm + 12.3 cm + 1 km = ______ km
1000 mm + 100 dm + 100 m = ______ km

Student's name: ____________________ Assignment date: ________________

Relating decimals to money

$1 = 100 cents (¢), 1 cent = 1 ¢ =$0.01
1 dime = 10 cents= 10 ¢, 1 nickel = 5 cents = 5 ¢
1 penny = 1 cent = 1 ¢

$1.55 + 5 cents = $ __________
$1.60 + ______ cents = $2.00
$1.400 + _____ cents = $5.00
400 ¢ + 900 ¢ = $ _______
692 ¢ + _____ cents = $9.01
$12.35 + _______ ¢ = $12.40
$ 12.40 + ______ cents = $13.50
$13.00 + $ _____ = $ 14.10
$5.15 – ______ cents = 232 cents
$1.10 – 99 cents = $ _______
$4.12 – $ ______ = 213 cents

Student's name: ____________________ Assignment date: ________________

Decimal word problems

1. A rope is 4.6 cm long. Another rope is 5.2 cm long. If the two ropes are connected, what is the maximum length of the rope?

2. An apple is 0.32 lb. An orange is 0.24 lb. What is the total weight of the two fruits?

3. A table is 0.8 m high. A box is 1.3 m high. If the box is put on the table, what is the height from the top of the box to the ground?

4. An ant walks 6.2 cm in one minute. A snail crawls 2.4 cm. How much further does an ant walk?

5. A shirt is $15.32. A hat is $7.45. What is the total price of the two items?

6. A watermelon is 3.6 kg. A pineapple is 1.2 kg. How much heavier is the watermelon?

7. Pauline bought 7 packs of jumbo gums for 79 cents each. How much change did she get from $7.00?

Student's name: ____________________ Assignment date: ________________

Rounding decimal number (5 up, 4 down)

The rounding decimal number is the same as rounding the whole number as long as we realize that the zeros after the decimal point do not make sense.

Question: Round the following numbers to the nearest tenths (one decimal place)	Step 1: Point to the place value (underlined) to be rounded.	Step 2: Look at the digit (single number) to the right of the pointed number.	Step 3: 5 up, 4 down If it is 5 or more, add 1 to the pointed number (round up); if it is less than 5, do not add 1 to the pointed number (round down).	Step 4: All digits to the right of the pointed number should be changed to 0.	Final answer
4128.59	4128.59	9	4128.6	4128.60	4128.6

Question:
Round the following numbers to the nearest tens (underlined)

4128.59	4128.59	8	4138.59	4130.00	4130

Question:
Round the following numbers to the nearest hundredths (2 decimal places)

4128.5987	4128.5987	8	4128.6087	4128.6000	4128.60

Round to the underlined place value

10.34	______	______	______	______	
0.355	______	______	______	______	

Student's name: ____________________ Assignment date: ________________

Test of rounding to the thousands

Circle the numbers from the list below that meet requirements. When rounded to tens, they equal 60. 51, 59, 56, 54, 55, 59, 54, 61, 67, 65, 60
Circle the numbers from the list below that meet requirements. When rounded to tens, they equal 100. 91, 99, 96, 94, 95, 90, 94, 101, 145, 151, 120, 110
Circle the numbers from the list below that meet requirements. When rounded to hundreds, they equal 100. 91, 99, 96, 94, 95, 90, 94, 101, 145, 151, 120, 110, 89, 199
Circle the numbers from the list below that meet requirements. When rounded to thousands, they equal 2000. 1991,1499,1896,1094, 2995, 2090, 1594, 2101, 1145, 1651, 1220, 2110, 2189, 2199

Find all possible numbers which meet the requirement: the numbers, when rounded to the nearest tens, are equal to 80.
Find all possible numbers between 350 to 499 which meet the requirement: the numbers, when rounded to the nearest hundreds, are equal to 400.
If a number 13?9 is rounded to 1300, what could be the tens?

Student's name: ____________________ Assignment date: ________________

***** Part 7 Pattern *****

Pattern attributes (for higher grades)

Figure pattern has some attributes such as colours, sizes, shapes, directions, and fonts. For example, the following pattern has the attributes of sizes, shapes, and colours.

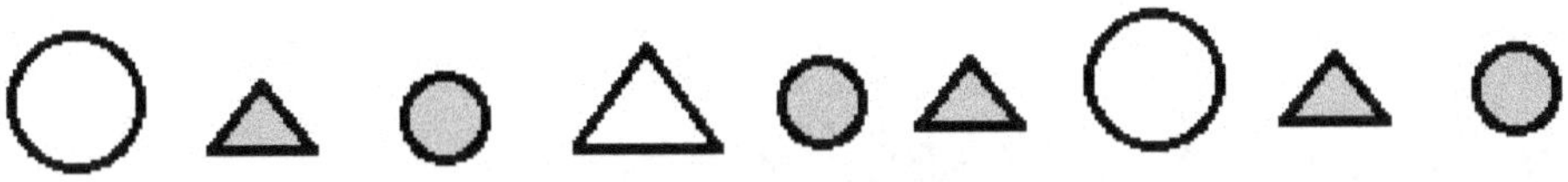

A. The above pattern has 3 attributes size, colour, shape.

B. How does the size change?
It changes in the order of Large, small, small, Large, small, small, ….

How does the shape change?
It changes in the order of large circle, small triangle, small circle, large circle, small triangle, small circle, ….

C. What are the next three shapes in the pattern?

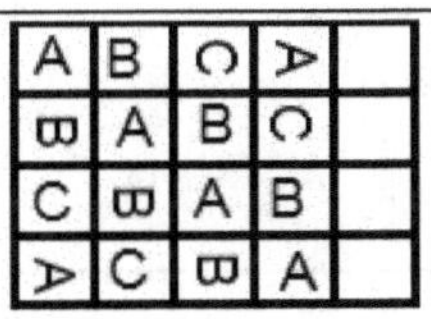

A	B	C	A	
B	A	B	C	
C	B	A	B	
A	C	B	A	

A. What attributes do they change in the above pattern?

B. What is the next column in the above pattern

…

A. What attributes do they change in the above pattern?
Shape and size

B. What is the next 3 column in the above pattern

Student's name: ____________________ Assignment date: ________________

Pattern core and pattern rule (for higher grades)

There are many different kinds of patterns such as all numbers pattern, pattern with figures, pattern with repeated core pattern or 2-dimensional pattern etc.

Pattern core

Example

What is the pattern core of the pattern ABCABCABCABCABC….?

The pattern core of the above pattern is ABC.

What is the 110th letter of the pattern ABCABCABCABCABC….?
Predict the colour of the 112th block of the following pattern. red | yellow | yellow | red | red | yellow | yellow | red | red | yellow | yellow | red .
predict the 57th term of A1B2A1B2A1B2… Each letter or number is considered as one term.
How many letters are in the 20th term in the following pattern? RY, RRYY, RRRYYY, RRRRYYYY, …

Student's name: ____________________ Assignment date: ________________

How to find the number pattern?

How to find the next number?

Step 1

To find the next number of a number pattern, it is often to use the difference or quotient (or called gap) between two adjacent numbers.

Step 2

To predict the next number, one should figure out the pattern rule.

1-dimensional pattern

3, 5, 7, 9, 11, _____

The gap is always 2 by using the larger – small number.
The pattern rule is as follows.
Start at 3, add 2 to get the next number.
The answer is 13.

2, 4, 8, 16, _________
The pattern rule is ________________

Row 1	1	2	3	4	5
Row 2	3	4	5	6	?

The pattern rule is ____________________________________.

Continue the pattern in the following table.

1			
3	6		
?	?	20	
7	14	?	56

Student's name: ____________________ Assignment date: ________________

In and out boxes

In	1	3	5	7
Out	3	5	7	?

Pattern rule: Out = In + 2

In	1	3	5	7
Out	3	5	7	?

Pattern rule: Out = In + 2

In	1	3	5	7
Out	3	5	7	?

Pattern rule: Out = In + 2

In	1	3	5	7
Out				

Pattern rule: Out = In + 2

In	1	3	5	7
Out				

Pattern rule: Out = In × 2

In	4	6	7	8
Out				

Pattern rule: Out = In - 1

In	Out
2	
4	
5	
7	

Pattern rule: Out = In × 3

In	Out
12	
9	
6	
5	

Pattern rule: Out = In add 2

In	Out
19	
18	
17	
13	

Pattern rule: Out = In subtract 6

Student's name: ____________________ Assignment date: ________________

Number patterns or letter pattern(for lower grades)

1.	1	2	3	_____	_____	_____
2.	2	4	6	_____	_____	_____
3.	5	10	15	_____	_____	_____
4.	10	100	1000	_____	_____	_____
5.	325	335	345	_____	_____	_____
6.	4236	5236	6236	_____	_____	_____
7.	270	280	290	_____	_____	_____
8.	1150	1200	1250	_____	_____	_____
9.	7385	7375	7365	_____	_____	_____
10.	4350	4250	4150	_____	_____	_____
11.	1007	1008	1009	_____	_____	_____
12.	4256	4506	4756	_____	_____	_____
13.	21	32	43	_____	_____	_____
14.	613	524	435	_____	_____	_____
15.	987	876	765	_____	_____	_____

Student's name: ____________________ Assignment date: ________________

Letters pattern

1. Continue the following patterns.

   B, D, F. H, ____
   ABAABA __ __ __ __ __ __ __ __
   GH1GH2GH3 __ __ __
   BAABBAAABBB___ ___ ___ ___ ___ ___ ___ ___

Student's name: ____________________ Assignment date: ________________

Looking for patterns

1.	3	_____	15	31	63	127	255
2.	10	20	40	80	160	_____	
3.	2	4	16	_____	65536		
4.	16	8	_____	_____	1		
5.	_____	12	36	108	324	972	
6.	_____	_____	20	24	96	100	400
7.	600	600	300	100	25	_____	
8.	784529	78452	7452	452	_____	_____	
9.	11	18	25	32	39	_____	53
10.	810	270	_____	30	10		
11.	1	4	16	64	256	_____	
12.	$400	$200	$100	$50	_____		
13.	100	99	97	94	90	_____	_____
14.	15	12	14	11	13	_____	_____
15.	1	3	7	15	31	_____	_____
16.	67	35	19	11	7	_____	_____

Student's name: ____________________ Assignment date: ________________

Looking for patterns.

1

2 2

3 4 3

4 7 __ 4

5 11 __ 11 5

6 __ 25 __ 16 6

7 22 41 __ 41 __ 7

The above is called the Pascal triangle if two 1's are added on both ends of each row.

1

2 4

3 9 27

4 16 __ 256

5 __ __ 625 3125

1

2 4

3 6 9

4 8 __ 16

5 __ 15 __ __

6 __ __ __ __ __

Student's name: ____________________ Assignment date: ________________

Figure pattern

Student's name: ____________________ Assignment date: ________________

Put R in the following board in such a way that each row, each column has one and only one R. Can you find more than one way?

1.

2.

3.

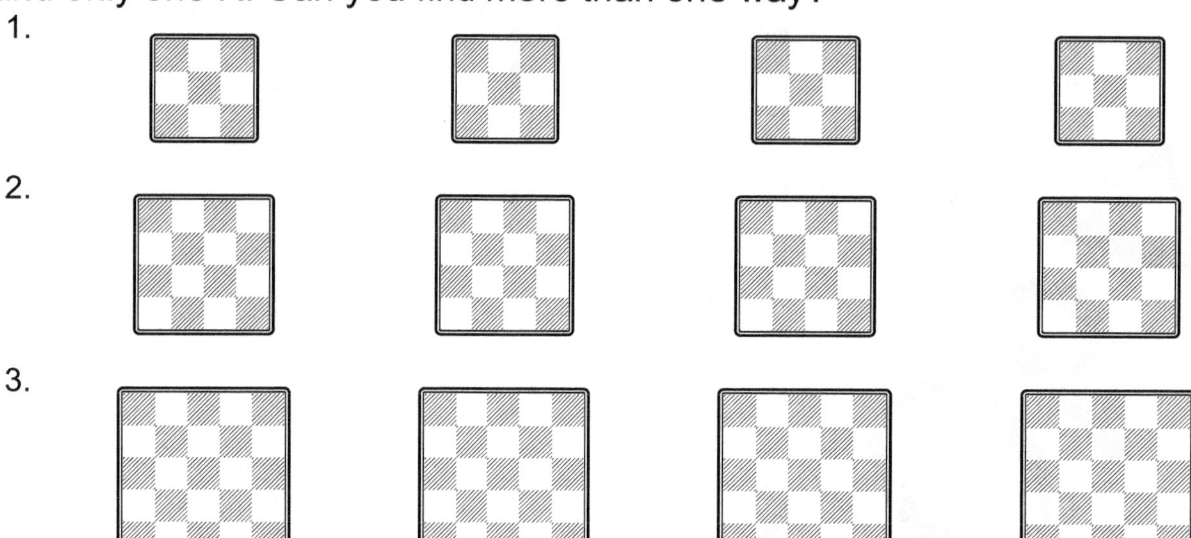

Put A,B,C in the following board in such a way that each row, each column has one and only one of each kind. Can you find more than one way?

Put A, B, C and D in the following board in such a way that each row, each column, and each main diagonal has one and only one of each kind. Can you find more than one way?

Student's name: ____________________ Assignment date: ________________

2-dimensional pattern

Look for Pattern and Complete T-table.

2.

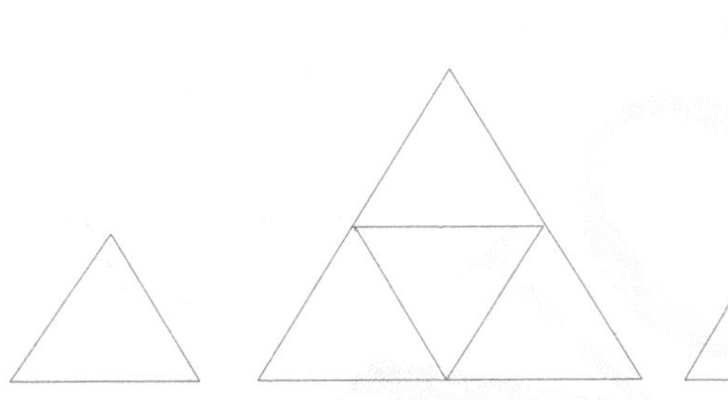

Number of columns	Number of squares
1	3
2	6
3	9
4	
5	
6	

3.

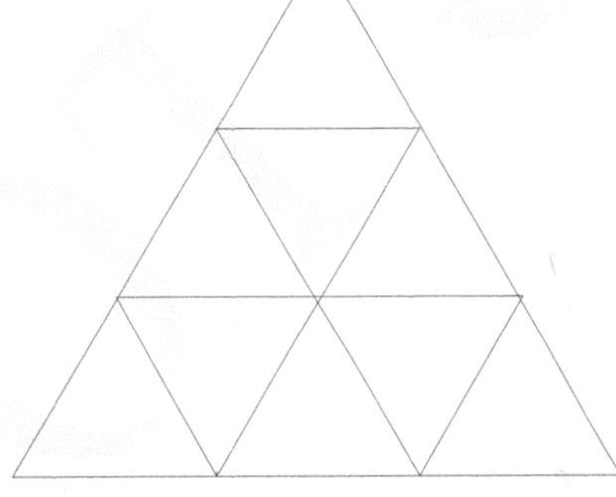

Number of rows	Number of triangles
1	1
2	4
3	9
4	
5	
6	

4.

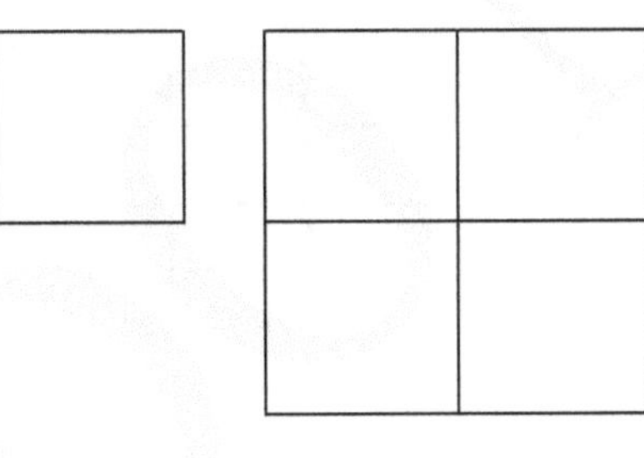

Number of rows	Number of squares
1	1
2	4
3	9
4	
5	
6	

Student's name: ____________________ Assignment date: ________________

Look for Pattern and Complete T-table.

5.

```
* * *      * * * *      * * * * *
*          *            *
*          *            *
           *            *
                        *
```

Number of rows	Number of apples
3	5
4	7
5	9
6	
7	
8	

6.

```
★ ★      ★ ★ ★      ★ ★ ★ ★
★ ★      ★   ★      ★     ★
         ★ ★ ★      ★     ★
                    ★ ★ ★ ★
```

Number of rows	Number of stars
2	4
3	8
4	12
5	
6	
7	

7.

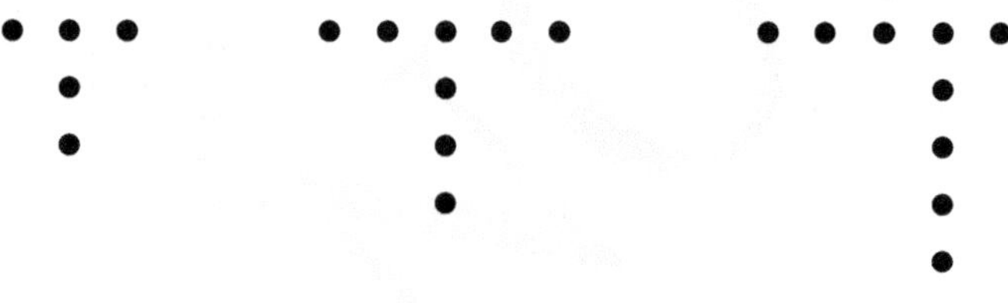

Number of rows	Number of dots
3	5
4	8
5	11
6	
7	
8	

Student's name: ____________________ Assignment date: ________________

Look for Pattern and Complete T-table.

8.

Number of rows	Number of apples
3	5
5	9
7	13
9	
11	
13	

9.

Number of rows	Number of stars
3	6
5	12
7	18
9	
11	
13	

10.

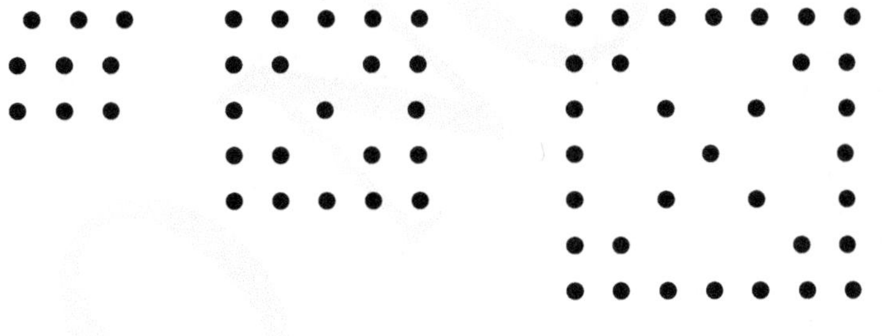

Number of rows	Number of dots
3	9
5	21
7	33
9	
11	
13	

Student's name: ____________________ Assignment date: ________________

Pattern word problems

Alvin saves $11 in February, and he saves $5 after that every month. How much will he have saved by the end of August?
Adam saves $17 in January and $5 each month after that. Bob saves $15 in January and $7 each month after that. Who has saved more money by the end of November?
Heather has biked 10 km from her home. After that, she cycles 7 km per hour. If she biked 38 km, how many more hours had she biked after the initial 10 km?
Kiko and Snow cats share cat food one can for every 5 days. How many cans should Frank buy in December if there are no more cans left?
Kiko, the cat, likes to go out in the very early morning. She will usually come back every 45 minutes, rest for 5 minutes, and then go out again until noon. Then she likes to take a nap. Suppose Kiko goes out at 6:30 a.m. If this pattern continues, how many times would she have gone out, and how many times would she have come back if Kiko stayed at home the last time before noon? 630 715, 720 805, 810 855, 900 945, 950 1035, 1040 1125.

Student's name: ____________________ Assignment date: ________________

The two cats Kiko and Snow, like to collect leaves. Yesterday Kiko collected 3 leaves, and Snow collected 1 leaf. If starting from today, Kiko collects 1 leaf every day and Snow collects 2 leaves every day, then on what day will they collect the same number of leaves?
In Ethan`s class, three out of every five students are male. There are 125 students in his class. How many of them are female
Today, Adam has read 8 pages of his book and will read one page after that. Bob has read 4 pages and will read 2 pages after that. How many days later will Adam and Bob read the same number of pages?
Kiko, the cat, goes out every 6 minutes, and the cat Snow goes out every 8 minutes. If both of them go out at 6:30 a.m. when would be the next time they go out altogether?
Banno has 8 books and buys 1 new book every week. Benni has 4 books and buys a new book every week. After how many weeks will Banno and Benni have the same number of books?

Student's name: ____________________ Assignment date: ________________

The pattern in **ax + by model**

Renee is working to raise money for her gymnastics competition trip. She has two options:
Option A – She works 7 days, and each day, she makes $8.
Option B – She makes different money each day.

Day 1	Day 2	Day 3	Day 4	Day 5	Day 6	Day 7
$1	$3	$5	$7	$9	?	?

To raise the most money, which option should Renee choose? Show all your work.

Renee wants to grow 50 seedlings in two kinds of trays. One tray can hold 4 seedlings, and the other tray can hold 6 seedlings. How many different ways can she fill in the two trays if each tray must be in full?

There are 4 ways to plant.

Student's name: ______________________ Assignment date: ________________

Pattern test

Figure out the pattern rule first, then write the next three numbers. 27, 24, 21, 18, _____, ______, ______
Figure out the pattern rule first, then write the next three numbers. 4, 5, 7, 10, 14, _____, ______, ______
Figure out the pattern rule first, then write the next three numbers. 31, 35, 39, _____, ______, ______

Look for patterns of the following pattern figure, then complete the number chain.

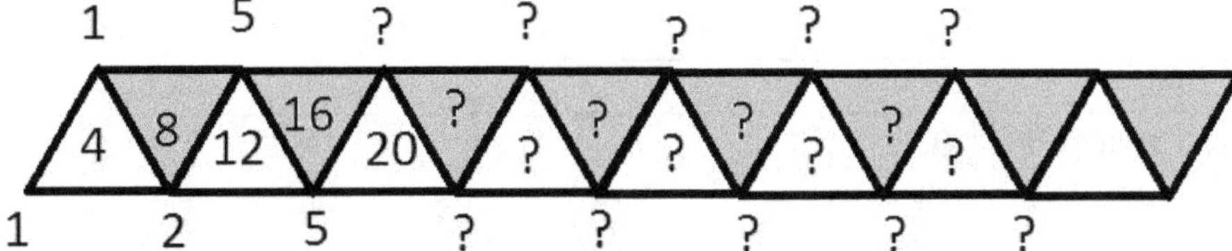

The pattern rule inside the chain. ________________________.
The pattern rule above the chain ________________________. The pattern below the chain ___________________________. The pattern of zigzagging numbers ___________________________.

Student's name: ____________________ Assignment date: ________________

Describe how the attributes change in the following diagram pattern?

□ ● □ ◇ □ ● □ ◇ □ ● □ ....

____

Repeat the pattern core
Draw the next three shapes. ____

Describe the pattern rule of the following T-chart. You should think about how to get the number of paws from the number of cats.

cats	paws
1	4
2	?
3	?
4?	?

The pattern rule is ______________________________

Describe the pattern rule of the following T-chart.

weeks	days
1	?
2	14
3	?
4?	?

____ dCreate a problem that can be solved by using the above pattern rule.

____

Student's name: ____________________ Assignment date: ________________

Renee can make 3 paper kites in 1 hour. Create a chart to show how many kites can make of increased hours each hour up to 5 hours.

hours	kites
1	3
?	?
?	?
?	?

____ Create a problem that can be solved by using the above pattern rule.

____

Student's name: ____________________ Assignment date: ________________

***** Part 8 Venn Diagram *****

Place the multiples of 3 in the following table and the multiples of 2 in the following table in the Venn diagram.

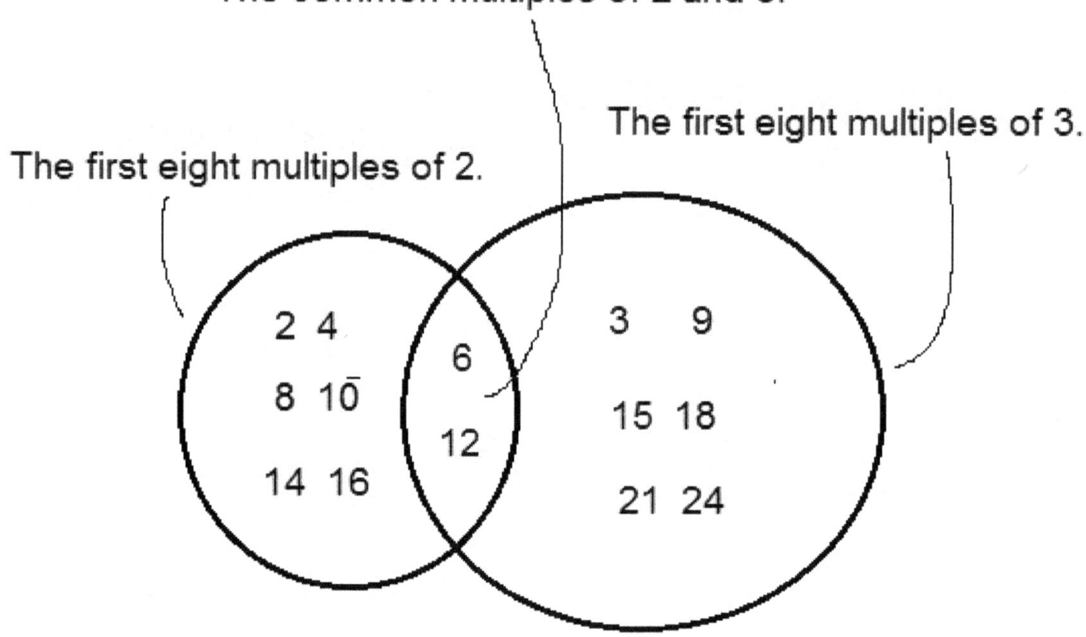

Place the first eight multiples of 6 in the following table and the first eight multiples of 9 in the following table in the Venn diagram.

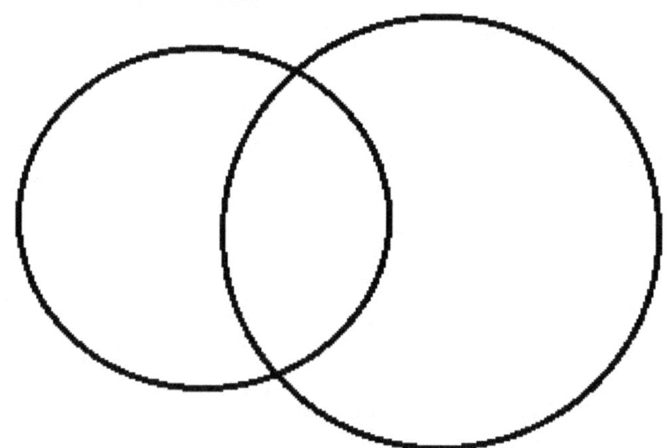

Student's name: ____________________ Assignment date: ________________

Venn diagram

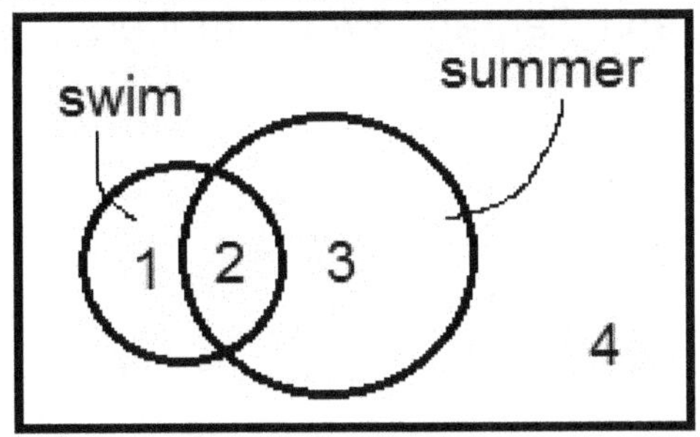

Use the above Venn diagram to answer the following questions.

A. In which part of the Venn diagram would you put on a summer swimming suit.
B. In which part of the Venn diagram would you put on your beachwear?
C. In which part of the Venn diagram would you swim outdoor?

Student's name: ____________________ Assignment date: ________________

Test of Venn diagram

There are some three-digit numbers sorted into the following Venn diagram. Write numbers into each circle to replace the question marks.

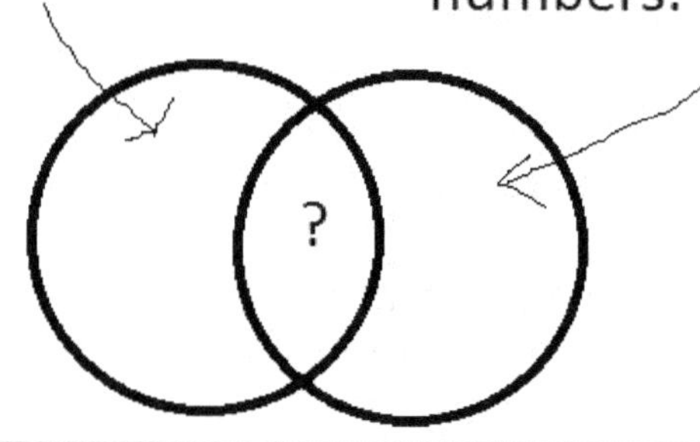

Use the following numbers to create a Venn diagram using the sorting rule (attributes) you created. Label each part of the circle and the intersection in the middle.
21, 27, 302, 80, 35, 235, 16, 107, 212
Answers may vary.

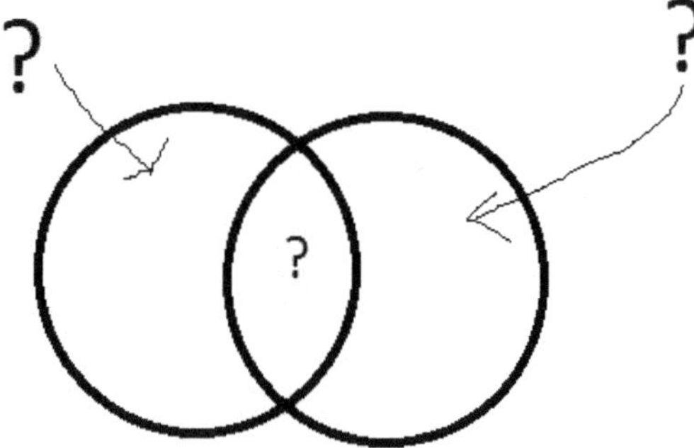

Student's name: ____________________ Assignment date: ________________

***** Part 9 Simple equation using figures *****

If ○ = 9 then ○ + 1 = ______. 10

If ○ = 11 then ○ – 2 = ______. 9

If ● = 1 then ○ = ●●● then ○ + ●●● = ______.

If ○ = ●●● then ○ + ●●● ●● = ______

If ○ = ●●● and ● = 1 then ○ + ●●● – ● = ______

Write a number in the box to make the equation true.

○ +7 = 11

○ + 6 = 13

○ + 9 = 16

2 + ○ = 13

6 + ○ = 14

11 = ○ + 2

17 = 8 + ○

○ – 8 = 3

○ – 2 = 9

13 – ○ – 8 = 3

6 – ○ – 1 = 3

Student's name: ____________________ Assignment date: ________________

Solving equation

Equations

It makes sense for students to learn some equations before ratio and proportion, so many students got confused on proportions simply because they do not know how to solve the equations of proportion, especially the method of using cross multiplication. This section aims to give students the knowledge of using equations to solve proportion and percent problems.

An equation is a mathematical sentence using = sign to connect two quantities. The left side of the = sign or the right side of the = sign is called an algebraic expression. The expression consists of numbers, operators, or variables (unknown quantity representing by a letter, normally by x). The operators can have brackets (parentheses), exponents, plus, minus, multiplication, or division,, which are used in elementary school mathematics. To solve an equation is to find all values of the variables so that both sides are equal.

To solve the equation, quite often, we use the following equation of properties:

The equation does not change when both sides add the same quantity.

The equation does not change when both sides subtract the same quantity.

The equation does not change when both sides multiply the same quantity.

The equation does not change when both sides are divided by the same quantity.

Student's name: ____________________ Assignment date: ________________

Arithmetic operations properties

A few properties govern the arithmetic operations with real numbers, and they are presented below.

Closure for addition, subtraction, and multiplication.
For real numbers a and b:

$a + b$ is a unique real number.
$a - b$ is a unique real number.
$a \times b$ Is a unique real number.

If two real numbers are added, subtracted, or multiplied, then the result is always a real number. The result is "enclosed" in the universe of the real numbers.
For division, it may not be true, such as $\frac{8}{0}$.

The commutative property for addition and multiplication of 2 numbers
(The associative property is used for 3 or more numbers)

For real numbers a and b.
$a + b = b + a$
$ab = ba$
The results are not changed when the order of 2 numbers is changed.

Which one of the following operations is commutative and which one is not?

Problems	Commutative or not
To put on soap and wash hands	☐
To put on gloves and put on a coat.	☐
To wash hands and eat.	☐

Student's name: ____________________ Assignment date: ________________

To wash clothes and dry them.	☐
To eat rice and eat chicken.	☐
To hang up the phone and say good-bye.	☐
To multiply 2 and 3.	☐
To mix blue and green paint.	☐
The number of different outfits of pairing pants and shirts.	☐
The number of ways of choosing food from a menu.	☐
To check and checkmate the king.	☐
To flip ⁘⁘ (2 × 4 array of dots) around	☐
To get an area of a rectangle.	☐

Student's name: ____________________ Assignment date: ________________

Associative property (grouping property) for addition and multiplication of 3 numbers

For real numbers a, b, c
$(a + b) + c = a + (b + c)$
$(ab)c = a(bc)$

Use the associative property to make 10 first and then add the third number.

4 6 + 3	4 3 + 6	9 7 + 1	4 8 + 2	7 8 + 3

Use the associative property to make a nice number (number with trailing zeros) first, then multiply the third number.

12 × 6 × 5 =	11 × 4 × 25 =	7 × 25 × 4 =
13 × 2 × 5 =	14 × 2 × 25 =	7 × 15 × 4 =
2 × 7 × 5 =	8 × 4 × 25 =	8 × 8 × 25 =

More problems can be found in this workbook under the heading multiplied by 5.

Student's name: ____________________ Assignment date: ________________

Addition by regrouping using the associative property

The order of operation is normally from left to right, but because the sign always goes with the number so the numbers can be regrouped for addition by using the associative property (1+7 + 9 = (1+9) +7= 10+7=17.

Example: 23 + 42 + 77 + 38 = (23 + 77) + (42 + 38) = 100 + 80 = 180

1. 42 + 73 + 27 + 58
=(42 + 58) + (73 + 27)
= 100 + 100
= 200

2. 26 + 39 + 44 + 61

3. 85 + 36 + 115 + 34

4. 51 + 23 + 49 + 57

5. 73 + 42 + 28 + 27

6. 49 + 36 + 51 + 74

7. 153 + 57 + 63 + 47

8. 535 + 58 + 52 + 65

9. 73 + 69 + 51 + 127

10. 56 + 368 + 32 + 84

Student's name: ____________________ Assignment date: ________________

Identity of addition

For real number a

$$a+0=0+a=a$$

Zero is the addition identity. Any number add a 0. Its answer is still the number itself.

Identity of multiplication

For real number a

$$a(1)=(1)a=a$$

One is the multiplication identity. Any number multiplies 1, and its answer is still the number itself.

Additive inverse

For any real number a, there exists a unique real number $-a$ such that

$a+(-a)=a-a=0$

The number $-a$ is known as the additive inverse.

a and $-a$ are additive inverse to each other and also the opposite of each other.

Multiplicative inverse

For any nonzero real number a, there exists a unique real number $\frac{1}{a}$ such that

$a\left(\frac{1}{a}\right)=\left(\frac{1}{a}\right)a=1$, the number $\frac{1}{a}$ is known as the multiplicative inverse or reciprocal of a.

a and $\frac{1}{a}$ are multiplicative inverse or reciprocal to each other. Since 1 is the product of $a\times\frac{1}{a}$ so to get $\frac{1}{\frac{a}{b}}$, we just have to inverse $\frac{a}{b}$ to get the answer $\frac{b}{a}$.

Student's name: ____________________ Assignment date: ________________

Distributive property

For real numbers a, b, c

$a(b+c)=ab+ac$	$a(b-c)=ab-ac$	$(a+b)c=ac+bc$	(a – b) c = ac - bc

The vertical multiplication is an example of using associative property.

$a(b+c)=ab+ac$	24 × 37 = 24 × (7 + 30) = 168 + 720 = 888 Note on the right-hand side, when 3 × 24, it means 30 × 24.	$\begin{array}{r} 24 \\ \times \quad 37 \\ \hline 168 \\ 72 \\ \hline 888 \end{array}$	One can clearly see the reason why the product lined up with tens place value when 3 × 24.
$a(b+c)=ab+ac$	24 × 37 = 24 × (30+7) = 720 + 168 = 888	$\begin{array}{r} 24 \\ \times \quad 37 \\ \hline 72 \\ 168 \\ \hline 888 \end{array}$	
	Note how 3 and 24 is multiplied first.		

Student's name: ____________________ Assignment date: ________________

Using distributive property to factor out common number on addition

Examples

$36 \times 8 + 36 \times 12$

$= 36 \times (8 + 12)$

$= 36 \times 20$

$= 720$

$56 \times 48 + 56 \times 52$

$= 56 \times (48 + 52)$

$= 56 \times 100$

$= 5600$

$73 \times 7 + 73 \times 3$

$81 \times 4 + 81 \times 6$

$693 \times 2 + 693 \times 8$

$239 \times 8 + 239 \times 2$

$421 \times 9 + 421 \times 1$

$326 \times 5 + 326 \times 5$

Student's name: ____________________ Assignment date: ________________

7. $43 \times 26 + 43 \times 74$

$61 \times 45 + 61 \times 55$

9. $48 \times 36 + 48 \times 64$

$68 \times 28 + 28 \times 32$

11. $57 \times 35 + 43 \times 35$

$69 \times 41 + 41 \times 31$

13. $58 \times 31 + 58 \times 69$

$29 \times 47 + 71 \times 47$

Student's name: ____________________ Assignment date: ________________

Using distributive property to factor out the common number on subtraction

Examples

$45 \times 13 - 45 \times 3$	$129 \times 147 - 129 \times 47$
$= 45 \times (13 - 3)$	$= 129 \times (147 - 47)$
$= 45 \times 10$	$= 129 \times 100$
$= 450$	$= 12900$

1. $61 \times 17 - 61 \times 7$

2. $87 \times 16 - 87 \times 6$

3. $52 \times 15 - 52 \times 5$

4. $43 \times 27 - 43 \times 7$

5. $67 \times 25 - 67 \times 5$

6. $66 \times 74 - 66 \times 4$

Student's name: ____________________ Assignment date: ________________

7. 48 × 132 – 48 × 32

8. 63 × 143 – 63 × 43

9. 77 × 124 – 77 × 24

10. 57 × 119 – 57 × 19

11. 48 × 265 – 48 × 65

12. 71 × 335 – 71 × 35

13. 63 × 47 – 47 × 13

14. 78 × 32 – 32 × 38

15. 53 × 26 – 33 × 26

16. 27 × 59 – 59 × 17

Student's name: ____________________ Assignment date: ________________

Variable and expression

In algebra, an unknown quantity or number is represented by a letter such as x, y. An algebraic expression is a mathematical sentence consisting of numbers, operators, or variables with no equal sign.

Fill in ____________ with an answer.

Word phrases	Expression	Comments
The product of 10 and a number	$10x$	Do not write the product as $10 \times x$. The number (called coefficient) is placed in front of the variable, and there is an implied $\times$ sign between the number and variable. $3x$ means 3 times x.
A number is doubled.	$2x$	Write variable (unknown) X as x or X since X looks like a multiplication sign. We normally use x, y, z as variables, but not always.
One hundred divided by a number	$\frac{100}{x}$	Do not write division as $a \div b$. Use $\frac{a}{b}$ as a division in algebra since we need to work with LCD in the future.

Student's name: ____________________ Assignment date: ________________

Variable and expression

Word phrases	Algebraic expression
A number is tripled.	$3x$
4 times x	$4x$
x times 2 (a number is doubled.)	$2x$
x times x (a number is multiplied by itself.)	x^2
one-sixth of a number (a number divided by 6)	____________
Maria's age 7 years from her age now	____________
1 times x	____________
x times 1	____________
$2x$ times 4	____________
2 times a	____________
a times 2	____________
thirty-one kilometres less than the distance	____________
4 times 2 x	____________
3 minus x	____________
1 more than a number	____________
a number decreased by four	____________

Student's name: ____________________ Assignment date: ________________

Writing algebraic expressions

Word phrase	Algebraic expression
99 subtracted from a number	
a number divided by 23	
The sum of a number y and 15	
one multiplies a number.	
the difference between a number and forty	
99 multiplied by a number	
a number multiplied by 1	x
the product of 2 and 5 and a number	
If x is an odd number, what is the next larger odd number?	
a number divided by 5523	
5523 divided by a number	
I rode roller coaster x times, and the total time is 300 minutes. What is the average time?	
It took me 30 minutes to finish my grocery shopping, and it included the time of x waiting in line. What is the time I actually spent on shopping?	

Student's name: ____________________ Assignment date: ________________

Writing algebraic expressions

Word phrase	Algebraic expression
Let t be the time taken between school and home round trip. How long did it take for 7 round trips?	______________
It took Stanley and Edward 5 hours altogether to finish typing a science project report. How much time did Stanley spend on typing, assume Edward typed x hours?	______________

Word phrase	Algebraic expression
____	$x + 9$
____	$5 - x$
____	$9x + 4$
____	$\frac{1}{2x}$
____	$5a$
a number x multiplied by itself	x^2
____	$x^2 + 30$

Student's name: ____________________ Assignment date: ________________

Writing word phrases

______________________________	$u+\frac{u}{4}$
111 less than a number	
______________________________	$200m$
______________________________	$\frac{1}{2x}$
______________________________	$3x-1$
______________________________	x^2
______________________________	$u-4u$

Student's name: ____________________ Assignment date: ________________

Evaluate the following expressions.

Expressions	Value	Comments
7 – 2 × 3		
7 – (2 × 3)		Are the brackets necessary? _____
(7 – 2) × 3		
2 × 7 – 3		
(2 × 7) – 3		Are the brackets necessary? _____
2 × (7 – 3)		
4 × 5 + 6 × 7		

Student's name: ____________________ Assignment date: ________________

Evaluate the following expressions

Expressions	Value	Comments
4 × (5 + 6) × 7		
4 × (5 + 6 × 7)		
(4 × 5 + 6) × 7		
45 ÷ 5 + 9 ÷ 3		
(45 ÷ 5) + (9 ÷ 3)		Are brackets necessary? ________
42 ÷ (5 + 9) ÷ 3		
48 ÷ (5 + 9 ÷ 3)		
(45 ÷ 5 + 9) ÷ 3		
1 + 2 + 3 ÷ 3 – 2 – 1		
(1 + 2 + 3) ÷ (3 – 2) – 1		
1 + 2 + 3 ÷ (3 – 2) – 1		
1 + 2 + 3 ÷ 3 × 2 – 1		
1 + 2 + 3 ÷ 3 × (2 – 1)		

Student's name: ____________________ Assignment date: ________________

Evaluate the following expressions

Evaluate. Use $x = 1$, $y = 2$, $z = 3$	Value	Comments
$1x$		$1x$ means x.
$y - x$		
$z - x$		
$z - x - y$		
$4x + 3x + 2x$		
$4x + 3x - 2x$		
$4x - 3x - 2x$		
$4x - 3x + 2x$		
$\frac{z}{3} + 9$		
$\frac{z}{3} + 9 + 2x$		
$2x + \frac{z}{3} - 1$		
$z + 2\frac{2}{3}$		
$-z + 2\frac{2}{3} + x$		
$\frac{x+y+z}{2} + 3$		

Student's name: ____________________ Assignment date: ________________

***** Part 10 Cross multiplication for proportion *****

When an equation is in the form of $\frac{a}{b}=\frac{c}{d}$, the cross multiplication method can be used to get the result. The basic idea is to get the cross product $ad=bc$.

Notice a and d, b and c can be exchanged in $\frac{a}{b}=\frac{c}{d}$ to get the same result. If $\frac{a}{b}=\frac{c}{d}$, a and d exchanged to get $\frac{d}{b}=\frac{c}{a}$ or if $\frac{a}{b}=\frac{c}{d}$, b and c exchanged to get $\frac{a}{c}=\frac{b}{d}$.

Proportion can be reduced in 2 ways, top with bottom (a,c) and (b,d) such as, for example, $\frac{x}{2}=\frac{\not{6}\,2}{\not{3}\,1}$ or left with right numbers such as $(a,b),(c,d)$, for example, $\frac{3}{\not{4}\,2}=\frac{x}{\not{2}\,1}$.

The technique of cross multiplication is very important, and it plays a very important role in elementary school math. Still, unfortunately, some students have ignored its importance when the elementary schools, later many problems students encountered in high school is because they did not master the technique of cross multiplication. Cross multiplication concept can be used to solve a large number of different types of problems. Some of them are as follows:

Proportions in ratio, rate, similarity, scale etc.

Solving equations in the form of $\frac{x}{a}=b$ or $\frac{x}{a}=\frac{b}{c}$ etc.

This method is extremely important in solving equations taught in elementary school. For example, the equations model in elementary school are all in the forms of $\frac{x}{a}=b$ or $\frac{x}{a}=\frac{b}{c}$, so a simple of the method of using cross multiplication could be used to solve all equation problems. If the model is changed to $\frac{x}{a}=\frac{b}{c}+dx$, then the cross multiplication concept will not work for the model $\frac{x}{a}=\frac{b}{c}+dx$

Rational equations in high school such as $\frac{x^2-3x+2}{x-2}=\frac{x}{2}$

Student's name: ____________________ Assignment date: ________________

Trinomial factoring in high school

Factor $x^2 + 3x - 2$

$$\begin{matrix} 1 & -2 \\ & \times \\ 1 & -1 \end{matrix}$$

Finding equations when the slope and one point are given in high school

$$\frac{y-1}{x-2} = \frac{3}{4}$$

Trigonometric ratios

For example, Sin 30° = $\frac{1}{2}$, the product concept could be used to get the answer when 2 of them are unknown and one of them is known, but the concept of cross multiplication still helps in solving trigonometric ratios.

Student's name: ____________________ Assignment date: ________________

Example

Tina bought 2 pencils for $2.50. At the same price rate, how much would a dozen of pencils cost?

Method 1: Use unit-rate

$\frac{2.50}{2} \times 12 = 2.5 \times 6 = 15$ dollars

Method 2: Use equivalent ratio

$\frac{2.50}{2} = \frac{x}{12}$ (× 6)

$x = 2.50 \times 6 = 15$

Since 12 is a multiple of 2, so it is easier to use multiple factors to figure out x.

Method 3: Use cross multiplication

When the equivalent ratio does not have an integral multiple factor then cross multiplication can be used.

$\frac{2.50}{2} = \frac{x}{12}$

$2x = 12 \times 2.5$

$x = 15$

Student's name: ____________________ Assignment date: ______________

Method 1 Multiply both sides by LCD	Method 2 Cross Multiplication
$\frac{x}{2}=\frac{3}{4}$ Multiply both sides by LCD, which is 4. (The reason the cross multiplication is introduced is because the above concept of multiplying 4 on both sides is difficult for the elementary students to understand: it involves equation property, fraction cancellation, and then numerator $\times$. It takes 3 extra steps to achieve the result of cross multiplication.) $4\times\frac{x}{2}=\frac{3}{4}\times 4$ $2x=3$ $x=\frac{3}{2}$	$\frac{x}{2}=\frac{3}{4}$ $4x$ 6 □ □ $\frac{x}{2}=\frac{3}{4}$ Cross multiply as shown above $4x=6$ $2x=3$ $x=\frac{3}{2}$
Multiply both sides by LCD is the more accurate and the general method to solve equation problems since it does not require further reducing later and it can also handle more complicated equation model such as $\frac{x}{a}=\frac{b}{c}+dx$ etc.	The cross multiplication method always assumes the LCD is the product of the 2 bottom numbers and in some cases it is not true. As we can see that the above cross multiplication assume the LCD is 8. so the reducing is required later. However, for elementary student the cross multiplication offers an advantage of being easily to operate for equation model like $\frac{x}{a}=\frac{b}{c}$.

Student's name: ____________________ Assignment date: ________________

Cross multiplication

After we understand how cross multiplication works using LCD in the last section, here 2 ways of cross multiplication is introduced. Do both method 1 and method 2 for the same question.

Method 1: Just blindly do cross multiplication without any analyzing.	Method 2: Only do cross multiplication on number × number and leave the side with variable alone and later exchange number and variable to get the answer.
$\frac{n}{2}=\frac{4}{3}$ $3n = 8$ $n=\frac{8}{3}$	$\frac{n}{2}=\frac{4}{3}$ We still do cross multiplication but only do the number and leave the variable side alone. 8 $\frac{n}{\not{2}}=\frac{\not{4}}{3}$ We did not do $3\times n$. So $n = \frac{8}{3}$
$\frac{x}{2}=\frac{4}{5}$	Only multiply 2 and 4 and leave 5 and x alone. Exchange 5 and x to get the answer.

Student's name: ____________________ Assignment date: ________________

Cross multiplication

Method 1: Just blindly do cross multiplication without any analysis.	Method 2: Only do cross multiplication on number and leave the side with variable alone and later exchange number and variable to get the answer.
$\frac{y}{3}=\frac{5}{7}$	
$\frac{3}{2}=\frac{x}{5}$	
$\frac{7}{2}=\frac{a}{13}$	
$\frac{9}{2}=\frac{y}{9}$	

Student's name: ____________________ Assignment date: ________________

Solve equations

Equations	Solve	Comments
$x + 1 = 2$	1. Isolate x by leaving x to the left side, but not always. Usually, we move x to the side, where it has a positive sign. We normally write the solution as x = a number, so it is a good idea to move x to the left. 2. Move the numbers to the right. There are 2 ways the number can be moved. Method 1 (adding/subtracting) $x + 1 = 2$ The first way is to add – 1 to both sides, so the number 1 on the left side disappears. $x + 1 - 1 = 2 - 1$ $x = 1$ Method 2 (moving numbers) Notice that the above, on the left side, the number added – 1 is cancelled with the original number 1. So we can really think of it as having moved the number 1 to the right side and changes its sign from – to +. So the 1 – 1 part on the left side can be omitted. $x + 1 = 2$ $x = 2 - 1$ $x = 1$	Method 1 (adding/subtracting) Subtract 1 on both sides so that 1 will be cancelled and x on the left side is isolated. $x + 1 = 2$ $x + 1 - 1 = 2 - 1$ $x + \cancel{1} - \cancel{1} = 2 - 1$ $x = 1$ Method 2 (moving numbers) Note the above the right-hand side 1 is cancelled with –1 anyway. An operation is just like to move 1 to the other side and also change its sign whenever the number is moved to the other side. $x + 1 = 2$ $x = 2 - 1$ $x = 1$

Student's name: ____________________ Assignment date: ________________

Fill in answer in □ and _______.

Equation	Unknown or variable	Comments
? + 1 = 3	? = 3 - □ = □	Subtract 1 from both sides. ? + 1– 1= 3 – 1 ? = 3 – 1 It can be thought as if it were moved to the right-hand side, and its sign is changed from + to –. ? + 1 = 3 (−1)
χ + 1 = 3	χ = 3 - □ = □	χ + 1 = 3 (−1)
χ + 2 = 3	χ = 3 - □ = □	
χ + 3 = 5	χ = 5 - □ = □	
χ + 4 = 7	χ = 7 - □ = □	

Student's name: ____________________ Assignment date: ________________

$5 + \chi = 9$	$\chi = 9 - \square$ $= \square$	Move 5 to the right side.
$\chi + 6 = 9$	$\chi = 9 - \square$ $= \square$	
$7 + \chi = 9$	$\chi = 9 - \square$ $= \square$	
$\chi + 8 = 9$	$\chi = 9 - \square$ $= \square$	
$\chi + 9 = 9$	$\chi = 9 - \square$ $= \square$	
$10 + \chi = 19$	$\chi = 19 - \square$ $= \square$	
$\chi + 12 = 19$	$\chi = 19 - \square$ $= \square$	

Student's name: ____________________ Assignment date: ________________

Equation	Unknown or variable	Comments
? – 1 = 3	? = 3 + □ = □	Add 1 from both sides. ? – 1 + 1 = 3 + 1 ? = 3 + 1 It can be thought as if 1 was moved to the right-hand side, and its sign is changed from – to +. ? – 1 = 3 (+1)
$\chi - 1 = 3$	$\chi = 3 + \square$ $= \square$	$\chi - 1 = 3$ (+1)
$\chi - 2 = 3$	$\chi = 3 + \square$ $= \square$	
$\chi - 3 = 5$	$\chi = 5 + \square$ $= \square$	
$-4 + \chi = 7$	$\chi = 7 + \square$ $= \square$	

Student's name: ____________________ Assignment date: ________________

$\chi - 5 = 9$	$\chi = 9 + \square$ $= \square$	Move 5 to the right side.
$-6 + \chi = 9$	$\chi = 9 + \square$ $= \square$	
$\chi - 7 = 9$	$\chi = 9 + \square$ $= \square$	
$\chi - 8 = 9$	$\chi = 9 + \square$ $= \square$	
$-9 + \chi = 9$	$\chi = 9 + \square$ $= \square$	
$\chi - 10 = 19$	$\chi = 19 + \square$ $= \square$	
$\chi - 12 = 19$	$\chi = 19 + \square$ $= \square$	

Student's name: ____________________ Assignment date: ________________

$2 \times ? = 6$	$? = \frac{6}{\square} = \square$	Divide both sides by 2. $\frac{2\times?}{2}=\frac{6}{2}$ $? = 3$ It can be thought as if 2 were moved to the right-hand side at the bottom position. Use the concept of cross multiplication. When moving a factor of a product, the factor always goes to the other side's denominator. It can be shown step by step as follows: $\frac{2\times?}{1}=\frac{6}{1}$ $\frac{?}{1}=\frac{6}{2\times1}$ $?=\frac{6}{2}$ $2\times?=\frac{6}{②}$
$2\chi = 8$	$\chi = \frac{6}{\square} = \square$	The idea of moving comes from the cross multiplication. $\frac{\not{2}x}{1}=\frac{8}{1}$ $\square$ 2
$\frac{3x}{1}=\frac{9}{1}$	$\frac{\not{3}x}{1}=\frac{9}{3} = \square$	

Student's name: ____________________ Assignment date: ________________

Without working on enough cross multiplication exercise, the concept of moving factor seems to be difficult for students to grasp. Alternatively, students could be taught by dividing the same number to both sides of the equation. The result x will be isolated any way after the division, so we do not really need to write an extra step for the division $\frac{3x}{3}=\frac{9}{3}$. For example, $3x=9$, both sides divide 3, then 3 x will become x. so on the left side, we could just write x and on the right side we write $\frac{9}{3}$. The equation becomes $x=\frac{9}{3}=3$.

$3\chi = 9$	$\chi = \frac{9}{\square} = \square$	
$\frac{3x}{1}=\frac{12}{1}$	$\frac{\cancel{3}x}{1}=\frac{12}{3} = \square$	
$3\chi = 12$	$\chi = \frac{12}{\square} = \square$	
$3\chi = 15$	$\chi = \frac{15}{\square} = \square$	
$3 \times \chi = 18$	$\chi = \frac{18}{\square} = \square$	
$4\chi = 16$	$\chi = \frac{16}{\square} = \square$	
$5 \times \chi = 20$	$\chi = \frac{20}{\square} = \square$	

Student's name: ____________________ Assignment date: ________________

$7\chi = 28$	$\chi = \frac{28}{\square} = \square$	
$9\chi = 36$	$\chi = \frac{36}{\square} = \square$	

Student's name: ____________________ Assignment date: ______________

Equation division

The idea of working on fractional equations (rational equations) is to convert the fractions to whole numbers by multiplying LCD to both sides of the equation. However, with the equation in $\frac{a}{b}=\frac{c}{d}$ form, the exchange of ad and bc could be used to solve the unknown.

$\frac{?}{2}=6$	? = 6 X □ = □	Multiply both sides by 2. ? = 2 X 6 = 12 It can be thought as if 2 were moved to the right-hand side and then multiply 6. $\frac{?}{2}=6$ The idea comes from cross multiplication and is demonstrated as follows. ? = 12 □ □ $\frac{?}{2}=\frac{6}{1}$
$\frac{\chi}{2}=6$	χ = 6 X □ = □	$\frac{\chi}{2}=6$
$\frac{x}{2}=8$	χ = 8 X □ = □	
$\frac{x}{3}=7$	χ = 7 X □ = □	

Student's name: ____________________ Assignment date: ________________

Equation division

$\frac{x}{4}=8$	$\chi= 8 \times \square$ $= \square$	
$\frac{x}{5}=10$	$\chi= 10 \times \square$ $= \square$	
$\frac{x}{6}=12$	$\chi= 12 \times \square$ $= \square$	
$\frac{x}{7}=13$	$\chi= 13 \times \square$ $= \square$	
$\frac{x}{8}=14$	$\chi= 14 \times \square$ $= \square$	
$\frac{x}{9}=11$	$\chi= 11 \times \square$ $= \square$	
$\frac{x}{10}=12$	$\chi= 12 \times \square$ $= \square$	

Student's name: ____________________ Assignment date: ________________

Solve Equations – addition and subtraction.
$x + 4 = 0$
$x - 4 = 0$
$x + 4 = 2$
$x - 4 = 2$
$4 + x = 0$
$4 - x = 0$
$4 + x = 2$
$4 - x = 2$

Student's name: ____________________ Assignment date: ________________

Solve Equations – addition and subtraction.
$x + 4 = 0$
$x - 4 = 0$
$x + 4 = 6$
$x - 4 = 2$
$4 + x = 0$
$4 - x = 0$
$4 + x = 2$
$4 - x = 2$

Student's name: ____________________ Assignment date: ________________

Solve Equations – multiplication and division
$4x = 12$
$x \times 4 = 16$
$4x + 4 = 2$
$6x - 4 = 8$
$4 + 2x = 0$
$4 - 8x = 0$
$4 + 4x = 2$
$4 - 4x = 2$

Student's name: ____________________ Assignment date: ________________

Addition problems

A number is 27 more than 35. What is the number?

The difference between a number and 49 is 137. What is the number?

A number minus 45 equals 132. What is the number?

Subtraction problems

The sum of a number and 37 is 961. What is the number?

The difference between 462 and a number is 344. What is the number?

A number plus 186 equals 251. What is the number?

A number is 18 less than 91. What is the number?

Student's name: ____________________ Assignment date: ________________

Multiplication problems

A number divided by 4 equals 502. What is the number?

How much is 456 multiplied by 12?

How much is 63 times 34?

What is the sum of nine 148's?

Number A is 128 and is twice as much as number B. How much is number B?

Student's name: ____________________ Assignment date: ________________

Division problems

9744 divided by 14, what is its quotient?

756 divided by a number. Its quotient is 3. What is the number?

How many times is 508 of 8?

A number multiplied by 9. Its product is 1458. What is the number?

8 multiplied by a number equals 356. What is the number?

The product of a number and 12 is 276. What is the number?

Number A is 128, and number B is twice as number A. How much is number B?

Number A is 48, and number B is 12. How many times is number A of number B?

Student's name: ____________________ Assignment date: ________________

Techniques in solving linear equations

To solve linear equations $(ax + b = 0)$, we rely on the equation properties as follows:

- Add a number to both sides of an equation
- Subtract a number from both sides of an equation.
- Multiply both sides of an equation by a number.
- Divide both sides of an equation by a non-zero number.

Move variable to the side where the sign will be positive

Move x to the left side	Move x to the right side
$3x = 2x + 2$	$2x + 2 = 3x$
$4x = 3x - 2$	$4x - 2 = 2x$
$5x = 2x - 2$	$3x = 5x + 2$
$5x = 2x - 2$	$4x = 5x + 2$
$6x + 2 = 5x$	$7x = 9x - 2$
$9x + 2 = 7x$	$6x = 8x - 2$

Student's name: ____________________ Assignment date: ________________

Advanced equation

$(\square \times 5) \div 3 = 4 + \square$
$2\square + 7 = 6\square - 9$
Solve $\square$. $2\square$ - 1 thousand + 3 hundreds + 8 tens + 7 hundredths = 5 hundredths
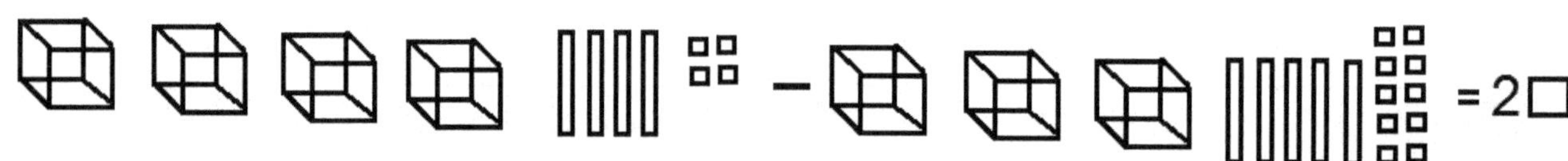
If $\frac{1}{3} \times x = 6$, then $x\frac{x+2}{2}$=?

Student's name: ____________________ Assignment date: ________________

Test of equation

If $5 \times x = 120$ and $\frac{x}{y} = 3$, then what is y?
Find N if $3 \times (25 + N - 13) = 96$.
What is x if there are three equations as follows: $x - y = 5$, $y + z = 4$, $z + 1 = 3$
What is n if $0 = 1 \times n \times 1$?
What is n if $1 = 1 \times n \times 1$?
What is $\square$ if $21 - \square = 54 \div 3$?
When a number is added to twice of itself, the result is the difference of the number less than 12, what is the number?

Student's name: ____________________ Assignment date: ________________

If □6 + 78 = 114, then what value is the missing part □? In this problem □6 is a 2-digit number.
If $\frac{28}{48} = \frac{\Delta}{12}$, what is the value of Δ?
If 1 + 2 × $p = 25$, then $p - 11 = ?$

Student's name: ____________________ Assignment date: ________________

Roman numerals

Complete the following table.

I	II	III	IV	V	VI	VII	VIII	IX	X
XI	XII			XV					XX
XXI									XXX
XXXI									XL
									L
									LX
									LXX
									LXXX
									XC
									C

Complete the following clock with Roman numerals.

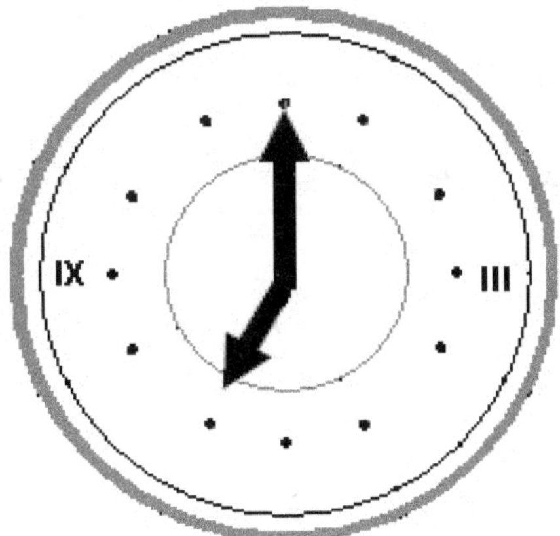

Ho Math Chess Primary Grades Math

Test Review assesssment 何数棋谜低年级数学测试複習考核

Student's name: ____________________ Assignment date: ________________

Connect the following drawings in order.

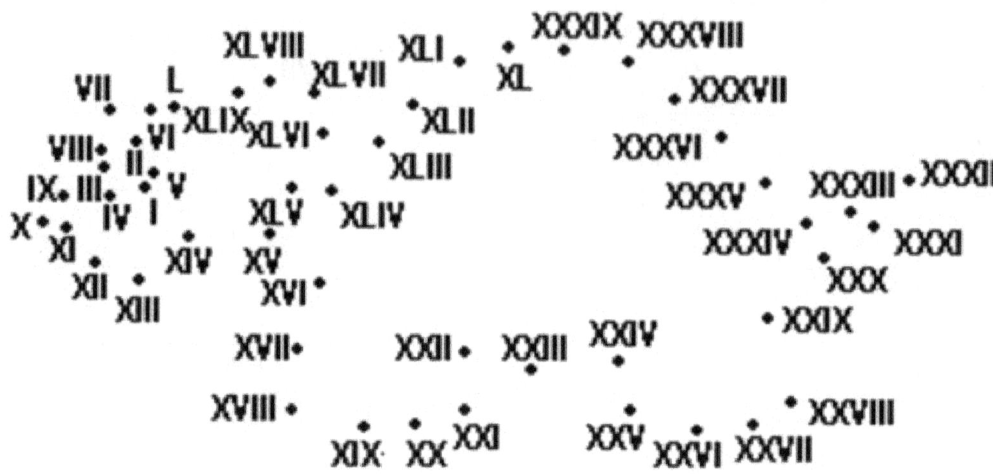

Translate the following Roman numerals to numbers.

1.	I	= ______	10.	X	= ______	19.	LX	= ______
2.	II	= ______	11.	XX	= ______	20.	LXX	= ______
3.	III	= ______	12.	XXX	= ______	21.	LXXX	= ______
4.	IV	= ______	13.	XL	= ______	22.	XC	= ______
5.	V	= ______	14.	L	= ______	23.	C	= ______
6.	IV	= ______	15.	VI	= ______	24.	VII	= ______
7.	IX	= ______	16.	XI	= ______	25.	XII	= ______
8.	XL	= ______	17.	LX	= ______	26.	LXX	= ______
9.	XC	= ______	18.	CX	= ______	27.	CXX	= ______

Student's name: ____________________ Assignment date: ________________

Translate the following numbers into Roman numerals.

1.	1	= _______	10.	10	= _______	19.	60	= _______
2.	2	= _______	11.	20	= _______	20.	70	= _______
3.	3	= _______	12.	30	= _______	21.	80	= _______
4.	4	= _______	13.	40	= _______	22.	90	= _______
5.	5	= _______	14.	50	= _______	23.	100	= _______
6.	11	= _______	15.	12	= _______	24.	14	= _______
7.	21	= _______	16.	22	= _______	25.	24	= _______
8.	31	= _______	17.	32	= _______	26.	34	= _______
9.	41	= _______	18.	42	= _______	27.	44	= _______

Translate the following numbers below.

1.	XII	= _______	10.	7	= _______	19.	9	= _______
2.	XXXIII	= _______	11.	3	= _______	20.	XXV	= _______
3.	XV	= _______	12.	19	= _______	21.	18	= _______
4.	XVI	= _______	13.	28	= _______	22.	75	= _______
5.	LI	= _______	14.	54	= _______	23.	LXVII	= _______
6.	VIII	= _______	15.	69	= _______	24.	LXXXV	= _______
7.	IX	= _______	16.	77	= _______	25.	42	= _______
8.	CC	= _______	17.	36	= _______	26.	63	= _______
9.	XCV	= _______	18.	81	= _______	27.	LV	= _______

Student's name: ____________________ Assignment date: ________________

***** Part 11 Measurement *****

Metric measurement ladder diagram

The Metric system uses the same prefix words to memorize all three weight, length, and capacity measurements. As you move the list of prefixes, the next unit is 10 times the current one. As you move down the list, the next unit is 10th of the current one. Every time, the measurement reduces 10 times by going up one step; the measurement increases 10 times by going down one step.

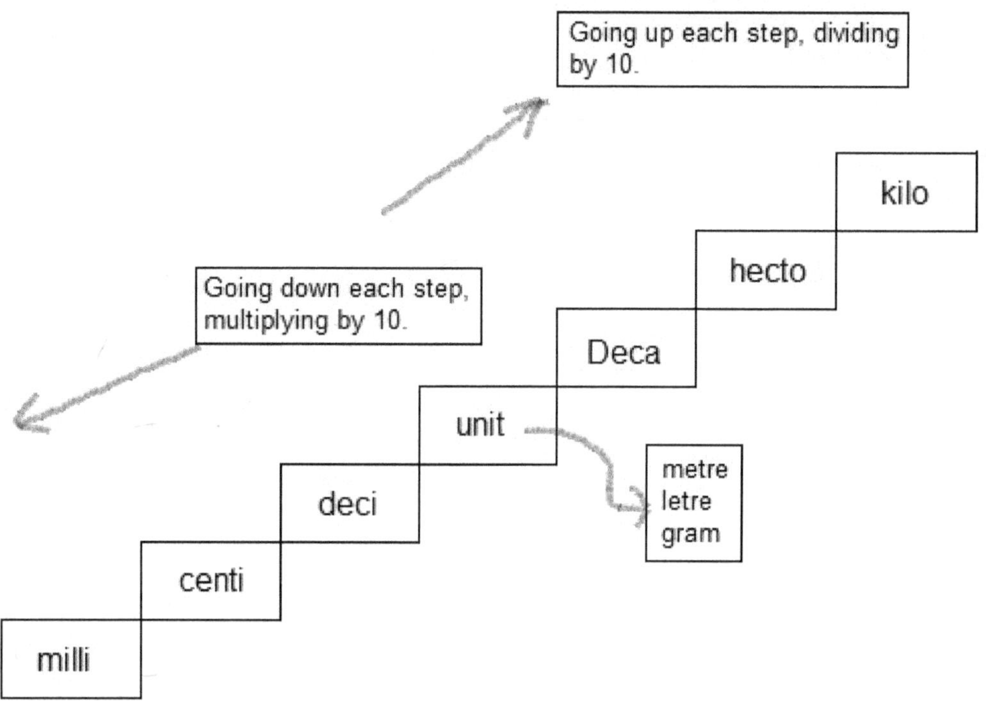

Length	kilometre (km) 1 km = 1000 m	hectometre (hm)	decametre (dam)	metre (m) 1 m = 100 cm	decimetre (dm)	centimetre (cm) 1 cm = 10 mm	millimetre (mm)
Weight (mass)	kilogram (kg) 1 kg = 1000 g 1 t = 1000 kg	hectogram	decagram	gram (g) 1 g = 1000 mg	decigram	centigram	milligram
Volume (Capacity)	kilolitre 1 kL = 1000 L	hectolitre	decalitre	Litre (L) 1 L = 10000 mL	decilitre	centilitre	millilitre

Student's name: ______________________ Assignment date: _________________

Capacity, volume, and mass

You will remember the following conversion formula, then convert it to get other units.
10 cm × 10 cm × 10 cm = 1000 cm^3 (volume) =1 L (capacity) = 1 kg (weight, mass)

Because 1 m = 100 cm, so 10 cm = 0.1 m, 0.001 m^3= 1 L

Because 1 L = 1000 mL so 10 cm × 10 cm × 10 cm = 1000 cm^3 = 1000 mL
so 1 mL = 1 cm^3

9800 cm^3= __________ L = _________kg
980 cm^3= __________ L = _________kg
8.6m^3= __________ L = _________kg
380 cm^3= __________ L = _________kg
38 cm^3= __________ L = _________kg
6.9 m^3= __________ L = _________kg
490 cm^3= __________ mL = _________ g
0.49 m^3= __________ L = _________kg
948 L = ________________ m^3 0.
8.6 mL = ________________ m^3
380 L = ________________ m^3
8000 L = ________________ m^3

Student's name: ____________________ Assignment date: ________________

km	m	cm	mm	t	kg	g	mg	kL	L	mL
1								5		
3		30,000	3,000,000		3600				37000	
	2300				2.11 kg+250 g			5.1		
0.409						5.2			3.8	
		4 cm+20 mm					3191			5000
	2 km+210 m				2500					3200
	300.02			3.1				1.1		
		198.21			3.5				2.2	
			3112.04			1000				3.3
512.12	512120	51212000					7000		400.21	

Student's name: ____________________ Assignment date: ________________

Test of measurement word problem

Melody wanted to buy some lunch meat that was priced per 100 g. if she wanted to buy $\frac{3}{4}$ kg of lunch meat, how many times the price per 100 g would she pay?
Shelby wanted to buy some roasted pumpkin seeds that were priced per 100 g. If she wanted to buy 1.2 kg of pumpkin seeds, how many times the price per 100 g would she pay?
Wayne bought some pieces of candies. Each piece weighed 150 g, and she bought 2.4 kg in total weight. How many pieces of candies did she buy in all?
If the total amount of juice in 7 containers was 24.5 L, how many millilitres of juice did one container hold on average?
I15 cm + 0.08 m + 1100 mm = ________ metres = _______ cm = ________ mm
0.8 L – 550 mL = ________ L = _____ mL
Ten-tenth of 100 cm + one-tenth of 2 metres = _______ cm
Han compared the costs of the following sizes of juice.

Size	Cost	calculation
250 mL	3 for $1.10	0.15 cents / mL
150 mL	4 for $2.50	1.56 cents / mL
1 L	$4.50	2.22 cents / mL, 1L = 1000 mL
2 L	$8.00	4 cents / mL

Which size would be the best to buy?

Student's name: ____________________ Assignment date: ________________

Each bag requires a piece of fabric 30 cm by 50 cm. What is the greatest number of bags that could be shown from a piece of fabric measuring 4 m by 5.5 m?
How can many cubed fudges with 3 inches side length be packed into an icebox 9 inches deep by 12 inches wide and 8 inches high such that the lid can still be closed?
One drawstring bag requires 150 cm of the cord. Cord for the drawstrings is sold in spools of 80 m. What is the greatest number of bags that can be completed with one spool of the cord?
If a ceramic tile costs $8.50 per square yard, what will a kitchen floor that is 12 feet by 15 feet long cost?
There are 8 ounces in a $\frac{1}{2}$ pound. How many ounces are in 5 $\frac{3}{4}$ lbs?
Grace and her friend walked from the parking lot to the beginning of a 4 km hiking trail. They realized that they left their water bottles in the car, so they went back to get their bottles, then they hiked the trail and returned to their car. How far did they walk in total?

Student's name: ____________________ Assignment date: ________________

Length

 THE LENGTH OF A SMALL CAR IS ABOUT 5 METRES.	 THE LENGTH OD A TENNIS RACQUET IS ABOUT 150 CENTIMETER.
 The length of a bed is about 2 metres.	 The height of a door is about 2 meters.
 A calculator is about 10 centimetres long.	 The diameter of a baseball is about 10 centimetres.

Student's name: ____________________ Assignment date: ________________

Length

1 km = 1000 m = 10,000 dm = 100,000 cm =1,000,000 mm
1 m = 10 dm = 100 cm = 1000 mm
1 dm = 10 cm = 100 mm
1 cm = 10 mm

1. Metre to decimetre.

1. 1 m = __________ dm
2. 5 m = __________ dm
3. 30 m = __________ dm
4. 60 m = __________ dm
5. 45 m = __________ dm
6. 67 m = __________ dm
7. 70 m = __________ dm
8. 88 m = __________ dm
9. 300 m = __________ dm
10. 400 m = __________ dm
11. 55 m = __________ dm
12. 19 m = __________ dm

2. Decimetre to the metre.

1. 10 dm = __________ m
2. 30 dm = __________ m
3. 100 dm = __________ m
4. 60 dm = __________ m
5. 300 dm = __________ m
6. 610 dm = __________ m
7. 150 dm = __________ m
8. 680 dm = __________ m
9. 1000 dm = __________ m
10. 740 dm = __________ m
11. 230 dm = __________ m
12. 600 dm = __________ m

Student's name: ____________________ Assignment date: ______________

3. Metre to Centimetre.

1. 1 m = __________ cm
2. 3 m = __________ cm
3. 10 m = __________ cm
4. 20 m = __________ cm
5. 15 m = __________ cm
6. 26 m = __________ cm
7. 50 m = __________ cm
8. 63 m = __________ cm
9. 100 m = __________ cm
10. 91 m = __________ cm
11. 40 m = __________ cm
12. 16 m = __________ cm

4. Centimetre to the metre.

1. 100 cm = __________ m
2. 700 cm = __________ m
3. 400 cm = __________ m
4. 2600 cm = __________ m
5. 5400 cm = __________ m
6. 7300 cm = __________ m
7. 2400 cm = __________ m
8. 14000 cm = __________ m
9. 1000 cm = __________ m
10. 53000 cm = __________ m
11. 5000 cm = __________ m
12. 3700 m = __________ m

5. Metre to the millimetre.

1. 1 m = __________ mm
2. 6 m = __________ mm
3. 60 m = __________ mm
4. 40 m = __________mm
5. 33 m = __________ mm
6. 55 m = __________ mm
7. 48 m = __________ mm
8. 89 m = __________ mm
9. 200 m = __________ mm
10. 900 m = __________ mm
11. 40 m = __________ mm
12. 18 m = __________ mm

Student's name: ____________________ Assignment date: ________________

6. Millimetre to the metre.

1. 1000 mm = __________ m
2. 8000 mm = __________ m
3. 33000 mm = __________ m
4. 72000 mm = __________ m
5. 29000 mm = __________ m
6. 16000 mm = __________ m
7. 57000 mm = __________ m
8. 60000 mm = __________ m
9. 45000 mm = __________ m
10. 90000 mm = __________ m
11. 20000 mm = __________ m
12. 66000 mm = __________ m

7. Kilometre to the metre.

1. 1 km = __________ m
2. 3 km = __________ m
3. 10 km = __________ m
4. 20 km = __________ m
5. 15 km = __________ m
6. 26 km = __________ m
7. 50 km = __________ m
8. 63 km = __________ m
9. 100 km = __________ m
10. 91 km = __________ m
11. 72 km = __________ m
12. 30 km = __________ m

8. Metre to a kilometre.

1. 1000 m = __________ km
2. 4000 m = __________ km
3. 5000 m = __________ km
4. 63000 m = __________ km
5. 34000 m = __________ km
6. 47000 m = __________ km
7. 52000 m = __________ km
8. 30000 m = __________ km
9. 180000 m = __________ km
10. 120000 m = __________ km
11. 30000 m = __________ km
12. 160000 m = __________ km

Student's name: ____________________ Assignment date: ________________

9. Centimetre to the millimetre.

1. 1 cm = __________ mm
2. 7 cm = __________ mm
3. 30 cm = __________ mm
4. 80 cm = __________ mm
5. 51 cm = __________ mm
6. 78 cm = __________ mm
7. 73 cm = __________ mm
8. 570 cm = __________ mm
9. 860 cm = __________ mm
10. 950 cm = __________ mm
11. 600 cm = __________ mm
12. 210 m = __________ mm

10. Millimetre to Centimetre.

1. 10 mm = __________ cm
2. 70 mm = __________ cm
3. 60 mm = __________ cm
4. 20 mm = __________ cm
5. 160 mm = __________ cm
6. 400 mm = __________ cm
7. 3700 mm = __________ cm
8. 5100 mm = __________ cm
9. 8400 mm = __________ cm
10. 5600 mm = __________ cm
11. 2500 mm = __________ cm
12. 4400 m = __________ cm

11. Metre to decimetre, centimetre, and millimetre.

1. 1m = __________ dm = __________ cm = __________ mm
2. 5m = __________ dm = __________ cm = __________ mm
3. 30m = __________ dm = __________ cm = __________ mm
4. 56m = __________ dm = __________ cm = __________ mm
5. 450m = __________ dm = __________ cm = __________ mm

Student's name: ____________________ Assignment date: ________________

Length

1. 9 m = __________ dm
2. 40 dm = __________ cm
3. 7 cm = __________ mm
4. 700 mm = __________ cm
5. 150 cm = __________ dm
6. 50 dm = __________ m
7. 5 m = __________ cm
8. 20 m = __________ cm
9. 56 dm = __________ mm
10. 8000 cm = __________ m
11. 9000 mm = __________ dm
12. 10 dm = __________ cm
13. 600 m = __________ dm
14. 800 dm = __________ m
15. 400 dm = __________ cm
16. 5000 cm = __________ dm
17. 6000 cm = __________ mm
18. 9000 mm = __________ cm
19. 30 km = __________ m
20. 50 m = __________ dm
21. 2000 m = __________ km
22. 8000 m = __________ km
23. 50 000 m = __________ km
24. 3000 km = __________ m
25. 6 dm = __________ cm
26. 7 cm = __________ mm
27. 7 m = __________ cm
28. 600 mm = __________ cm
29. 400 dm = __________ m
30. 40 cm = __________ dm
31. 8 km = __________ m
32. 60 000 m = __________ km
33. 30 dm = __________ mm
34. 60 m = __________ cm
35. 3000 mm = __________ dm
36. 8000 cm = __________ m
37. 5 dm = __________ cm
38. 8 dm = __________ cm

Student's name: ____________________ Assignment date: ________________

Length

1. 9 cm = __________ mm
2. 3 m = __________ cm
3. 35 dm = __________ mm
4. 3 km = __________ m
5. 400 cm = __________ dm
6. 5000 cm = __________ dm
7. 90 mm = __________ cm
8. 4000 cm = __________ m
9. 5000 mm = __________ m
10. 560 000 dm = __________km
11. 70 cm = __________ mm
12. 12 m = __________ cm
13. 102 dm = __________ mm
14. 40 km = __________ m
15. 6200 cm = __________ dm
16. 780 cm = __________ dm
17. 690 mm = __________ cm
18. 42000 cm = __________ m
19. 56000 mm = __________ m
20. 470 000 dm = __________ km
21. 45000 m = __________ km
22. 60 000 m = __________ km
23. 780 000 m = __________ km
24. 150 000 km = __________ m
25. 120 dm = __________ cm
26. 510 cm = __________ mm
27. 690 m = __________ cm
28. 4 600 mm = __________ cm
29. 47 000 dm = __________ m
30. 29 000 cm = __________ dm
31. 830 cm = __________ mm
32. 8 700 mm = __________ cm
33. 11 000 cm = __________ dm
34. 450 dm = __________ m
35. 60 m = __________ cm
36. 22 000 m = __________ cm
37. 730 dm = __________ mm
38. 8800 cm = __________ m

Student's name: ____________________ Assignment date: ________________

Fill in ( ) with >, < or =.

1. 2000 mm _____ 2 m
2. 30 dm _____ 4 m
3. 15 dm _____ 110 cm
4. 40 cm _____ 4 dm
5. 60 m _____ 6 km
6. 80 mm _____ 8 cm
7. 8 m _____ 80 km
8. 90 mm _____ 9 dm
9. 50 000 dm _____ 6 km
10. 3 km _____ 400 m

Fill in the following blank.

1.	km	m	dm	cm	mm
2.					5 000 000
3.			400 000		
4.				300 000	
5.	80				
6.		9 000			
7.					45 000 000
8.			5600 000		
9.			340 000		
10.				7 200 000	
11.		43 000			
12.					90 000 000
13.	220				
14.			660 000		
15.	52				

Student's name: ____________________ Assignment date: ________________

Choose the appropriate answer.

1.	The length of a book is	a. 20 cm	b. 2 m	c. 20 m	__
2.	The length of a desk is	a. 20 cm	b. 2 m	c. 20 m	__
3.	The length of a bed is	a. 20 cm	b. 2 m	c. 20 m	__
4.	The height of a door is	a. 20 cm	b. 2 m	c. 20 m	__
5.	The length of a swimming pool is	a. 20 cm	b. 2 m	c. 20 m	__
6.	The length of a soccer field is	a. 20 cm	b. 2 m	c. 20 m	__
7.	The length of a bus is	a. 10 cm	b. 1 m	c. 10 m	__
8.	The length of a car is	a. 50 cm	b. 5 m	c. 50 m	__
9.	The length of your feet is about	a. 20 cm	b. 2 m	c. 20 m	__
10.	The thickness of a piece of 2 x 4 board is	a. 1 mm	b. 1 cm	c. 1 dm	__
11.	The thickness of a laptop computer	a. 5 mm	b. 5 cm	c. 5 dm	__
12.	The thickness of a piece of CD is	a. 1 mm	b. 1 cm	c. 1 m	__
13.	The height of Seymour mountain is	a. 15 cm	b. 15 m	c. 1500 m	__
14.	The height of a house door is about	a. 2 m	b. 2 m	c. 1500 m	__
15.	Car distance of travelling for one hour is	a 2 km	b. 2 m	c. 60 km	__
16.	The length of a cell phone is about	a 10 cm	b. 2 m	c. 10 km	__
17.	The diameter of the earth is about	a. 13 m	b. 13 km	c. 13000 km	__

1.

Student's name: ____________________ Assignment date: ________________

Test of measuring length

km	m	cm	mm	comment
0.00004				
	0.02			
		200000		
			20000	
0.04				
	80000			
0.0007×1000				
5×0.01				

Student's name: ____________________ Assignment date: ________________

Capacity

 ONE CARTON CAN HOLD ABOUT 1 LITRE OF MILK.	 A CAN OF POP MIGHT CONTAIN 350 MILLILITERS.
 A small car oil container can hold 20 litres of gasoline.	 A small bottle of medicine is about 30 millilitres.
 A bottle of water is about 20 litres.	 A kettle can hold about 3 litres of water.

Student's name: ____________________ Assignment date: ________________

Capacity

1 L = 1000 mL	1000 mL = 1L

1. Litre to millilitre.

1. 1 l = __________ ml
2. 4 l = __________ ml
3. 7 l = __________ ml
4. 10 l = __________ ml
5. 81 l = __________ ml
6. 210 l = __________ ml
7. 700 l = __________ ml
8. 305 l = __________ ml
9. 380 l = __________ ml
10. 402 l = __________ ml
11. 54 l = __________ ml
12. 800 l = __________ ml
13. 70 l = __________ ml
14. 26 l = __________ ml

2. Millilitre to litre.

1. 1 000 ml = __________ l
2. 3 000 ml = __________ l
3. 5 000 ml = __________ l
4. 10 000 ml = __________ l
5. 35 000 ml = __________ l
6. 41 000 ml = __________ l
7. 67 000 ml = __________ l
8. 605 000 ml = __________ l
9. 740 000 ml = __________ l
10. 706 000 ml = __________ l
11. 880 000 ml = __________ l
12. 510 000 ml = __________ l
13. 60 000 ml = __________ l
14. 94 000 ml = __________ l

Student's name: ____________________ Assignment date: ________________

Capacity

1. 5 000 ml = __________ l
2. 8 000 ml = __________ l
3. 70 l = __________ ml
4. 4 l = __________ ml
5. 60 000 ml = __________ l
6. 10 000 ml = __________ l
7. 18 l = __________ ml
8. 64 l = __________ ml
9. 309 000 ml = __________ l
10. 203 000 ml = __________ l
11. 6000 l = __________ ml
12. 4000 l = __________ ml
13. 12 000 ml = __________ l
14. 58 l = __________ ml
15. 76 l = __________ ml
16. 91 000 ml = __________ l
17. 430 000 ml = __________ l
18. 200 l = __________ ml
19. 504 l = __________ ml
20. 35 000 ml = __________ l
21. 700 l = __________ ml
22. 2000 l = __________ ml
23. 4000 l = __________ ml
24. 4070 l = __________ ml
25. 45 000 ml = __________ l
26. 50 000 ml = __________ l
27. 67 l = __________ ml
28. 48 000 ml = __________ l
29. 20 l = __________ ml
30. 123 l = __________ ml
31. 508 l = __________ ml
32. 612 l = __________ ml
33. 97 000 ml = __________ l
34. 1 l = __________ ml
35. 60 000 ml = __________ l
36. 33 000 ml = __________ l
37. 28 l = __________ ml
38. 43 000 ml = __________ l

Student's name: ____________________ Assignment date: ________________

Mass (weight)

 AN APPLE HAS A MASS OF ABOUT 200 GRAMS.	 AN EGG HAS A MASS OF ABOUT 50 GRAMS.
 A book is about 1 kilogram.	 A piece of paper has a mass of about 5 grams.
 A bag of rice has a mass of about 10 kilograms.	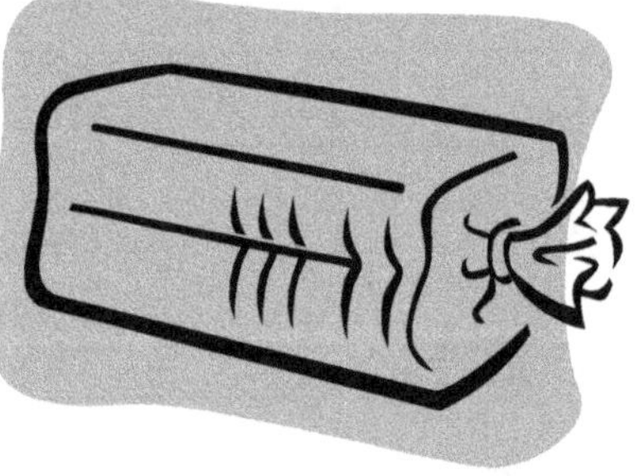 A loaf of bread is about 500 grams.

Student's name: ____________________ Assignment date: ________________

Mass

1kg=1000 g	1000 g= 1 kg

1. Kilogram to the gram.

1. 1 kg = __________ g
2. 5 kg = __________ g
3. 12 kg = __________ g
4. 20 kg = __________ g
5. 200 kg = __________ g
6. 3300 kg = __________ g
7. 305 kg = __________ g
8. 409 kg = __________ g
9. 600 kg = __________ g
10. 70 kg = __________ g
11. 43 kg = __________ g
12. 607 kg = __________ g

2. Gram to the kilogram.

1. 1 000 g = __________ kg
2. 3 000 g = __________ kg
3. 15 000 g = __________ kg
4. 45 000 g = __________ kg
5. 201 000 g = __________ kg
6. 307 000 g= __________ kg
7. 280 000 g = __________ kg
8. 606 000 g = __________ kg
9. 6 000 000 g = __________ kg
10. 9 006 000 g = __________ kg
11. 48 000 g = __________ kg
12. 5 060 000 g = __________ kg

Student's name: ____________________ Assignment date: ________________

Mass

1. 5 000 g = __________ kg
2. 6 000 g = __________ kg
3. 43 000 g = __________ kg
4. 65 kg = __________ g
5. 77 kg = __________ g
6. 80 kg = __________ g
7. 80 000 g = __________ kg
8. 75 kg = __________ g
9. 3 000 000 g = __________ kg
10. 2 006 000 g = __________ kg
11. 48 000 kg = __________ g
12. 5 060 000 g = __________ kg
13. 505 kg = __________ g
14. 6 000 kg = __________ g
15. 70 kg = __________ g
16. 90 kg = __________ g
17. 201 000 g = __________ kg
18. 307 000 g= __________ kg
19. 28 000 kg = __________ g
20. 606 000 g = __________ kg
21. 71 000 g = __________ kg
22. 480 kg = __________ g
23. 810 kg = __________ g
24. 70 000 g = __________ kg

Fill in the blank with >, < or =

1. 5 kg ____ 500 g
2. 200 kg ____ 200 g
3. 30 kg ____ 3000 g
4. 53 kg ____ 53000 g
5. 2 kg ____ 99 g
6. 8000 g ____ 80 kg
7. 5 kg ____ 6000 g
8. 5 kg ____ 4 000 g
9. 7 kg ____ 30 000 g
10. 9 kg ____ 9 000 g
11. 7 kg ____ 900 g
12. 6000 g ____ 40 kg

Student's name: ____________________ Assignment date: ________________

Choose the appropriate answer. All numbers are approximate.

1.	A box of table salt (10 cm by 5 cm by 17 cm) weighs	a. 1 g	b. 1 kg	__
2.	The mass of an egg is	a. 50 g	b. 50 kg	__
3.	A loaf of bread weighs	a. 500 g	b. 500 kg	__
4.	A jellybean weighs	a. 1 g	b. 1 kg	__
5.	The average mass of an adult is about	a. 70 g	b. 70 kg	__
6.	The mass of a muffin is about	a. 100 g	b. 100 kg	__
7.	The mass of a notebook computer is	a. 3 g	b. 3 kg	__
8.	The mass of a poker chip	a. 10 g	b. 10 kg	__
9.	The mass of a can of juice is about	a. 300 g	b. 300 kg	__
10.	The mass of a jar of peanut butter is	a. 1 g	b. 1 kg	__
11.	The mass of a 30 cm ruler is	a. 50 g	b. 10 kg	__
12.	A litre of juice has a mass of about	a. 1 g	b. 1 kg	__
13.	A hen has a mass of about	a. 3 g	b. 3 kg	__
14.	A miniature Yorkshire terrier is about	a. 1 g	b. 1 kg	__
15.	The mass of an apple is about	a. 200 g	b. 200 kg	__
16.	A newborn baby has a mass of about	a. 3 g	b. 3 kg	__
17.	The mass of a large bag of cat food is about	a. 8 g	b. 8 kg	__
18.	The mass of an orange is about	a. 50 g	b. 50 kg	

Student's name: ____________________ Assignment date: ________________

Conversion of units

1. 6 km + 2 km = ____________ km
2. 4 km + 300 m = ____________ m
3. 5 dm + 1 cm = ____________ cm
4. 9 m + 5 dm + 3 cm = ____________ cm
5. 8 m + 6 dm + 5 cm + 4 mm = ____________ mm
6. 7 km – 1300 m = ____________ m
7. 12 km – 4500 m = ____________ m
8. 72 m + 8 dm + 15 cm = ____________ cm
9. 10 m + 78 cm + 17 mm= ____________ mm
10. 35 m – 4 dm – 18 mm= ____________ mm
11. 3 kg + 400 g = ____________ g
12. 4 kg – 120 g = ____________ g
13. 33 kg – 2500 g = ____________ g
14. 27 kg + 560 g – 3 kg = ____________ g
15. 6 L + 18 L = ____________ mL
16. 52 L + 1600 mL = ____________ mL
17. 35000 mL + 69000 mL= ____________ L
18. 7 l – 780 mL = ____________ mL
19. 3 L – 20 mL = ____________ mL

Student's name: ____________________ Assignment date: ________________

Imperial system

Length
1 foot = 12 inches
1 yard = 3 feet
1 mile = 5289 feet

Volume

1 gallon = 4 quarts

Mass and Weight

1 pound (lb) = 16 ounces (oz)

Student's name: ____________________ Assignment date: ________________

***** Part 12 Perimeter and Area *****

Perimeter is the distance around the figure.

1. Trace the perimeter of the following figure with a colour pen.

2. The side of each small square is 1 cm. Find the perimeters of the following shapes.

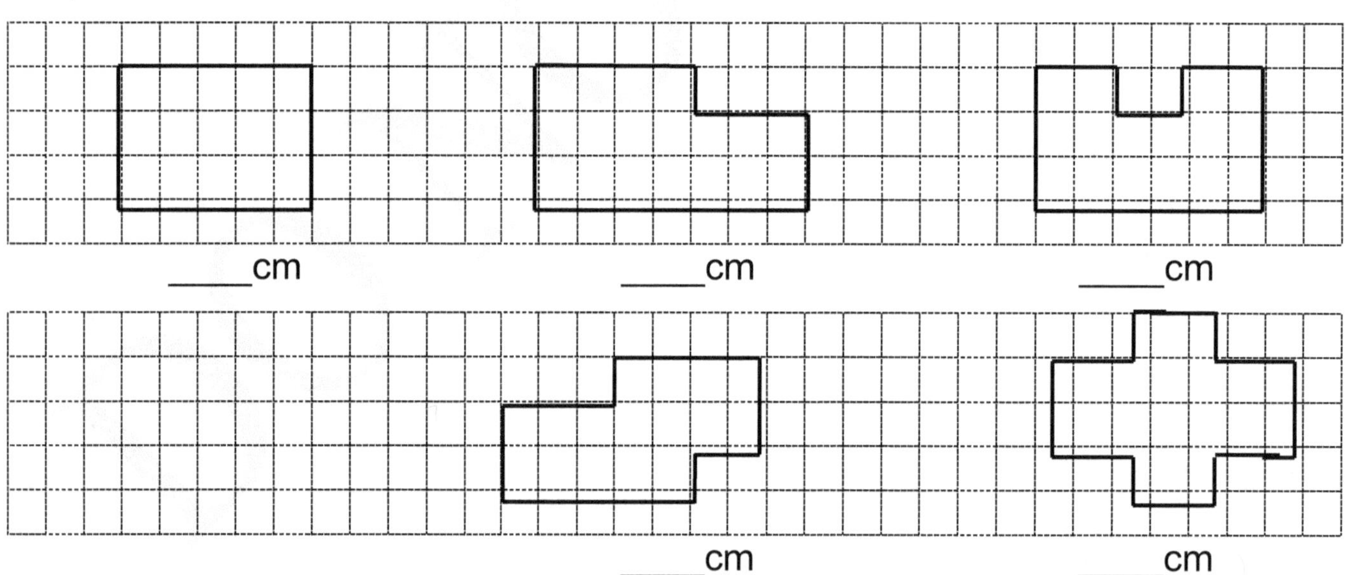

_____cm _____cm _____cm

_____cm _____cm

Student's name: ____________________ Assignment date: ________________

Perimeter

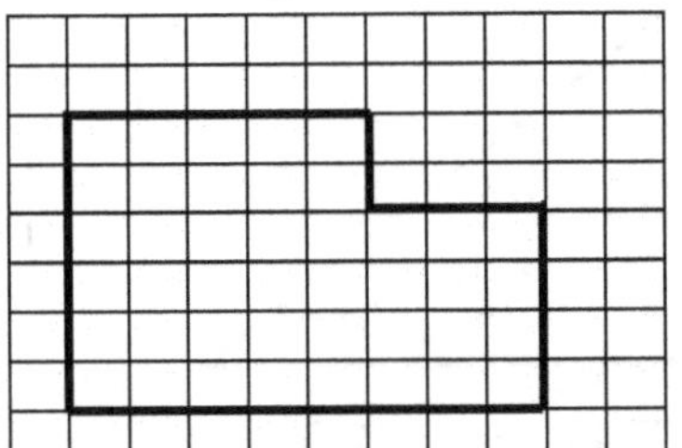

Perimeter =

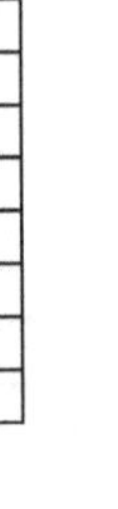

Perimeter =

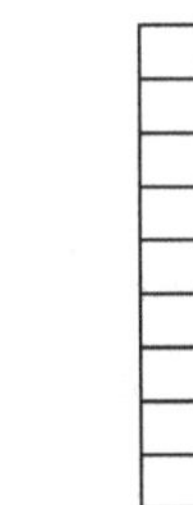

Perimeter =

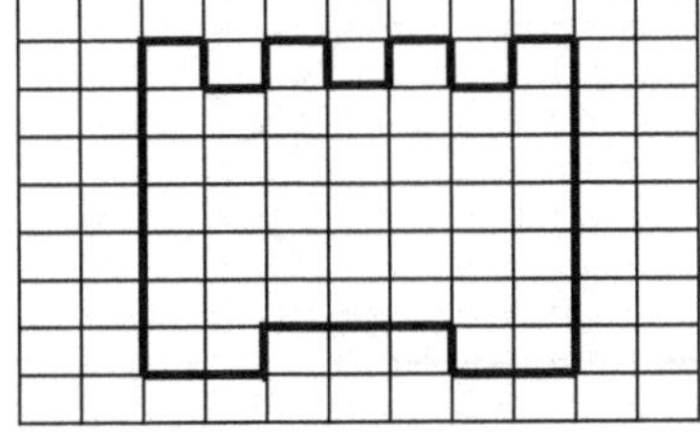

Perimeter =

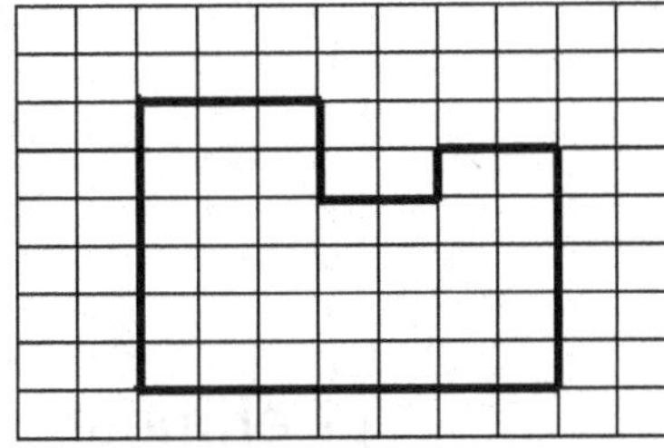

Perimeter =

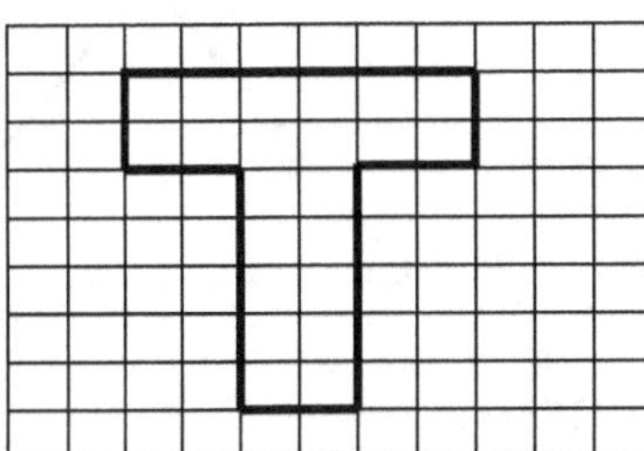

Perimeter =

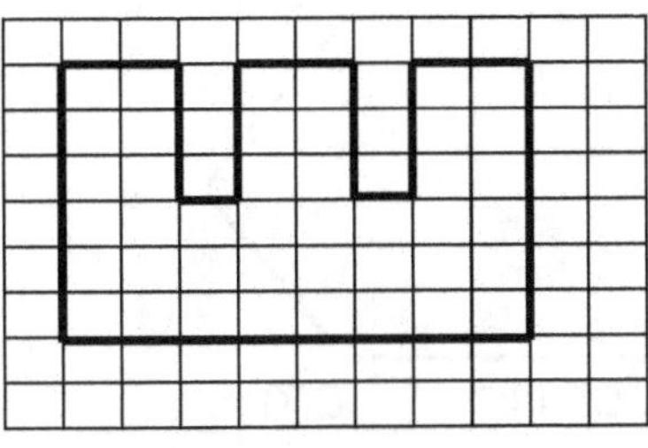

Perimeter =

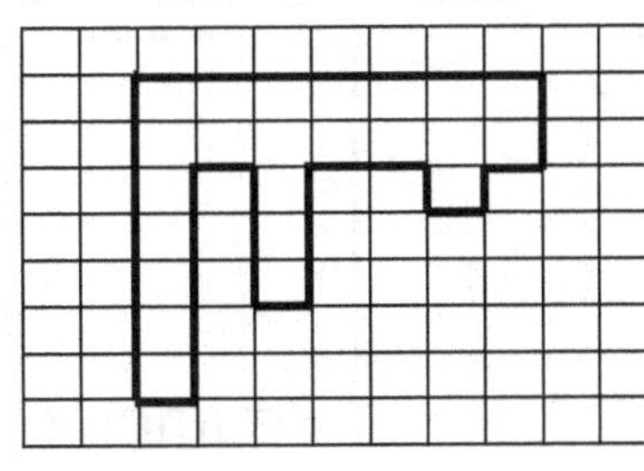

Perimeter =

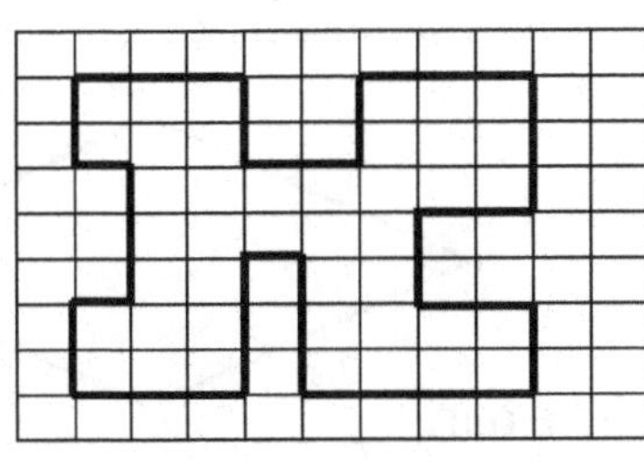

Perimeter =

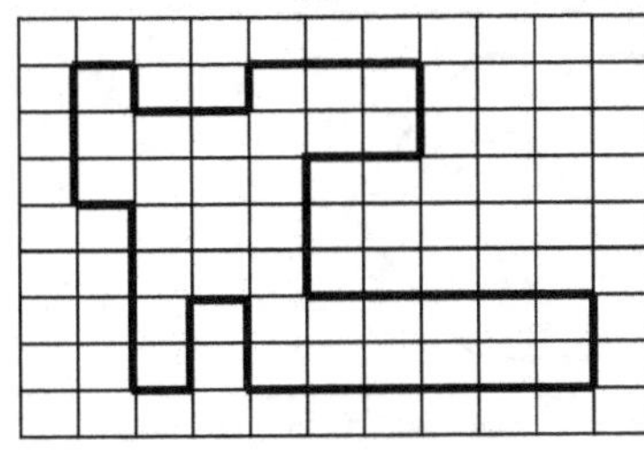

Perimeter =

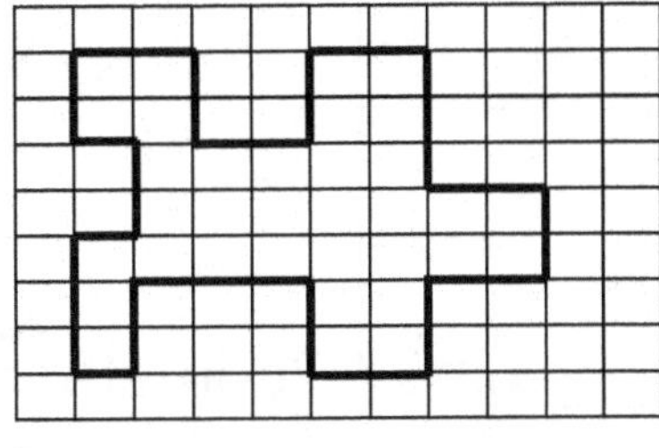

Perimeter =

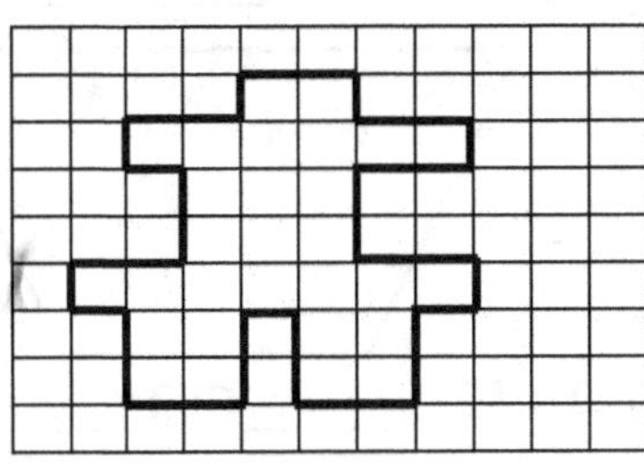

Perimeter =

Student's name: ____________________ Assignment date: ________________

Measure the lengths of the sides. Then find the perimeters of the figures.

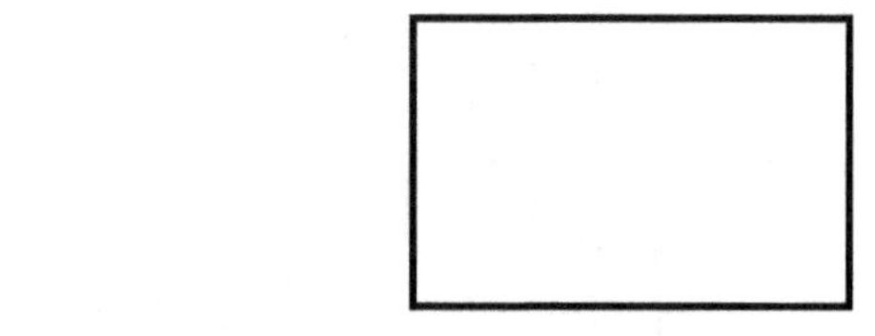

Perimeter
=____cm+____cm+____cm+____cm
=

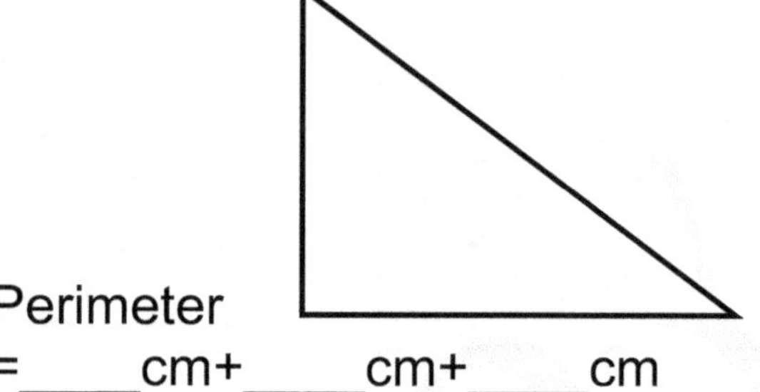

Perimeter
=____cm+____cm+____cm
=

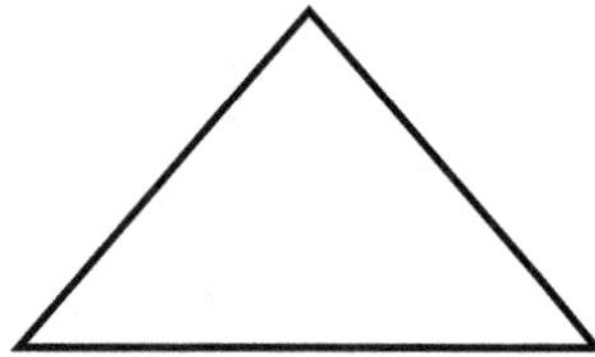

Perimeter
=____cm+____cm+____cm
=

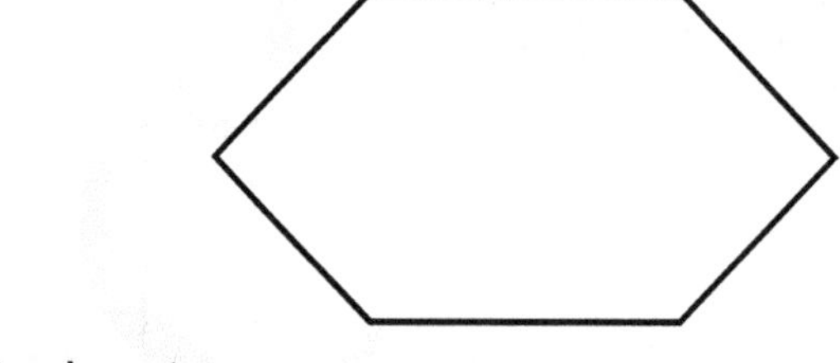

Perimeter =
____cm+____cm+____cm+ ____cm
+____cm+____cm
=

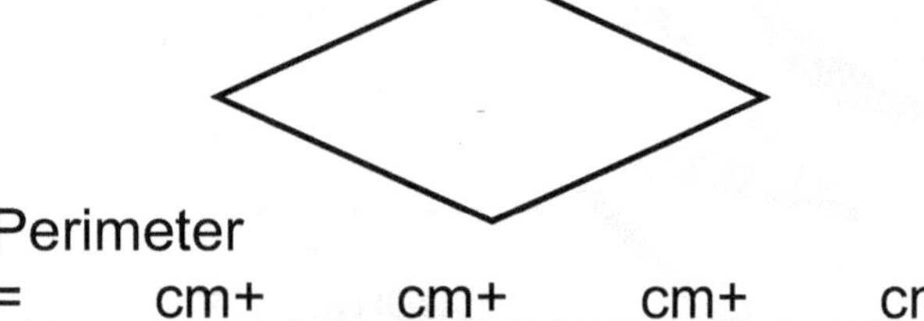

Perimeter
=____cm+____cm+____cm+____cm
=

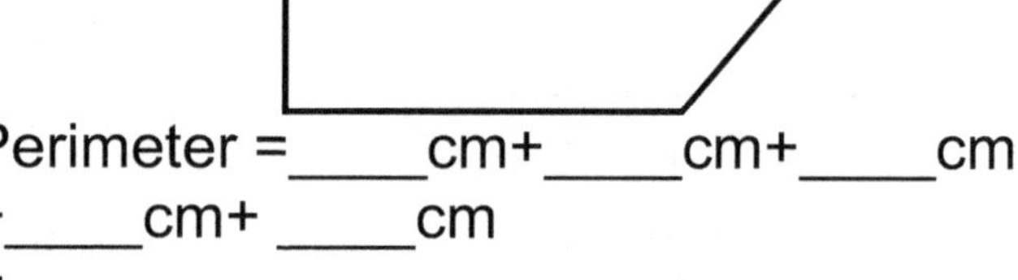

Perimeter =____cm+____cm+____cm
+____cm+ ____cm
=

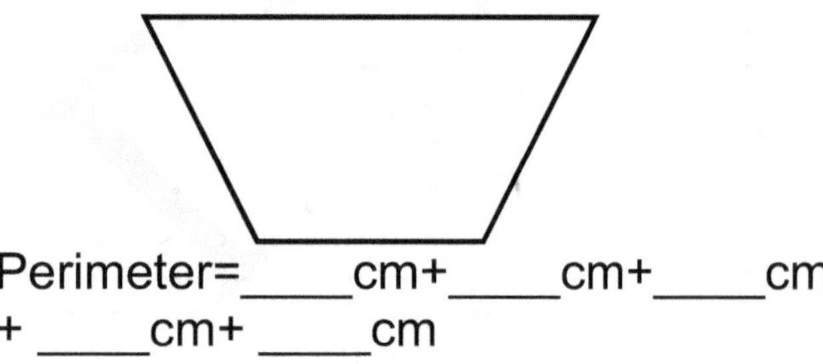

Perimeter=____cm+____cm+____cm
+ ____cm+ ____cm
=

Perimeter =____cm+____cm+____cm
+____cm + ____cm + ____cm
=

Student's name: ____________________ Assignment date: ________________

The perimeter of a Rectangle

Perimeter of a rectangle = 2 × (Length + Width)

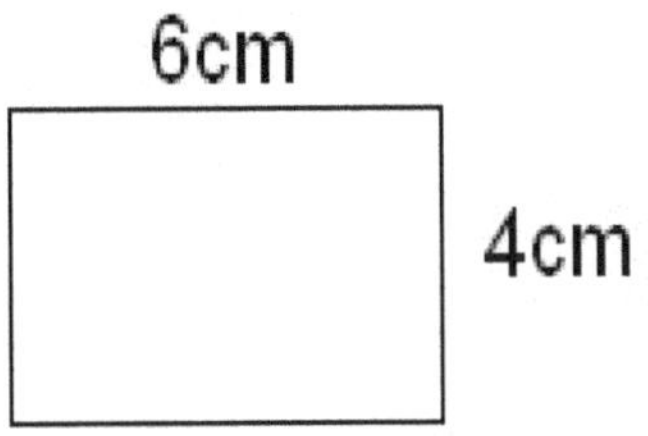

6cm, 4cm

Perimeter = 2 × (___ + ___)
= _____cm

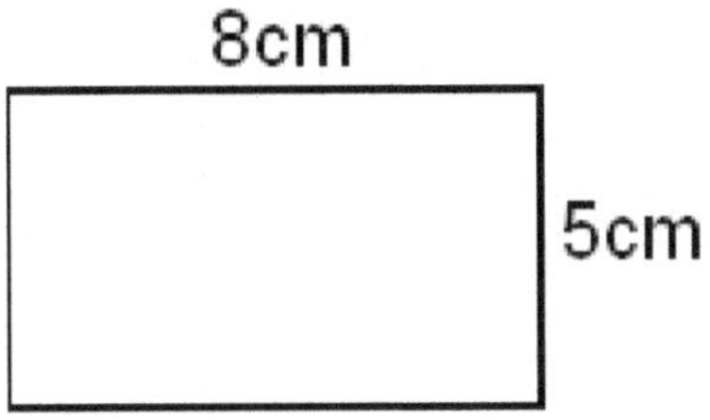

8cm, 5cm

Perimeter = 2 × (___ + ___)
= _____cm

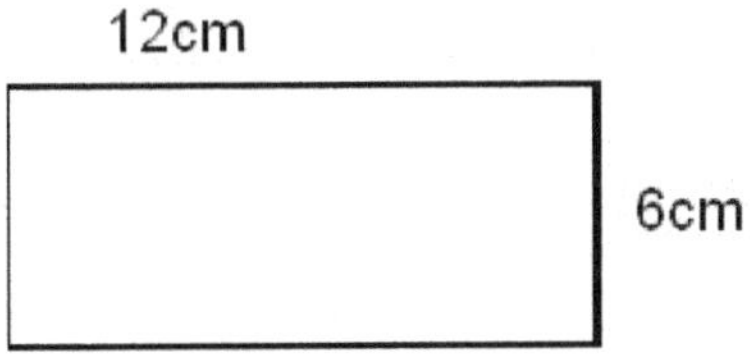

12cm, 6cm

Perimeter =

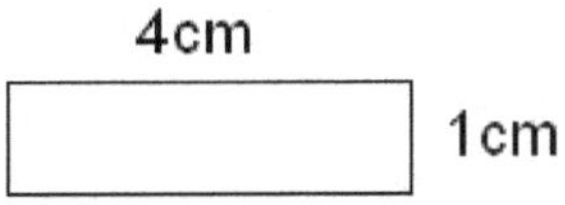

4cm, 1cm

Perimeter =

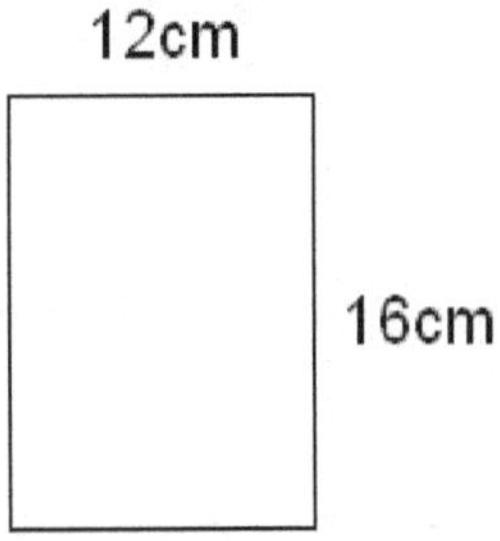

12cm, 16cm

Perimeter =

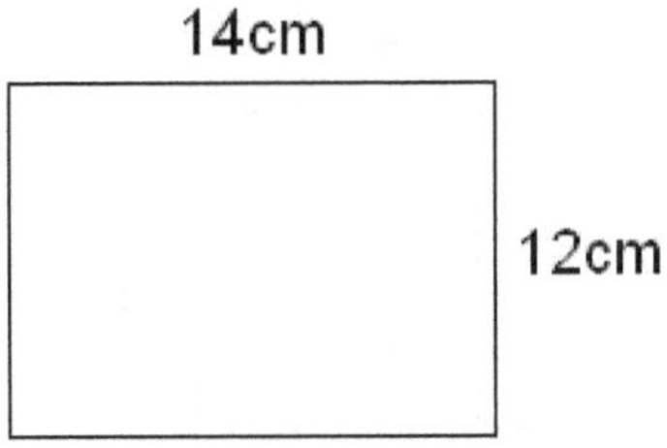

14cm, 12cm

Perimeter =

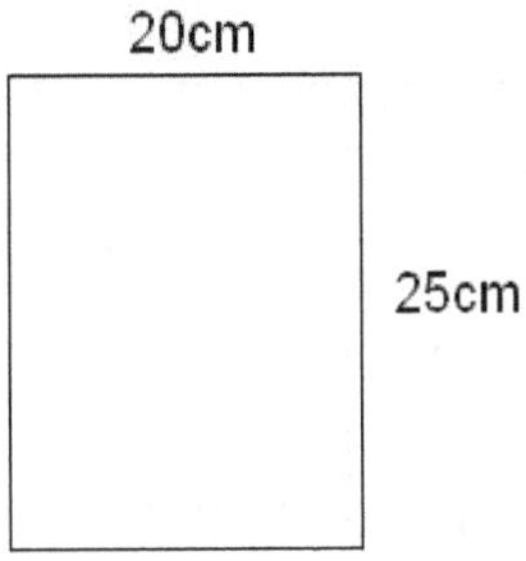

20cm, 25cm

Perimeter =

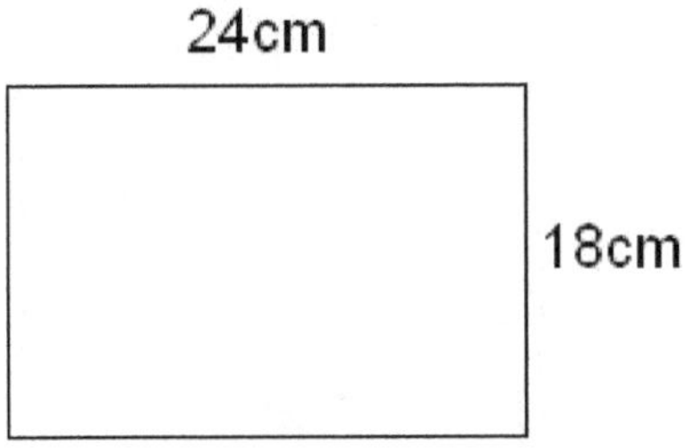

24cm, 18cm

Perimeter =

Student's name: ____________________ Assignment date: ________________

The perimeter of a Square

The perimeter of a square = 4 × side Length

4cm

Perimeter = 4 × ___ =_____cm

7cm

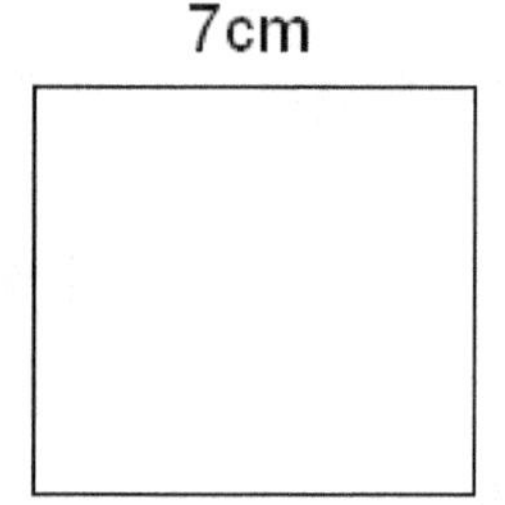

Perimeter = 4× ___ =_____cm

20cm

Perimeter =

14cm

Perimeter =

26cm

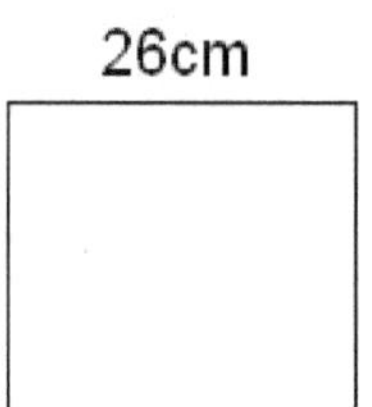

Perimeter =

32cm

Perimeter =

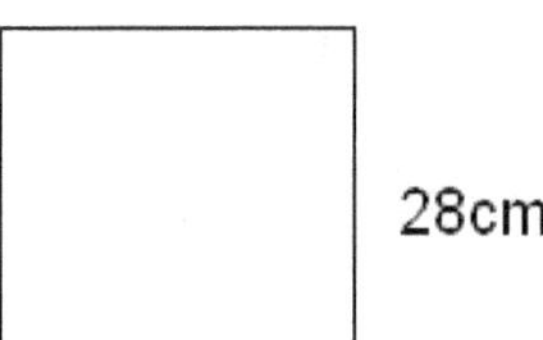

28cm

Perimeter =

42cm

Perimeter =

Ho Math Chess Primary Grades Math

Test Review assesssment 何数棋谜低年级数学测试複習考核

Student's name: ______________________ Assignment date: _________________

Areas of rectangles or squares

Student's name: ____________________ Assignment date: ________________

Area of a triangle

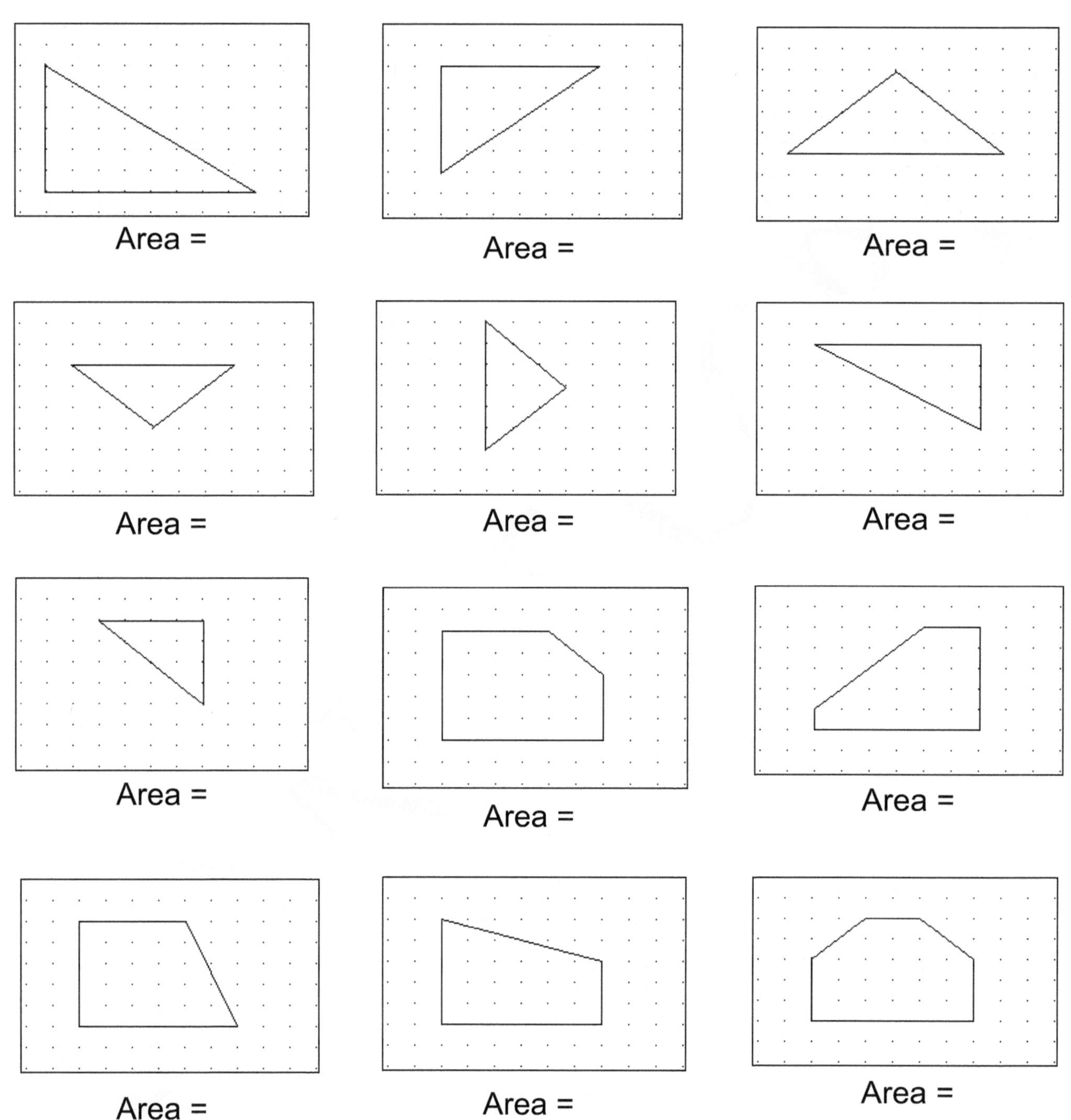

Student's name: ____________________ Assignment date: ________________

Area

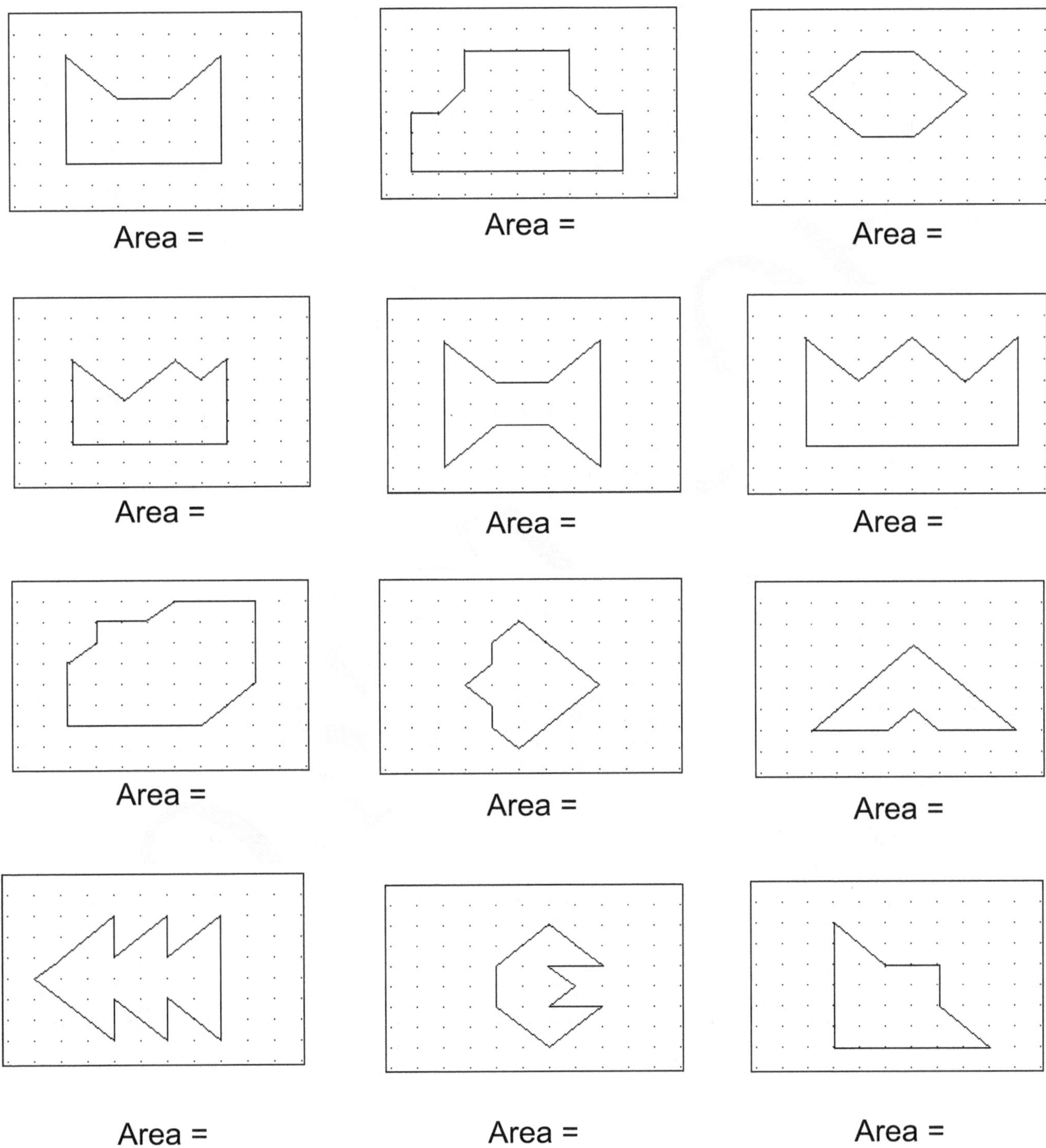

Ho Math Chess Primary Grades Math

Test Review assesssment 何数棋謎低年级数学测试複習考核

Student's name: ____________________ Assignment date: ________________

Area of a Rectangle

Area of a rectangle = Length × Width

7cm

4cm

Area = ___ ×___ =_____cm^2

13cm

16cm

Area = ___ × ___ =_____cm^2

28cm

15cm

Area = cm^2

24m

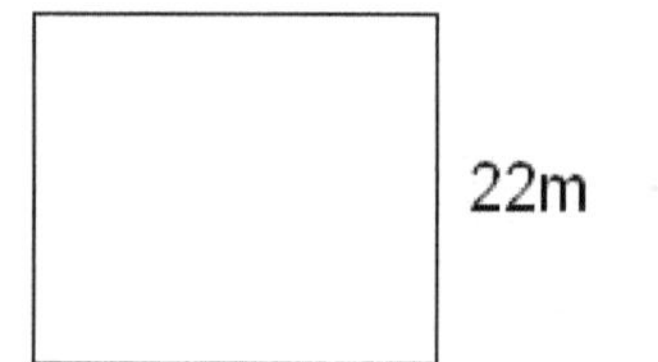

22m

Area = m^2

16cm

5cm

Area = cm^2

20m

10m

Area = m^2

11cm

25cm

Area = cm^2

33m

21m

Area = m^2

Student's name: ____________________ Assignment date: ________________

Find the perimeter and area of each rectangle.

1. 12 cm in wide, 15 cm in long Perimeter = ________cm Area = ________ cm^2	2. 14 cm in wide, 20 cm in long Perimeter = ________cm Area = ________ cm^2
3. 24 cm in wide, 36 cm in long Perimeter = ________ Area = ________	4. 31 cm in wide, 40 cm in long Perimeter = ________ Area = ________
5. 32 m in wide, 45 m in long Perimeter = ________ Area = ________	6. 100 m in wide, 120 m in long Perimeter = ________ Area = ________
7. 15 km in wide, 30 km in long Perimeter = ________ Area = ________	8. 40 km in wide, 140 km in long Perimeter = ________ Area = ________
9. 400 cm in wide, 500 cm in long Perimeter = ________ Area = ________	10. 72 km in wide, 150 km in long Perimeter = ________ Area = ________
11. Find the following rectangular area with the dimension of width 50 cm and the length 5 m.	12. Find the following rectangular area with the dimension of width 2 m and the length 900 cm.

Student's name: ____________________ Assignment date: ________________

Area of a rectangle and square

Area of a rectangle = Length × width
Area of a square = side Length × side length

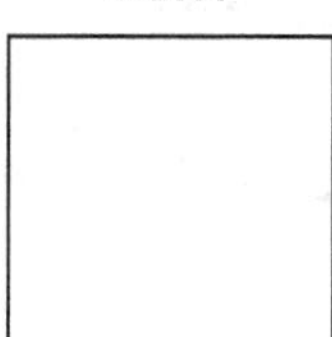
6cm

Area = ___ × ___ =_____cm^2

12cm

Area = ___ × ___ =_____cm^2

15m

Area = m^2

25cm

Area = cm^2

18m

Area = m^2

28cm

Area = cm^2

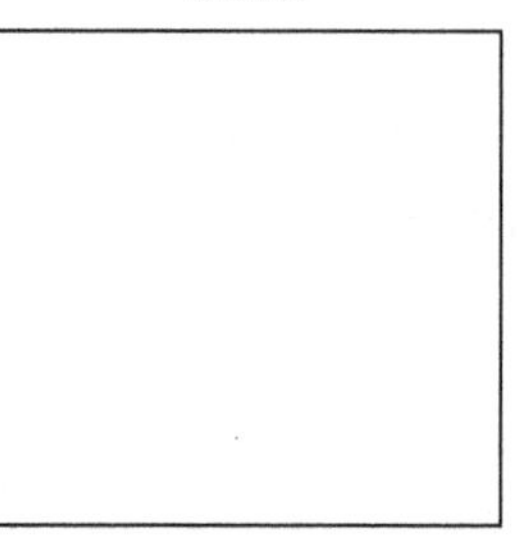
33m

Area = m^2

42cm

Area = cm^2

Student's name: ____________________ Assignment date: ________________

Find the perimeter and area of each square.

1. Side length is 20 cm Perimeter = ________cm Area = ________ cm^2	2. Side length is 50 cm Perimeter = ________cm Area = ________ cm^2
3.Side length is 13 cm Perimeter = ________ Area = ________	4. Side length is 48 m Perimeter = ________ Area = ________
5. Side length is 63 km Perimeter = ________ Area = ________	6. Side length is 36 km Perimeter = ________ Area = ________
7. Side length is 28 cm Perimeter = ________ Area = ________	8. Side length is 32 m Perimeter = ________ Area = ________
9. Side length is 37 km Perimeter = ________ Area = ________	10. Side length is 93 km Perimeter = ________ Area = ________

Student's name: ____________________ Assignment date: ________________

Area and Perimeter

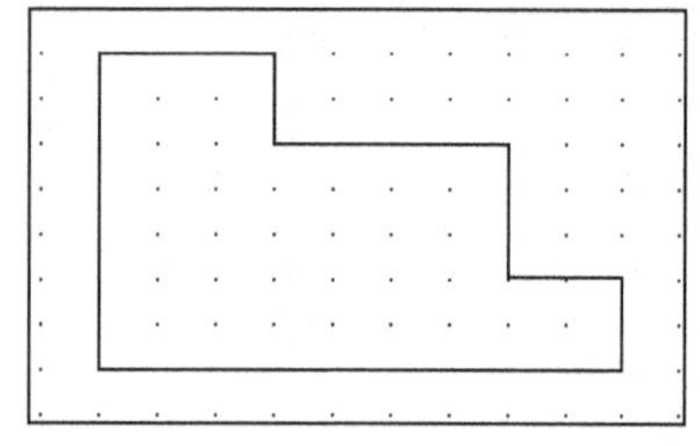

Perimeter _______ units
Area _______units^2

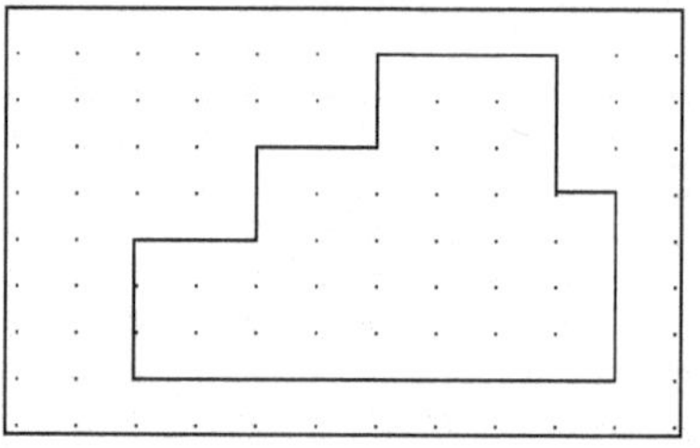

Perimeter _______ units
Area _______units^2

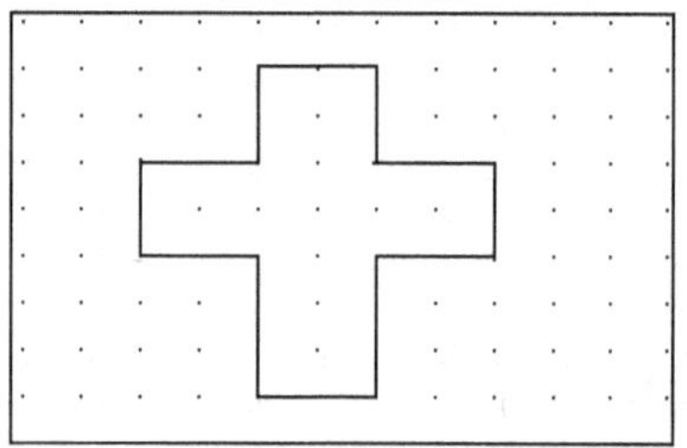

Perimeter _______ units
Area _______units^2

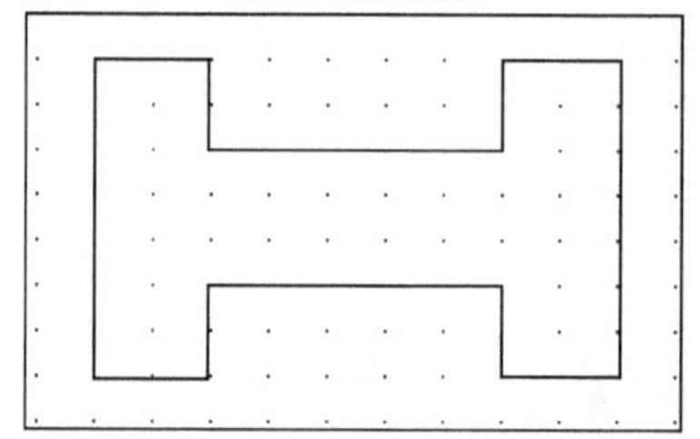

Perimeter _______ units
Area _______units^2

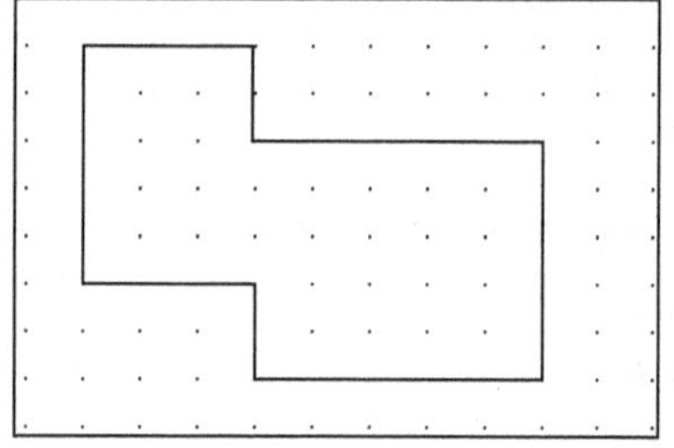

Perimeter _______ units
Area _______units^2

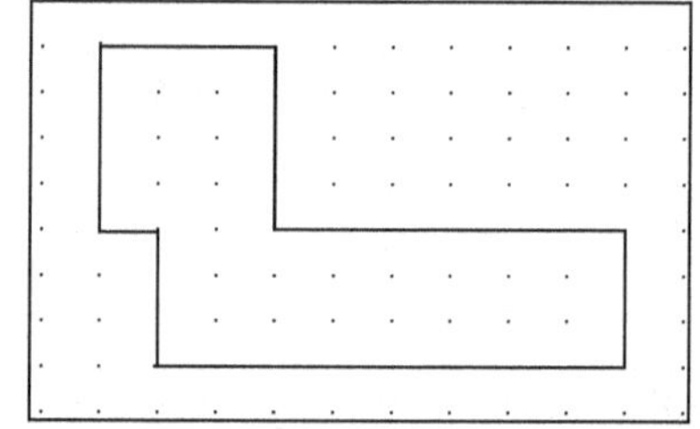

Perimeter _______ units
Area _______units^2

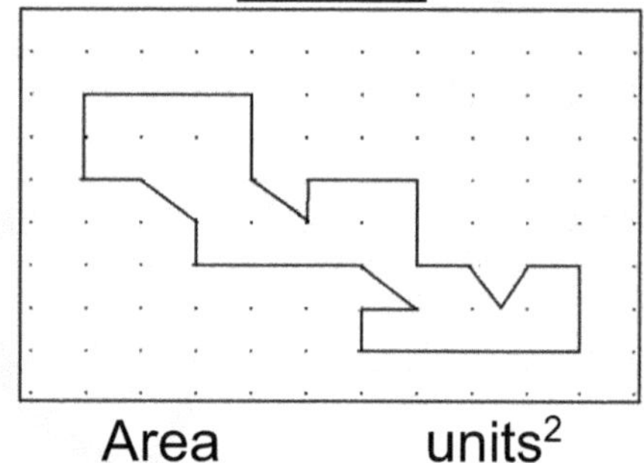

Area _______units^2

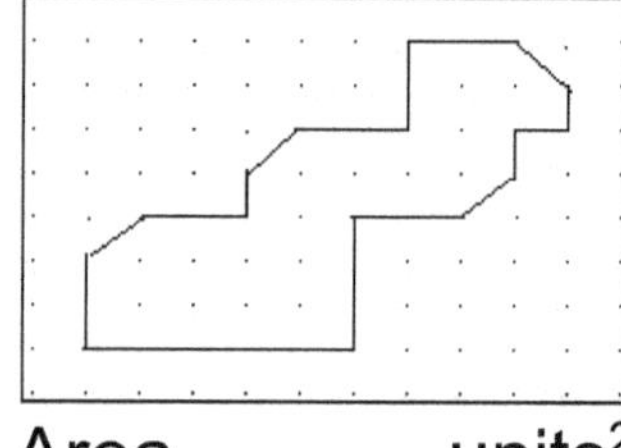

Area _______units^2

Student's name: ____________________ Assignment date: ________________

Fill in the missing values for a rectangle.

	Length	Width	Perimeter	Area
1.	8	4		
2.	12	7		
3.	8		24	
4.		6	30	
5.	8			56
6.		5		65
7.			20	24
8.			48	80

Fill in the missing values for a square.

	Side length	Perimeter	Area
1.	4		
2.	7		
3.		36	
4.		48	
5.			49
6.			81

Student's name: ____________________ Assignment date: ________________

Area and perimeter word problems

1. Averill Garden is in the shape of a rectangle with 30 m in length and 40m in width. The owner wants to fence the Garden. How many meters of the fence does he need to buy?

____

2. Mystery City is in the shape of a square. The length of one side is 180 km. There is a road around the city. How long is the road?

____

3. A tower is in the shape of a triangle. The total distance around the tower is 480 m. What is the length of the missing side?

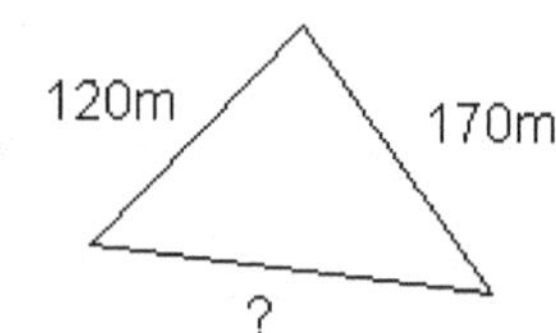

____

4. Janet walks her dog around a block 4 times a day. The block is 240 m long and 320m wide. What is the total distance does she walk with her dog every day?

____

5. A table is 120 cm long and 60 cm wide. Lucy wants to cover the table with a table cloth. At least how much cloth does she need?

____

6. Nick wants to floor his bedroom. His bedroom is 15 m long and 11 m wide. How many square meters of the wood panel does he need?

____

Student's name: ____________________ Assignment date: ________________

7. A basketball court measures 40 m by 20 m.

What is the perimeter? ________________

What is the area? ________________

8. A volleyball court measures 18 m by 9 m.

What is the perimeter? ________________

What is the area? ________________

9. The distance around a tennis court is 100 m. It is 30 meters long. What is its width?

____

10. A bear pen is 9 m long if its area is 108 m^2.

What is its width? ________________

What is its perimeter? ________________

11. Linda wants to build a fence for her backyard against the wall of her house. The wall is 12 m long. Suppose she needs a 30 m fence. What is the width of her backyard?

____

What is the area of her backyard? ________________

12. Lois wants to fence his rectangular garden against the river. No fence is needed along the river. The area of the garden is 240 m^2. The length along the river is 40 m. . What is the width of his garden?

____

What is the total length of his fence? ________________

Student's name: ____________________ Assignment date: ________________

Advanced word problems of areas for rectangles or squares
Answers are in whole numbers only.

<table>
<tr><td>shapes</td><td>perimeter</td><td>area</td><td>What could be the dimension of the shape?</td></tr>
<tr><td>rectangle</td><td>48 m

$48 \div 2 = 24$
<table>
<tr><td>length</td><td>width</td></tr>
<tr><td>23</td><td>1</td></tr>
<tr><td>22</td><td>2</td></tr>
<tr><td>21</td><td>3</td></tr>
<tr><td>20</td><td>4</td></tr>
<tr><td>19</td><td>5</td></tr>
<tr><td>18</td><td>6</td></tr>
<tr><td>17</td><td>7</td></tr>
<tr><td>16</td><td>8</td></tr>
<tr><td>15</td><td>9</td></tr>
<tr><td>14</td><td>10</td></tr>
<tr><td>13</td><td>11</td></tr>
<tr><td>12</td><td>12</td></tr>
</table></td><td>What could be the areas?</td><td>Not applicable</td></tr>
<tr><td>rectangle</td><td>What could be the largest perimeter?

What could be the least perimeter?</td><td>36 m^2</td><td>Not applicable</td></tr>
</table>

Student's name: ____________________ Assignment date: ________________

shapes	perimeter	area	What could be the dimension of the shape?
rectangle	6 m	2 m^2	What could be the dimensions of the shape?
Rectangle	12 m		What could be the dimension of the square?
square		49 m^2	What could be the dimension of the square?

Student's name: ____________________ Assignment date: ________________

Volume of a rectangle and a square

The volume of a rectangle or cube = LWH (Length × Width × Height)

A rectangular tank has dimensions 5 feet by 10 feet by 15 feet. The tank will be filled with water at a rate of 5 cubic feet per minute. How long will it take to fill up the tank?

Student's name: ____________________ Assignment date: ________________

Temperature

Write the temperatures.

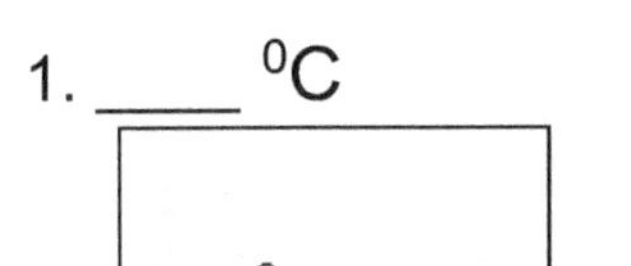
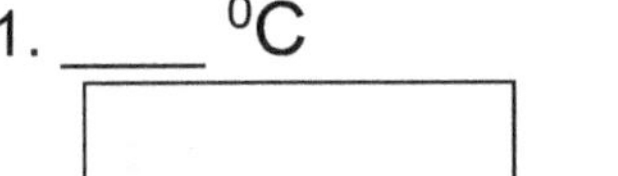
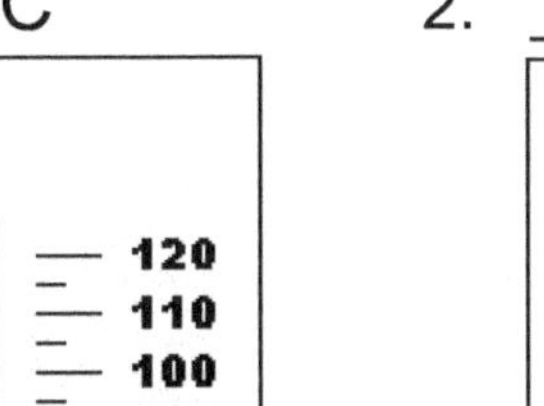

1. ____ °C

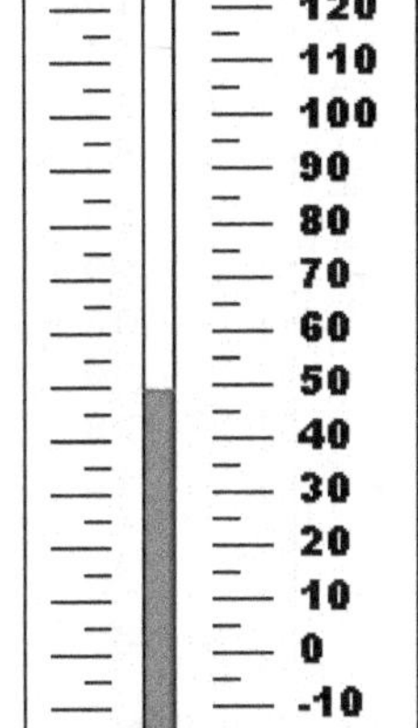

2. ____ °C

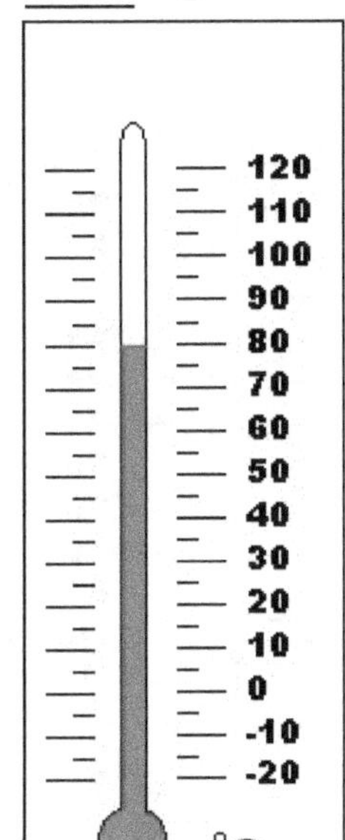

3. ____ °C

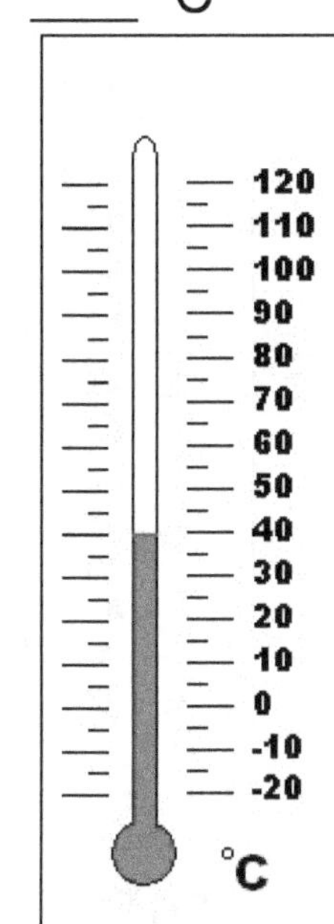

4. ____ °C

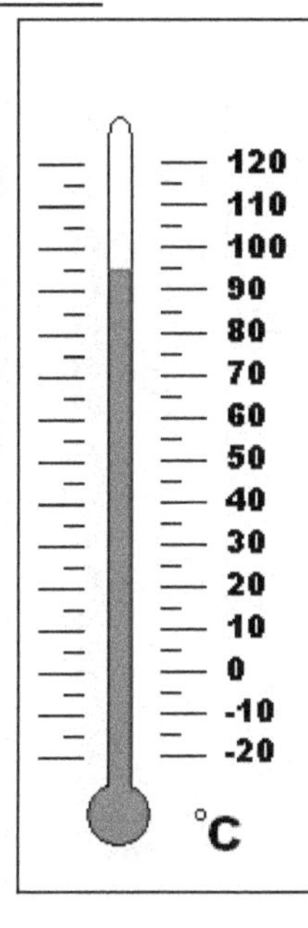

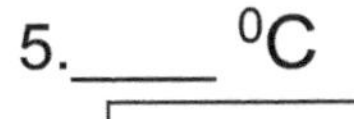

5.____ °C

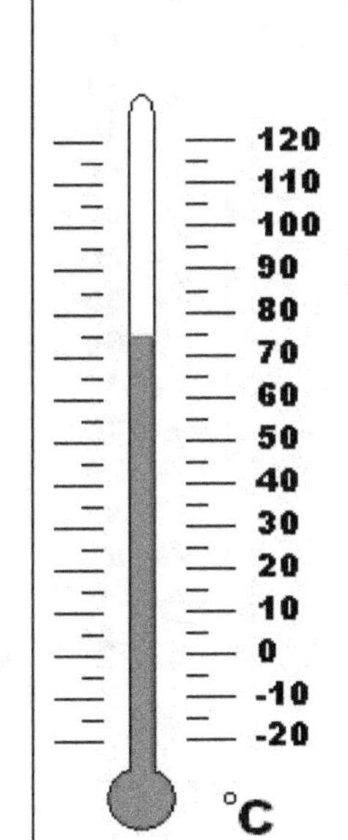

6. ____ °C

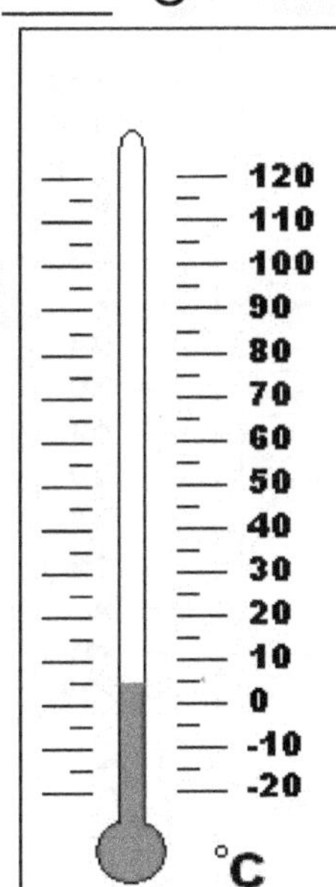

7.____ °C

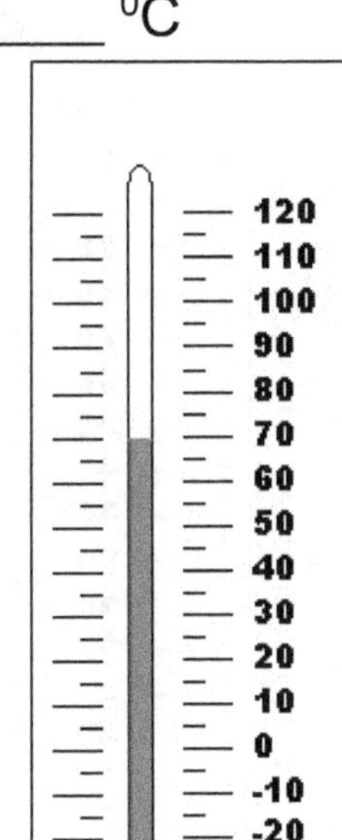

8. ____ °C

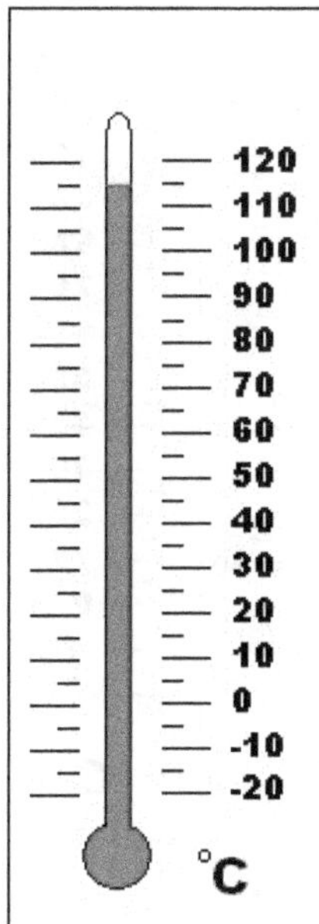

Student's name: ____________________ Assignment date: ________________

Colour the thermometer to show the temperature.

1. 
40 °C

2. 80 °C

3. 55 °C

4. 75 °C

5. 
5 °C

6. 
60 °C

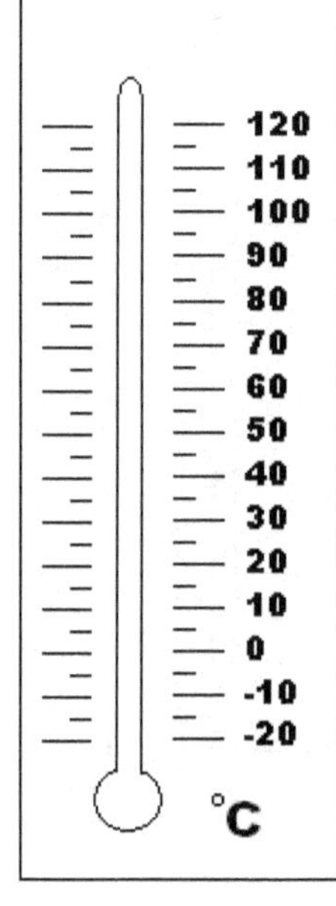

7. 95 °C

8. 100 °C

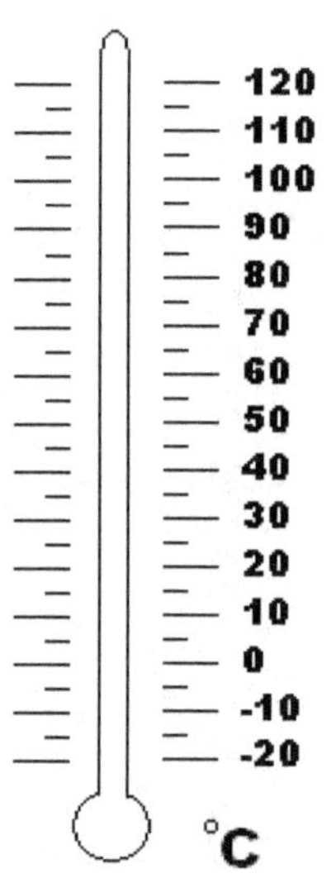

Student's name: ____________________ Assignment date: ________________

The following thermometers show the temperatures of midnight in four different cities: Vancouver, Winnipeg, Chicago, and San Carlos.

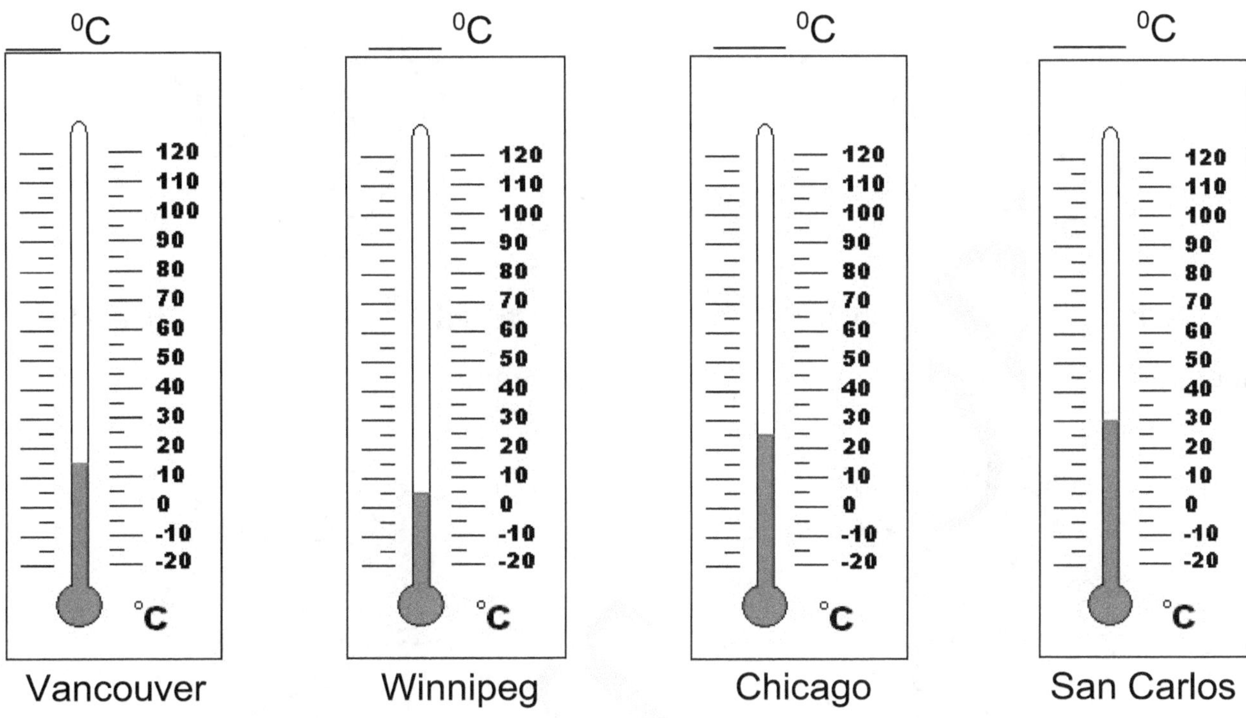

1. What is the temperature of Vancouver?
2. What is the temperature of Chicago?
3. What is the highest temperature? Which city?
4. What is the lowest temperature? Which city?
5. How many ^{0}C higher is the temperature of San Carlos than Winnipeg?
6. How many ^{0}C lower is the temperature of Vancouver than Chicago?

Student's name: ____________________ Assignment date: ________________

Cold or hot? Then estimate the temperature.

a. hot b. cold

Temperature: ____________

a. hot b. cold

Temperature: ____________

a. hot b. cold

Temperature: ____________

a. hot b. cold

Temperature: ____________

a. hot b. cold

Temperature: ____________

a. hot b. cold

Temperature: ____________

Student's name: ____________________ Assignment date: ______________

***** Part 13 Money *****

Even though Canadian money is represented here, its math knowledge can be transferred into any country's money system. Only dollar sign ($) or cent sign (¢) are used in presenting money amount.

	Money cent notation	Money dollar notation
One hundred cents	100¢	$1.00 10 cents (dimes) $1.00 dollar cents (pennies) A dime is a tenth of a dollar. A penny is a hundredth of a dollar or a tenth of a dime, A dollar is 10 dimes or a 100 dents. A dime is 10 cent.

Student's name: ____________________ Assignment date: ________________

Write each amount in two ways (dollars and cents).

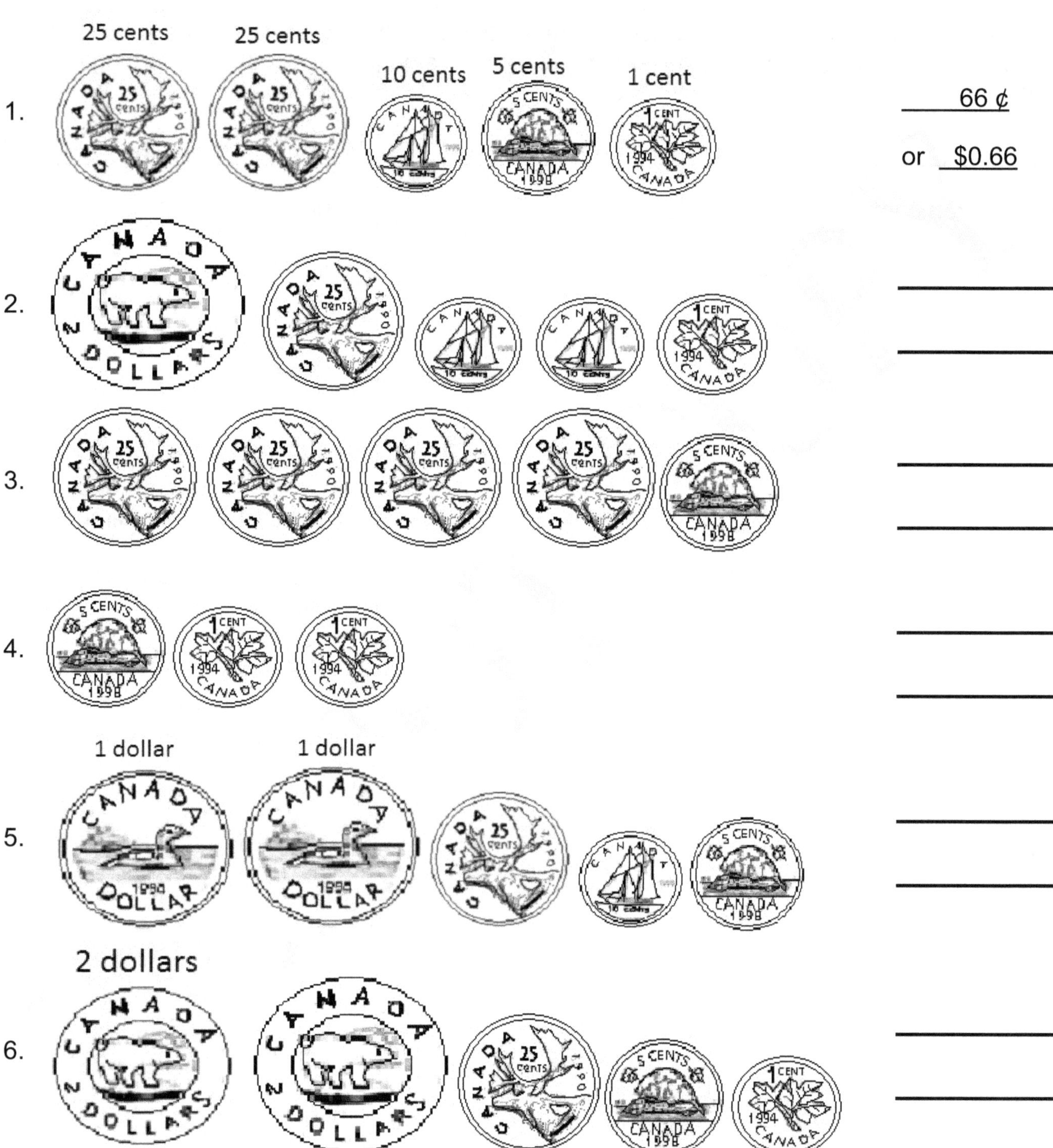

Student's name: ____________________ Assignment date: ________________

Write each amount in two ways.

7. ________
____

8. ________
____

9. ________
____

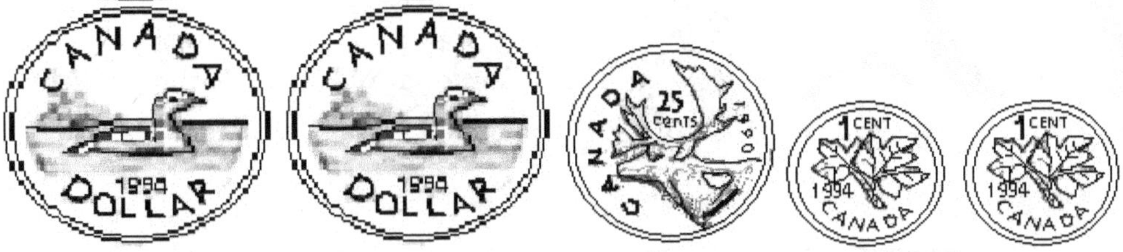

10. ________
____

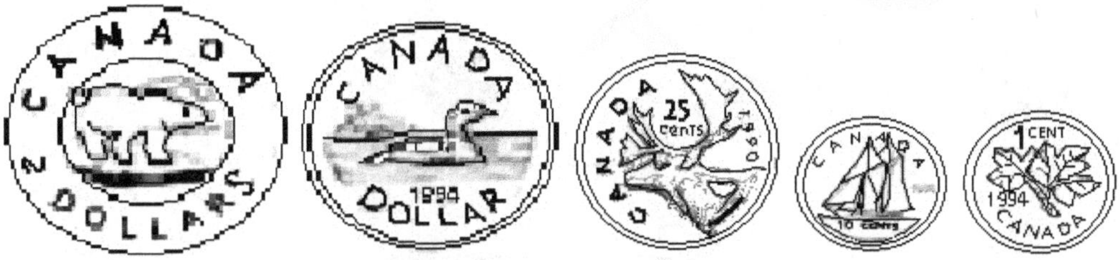

11. ________
____

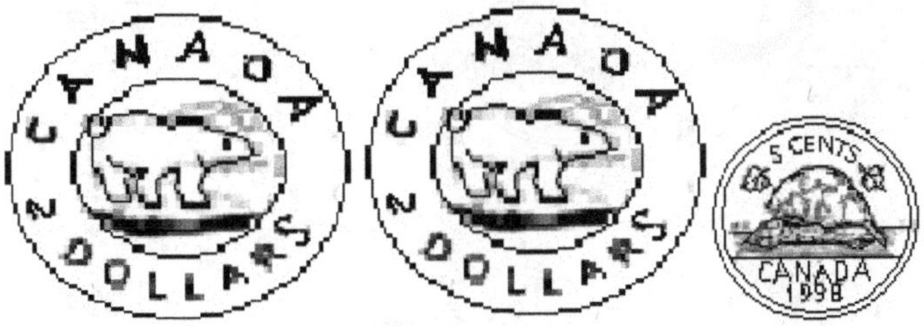

12. ________
____

Student's name: ____________________ Assignment date: ________________

Fill in the missing number.

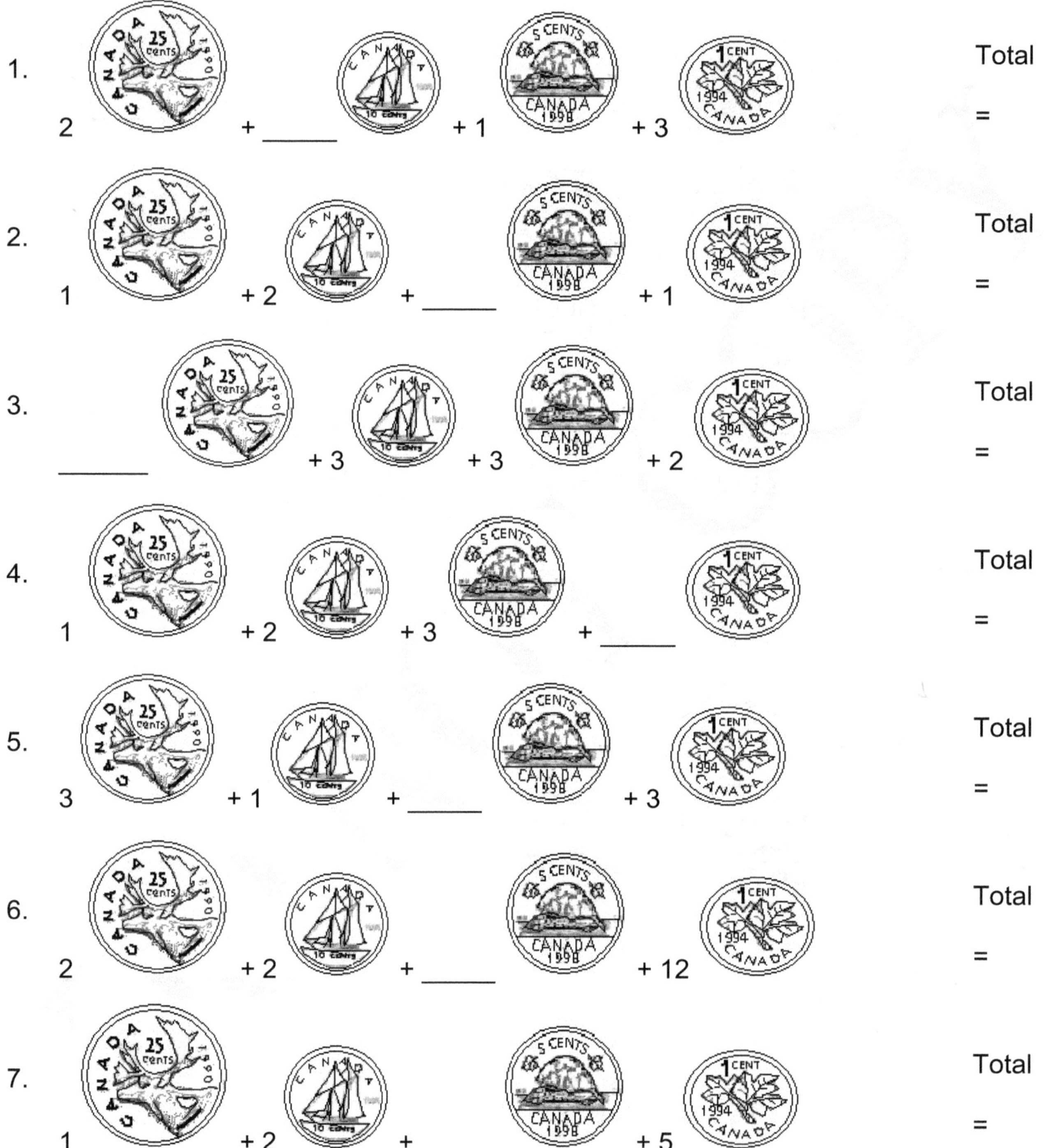

Student's name: ____________________ Assignment date: ________________

Fill in the missing number.

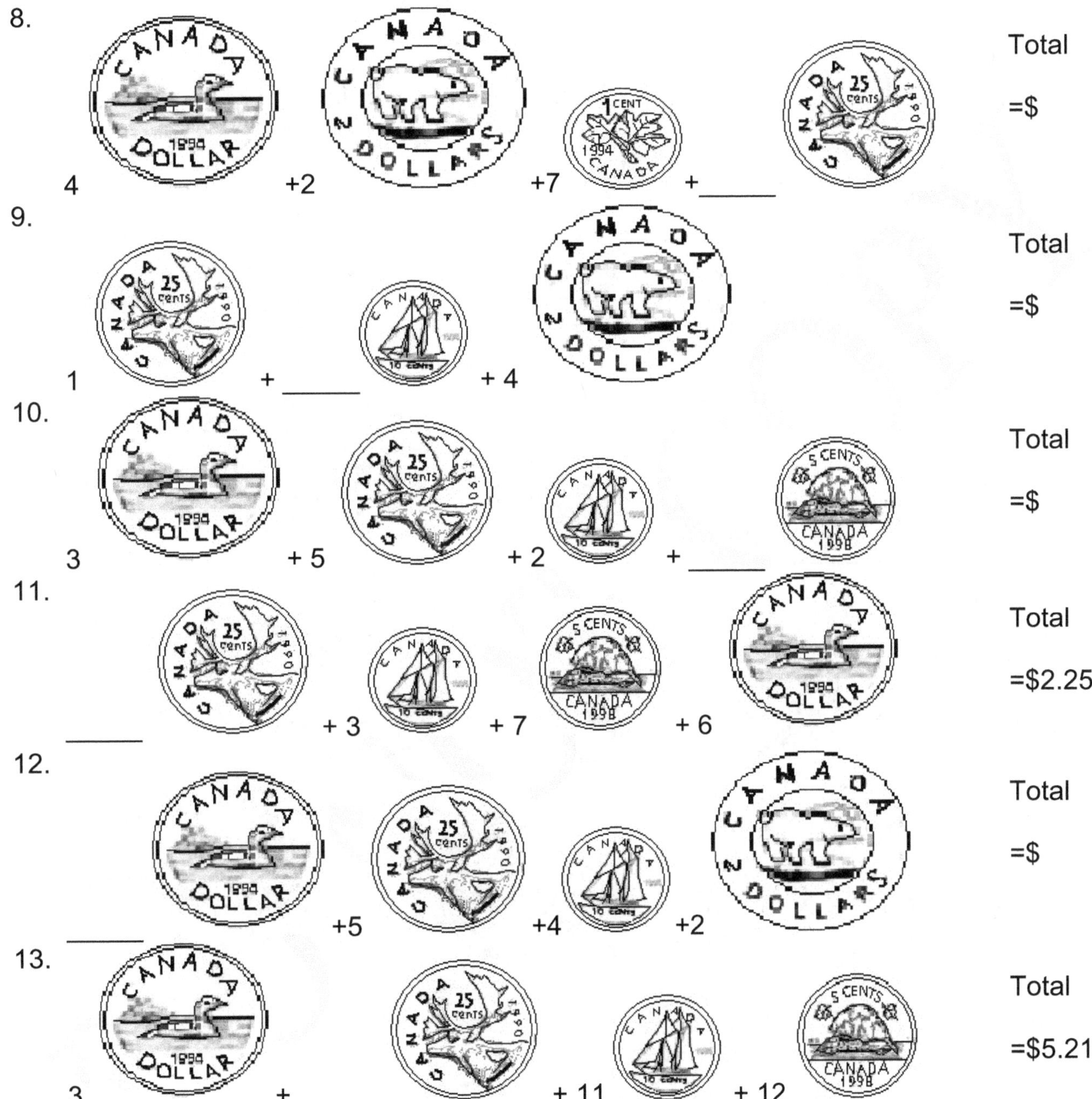

8. 4 +2 +7 + ____ Total =$

9. 1 + ____ + 4 Total =$

10. 3 + 5 + 2 + ____ Total =$

11. ____ + 3 + 7 + 6 Total =$2.25

12. ____ +5 +4 +2 Total =$

13. 3 + ____ + 11 + 12 Total =$5.21

Student's name: ____________________ Assignment date: ________________

Fill in the missing number.

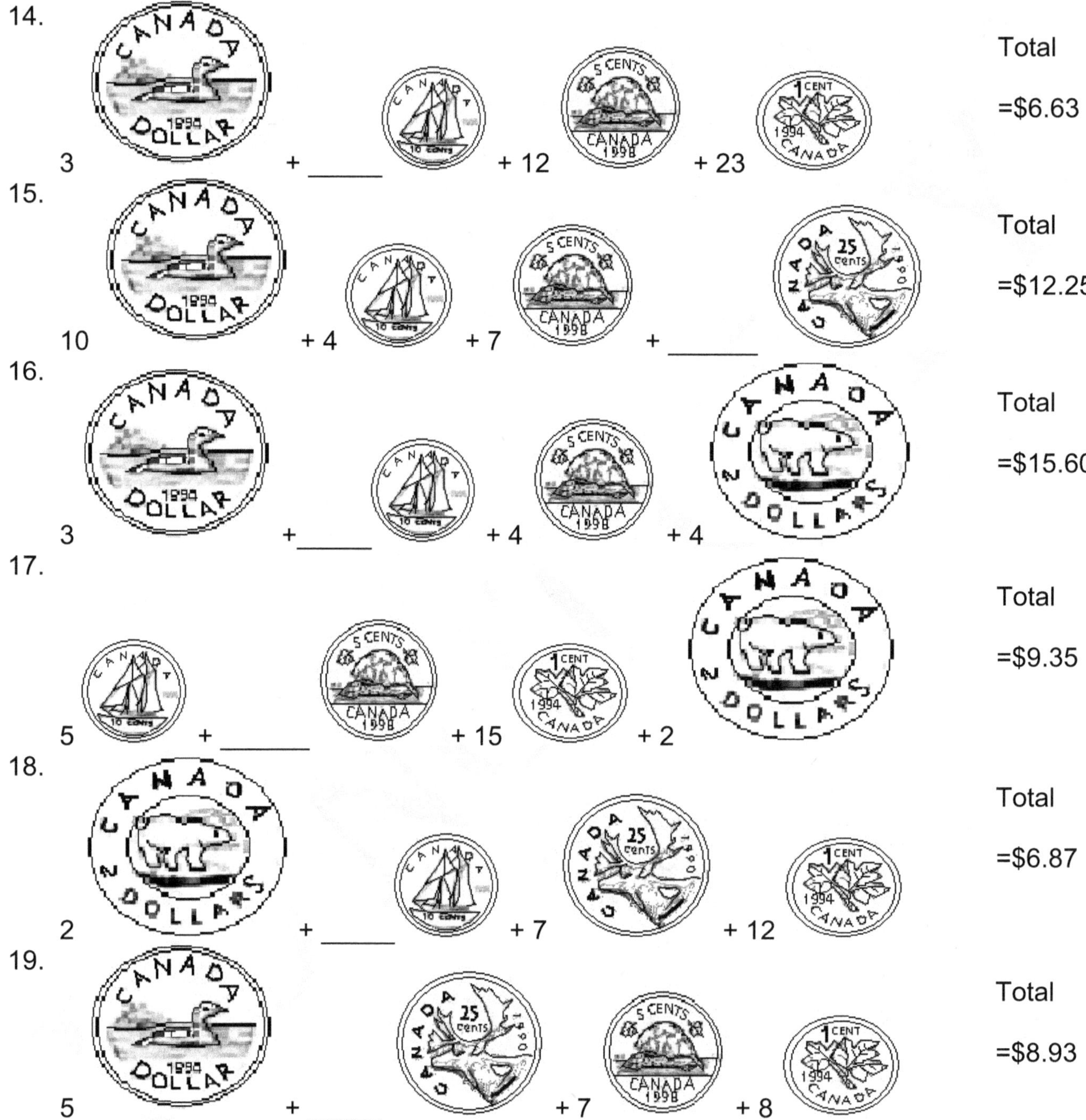

14. 3 + _____ + 12 + 23 Total =$6.63

15. 10 + 4 + 7 + ______ Total =$12.25

16. 3 + _____ + 4 + 4 Total =$15.60

17. 5 + ______ + 15 + 2 Total =$9.35

18. 2 + _____ + 7 + 12 Total =$6.87

19. 5 + _____ + 7 + 8 Total =$8.93

Student's name: ____________________ Assignment date: ________________

Write each amount in decimal form.

1. 2 quarters, 3 dimes, 4 nickels, 5 pennies ________________	2. 4 quarters, 1 nickel, 2 dimes, 3 pennies ________________
3. 1 quarter, 6 dimes, 2 nickels, 7 pennies ________________	4. 3 quarters, 8 dimes, 12 pennies ________________
5. 2 quarters, 7 nickels, 9 pennies ________________	6. 6 quarters, 2 nickels, 1 dime, 22 pennies ________________
7. 2 loonies, 1 quarter, 4 nickels, 4 pennies ________________	8. 1 toonie, 3 loonies, 5 nickels, 6 dimes ________________
9. 3 toonies, 5 quarters, 6 nickels, 8 pennies ________________	10. 5 loonies, 2 quarters, 6 dimes, 1 nickel ________________
11. 1 10-dollar bill, 3 toonies, 2 loonies, 1 quarter, 4 nickels, 3 dimes, 12 pennies ________________	12. 3 5-dollar bills, 2 toonies, 3 loonies, 5 quarters, 2 nickels, 8 pennies ________________
13. 2 10-dollar bills, 3 5-dollar bills, 4 toonies, 6 loonies, 2 quarters, 5 dimes, 8 pennies ________________	14. 2 20-dollar bills, 5 5-dollar bills, 3 toonies, 7 quarters, 9 dimes, 31 pennies ________________
15. 2 20-dollar bills, 3 10-dollar bills, 4 loonies, 8 nickels, 3 dimes, 24 pennies ________________	16. 3 10-dollar bills, 6 toonies, 3 loonies, 7 quarters, 5 nickels, 5 pennies ________________

Student's name: ____________________ Assignment date: ________________

Use the fewest number of coins to make each amount.

1. 62 ¢

______ pennies ______ dimes

______ nickels ______ quarters

2. 36 ¢

______ pennies ______ dimes

______ nickels ______ quarters

3. 48 ¢

______ pennies ______ dimes

______ nickels ______ quarters

4. 74 ¢

______ pennies ______ dimes

______ nickels ______ quarters

5. 91 ¢

______ pennies ______ dimes

______ nickels ______ quarters

6. 56 ¢

______ pennies ______ dimes

______ nickels ______ quarters

7. 87 ¢

______ pennies ______ dimes

______ nickels ______ quarters

8. 19 ¢

______ pennies ______ dimes

______ nickels ______ quarters

9. $ 1.45

______ pennies ______ dimes

______ nickels ______ quarters

______ loonies ______ toonies

10. $ 5.39

______ pennies ______ dimes

______ nickels ______ quarters

______ loonies ______ toonies

11. $ 6.72

______ pennies ______ dimes

______ nickels ______ quarters

______ loonies ______ toonies

12. $ 3.56

______ pennies ______ dimes

______ nickels ______ quarters

______ loonies ______ toonies

Student's name: ____________________ Assignment date: ________________

Use exactly the number of coins to make each amount.

1. 47 ¢ with 5 coins

______ pennies ______ dimes

______ nickels ______ quarters

2. 53 ¢ with 5 coins

______ pennies ______ dimes

______ nickels ______ quarters

3. 36 ¢ with 4 coins

______ pennies ______ dimes

______ nickels ______ quarters

4. 51 ¢ with 7 coins

______ pennies ______ dimes

______ nickels ______ quarters

5. 53 ¢ with 8 coins

______ pennies ______ dimes

______ nickels ______ quarters

6. 58 ¢ with 9 coins

______ pennies ______ dimes

______ nickels ______ quarters

7. 86 ¢ with 14 coins

______ pennies ______ dimes

______ nickels ______ quarters

8. 71 ¢ with 11 coins

______ pennies ______ dimes

______ nickels ______ quarters

9. $ 1.25 with 10 coins

______ pennies ______ dimes

______ nickels ______ quarters

______ loonies ______ toonies

10. $ 2.08 with 6 coins

______ pennies ______ dimes

______ nickels ______ quarters

______ loonies ______ toonies

11. $ 3.21 with 10 coins

______ pennies ______ dimes

______ nickels ______ quarters

______ loonies ______ toonies

12. $ 5.81 with 10 coins

______ pennies ______ dimes

______ nickels ______ quarters

______ loonies ______ toonies

Student's name: ____________________ Assignment date: ________________

Use two ways to present each amount. (Use 'P' present penny, 'N' present nickel, 'D' present dime, 'Q' present quarter and 'T' present total.)

1. 30 ¢ with 6 coins	2. 40 ¢ with 4 coins
3. 45 ¢ with 9 coins	4. 55 ¢ with 7 coins
5. 80 ¢ with 8 coins	6. 85 ¢ with 13 coins

Student's name: ____________________ Assignment date: ________________

How many ways can you make each amount? ('P' present penny, 'N' present nickel, 'D' present dime, 'Q' present quarter and 'T' present total)

1. 57 ¢ with 9 coins

	P	N	D	Q	T
1.					
2.					
3.					
4.					
5.					
6.					
7.					

____________ ways

2. 85 ¢ with 12 coins

	P	N	D	Q	T
1.					
2.					
3.					
4.					
5.					
6.					
7.					

____________ ways

3. 73 ¢ with 15 coins

	P	N	D	Q	T
1.					
2.					
3.					
4.					
5.					
6.					
7.					
8.					
9.					

____________ ways

4. $ 1.00 with 18 coins

	P	N	D	Q	T
1.					
2.					
3.					
4.					
5.					
6.					
7.					
8.					
9.					

____________ ways

Student's name: ____________________ Assignment date: ________________

Money calculation by making changes

A good way of learning decimal calculations.

	Purchase	paid	Change
1.	$3.12	5	
2.	$0.89	CANADA 2 DOLLARS	
3.	$4.58	10	
4.	$6.12	10	
5.	$15.68	20	
6.	$12.45	20	
7.	$0.69	CANADA 2 DOLLARS	
8.	$12.68	20	

Student's name: ____________________ Assignment date: ________________

Money calculation by making changes

	Purchase	paid	Change
9.	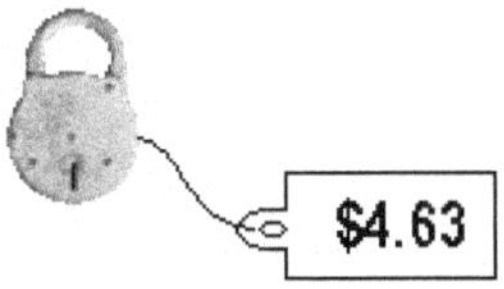 $4.63		
10.	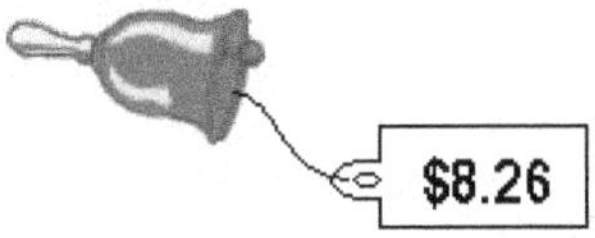 $8.26	 5 5	
11.	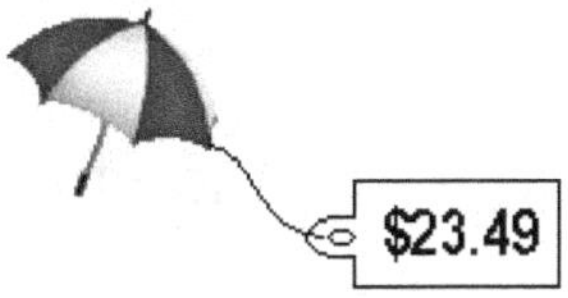 $23.49	 10 20	
12.	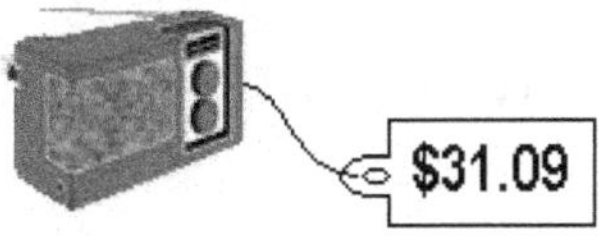 $31.09	 20 10	
13.	 $11.43	 20 5	
14.	 $46.18	 20 20 20	
15.	 $17.93	 10 5	

Student's name: ____________________ Assignment date: ________________

Money word problems

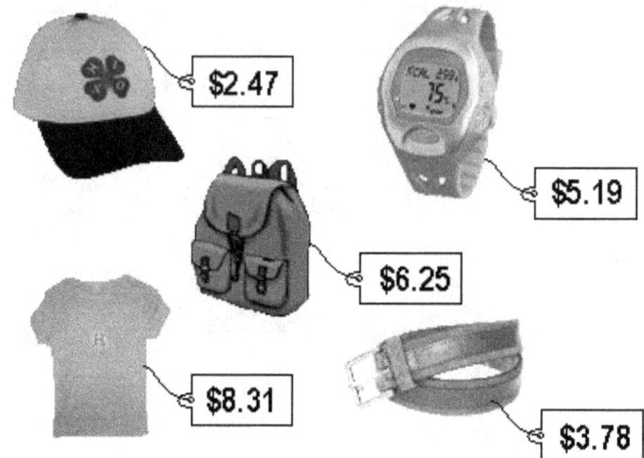

1. Linda bought a T-shirt and paid $10. How much change would she get?

2. Grace gave the clerk $6.25 for two items. Which two items did she buy?

3. Tom bought a bag and a watch. How much did the two items cost him?

   If he gave the clerk $15. How much change should he get?

4. Steve bought 2 T-shirt and a bag. He had $20 with him. Is it enough? How much should he borrow to make the deal?

5. Isabel bought 3 items with $12. Which 3 items did she buy? How much change did she get?

Student's name: ____________________ Assignment date: ________________

Money word problems

1. James bought a notebook for $1.75 and a pen for $2.46. How much did he spend?

2. Lollipop is $2.58 per pound. Chocolate bar is $7.84 per pound. Frank bought 5 pounds of lollipop and 2 pounds of chocolate bar. How much did it cost him?

3. Kevin has some coins in his purse: 3 toonies, 4 loonies, 7 quarters, 3 dimes, 5s, and 15 pennies. How much does he have?

4. Three friends went for shopping for picnic. They bought 3 loaves of bread for $1.27 each, 5 bottles of juice for $2.35 each, 2 pounds of sausage for &7.46 per pound. How much should each person pay?

5. Aaron bought four goldfish for $0.28 each and a bag of fish food for $1.63. He gave the clerk $5. How much change did he get?

Student's name: ____________________ Assignment date: ________________

Rounding to the nearest dollar

Example: Is $3.42 is closer to $3 or $4?

$3 $3.42 $4

$0.42 $0.58

The difference between $3 and $3.42 is: $3.42 - $3 = $0.42
The difference between $4 and $3.42 is: $4 - $3.42 = $0.58
And we know that 0.58 > 0.42. So when $3.42 is rounded to nearest dollar, the answer is $3.

1. $ 4.78 ____________ 2. $ 0.63 ____________

3. $ 23.52 ____________ 4. $ 8.41 ____________

5. $ 7.89 ____________ 6. $ 5.09 ____________

7. $ 27.91 ____________ 8. $ 81.32 ____________

9. $ 48.19 ____________ 10. $ 31.87 ____________

11. $ 157.37 ____________ 12. $ 642.61 ____________

Round to the nearest ten dollar or tens place.

1. $ 36.72 $40 2. $ 81.32 ____________

3. $ 68.07 ____________ 4. $ 55.67 ____________

5. $ 43.98 ____________ 6. $ 37.21 ____________

7. $ 582.71 ____________ 8. $ 695.86 ____________

9. $ 472.96 ____________ 10. $ 892.65 ____________

11. $ 531.53 ____________ 12. $ 637.09 ____________

Student's name: ____________________ Assignment date: ________________

Rounding to the nearest dime

Example: Is \$3.42 is closer to \$3.4 or \$3.5?

\$3 \$3.42 \$4

\$0.42 \$0.58

The difference between \$3.4 and \$3.42 is: \$0.42 \$3.42 - \$3.4 = \$0.02
The difference between \$3.5 and \$3.42 is: \$3.5 - \$3.42 = \$0.08
We know that 0.08 > 0.02, so when \$3.42 is rounded to nearest dime, the answer is \$3.4

13. \$ 4.78 ____________ 14. \$ 0.63 ____________

15. \$ 23.52 ____________ 16. \$ 8.41 ____________

17. \$ 7.89 ____________ 18. \$ 5.09 ____________

19. \$ 27.91 ____________ 20. \$ 81.32 ____________

21. \$ 48.19 ____________ 22. \$ 31.87 ____________

23. \$ 157.37 ____________ 24. \$ 642.61 ____________

Circle the amount where the cent is more than 50 cents.

13. \$ 36.72 14. \$ 81.32

15. \$ 68.07 16. \$ 55.67

17. \$ 43.98 18. \$ 37.21

19. \$ 582.71 20. \$ 695.86

21. \$ 472.96 22. \$ 892.65

23. \$ 531.53 24. \$ 637.09

Student's name: ____________________ Assignment date: ________________

***** Part 14 Estimating *****

Estimating the sums or differences.

Example:

	$2 . 3 7	→		$2 . 0 0
+	$3 . 8 2	→		$4 . 0 0
			about	$6 . 0 0

	$6 . 6 7	→		$7 . 0 0
-	$2 . 7 1	→	-	$3 . 0 0
			about	$4 . 0 0

$ 2.74 + $ 5.08 + $ 12.57

= $ 3 + $ 5 + $ 13

= $21

$ 15.63 - $ 6.98

= $ 16 - $ 7

= $ 9

1.

	$7 . 4 6	→		
+	$4 . 7 3	→	+	

2.

	$9 . 8 6	→		
-	$5 . 4 7	→	-	

3.

	$3 2. 6 5	→		
+	$6 7. 2 8	→	+	

4.

	$7 2. 5 8	→		
-	$1 8. 3 6	→	-	

5. $ 4.75 + $ 3.17 + $ 8.69

=

=

6. $ 6.85 + $ 0.26 + $ 7.94

=

=

7. $ 17.95 - $ 3.62

=

=

8. $ 25.73 - $ 12.39

=

=

Student's name: ____________________ Assignment date: ________________

Estimating the products.

Example:

$2 . 8 3 × 6 ——— .	$3 . 0 0 × 6 ——— about $1 8 . 0 0	$ 18.93 × 52 = $20 × 50 = $ 1000

1.

$5 . 0 8 → ______
× 9 → × ______

2.

$8 . 7 3 → ______
× 4 → × ______

3.

$1 2. 6 6 → ______
× 7 → × ______

4.

$4 7. 2 3 → ______
× 8 → × ______

5. $ 5.14 × 12

=

=

6. $ 6.71 × 8

=

=

7. $ 15.31 × 5

=

=

8. $ 19.57 × 13

=

=

9. $ 21.47 × 32

=

=

10. $ 68.04 × 79

=

=

Student's name: ____________________ Assignment date: ________________

Estimating the quotients.
Example:

$6\overline{)\$23.27}$ *use compatible number* $6\overline{)\$24.00}$ = \$4.00 (24, 0)

\$ 46.73 ÷ 7
= \$ 49.00 ÷ 7 (round dividend with compatible number)
= \$ 7

1. $5\overline{)\$62.73}$ →

2. $4\overline{)\$33.59}$ →

3. $8\overline{)\$67.23}$ →

4. $7\overline{)\$81.36}$ →

5. \$ 53.87 ÷ 6
=
=

6. \$ 70.62 ÷ 9
=
=

7. \$ 43.09 ÷ 5
=
=

8. \$ 68.47 ÷ 6
=
=

9. \$ 39.72 ÷ 4
=
=

10. \$ 61.78 ÷ 7
=
=

Student's name: ____________________ Assignment date: ________________

***** Part 15 Rounding whole numbers *****

Example:

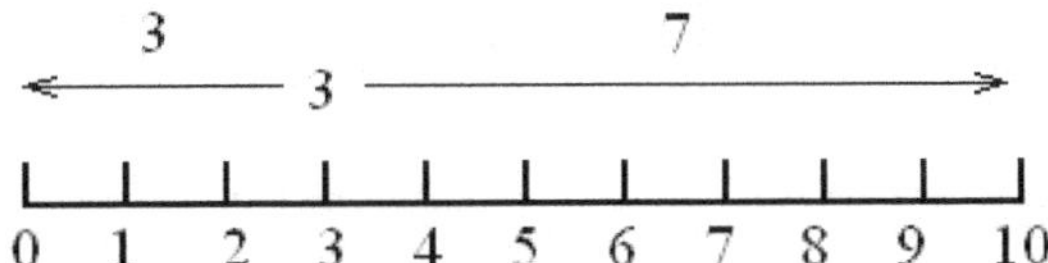

From 3 to 0 is 3, from 3 to 10 is 7, so 3 is closer to 0.

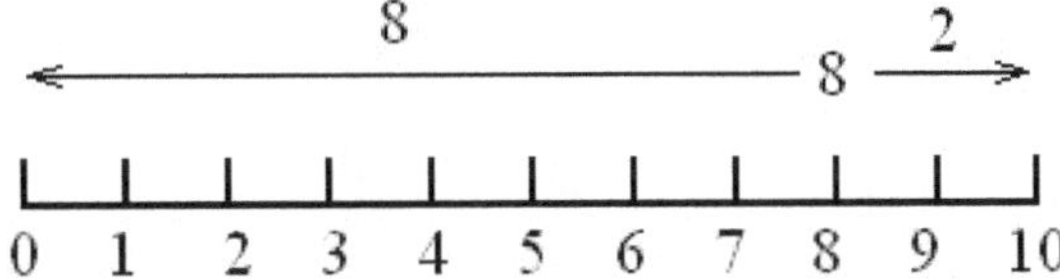

From 8 to 0 is 8, from 8 to 10 is 2, so 8 is closer to 10.

The number 1, 2, 3, 4 are rounded down to 0.

The umber 5, 6, 7, 8, 9 are rounded up to 10.

Rounding the following numbers to either 0 or 10

1.	2 $\xrightarrow{\text{rounded}}$	2.	8 $\xrightarrow{\text{rounded}}$
3.	4 $\xrightarrow{\text{rounded}}$	4.	3 $\xrightarrow{\text{rounded}}$
5.	9 $\xrightarrow{\text{rounded}}$	6.	7 $\xrightarrow{\text{rounded}}$
7.	6 $\xrightarrow{\text{rounded}}$	8.	5 $\xrightarrow{\text{rounded}}$

Rounding the following numbers to the nearest ten

We look at the tens place digit, if it is less than five, then round it up; otherwise, rounded it down.

5<u>4</u> is rounded down to 50; 6<u>7</u> is rounded up to 70.

1.	32 $\xrightarrow{\text{rounded}}$	2.	47 $\xrightarrow{\text{rounded}}$
3.	38 $\xrightarrow{\text{rounded}}$	4.	24 $\xrightarrow{\text{rounded}}$
5.	19 $\xrightarrow{\text{rounded}}$	6.	76 $\xrightarrow{\text{rounded}}$
7.	52 $\xrightarrow{\text{rounded}}$	8.	65 $\xrightarrow{\text{rounded}}$

Student's name: ____________________ Assignment date: ________________

Rounding the following numbers to the nearest hundred

We look at the hundreds place digit, if it is less than five, then round it up; otherwise, rounded it down.

683 is rounded down to 700; 239 is rounded up to 200.

1. 256 $\xrightarrow{rounded}$
2. 218 $\xrightarrow{rounded}$
3. 363 $\xrightarrow{rounded}$
4. 649 $\xrightarrow{rounded}$
5. 409 $\xrightarrow{rounded}$
6. 832 $\xrightarrow{rounded}$
7. 271 $\xrightarrow{rounded}$
8. 551 $\xrightarrow{rounded}$
9. 759 $\xrightarrow{rounded}$
10. 725 $\xrightarrow{rounded}$
11. 647 $\xrightarrow{rounded}$
12. 527 $\xrightarrow{rounded}$

Rounding the following numbers to the nearest thousand

We look at the thousands place digit, if it is less than five, then round it up; otherwise, rounded it down.

2464 is rounded down to 2000; 6837 is rounded up to 7000.

1. 4680 $\xrightarrow{rounded}$
2. 1843 $\xrightarrow{rounded}$
3. 3279 $\xrightarrow{rounded}$
4. 8419 $\xrightarrow{rounded}$
5. 1862 $\xrightarrow{rounded}$
6. 6708 $\xrightarrow{rounded}$
7. 7498 $\xrightarrow{rounded}$
8. 5275 $\xrightarrow{rounded}$
9. 2673 $\xrightarrow{rounded}$
10. 2751 $\xrightarrow{rounded}$
11. 4501 $\xrightarrow{rounded}$
12. 9999 $\xrightarrow{rounded}$

Student's name: ____________________ Assignment date: ________________

Filling the following blank

1. 296 is composed of _____ hundreds, _____ tens and _____ ones.
2. 698 is composed of _____ hundreds, _____ tens and _____ ones.
3. 513 is composed of _____ hundreds, _____ tens and _____ ones.
4. 203 is composed of _____ hundreds, _____ tens and _____ ones.
5. 716 is composed of _____ hundreds, _____ tens and _____ ones.
6. 1238 is composed of ___ thousands, ___ hundreds, ___ tens and ___ ones.
7. 4368 is composed of ___ thousands, ___ hundreds, ___ tens and ___ ones.
8. 9861 is composed of ___ thousands, ___ hundreds, ___ tens and ___ ones.
9. 14 321 is composed of _____ ten thousands, _____ thousands,

   _____ hundreds, _____ tens and _____ ones.
10. 99 999 is composed of _____ ten thousands, _____ thousands,

    _____ hundreds, _____ tens and _____ ones.
11. 396 is nearly _____ hundred.
12. 91 is nearly _____ ten.
13. 3003 is nearly _____ thousand.
14. 1997 is nearly _____ thousand.

Student's name: ____________________ Assignment date: ________________

15. 301 is nearly _____ hundred.

16. 19 is nearly _____ ten.

17. 396 is nearly _____ hundred.

18. 531 is nearly _____ hundred.

19. 698 is nearly _____ hundred.

20. 203 is nearly _____ hundred.

21. 716 is nearly _____ hundred.

22. 1238 is nearly _____ thousand, _____ hundred, _____ ten.

23. 4368 is nearly _____ thousand, _____ hundred, _____ ten.

24. 9861 is nearly _____ thousand, _____ hundred, _____ ten.

25. 14 321 is nearly ___ ten thousands, ___ thousand, ___ hundred, ___ ten.

26. 99 989 is nearly ___ ten thousands, ___ thousand, ___ hundred, ___ ten.

27. 2002 is nearly _____ thousands.

28. 2998 is nearly _____ thousands.

29. 898 is nearly _____ hundreds.

30. 489 is nearly _____ hundreds.

31. 58 is nearly _____ tens.

32. 82 is nearly _____ tens.

Student's name: ____________________ Assignment date: ________________

Estimating Sums

351 →	400	351 is close to 400
+ 168 →	+ 200	168 is close to 200
	600	400 + 200 = 600.
		So 351 + 168 is about 600.

13. 252 → ______
+ 476 → + ______

14. 337 → ______
+ 575 → + ______

15. 537 → ______
+ 159 → + ______

16. 379 → ______
+ 582 → + ______

17. 373 → ______
+ 727 → + ______

18. 368 → ______
+ 208 → + ______

19. 347 → ______
+ 563 → + ______

20. 358 → ______
+ 537 → + ______

21. 306 → ______
+ 247 → + ______

22. 369 → ______
+ 274 → + ______

23. 281 → ______
+ 435 → + ______

24. 628 → ______
+ 241 → + ______

Student's name: ____________________ Assignment date: ________________

Estimate Sums

$$\begin{array}{r} 352 \\ +\ 79 \\ \hline \end{array} \rightarrow \begin{array}{r} 350 \\ +\ 80 \\ \hline 430 \end{array}$$

352 is close to 350
79 is close to 80
350 + 80 = 430.
So 352 + 79 is about 430.

25 $\begin{array}{r} 469 \\ +\ 26 \\ \hline \end{array} \rightarrow \begin{array}{r} \\ +\ \_\_\_ \end{array}$

26. $\begin{array}{r} 479 \\ +\ 47 \\ \hline \end{array} \rightarrow \begin{array}{r} \\ +\ \_\_\_ \end{array}$

27 $\begin{array}{r} 361 \\ +\ 57 \\ \hline \end{array} \rightarrow \begin{array}{r} \\ +\ \_\_\_ \end{array}$

28. $\begin{array}{r} 362 \\ +\ 34 \\ \hline \end{array} \rightarrow \begin{array}{r} \\ +\ \_\_\_ \end{array}$

29 $\begin{array}{r} 637 \\ +\ 68 \\ \hline \end{array} \rightarrow \begin{array}{r} \\ +\ \_\_\_ \end{array}$

30. $\begin{array}{r} 309 \\ +\ 31 \\ \hline \end{array} \rightarrow \begin{array}{r} \\ +\ \_\_\_ \end{array}$

31 $\begin{array}{r} 81 \\ +\ 352 \\ \hline \end{array} \rightarrow \begin{array}{r} \\ +\ \_\_\_ \end{array}$

32. $\begin{array}{r} 18 \\ +\ 376 \\ \hline \end{array} \rightarrow \begin{array}{r} \\ +\ \_\_\_ \end{array}$

33 $\begin{array}{r} 372 \\ +\ 9 \\ \hline \end{array} \rightarrow \begin{array}{r} \\ +\ \_\_\_ \end{array}$

34. $\begin{array}{r} 408 \\ +\ 3 \\ \hline \end{array} \rightarrow \begin{array}{r} \\ +\ \_\_\_ \end{array}$

35 $\begin{array}{r} 481 \\ +\ 16 \\ \hline \end{array} \rightarrow \begin{array}{r} \\ +\ \_\_\_ \end{array}$

36. $\begin{array}{r} 372 \\ +\ 44 \\ \hline \end{array} \rightarrow \begin{array}{r} \\ +\ \_\_\_ \end{array}$

Student's name: ____________________ Assignment date: ________________

Estimating Differences

Example:

```
  5 7 9 →       6 0 0
– 3 1 2 →     – 3 0 0
                3 0 0
```

```
  5 4 2 →       5 4 0
–   7 5 →     –   8 0
                4 6 0
```

1.
```
  4 8 1 →
– 2 2 6 →   –  ______
```

2.
```
  7 3 1 →
– 4 7 2 →   –  ______
```

3.
```
  4 8 2 →
– 3 6 9 →   –  ______
```

4.
```
  4 6 5 →
– 2 7 3 →   –  ______
```

5.
```
  5 3 8 →
– 4 0 7 →   –  ______
```

6.
```
  6 2 9 →
– 1 2 4 →   –  ______
```

7.
```
  6 2 4 →
–   6 4 →   –  ______
```

8.
```
  3 8 3 →
–   5 8 →   –  ______
```

9.
```
  5 3 9 →
–   2 7 →   –  ______
```

10.
```
  7 4 1 →
–   7 3 →   –  ______
```

11.
```
  5 8 2 →
– 1 0 5 →   –  ______
```

12.
```
  5 3 7 →
– 3 6 2 →   –  ______
```

Student's name: ____________________ Assignment date: ________________

Estimating Products

$$\begin{array}{r} 325 \\ \times \quad 24 \\ \hline \end{array} \rightarrow \begin{array}{r} 300 \\ \times \quad 20 \\ \hline 6000 \end{array}$$

325 is close to 300
24 is close to 20
325 × 20 = 6000.
So 325 × 20 is about 6000.

1. 460 → ____
× 29 → × ____

2. 391 → ____
× 32 → × ____

3. 417 → ____
× 53 → × ____

4. 716 → ____
× 61 → × ____

5. 826 → ____
× 209 → × ____

6. 431 → ____
× 572 → × ____

7. 280 → ____
× 72 → × ____

8. 328 → ____
× 183 → × ____

9. 631 → ____
× 826 → × ____

10. 495 → ____
× 52 → × ____

11 274 → ____
× 33 → × ____

12. 472 → ____
× 83 → × ____

Student's name: ____________________ Assignment date: ________________

Estimating Products

If the multiplier or multiplicand is close to 15, 25, 35 (or 150, 250, 350), etc., use the first digit times the other number, plus half of the other number times ten.

Example:

630 × 24	630 is close to 600 24 is close to 25	600 × 20 = 12000 600 ÷ 2 × 10 = 3000 12000 + 3000 = 15000	So, 630 × 24 is about 15000.

1. 483 × 15

   → 500 × 10 + 500 ÷ 2 × 10

   = 5000 + 2500

   = 7500

2. 692 × 16

   →

3. 417 × 25

   →

4. 306 × 35

   →

5. 782 × 34

   →28

6. 487 × 153

   →

7. 242 × 793

   →

8. 156 × 389

   →

9. 245 × 421

   →

10. 784 × 257

    →

11. 320 × 348

    →

12. 247 × 721

    →

Student's name: ____________________ Assignment date: ________________

Estimating Quotients with 1-digit divisors

Example:

3747 ÷ 6 Round the front-end of dividend to the nearest multiple of divisor.

Round front-end 37 hundred to nearest multiple of 6. 3747 → 3600, and 3600 ÷ 6 = 600

1. 372 ÷ 5

→ 350 ÷ 5

= 70

2. 572 ÷ 7

→

3. 4726 ÷ 6

→

4. 3729 ÷ 9

→

5. 4371 ÷ 5

→

6. 5231 ÷ 9

→

7. 6217 ÷ 8

→

8. 2416 ÷ 5

→

9. 4642 ÷ 3

→

10. 5725 ÷ 2

→

11. 6438 ÷ 7

→

12. 5373 ÷ 9

→

Student's name: ____________________ Assignment date: ________________

Estimating Quotients with 2-digit divisors

Example:

6429 ÷ 28

Round the divisor first. Then round the front-end of dividend to the nearest multiple of divisor.

28 is rounded to 30. Round front-end 64 hundred to nearest multiple of 30. 6429 → 6300, and 6300 ÷ 30 = 210

1.	2351 ÷ 32 →	2.	4725 ÷ 73 →
3.	3825 ÷ 93 →	4.	7925 ÷ 87 →
5.	5330 ÷ 62 →	6.	6528 ÷ 78 →
7.	3709 ÷ 59 →	8.	3642 ÷ 51 →
9.	3178 ÷ 38 →	10.	5189 ÷ 42 →
11.	6235 ÷ 73 →	12.	4627 ÷ 19 →

Student's name: ____________________ Assignment date: ________________

Test of rounding word problems

1. I'm a 3-digit number. The sum of my digits is 10. When rounded to the nearest hundred, I am 900. When rounded to the nearest ten, I am 900 too. What number am I?
2. When a number is rounded to the nearest thousand, it round to 4000. All of its digits are the same. What number is it?

3. Rounding a number to the nearest ten, hundred, or thousand will give the same answer 3000. The number is not 3000. What is the number?

4. When a number is rounded to the nearest hundred, the number is doubled. What is the number?

5. To the nearest hundred, a number round to 2800. Three digits of the number are the same. What is the number?

6. When a number is rounded to the nearest tens, hundreds, or thousands place, it gives the same answer 1000. When you read it forward, it sounds the same as you read it backwards. What is the number?

7. Austin has $1 with at least one kind of quarters, dimes, and nickels. What could be the greatest number of coins he could have?

8. The sum of 89297 + 98729 = _______
   The difference of 270270 – 3 = ________
   The product of 270270 × 3 = __________
   The quotient of 270270 ÷ 3 = ___________

Student's name: ____________________ Assignment date: ________________

9. Johnny would like to place 15 chocolates into 4 boxes. Each box can hold 4 or 3 chocolates. How many boxes will hold exactly 3 chocolates.

bbb

Student's name: ____________________ Assignment date: ________________

***** Part 16 Fractions *****

Fraction can be represented by the following two models.

Model 1 – Choosing one or more equal parts of 1 whole.

A fraction is shown by $\frac{a}{b}$. The top part is <u>*numerator*</u> which tells how many parts are chosen. The bottom part is called *denominator* which tells how many parts are in a whole. The *denominator* is also the fraction unit of that fraction. For example, the following fraction three-quarter example shows that there are three of one quarter (basic fraction unit) .

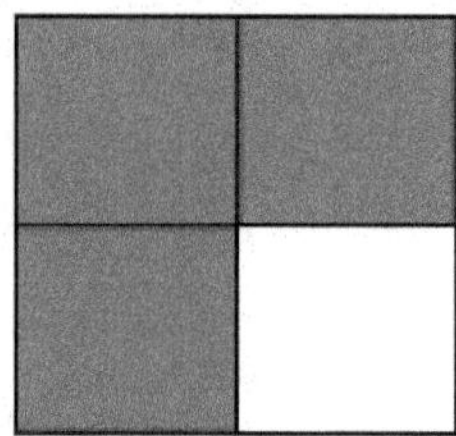

What is meaning of 2 in the following fraction?
$\frac{1}{2}$

The above digit is 2 but the real meaning is actually "half", so $\frac{3}{2}$ means there are three of half. The fraction unit concept can be used to understand fraction addition or subtraction better. For example, $\frac{2}{2} + \frac{1}{2}$ = two of half plus 1 of half = 3 of half = $\frac{3}{2}$.

Model 2 – Choosing one or more equal parts of a set.

What part is the circle figure in the following set?

The answer is $\frac{2}{7}$.

Student's name: ____________________ Assignment date: ________________

Model 1 – Choosing one or more equal parts of 1 whole.
Example: Divide 1 whole into equal parts.

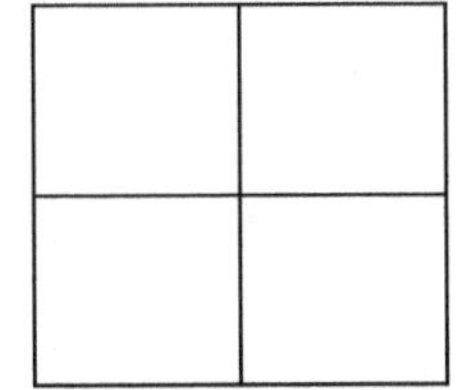

4 equal parts
4 fourth or 4 quarters

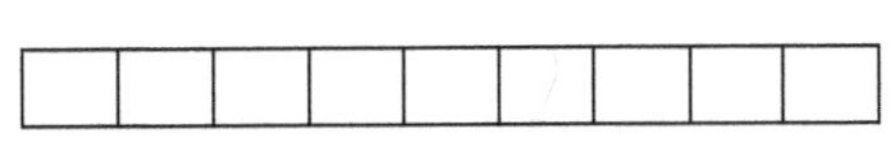

9 equal parts
Nine ninth

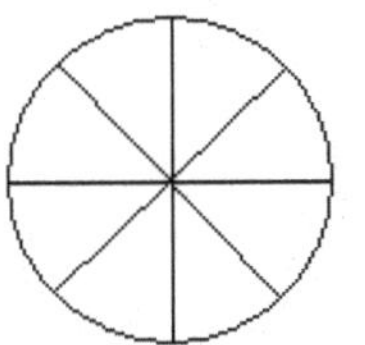

8 equal parts
10 eighth

1. Circle the following figures with equal parts.

1.
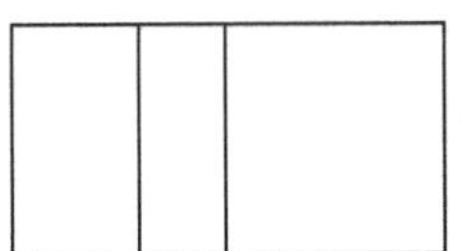

2.
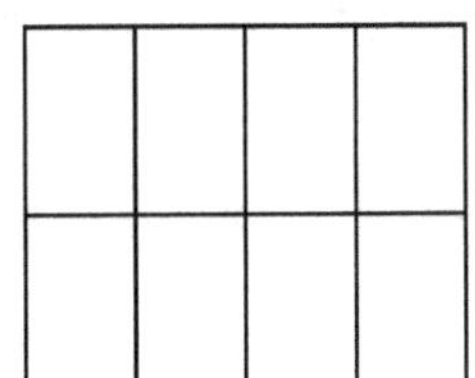

3.
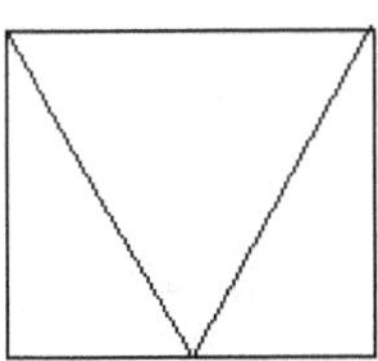

4.
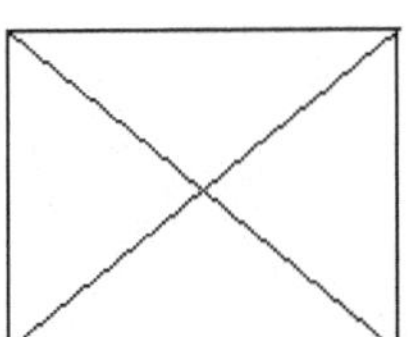

5.
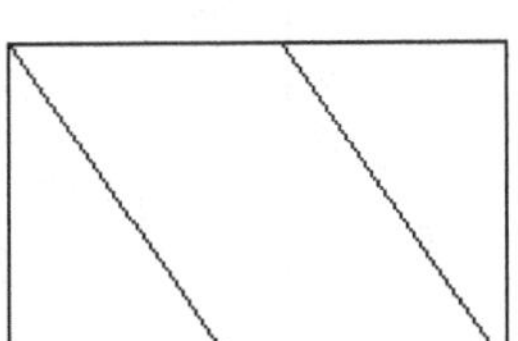

6.
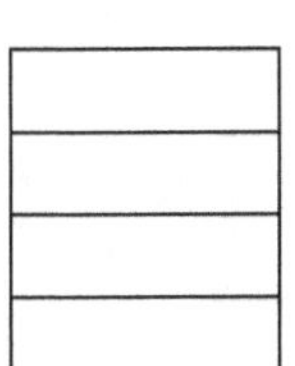

7.
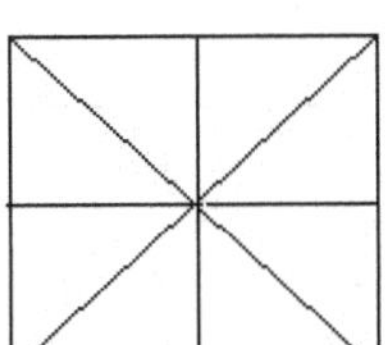

8.
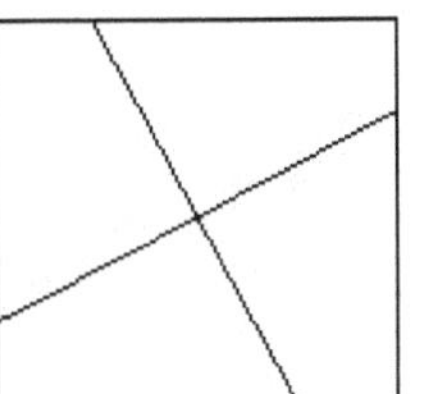

9.
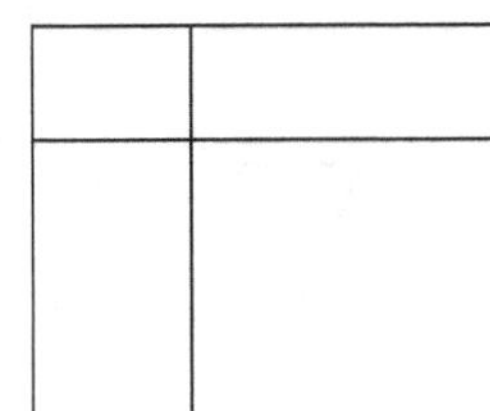

10.
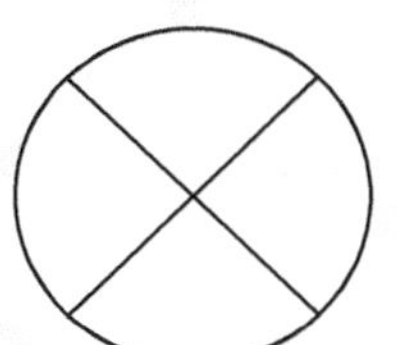

11
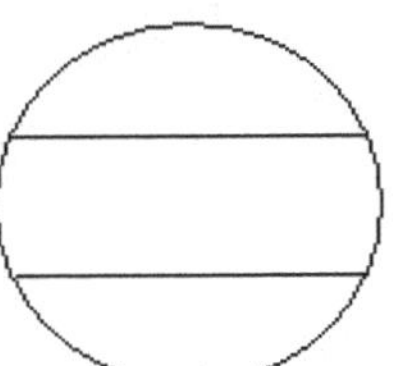

12.
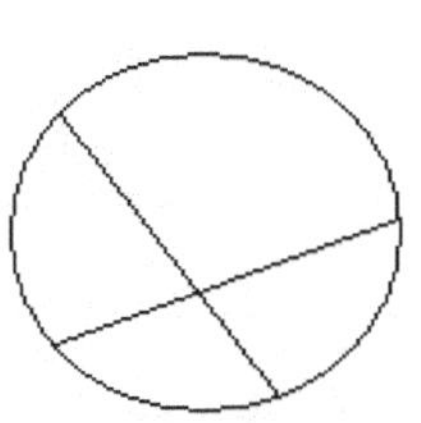

13.
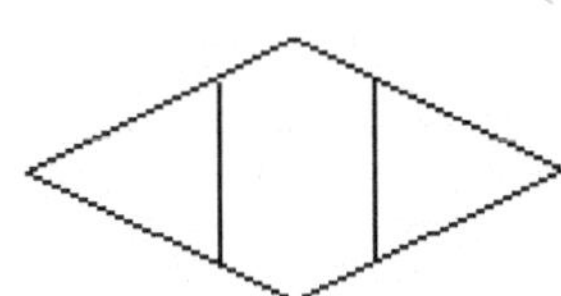

14
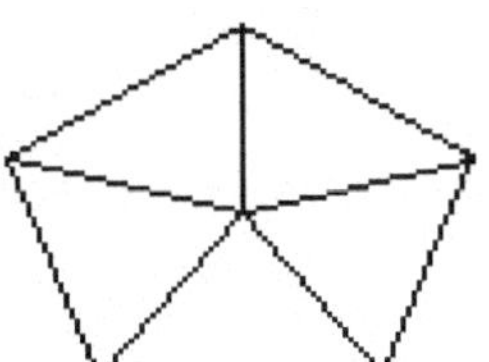

15.
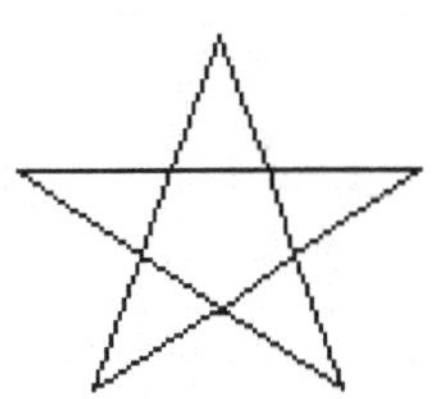

Student's name: ____________________ Assignment date: ________________

2. Name the equal parts of each whole.

1.
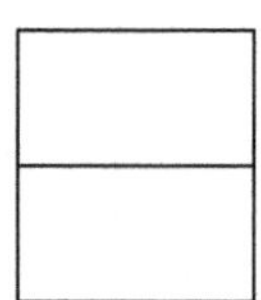

2 halves

2.
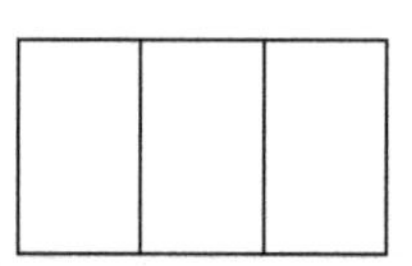

____

3.
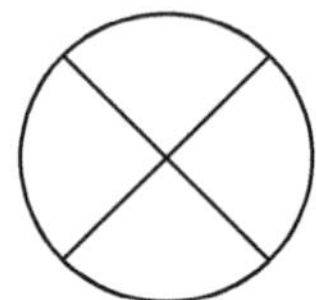

____

4.
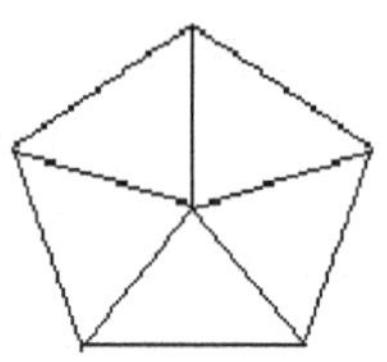

____

5.
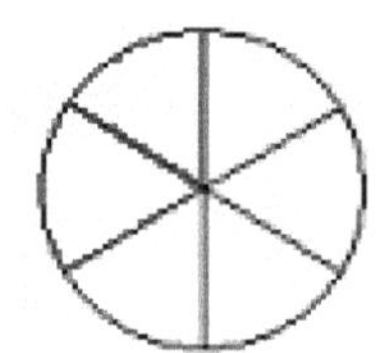

____

6.
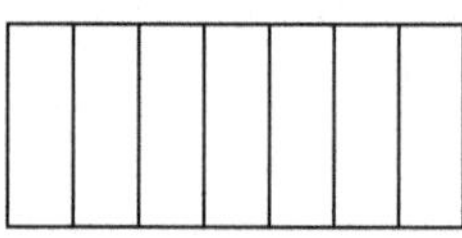

____

7.
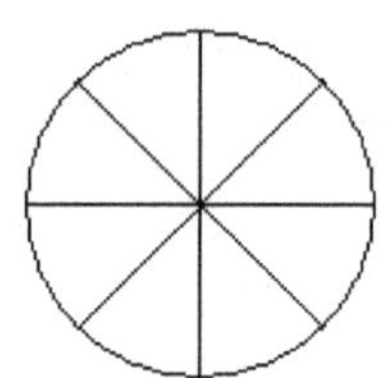

____

8.
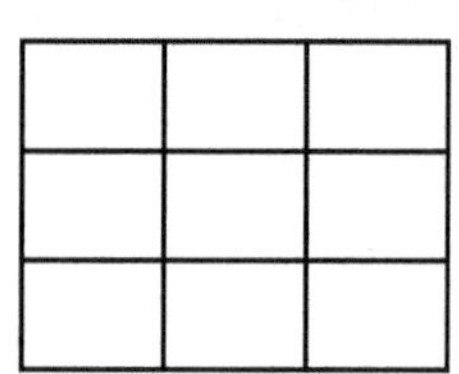

____

9.
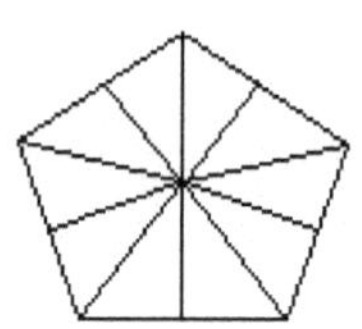

____

10.
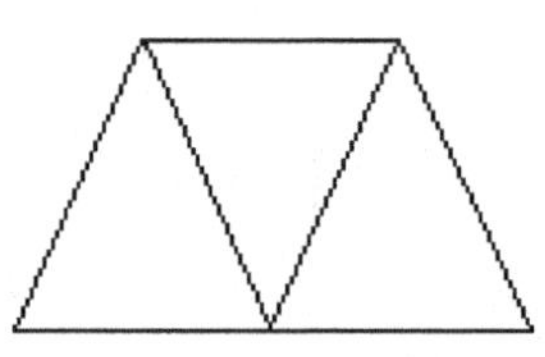

____

11.
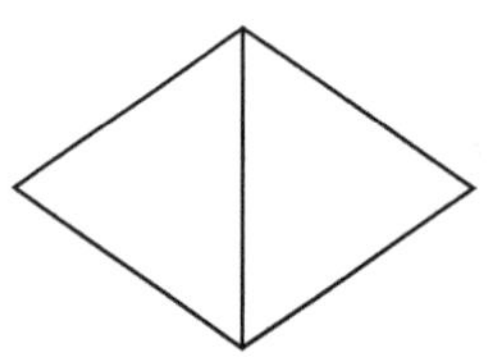

____

12.
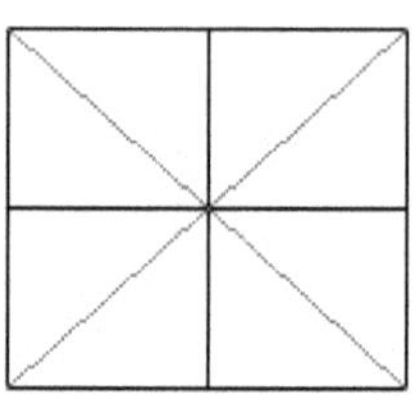

____

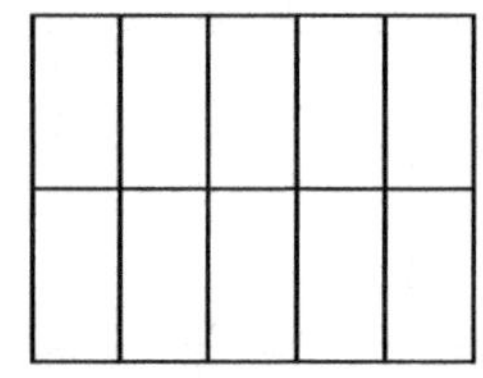

____

____

____

Student's name: ____________________ Assignment date: ________________

Equal Parts

1. Name the equal parts of each whole.

Example: 3 equal parts three thirds

1.

2.

3.

4.

5.

6.

2. Divide each square into 2 halves (at least the same size) in five ways.

3. Divide each square into four fourths (the same size and shape) in five ways.

4. Divide each square into six sixths (at least the same size) in four ways.

Student's name: ____________________ Assignment date: ________________

Representing Fractions

$$\frac{\text{numerator}}{\text{denominator}} = \frac{\text{the number of favorite parts}}{\text{the number of equal parts in a whole}}$$

1. What fraction of each figure is shaded?

1. 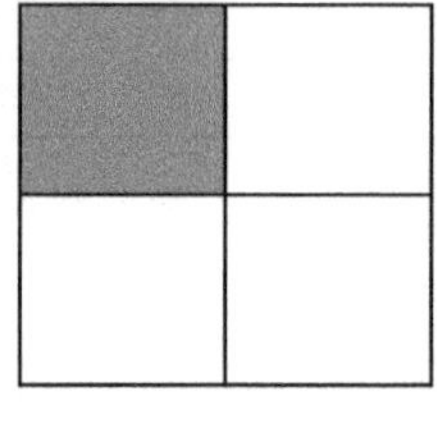
____

2. 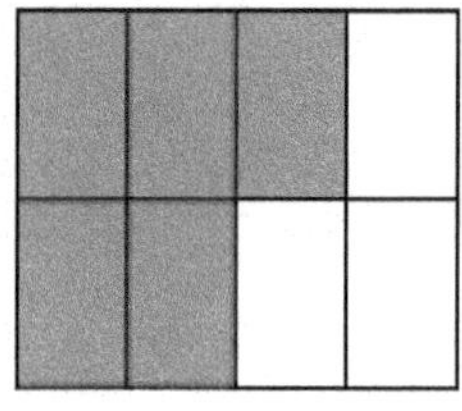
____

3. 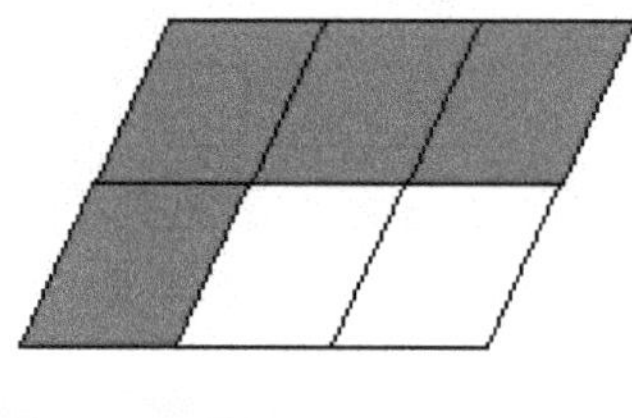
____

4. 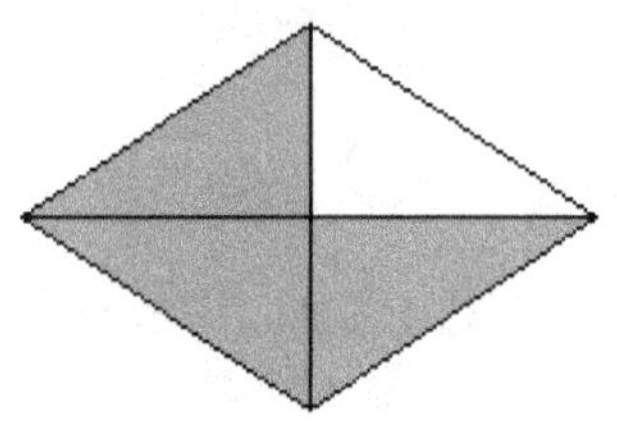
____

5. 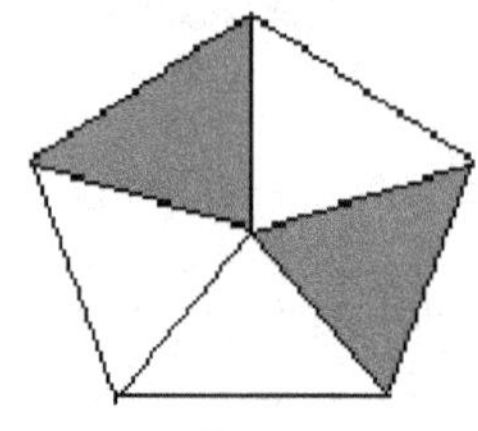
____

6. 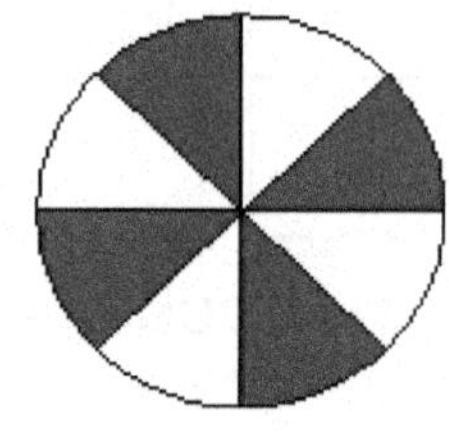
____

7. 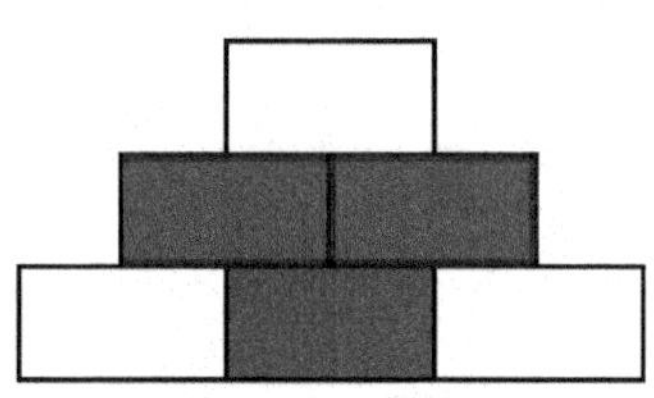
____

8. 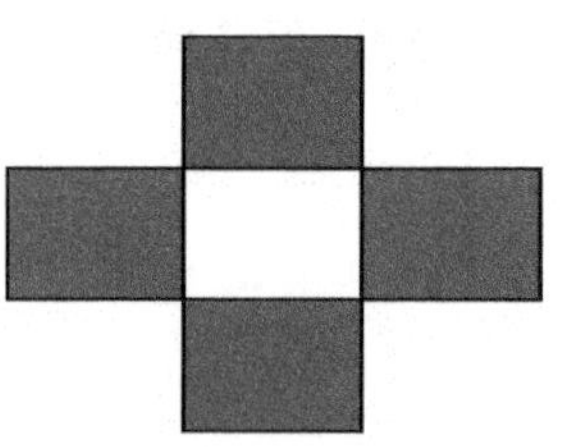
____

9. 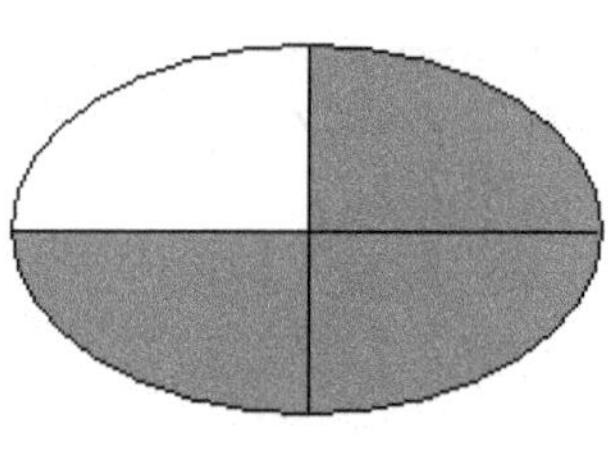
____

10. 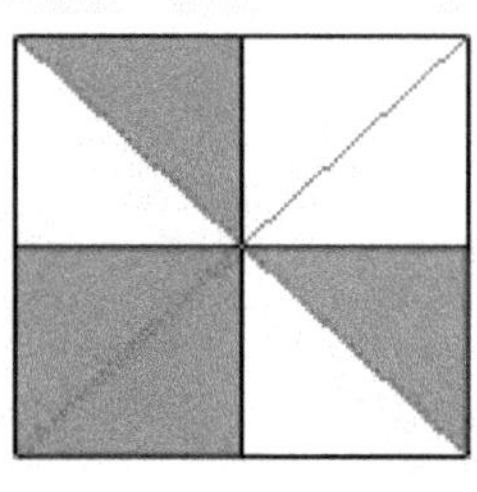
____

11. 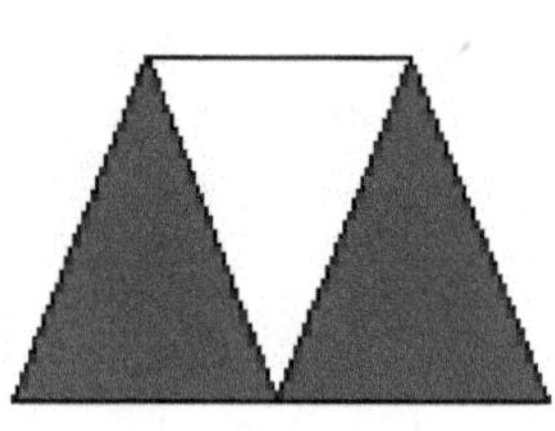
____

12. 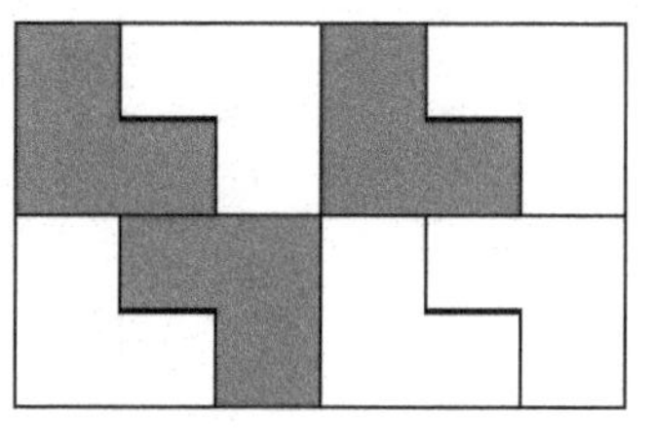
____

Student's name: ____________________ Assignment date: ________________

2. What fraction of each figure is shaded? Express in words and in fraction form.

1.  two thirds $\frac{2}{3}$

2. 

3. 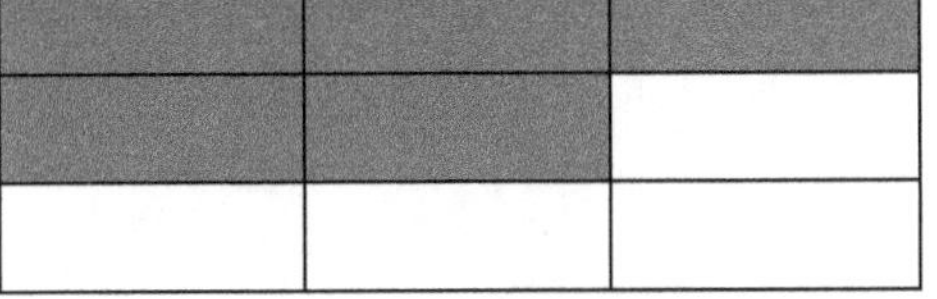

4. 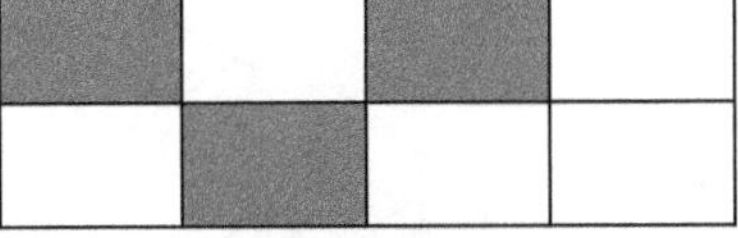

5. 

6. 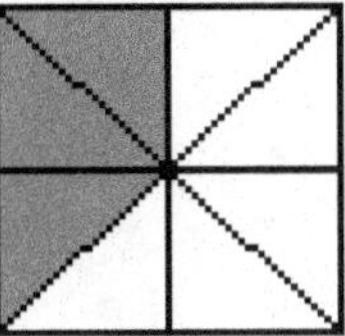

7. 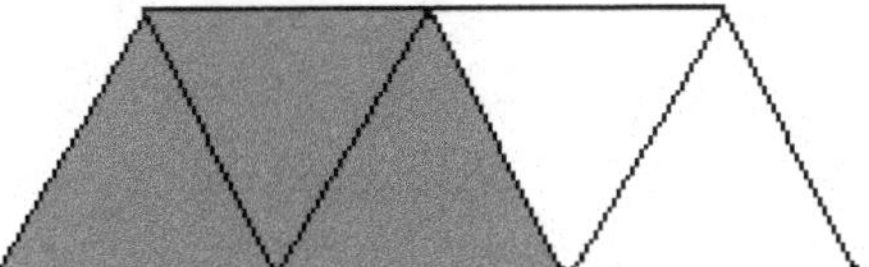

8. 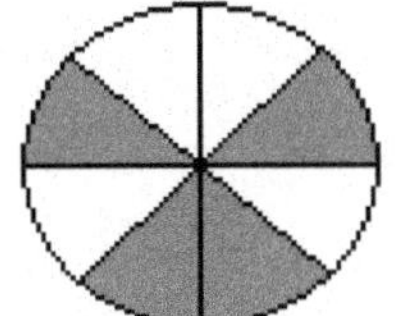

Student's name: ____________________ Assignment date: ________________

1. Divide each figure and shade the portion the fraction presented.

1.

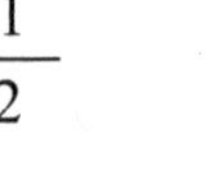

$\frac{1}{2}$

2.

$\frac{2}{4}$

3.

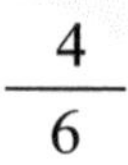

$\frac{4}{6}$

4.

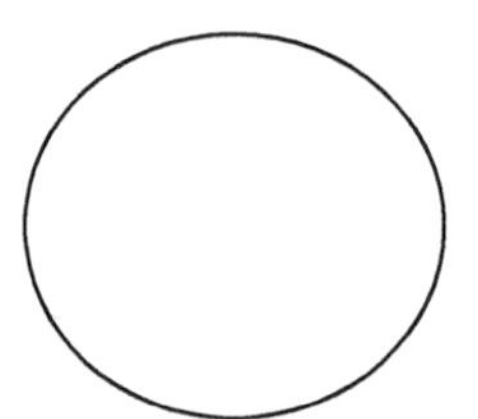

$\frac{3}{4}$

5.

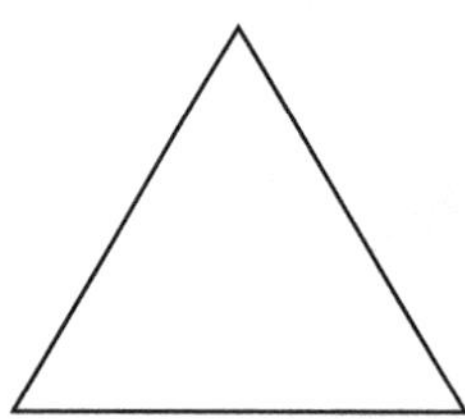

$\frac{1}{4}$

6.

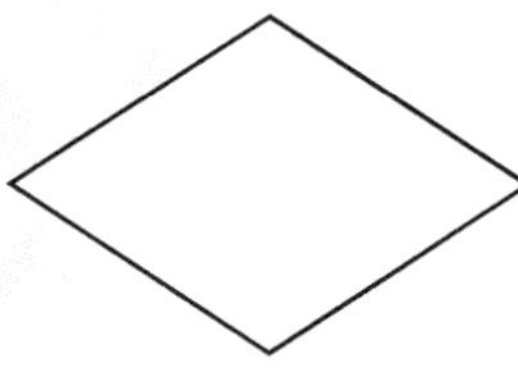

$\frac{3}{4}$

7.

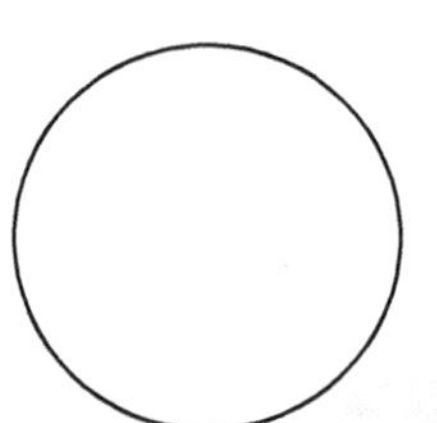

$\frac{5}{6}$

8.

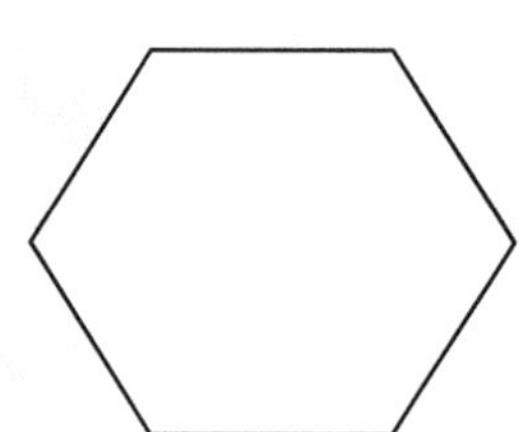

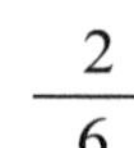

$\frac{2}{6}$

9.

$\frac{2}{5}$

10.

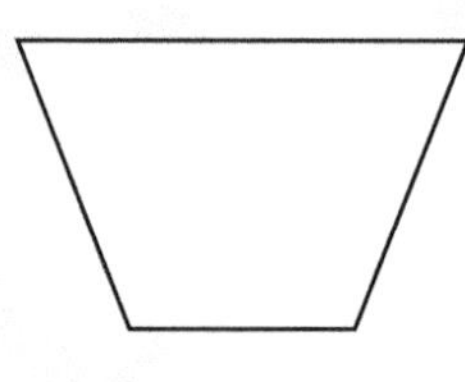

$\frac{1}{3}$

11.

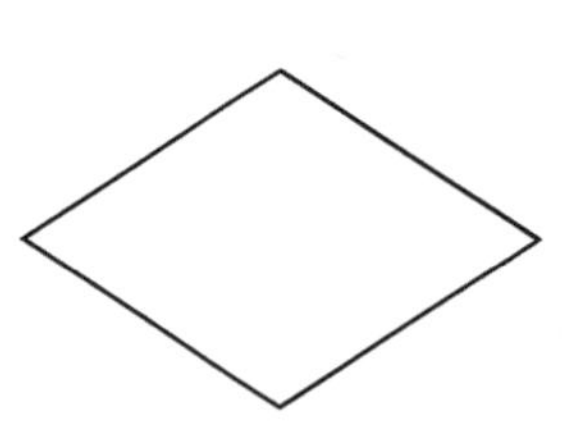

$\frac{7}{8}$

12.

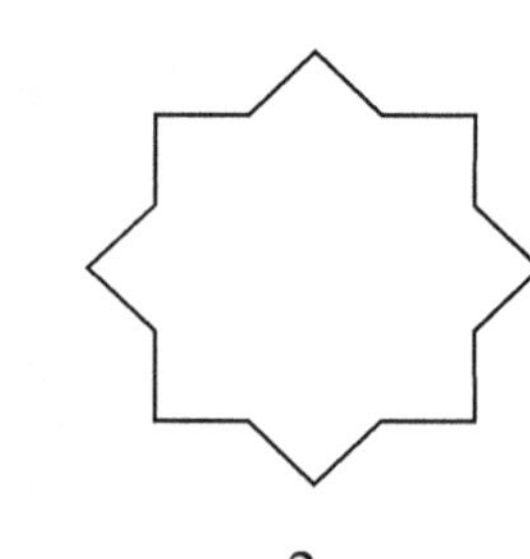

$\frac{2}{4}$

Student's name: ____________________ Assignment date: ________________

2. Divide each figure and shade it as indicated.

1. one half

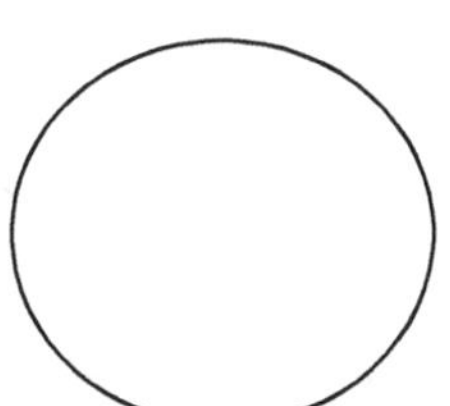

2. two fifths

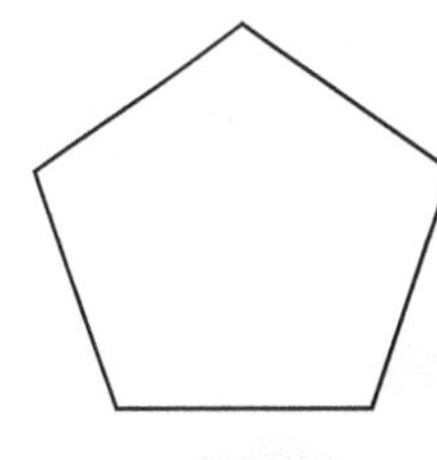

3. three eighths

4. one fourth

5. three fourths

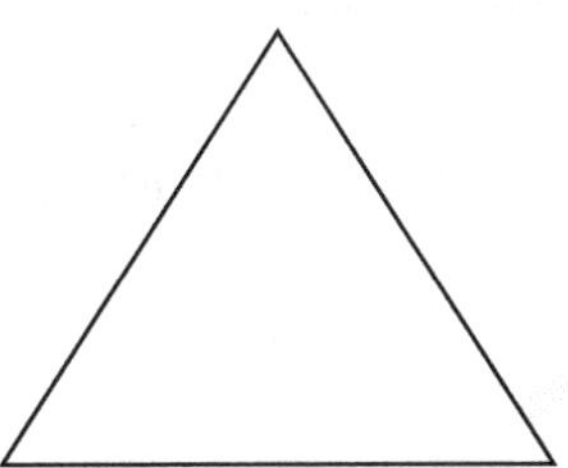

6. two thirds

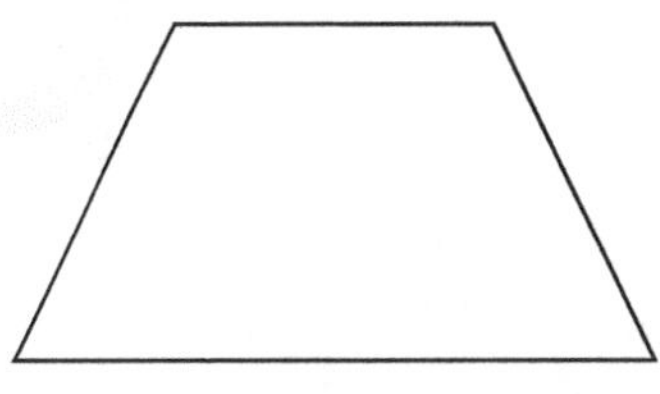

7. four fifteenths

8. seven eighths

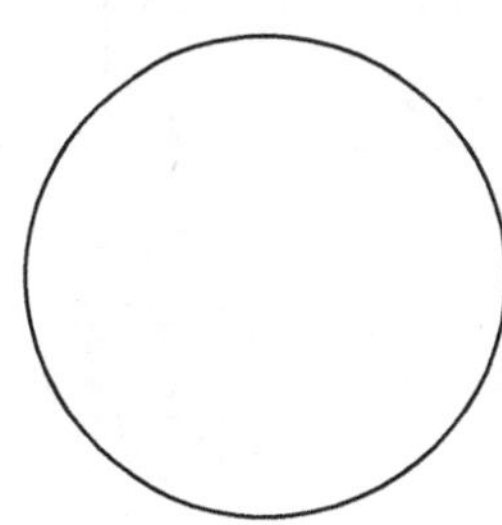

9. three fifths

10. two halves

Student's name: ____________________ Assignment date: ________________

Proper fraction, improper fraction and mixed numbers using models

Here are two type of fractions as follows.

Proper Fraction	$\frac{\text{small numerator}}{\text{big denominator}}$		$\frac{3}{4}$
Improper fraction	$\frac{\text{big numerator}}{\text{small denominator}}$		$\frac{9}{4}$

Mixed number	$\text{whole number} + \frac{\text{numerator}}{\text{denominator}} \text{ of whole} = \text{whole number}\frac{\text{numerator}}{\text{denominator}}$		$2\frac{1}{4}$

1. Write each as an improper fraction and a mixed number.

	figure	Improper fraction	Mixed number
1.		________	________
2.		________	________
3.		________	________
4.		________	________
5.		________	________
6.		________	________

Student's name: ____________________ Assignment date: ________________

2. Draw pictures to show each improper fraction and write a mixed number.

	Improper fraction	Figure	Mixed number
1.	$\frac{5}{2}$	____________________	________
2.	$\frac{5}{3}$	____________________	________
3.	$\frac{7}{4}$	____________________	________
4.	$\frac{8}{5}$	____________________	________
5.	$\frac{10}{3}$	____________________	________

2. Draw pictures to show each mixed number and write an improper fraction.

	Mixed number	Figure	Improper fraction
1.	$1\frac{1}{3}$	____________________	________
2.	$1\frac{4}{5}$	____________________	________
3.	$2\frac{3}{4}$	____________________	________
4.	$3\frac{1}{2}$	____________________	________
5.	$2\frac{5}{6}$	____________________	________

Student's name: ____________________ Assignment date: ________________

Proper fraction, improper fraction and mixed numbers using division

Mixed number	Improper fraction	Division	Ratio	Ratio converted to Part to whole fractions
$2\frac{1}{3}$	$\frac{7}{2}$	$\begin{array}{r} 3 \\ 2\overline{)\,7} \\ \underline{6} \\ 1 \end{array}$	7 to 2	$\frac{7}{9}$ *to* $\frac{2}{9}$
	$\frac{13}{3}$			
	$\frac{17}{4}$			
$4\frac{2}{7}$				
		$\begin{array}{r} 6 \\ 3\overline{)\,20} \\ \underline{18} \\ 2 \end{array}$		
			21 : 2	

Student's name: ____________________ Assignment date: ________________

Equivalent Fractions

Example:

$\frac{1}{2}$  is equivalent to (the same as) $\frac{2}{4}$ 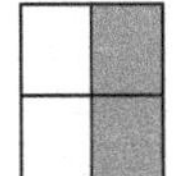 We say, $\frac{1}{2}=\frac{2}{4}$

1. Write an equivalent fraction for each fraction.

$\frac{1}{3}$		$\frac{1}{3}$		$\frac{1}{3}$	
$\frac{1}{6}$	$\frac{1}{6}$	$\frac{1}{6}$	$\frac{1}{6}$	$\frac{1}{6}$	$\frac{1}{6}$

$\frac{1}{3}=$ ________ $\frac{2}{3}=$ ________ $\frac{3}{3}=$ ________

$\frac{1}{4}$		$\frac{1}{4}$		$\frac{1}{4}$		$\frac{1}{4}$	
$\frac{1}{8}$	$\frac{1}{8}$	$\frac{1}{8}$	$\frac{1}{8}$	$\frac{1}{8}$	$\frac{1}{8}$	$\frac{1}{8}$	$\frac{1}{8}$

$\frac{1}{4}=$ ________ $\frac{2}{4}=$ ________ $\frac{3}{4}=$ ________ $\frac{4}{4}=$ ________

2. Shade the second figure which is equivalent to the first figure and fill in blank.

1. 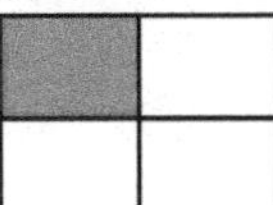 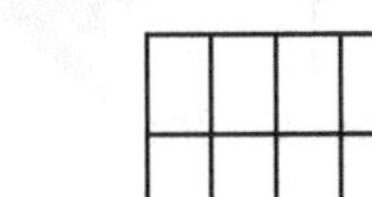

$\frac{1}{4}=$ ________

2. 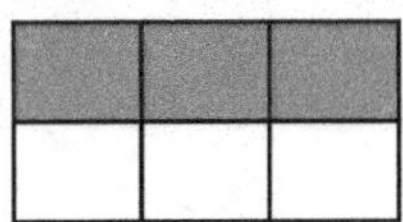 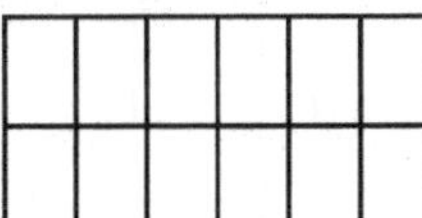

$\frac{3}{6}=$ ________

  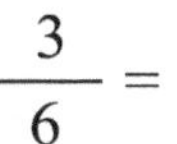

3. 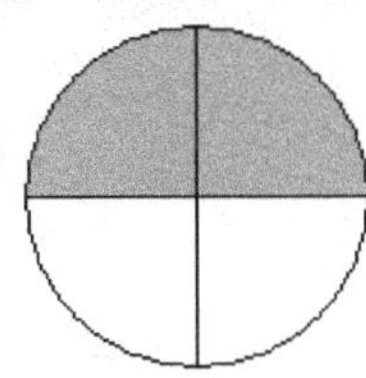 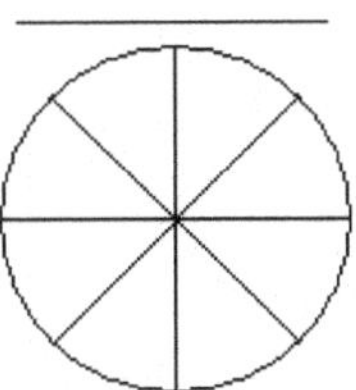

$\frac{2}{4}=$ ________

4. 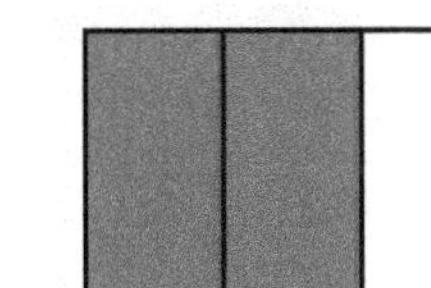 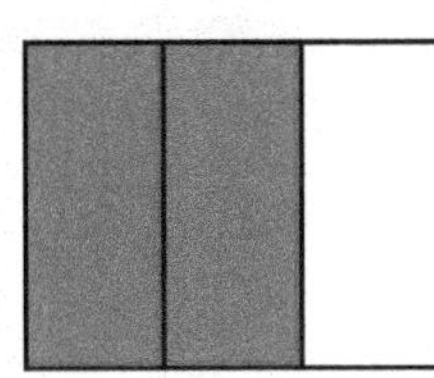 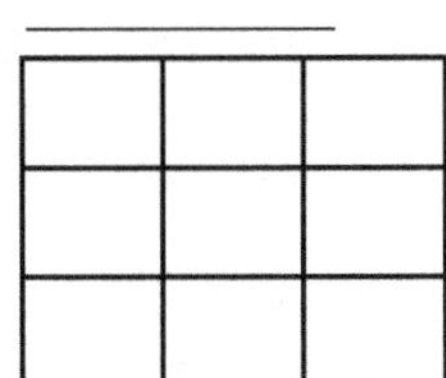

$\frac{2}{3}=$ ________

Student's name: ____________________ Assignment date: ________________

3. Complete the chart then write an equivalent fraction for each fraction.

<table>
<tr><td colspan="60">1 whole</td></tr>
<tr><td colspan="30">$\frac{1}{2}$</td><td colspan="30">$\frac{1}{2}$</td></tr>
<tr><td colspan="20">$\frac{1}{3}$</td><td colspan="20">$\frac{1}{3}$</td><td colspan="20"></td></tr>
<tr><td colspan="15">$\frac{1}{4}$</td><td colspan="15"></td><td colspan="15"></td><td colspan="15"></td></tr>
<tr><td colspan="12">$\frac{1}{5}$</td><td colspan="12"></td><td colspan="12"></td><td colspan="12"></td><td colspan="12"></td></tr>
<tr><td colspan="10">$\frac{1}{6}$</td><td colspan="10"></td><td colspan="10"></td><td colspan="10"></td><td colspan="10"></td><td colspan="10"></td></tr>
<tr><td colspan="6"></td><td colspan="6"></td><td colspan="6"></td><td colspan="6"></td><td colspan="6"></td><td colspan="6"></td><td colspan="6"></td><td colspan="6"></td><td colspan="6"></td><td colspan="6"></td></tr>
</table>

1. $\frac{3}{4} =$ ____________
2. $\frac{2}{5} =$ ____________
3. $\frac{2}{3} =$ ____________
4. $\frac{6}{10} =$ ____________
5. $\frac{4}{6} =$ ____________
6. $\frac{6}{9} =$ ____________
7. $\frac{2}{8} =$ ____________
8. $\frac{3}{5} =$ ____________
9. $\frac{3}{9} =$ ____________
10. $\frac{8}{10} =$ ____________
11. $\frac{3}{6} =$ ____________
12. $\frac{1}{4} =$ ____________
13. $\frac{1}{5} =$ ____________
14. $\frac{2}{6} =$ ____________
15. $\frac{4}{10} =$ ____________
16. $\frac{4}{8} =$ ____________

Student's name: ____________________ Assignment date: ________________

Comparing fractions using models

1. 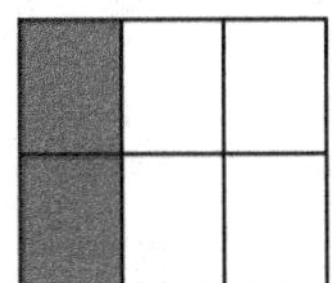 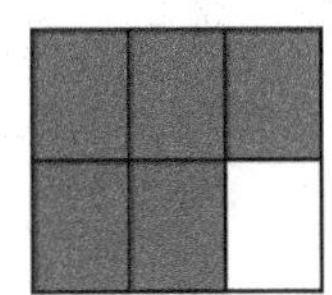

$\frac{2}{6} < \frac{5}{6}$

2. 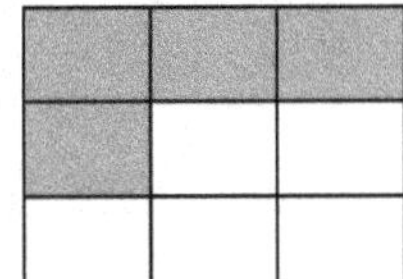 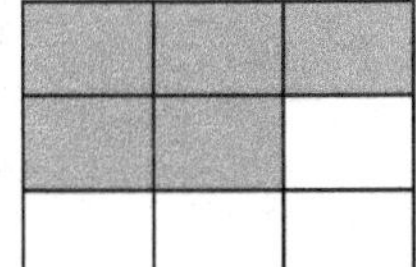

____

3. 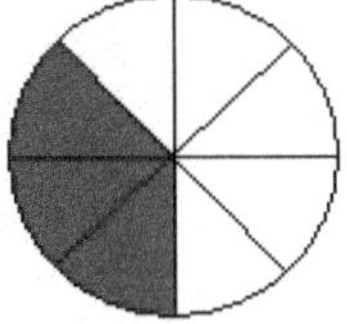 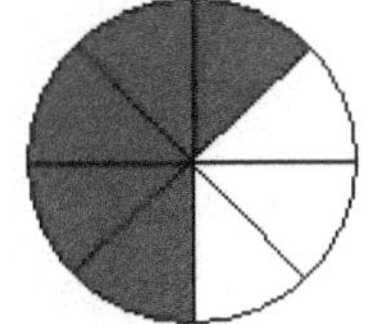

____

4. 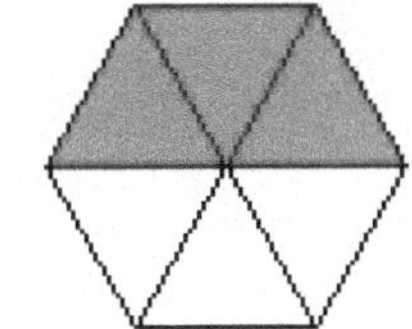 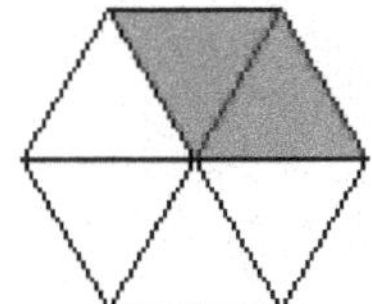

____

5. 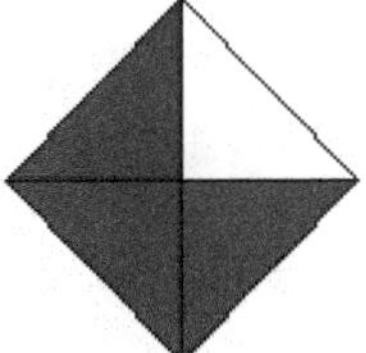 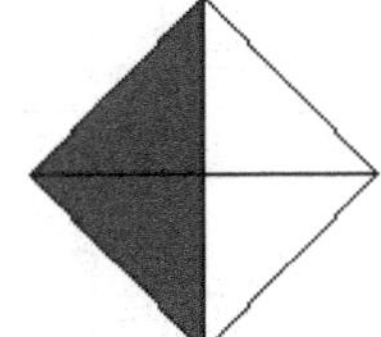

____

6. 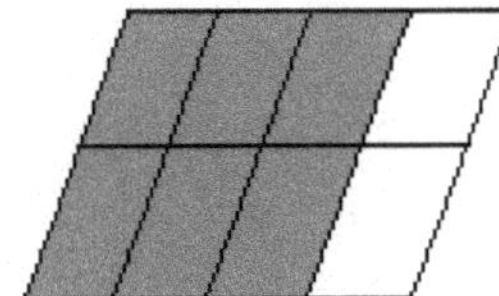 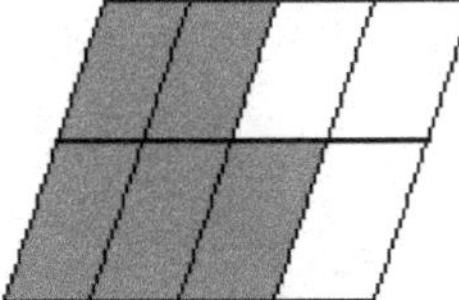

____

7. 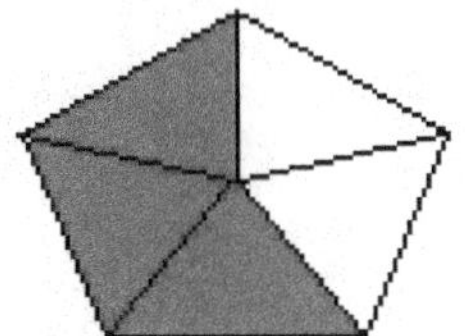 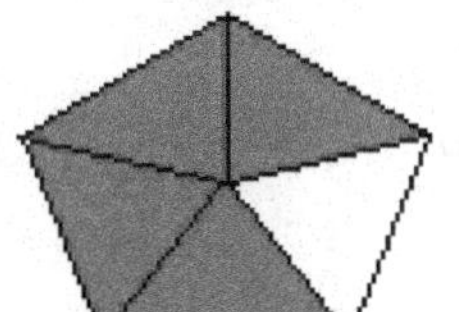

____

8. 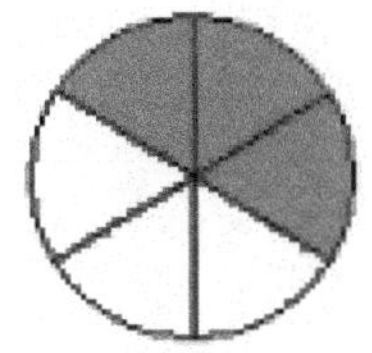 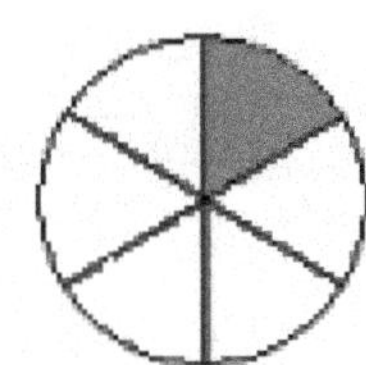

____

9. 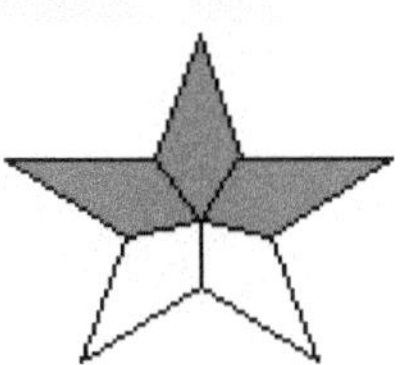

____

10. 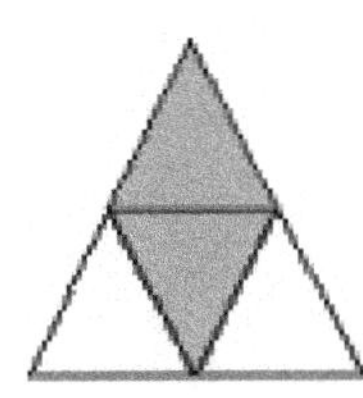 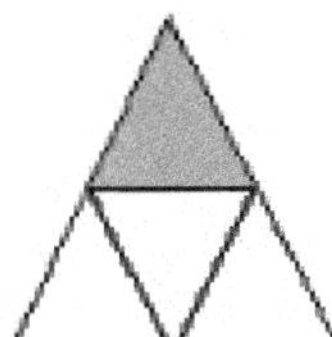

$\frac{2}{4} > \frac{1}{4}$ ____________________

Student's name: ____________________ Assignment date: ________________

Compare fractions.

1. $\frac{4}{8}$ [>] $\frac{3}{8}$

2. $\frac{3}{5}$ ☐ $\frac{4}{5}$

3. $\frac{1}{4}$ ☐ $\frac{3}{4}$

4. $\frac{3}{3}$ ☐ $\frac{2}{3}$

5. $1\frac{1}{5}$ ☐ $\frac{3}{5}$

6. $2\frac{3}{4}$ ☐ $3\frac{2}{4}$

7. $\frac{5}{8}$ ☐ $4\frac{2}{8}$

8. $6\frac{1}{2}$ ☐ $3\frac{1}{2}$

9. $2\frac{4}{7}$ ☐ $2\frac{2}{7}$

10. $5\frac{4}{9}$ ☐ $5\frac{5}{9}$

11. $7\frac{1}{8}$ ☐ $1\frac{7}{8}$

12. $4\frac{3}{5}$ ☐ $3\frac{4}{5}$

13. $\frac{15}{7}$ ☐ $\frac{14}{7}$

14. $2\frac{2}{9}$ ☐ $1\frac{7}{9}$

15. $8\frac{5}{6}$ ☐ $4\frac{1}{6}$

16. $\frac{11}{3}$ ☐ $\frac{13}{3}$

17. $7\frac{3}{4}$ ☐ $4\frac{1}{4}$

18. $9\frac{1}{5}$ ☐ $7\frac{4}{5}$

19. $1\frac{1}{7}$ ☐ $2\frac{3}{7}$

20. $4\frac{3}{8}$ ☐ $3\frac{4}{8}$

21. $2\frac{1}{5}$ ☐ $3\frac{4}{5}$

22. $7\frac{5}{8}$ ☐ $7\frac{7}{8}$

23. $3\frac{1}{9}$ ☐ $2\frac{5}{9}$

24. $3\frac{6}{8}$ ☐ $4\frac{7}{8}$

25. $\frac{7}{4}$ ☐ $\frac{8}{4}$

26. $\frac{6}{5}$ ☐ $\frac{2}{5}$

Student's name: ____________________ Assignment date: ________________

Circling fraction models to match fraction on the left

$\frac{6}{9}$	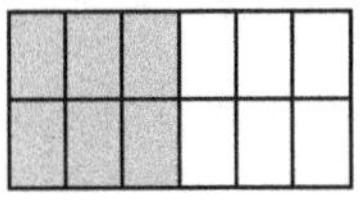 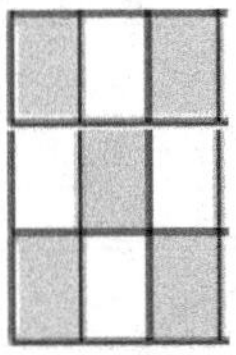 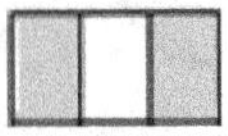
$\frac{2}{3}$	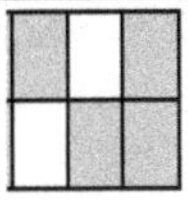 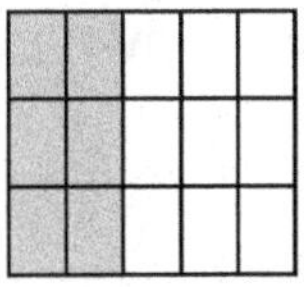 (Think the figure as $\frac{2\ coluns}{5\ columns}$ not $\frac{6}{15}$) 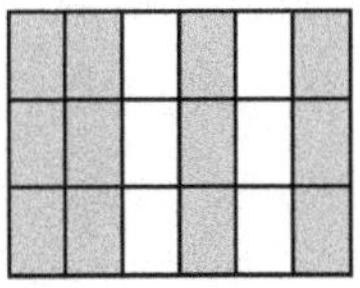 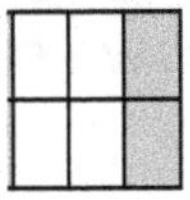
$\frac{3}{9}$	.

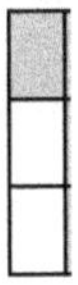

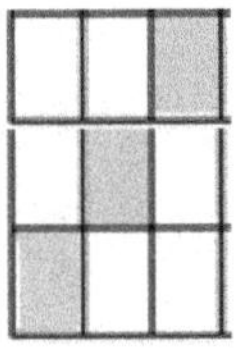

Student's name: ____________________ Assignment date: ________________

Circling fraction models to match fraction on the left

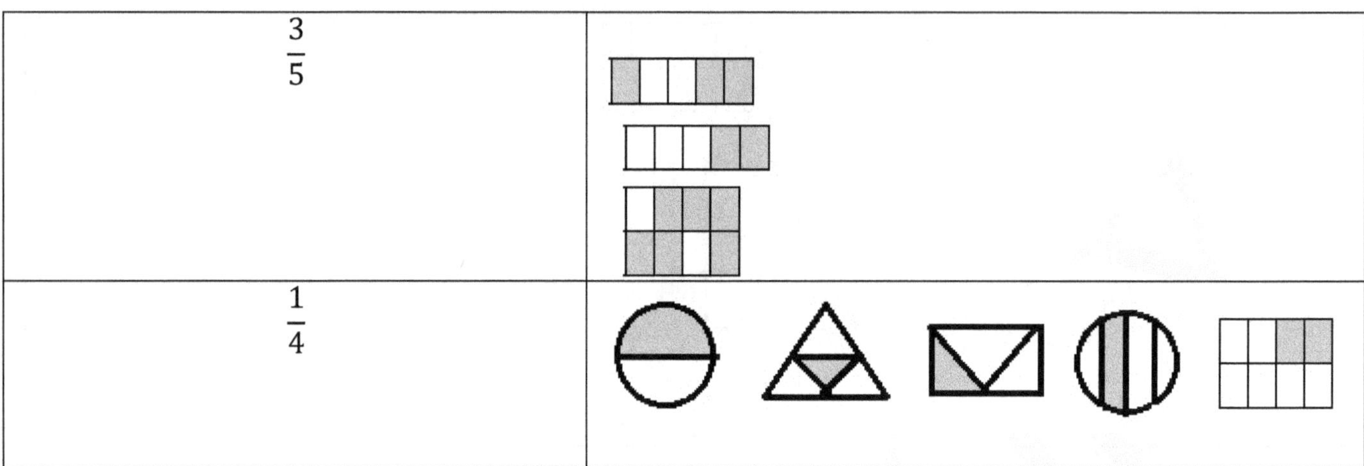

$\frac{3}{5}$	
$\frac{1}{4}$	

Use equivalent fraction to do prediction

Lucy finished $\frac{1}{15}$ of a black and white quilt as shown below. How many white rectangles will be in the finished quilt?  .
Lucy finished $\frac{1}{21}$ of a black and white quilt as shown below. How many white rectangles will be in the finished quilt? 

Student's name: ____________________ Assignment date: ________________

Order the following fractions from least to greatest.

1. $\frac{6}{8}, \frac{3}{8}, \frac{5}{8}$

____

2. $\frac{2}{7}, \frac{6}{7}, \frac{5}{7}$

____

3. $\frac{6}{9}, \frac{3}{9}, \frac{7}{9}$

____

4. $\frac{8}{5}, \frac{3}{5}, \frac{1}{5}$

____

5. $2\frac{1}{3}, 3\frac{2}{3}, 1\frac{1}{3}$

____

6. $2\frac{6}{7}, 1\frac{3}{7}, 3\frac{2}{7}$

____

Order the following fractions from greatest to least.

1. $\frac{2}{6}, \frac{3}{6}, \frac{5}{6}$

____

2. $\frac{7}{9}, \frac{3}{9}, \frac{6}{9}$

____

3. $\frac{6}{5}, \frac{9}{5}, \frac{4}{5}$

____

4. $\frac{15}{8}, \frac{13}{8}, \frac{7}{8}$

____

5. $1\frac{3}{7}, 3\frac{2}{7}, 2\frac{5}{7}$

____

6. $5\frac{1}{8}, 1\frac{7}{8}, 3\frac{5}{8}$

____

Student's name: ____________________ Assignment date: ________________

Order the following fractions from least to greatest.

1. 13 $\frac{6}{8}, \frac{3}{8}, \frac{5}{8}$

____

2. $\frac{2}{7}, \frac{6}{7}, \frac{5}{7}$

____

3. $\frac{6}{9}, \frac{3}{9}, \frac{7}{9}$

____

4. $\frac{8}{5}, \frac{3}{5}, \frac{1}{5}$

____

5. $2\frac{1}{3}, 3\frac{2}{3}, 1\frac{1}{3}$

____

6. $2\frac{6}{7}, 1\frac{3}{7}, 3\frac{2}{7}$

____

Student's name: ____________________ Assignment date: ______________

Order fractions with different denominators

$\frac{7}{13}, \frac{6}{10}, \frac{3}{7}$
$\frac{4}{8}, \frac{5}{9}, \frac{3}{6}$
$\frac{4}{5}, \frac{7}{10}, \frac{7}{9}$
$\frac{10}{12}, \frac{8}{10}, \frac{3}{7}$
$\frac{10}{11}, \frac{8}{9}, \frac{3}{8}$
$\frac{8}{12}, \frac{8}{9}, \frac{5}{7}$

Student's name: ____________________ Assignment date: ________________

Model 2 – Choosing one or more equal parts of a set.

The fraction of a set

Example: Find $\frac{2}{4}$ of 12

1. Divide 12 into 4 equal groups.
2. Count the number in each group, which is "3".
3. Times the number with a numerator.
 3 × 2 = 6

○	○	○	○
○	○	○	○
○	○	○	○
$\frac{1}{4}$	$\frac{1}{4}$	$\frac{1}{4}$	$\frac{1}{4}$

$\frac{1}{4}$ $\frac{2}{4}$

Shade or divide the following squares such that the shaded area matches the fraction shown.

□□□□ □□□□ $\frac{1}{2}$	□□□ $\frac{5}{6}$	□□□□ □□□□ $\frac{9}{16}$
□□□□□ $\frac{1}{2}$	□□□□□ $\frac{3}{10}$	□□□□ $\frac{1}{3}$

Student's name: ____________________ Assignment date: ________________

Shade or divide the following squares such that the shaded area matches the fraction shown.

1. □□□□□ □□□□□ $\frac{3}{10}$ ______

2.  $\frac{3}{14}$ ______

3. □□□□□□ $\frac{5}{6}$ ______

4. □□□□□ $\frac{2}{5}$ ______

5. □□□□□□□ $\frac{4}{7}$ ______

6. □□□□□□ $\frac{4}{6}$ ______

7. □□□□ $\frac{2}{4}$ ______

8. □□□□□ $\frac{3}{5}$ ______

9. □□□□□ □□□□□ $\frac{6}{10}$ ______

10. □□□□ □□□□□ $\frac{4}{9}$ ______

11. □□□ □□□□□ $\frac{3}{8}$ ______

12. □□□□ □□□□□□ $\frac{5}{10}$ ______

13. □□□ □□□□□ $\frac{2}{8}$ ______

14. □□□ □□□□ $\frac{5}{7}$ ______

15. □□□□ $\frac{4}{4}$ ______

16. □□□□□ $\frac{0}{5}$ ______

17. □□□ □□ $\frac{4}{5}$ ______

18. □□ □□□□ $\frac{2}{6}$ ______

Student's name: ____________________ Assignment date: ________________

Converting fraction addition or subtraction to $\frac{a}{b}$

Fraction addition	Fraction subtraction
$1+\frac{1}{3}=\frac{1\times3+1}{3}=\frac{4}{3}$	$1-\frac{1}{3}=\frac{1\times3-1}{3}=\frac{2}{3}$
$1+\frac{1}{4}=$	$1-\frac{1}{4}=$
$1+\frac{1}{6}=$	$1-\frac{1}{6}=$
$1+\frac{1}{6}=$	$1-\frac{1}{6}=$
$1+\frac{1}{7}=$	$1-\frac{1}{7}=$
$1+\frac{1}{10}=$	$1-\frac{1}{10}=$
$2+\frac{1}{6}=$	$2-\frac{1}{6}=$
$3+\frac{1}{6}=$	$3-\frac{1}{6}=$
$2+\frac{1}{7}=$	$2-\frac{1}{7}=$
$2+\frac{1}{8}=$	$2-\frac{1}{8}=$

Student's name: ____________________ Assignment date: ________________

Find the fractional part of the number.

Lower-grade students should master $\frac{1}{a} \times$ amount first.

1. $\frac{1}{8}$ *of* 16 = ____________

2. $\frac{1}{3}$ *of* 15 = ____________

3. $\frac{2}{5}$ *of* 20 = ____________

4. $\frac{3}{4}$ *of* 16 = ____________

5. $\frac{2}{3}$ *of* 18 = ____________

6. $\frac{2}{6}$ *of* 30 = ____________

7. $\frac{3}{4}$ *of* 12 = ____________

8. $\frac{1}{5}$ *of* 45 = ____________

9. $\frac{3}{6}$ *of* 24 = ____________

10. $\frac{7}{9}$ *of* 54 = ____________

11. $\frac{3}{10}$ *of* 30 = ____________

12. $\frac{6}{10}$ *of* 50 = ____________

13. $\frac{2}{7}$ *of* 28 = ____________

14. $\frac{7}{8}$ *of* 32 = ____________

15. $\frac{3}{5}$ *of* 50 = ____________

16. $\frac{7}{10}$ *of* 80 = ____________

17. $\frac{5}{9}$ *of* 36 = ____________

18. $\frac{2}{11}$ *of* 33 = ____________

19. $\frac{5}{8}$ *of* 80 = ____________

20. $\frac{5}{30}$ *of* 180 = ____________

21. $\frac{1}{4}$ *of* 40 = ____________

22. $\frac{3}{4}$ *of* 12 = ____________

23. $\frac{3}{7}$ *of* 70 = ____________

24. $\frac{7}{11}$ *of* 55 = ____________

Student's name: ____________________ Assignment date: ________________

Fraction and division

$\frac{1}{10}$=0.1	$1\frac{1}{10}$=1.1	$1\frac{1}{100}$=1.01	$1\frac{1}{1000}$=1.001
$\frac{2}{10}$=	$1\frac{12}{10}$=	$1\frac{2}{100}$=	$1\frac{2}{1000}$=
$\frac{3}{10}$=	$1\frac{3}{10}$=	$1\frac{3}{100}$=	$1\frac{3}{1000}$=
$\frac{4}{10}$=	$1\frac{4}{10}$=	$1\frac{4}{100}$=	$1\frac{4}{1000}$=
$\frac{5}{10}$=	$1\frac{5}{10}$=	$1\frac{5}{100}$=	$1\frac{5}{1000}$=
$\frac{6}{10}$=	$1\frac{6}{10}$=	$1\frac{6}{100}$=	$1\frac{6}{1000}$=
$\frac{7}{10}$=	$1\frac{7}{10}$=	$1\frac{7}{100}$=	$1\frac{7}{1000}$=

Student's name: ____________________ Assignment date: ________________

Commonly used unit fractions

Lower grades students are not taught how to do fraction divisions, but sometimes the commonly used unit fractions will appear in the word problems. Some problems do not need division but to think a bit more.

Pauline bus 6 pounds of candy and packs them into $\frac{1}{2}$-pound per bag. How many pounds can she pack?
Pauline bus 6 pounds of candy and packs them into $\frac{1}{3}$-pound per bag. How many pounds can she pack?
10% + 10% = ? (Answer in fraction)
10% + 1% = ? (Answer in fraction)
100% – 10% = ? (Answer in fraction)
10% × 100% = ? (Answer in fraction)
100% ÷ 10% = ? (Answer in fraction)

Student's name: ____________________ Assignment date: ________________

Test of fraction word problems

Rank the following data from least to greatest in the original data format. $\frac{4}{4}, \frac{3}{4}. 0.6, 0.8, 25\%, 0.09$
Kitty started to prepare for her final test from 6 p.m. to 8 p.m. She took a break $\frac{1}{4}$ of the way during her study until the middle of the second half of the study. How many minutes did she take her break during the studyÉ
A bathtub is $\frac{3}{4}$ full after 15 gallons of water have been drained. How much water can it hold when it is full?
A bathtub is $\frac{3}{4}$ full. After 15 gallons of water have been drained, it is half full. How much water can it hold when it is full?
$\frac{1}{3}$ of tulips are red. The rest are 40 white tulips. How many red tulips are there? .

Student's name: ____________________ Assignment date: ________________

Finding the original amount using fraction or ratio

A ratio could often be converted to a fraction, then a Line Segment Diagram or a Division Method (work backwards) could be used to solve the original amount problems.

Cher spent \$10 to buy a gift for her sister. This was $\frac{2}{2}$ of her money in her purse. How much did she have originally in her purse?
Jessica went shopping and spent $\frac{1}{3}$ of her money at her lunch break. She had 316 left. How much did she spend on her lunch break?

Student's name: ____________________ Assignment date: ________________

Estimation of fractions 0, $\frac{1}{2}$, and 1 (Faction benchmark)

Example:

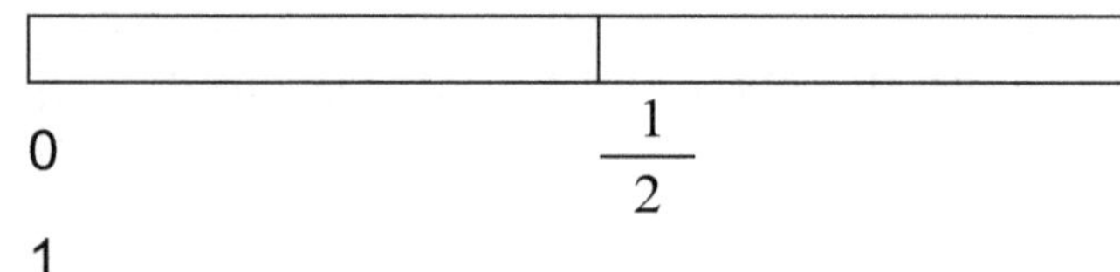

Decide whether each fraction is close to 1, $\frac{1}{2}$, or 1

$\frac{3}{5}$ is closer to $\frac{1}{2}$.

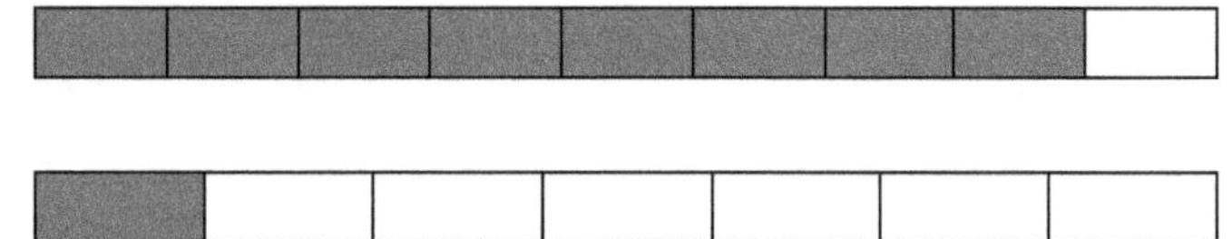

$\frac{8}{9}$ is closer to 1.

$\frac{1}{7}$ is closer to 0.

Divide each strip to show a fraction and decide whether it is closer to 0, $\frac{1}{2}$ or 1.

1. $\frac{1}{5}$ is closer to ________

2. $\frac{3}{8}$ is closer to ________

3. $\frac{5}{6}$ is closer to ________

4. $\frac{3}{5}$ is closer to ________

5. $\frac{2}{9}$ is closer to ________

6. $\frac{6}{7}$ is closer to ________

7. $\frac{1}{3}$ is closer to ________

Student's name: ____________________ Assignment date: ________________

Divide each strip to show a fraction and decide whether it is "more than half", "half", or "less than half".

1. $\frac{1}{5}$ [ ] is ________ ______

2. $\frac{3}{8}$ [ ] is ________ ________

3. $\frac{5}{6}$ [ ] is ________ ________

4. $\frac{3}{5}$ [ ] is ________ ________

5. $\frac{2}{9}$ [ ] is ________ ________

6. $\frac{6}{7}$ [ ] is ________ ________

7. $\frac{1}{3}$ [ ] is ________ ________

8 $\frac{5}{10}$ [ ] is ________

Student's name: ____________________ Assignment date: ________________

Fraction word problem

1. Today is Linda's birthday. She shared her birthday cake with five friends equally. Draw a graph to show how she divided her cake.

2. Sam bought a pizza. He ate 2 eighths of the pizza and gave Linda 3 eighths. What fraction of the pizza did he give to Linda?

3. There are 5 girls and 3 boys in the playground. What fraction of the children are girls?

4. There are 5 apples, 3 pears and 4 oranges in a basket. What fraction of the fruits are pears?

5. There are 7 pieces in a Tangram. Three of them are triangles. The rest are quadrilaterals. What fraction of the Tangram are quadrilaterals?

6. Adam has ten marbles. 2 tenths of them are blue. 3 tenths of them are red. The rest are yellow. Draw a picture to show the marbles. What fraction of the marbles are yellow?

7. 20 minutes is what fraction of an hour?

8. 3 days is what fraction of a week?

Student's name: ____________________ Assignment date: _______________

9. 7 eggs are what fraction of a dozen eggs?

10. How many centimetres are there in 17 millimetres? Write a fraction and a mixed number.

11. How many centimetres are there in 25 millimetres? Write a fraction and a mixed number.

12. How many years are there in 18 months? Write a fraction and a mixed number.

13. Emma had 12 candies. She ate half of them. How many candies did she eat?

14. Stanley has 20 books. He gave 2 fifths of them to his sister. How many books did he give to his sister?

15. Shirley has a ribbon 50 cm long. She cut 2 fifths of it off. How long is the ribbon now?

16. Marko had 15 chocolate bars. He ate 1 fifth of them and gave 3 to Fiona. How many chocolate bars did he leave?

Student's name: ____________________ Assignment date: ________________

17. Pauline has walked 7 blocks, and she must walk 10 blocks in total to reach her school. What fraction of distance is left for her to walk?

18. Amanda says $\frac{2}{4}$ of a pie, size is the same as to say $\frac{2}{4}$ of the same pie. Is she right? Explain your reason by drawing a model.

19. What fraction of a pit must you order to $\frac{2}{5}$ of a pie, you already ordered to make a whole pie?

Student's name: ______________________ Assignment date: __________________

Test of fractions

Result of fraction in English	Arithmetic computation	Graphic representation
	Not available	
	Not available	
	Not available	0 1
		0 1
		–
		+ ? = 1
		2 of $\frac{1}{4}$ =

Student's name: ____________________ Assignment date: ________________

Test of fractions

Fractions	Write the fractions from the least to the greatest
$\frac{9}{2}$ $4\frac{1}{3}$	
$2\frac{2}{3}$ $\frac{7}{3}$	
$\frac{23}{27}$, $\frac{11}{27}$, $\frac{25}{27}$, $\frac{26}{27}$	
$3\frac{3}{7}$, $4\frac{1}{7}$, $3\frac{5}{7}$, $2\frac{6}{7}$	
$\frac{3}{7}$, $\frac{3}{5}$, $\frac{3}{4}$, $\frac{3}{6}$	
$\frac{6}{7}$, $\frac{6}{5}$, $\frac{6}{4}$, $\frac{6}{6}$	
$\frac{8}{9}$, $\frac{8}{11}$, $\frac{8}{13}$, $\frac{8}{10}$	

Write a fraction or a mixed number to make each statement true (more than one answers).

$\frac{8}{8}$ > ______
$1\frac{1}{1}$ < ______
______ > $\frac{4}{7}$
______ < $1\frac{2}{3}$

Student's name: ____________________ Assignment date: ________________

Test of fractions

The following figure represents $\frac{3}{7}$ of one whole. It has some part missing, so complete the figure and shaded it, so it shows the shaded part is $\frac{3}{7}$. 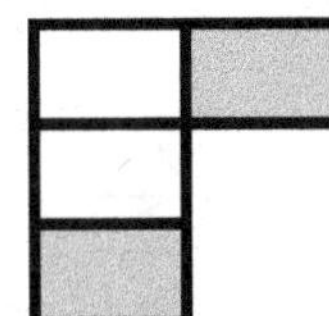
A. Write a fraction between 0 and 1 that is neither closer to 0 nor closer to 1. ________ B. Write a fraction between 0 and $\frac{1}{2}$ that is neither closer to 0 nor closer to $\frac{1}{2}$. ________ C. Write a fraction between 1 and $\frac{1}{2}$ that is neither closer to 1 nor closer to $\frac{1}{2}$. ________

Fraction equation	Fraction multiplication model
$\frac{1}{2} \times 6 = 3$	$\frac{1}{2}$ of 6
$\frac{3}{5} \times 20 = ?$	?
?	
?	

Student's name: ____________________ Assignment date: ________________

Test of fractions and fraction pictures

Mixed number	Improper fraction	Fraction picture

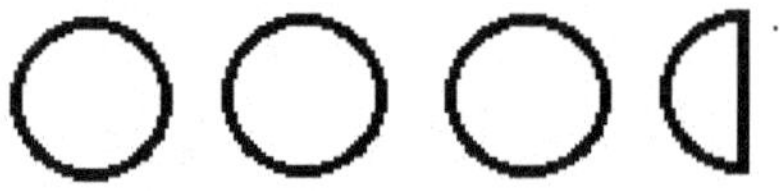

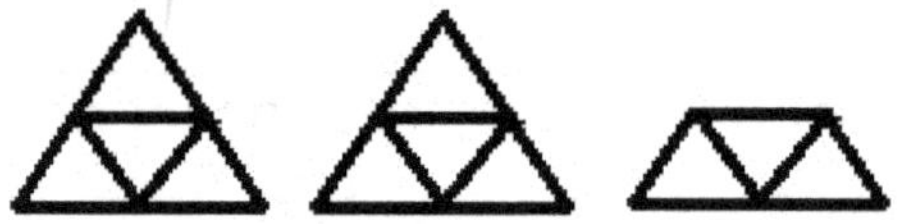

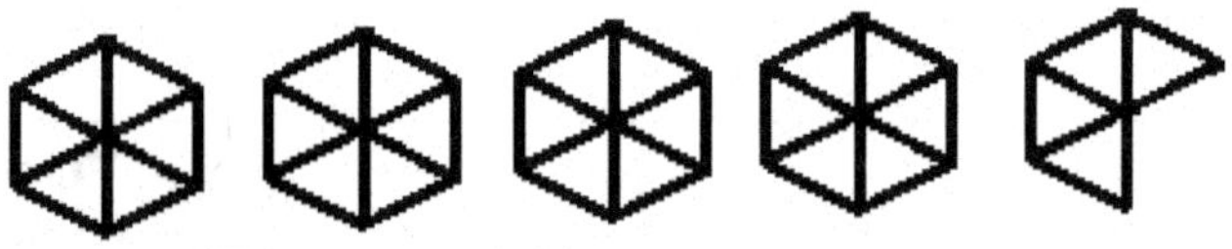

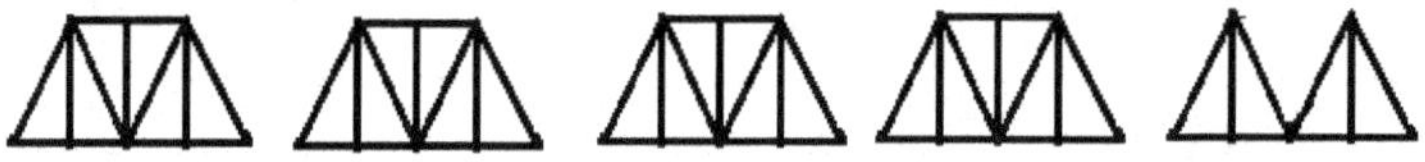

One-half plus one and three-quarter is equal to ____________.
Shade $\frac{3}{5}$ of 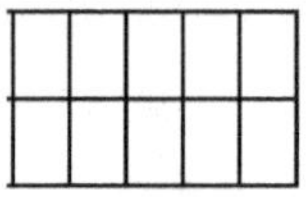
Shade $\frac{4}{10}$ of
Shade $\frac{4}{10}$ of
Shade $2\frac{4}{6}$ of 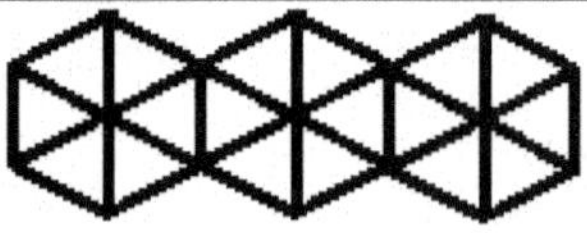

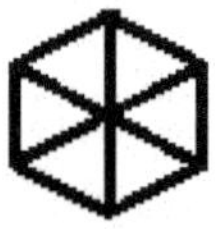

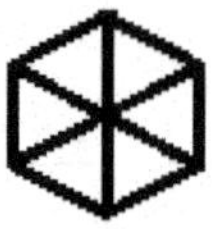

Student's name: ____________________ Assignment date: ________________

Test of fractions using the number line

Fill in the missing fractions on the following number lines.

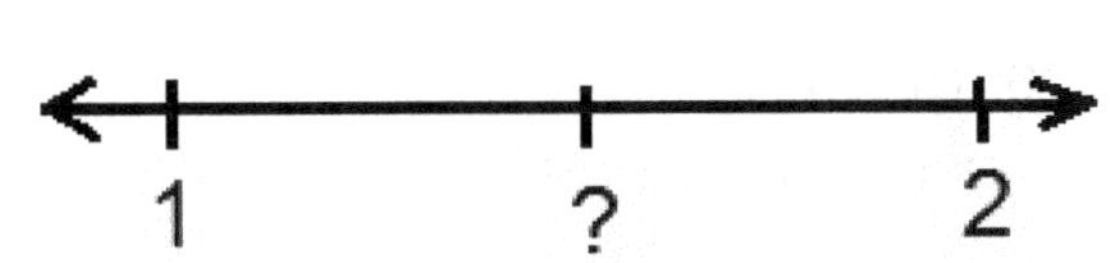

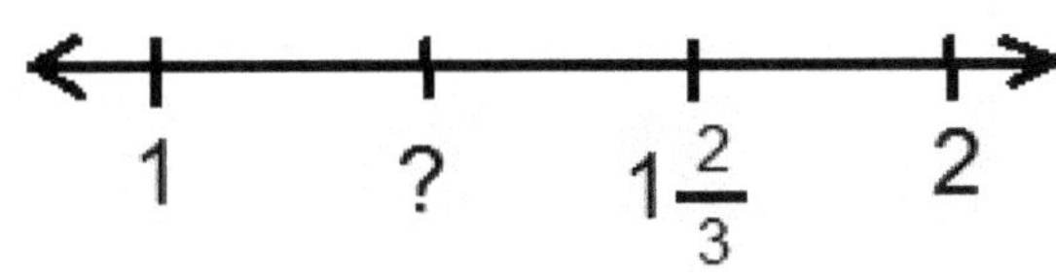

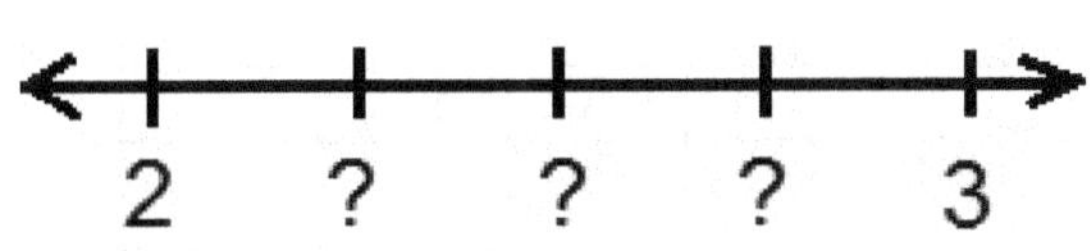

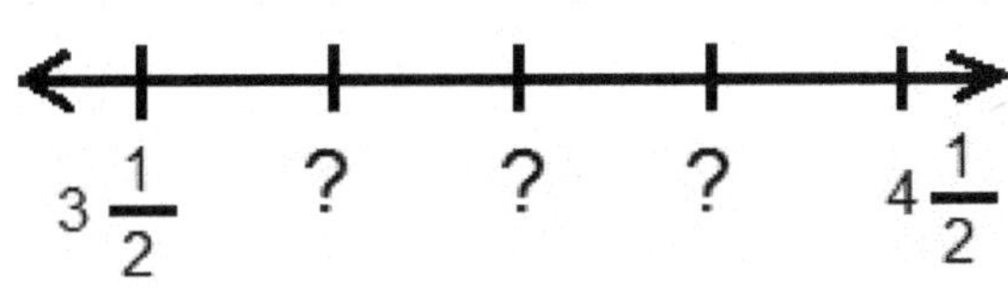

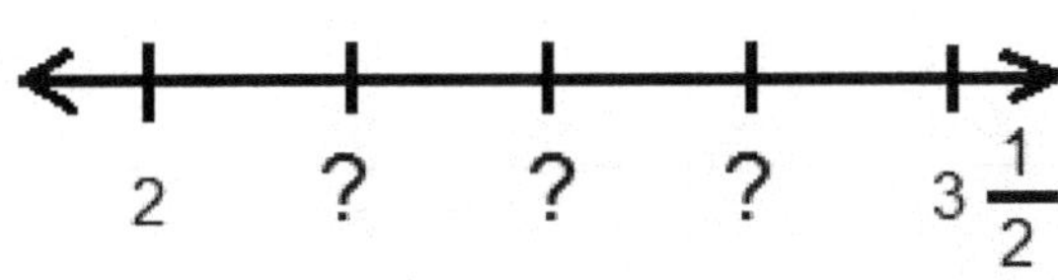

Student's name: ____________________ Assignment date: ________________

***** Part 17 Percent *****

Percent means "per hundred" or "out of 100". When a fraction $\frac{a}{100}$ is expressed as a out of 100, then it is called a %. For example, $\frac{2}{100}$ = 2%. The notation is used for easy communication, so the % is often converted to decimal for computation purposes. Since $\frac{2}{100} = 0.02$, We now established the conversion relationship between fraction, percent, and decimal.

When $\frac{a}{b}$ (a over b) is not explained, it could mean the following different meanings:

- a out of b
- a to b (a : b)
- a divided by b
- a times $\frac{1}{b}$
- a favourable outcome out of b possible outcome

For computation purposes, a percent normally is converted to decimal.

fraction	%	decimal	Division
$\frac{1}{10}$			$10\overline{)1}$
$\frac{1}{20}$			
$\frac{1}{8}$			
$\frac{1}{2}$			
$\frac{3}{4}$			
$\frac{2}{3}$			

Student's name: ____________________ Assignment date: ________________

fraction	%	decimal	Division
		0.4	
		0.12	
		0.01	
		1.5	
		1.05	
6 out of 10			
$2\frac{1}{5}$			
	$33\frac{1}{3}\%$		
X		$0.\overline{3}$	
	455		

Student's name: ____________________ Assignment date: ________________

Computation of percent

Often we translate percent to either divided by 100 or multiplied by $\frac{1}{100}$ in the computation of %.

Original amount × percent = partial amount

In lower grades, most problems are to find the partial amount when a percent is given. A direct method using multiplication could be used to solve it.

Example 1

A dress is selling for $20. If Sophie buys it at a 20% discount, how much will she save and how much will she have to pay?

20 × 0.2 = 4 …… The Amount Sophie will save.
20- 4 = 16 …….. The amount Sophie will have to pay.

Use one statement

Students should also understand that without getting the amount of discount, use the concept of a whole in fraction. How much does Sophie have to pay could also be solved by using only one statement?

20 × 0.8 = 16 … Sophie only pays 80%.

Student's name: ____________________ Assignment date: ________________

Example 2

Twelve students of Alvin's borrowed books for the library, which is 75% of the entire class. How many students in Alvin's class did not borrow any books?

Method 1

Convert the percent to fraction and then convert fraction to groups.

75% = $\frac{3}{4}$ which could mean Alvin's class is divided into 4 groups, and 3 groups of them borrowed books, and the number of students in that 3 groups is 12. To find how many students in each group, we just use $\frac{12}{3}$=4. We know there is only one group of students who did not borrow any books, so the answer is 4.

Method 2

Use the Line Segment Method by drawing line segments.

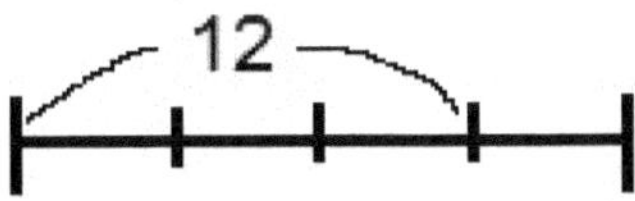

Method 3

A quantity divided by its corresponding value (to work backwards to get the original amount.)

This method is difficult for lower grades students to understand, so we suggest this method for higher grades students.

12 ÷ 0.75 = 12 × $\frac{4}{3}$ = 16 …. The number of students for the entire class

16 – 12 = 4

Student's name: ____________________ Assignment date: ________________

Test of Percent

Information		Problem	Answer
(2 × 2 grid, 1 square shaded)		Find the % of the shaded area. Find % of the not shaded area.	
Annie		Find the letter of n`s percentage in the name as spelled on the left.	
25% 50%		Which one is a larger percentage?	
(2 × 4 grid, all squares shaded)		Find the percent of shaded squares.	
Annie`s class has 10 boys and 15 girls.		Find the percent of boys in Annie`s class.	

Student's name: ____________________ Assignment date: ________________

Finding equal to, more than, less than of the originals

Emily has 20% of Mable's money. Mable has \$15. How much money does Emily have?
Emily has 20% more money than Mable. Mable has \$15. How much money does Emily have?
Emily has 20% less money than Mable. Mable has \$15. How much money does Emily have?
Emily has as much as $\frac{2}{5}$ of Mable's money. Mable has \$15. How much money does Emily have?
Emily has $\frac{2}{5}$ more money than Mable. Mable has \$15. How much money does Emily have?
Emily has $\frac{2}{5}$ less than Mable. Mable has \$15. How much money does Emily have?

Student's name: ____________________ Assignment date: ________________

Percent and line number

Find the answer to each question.

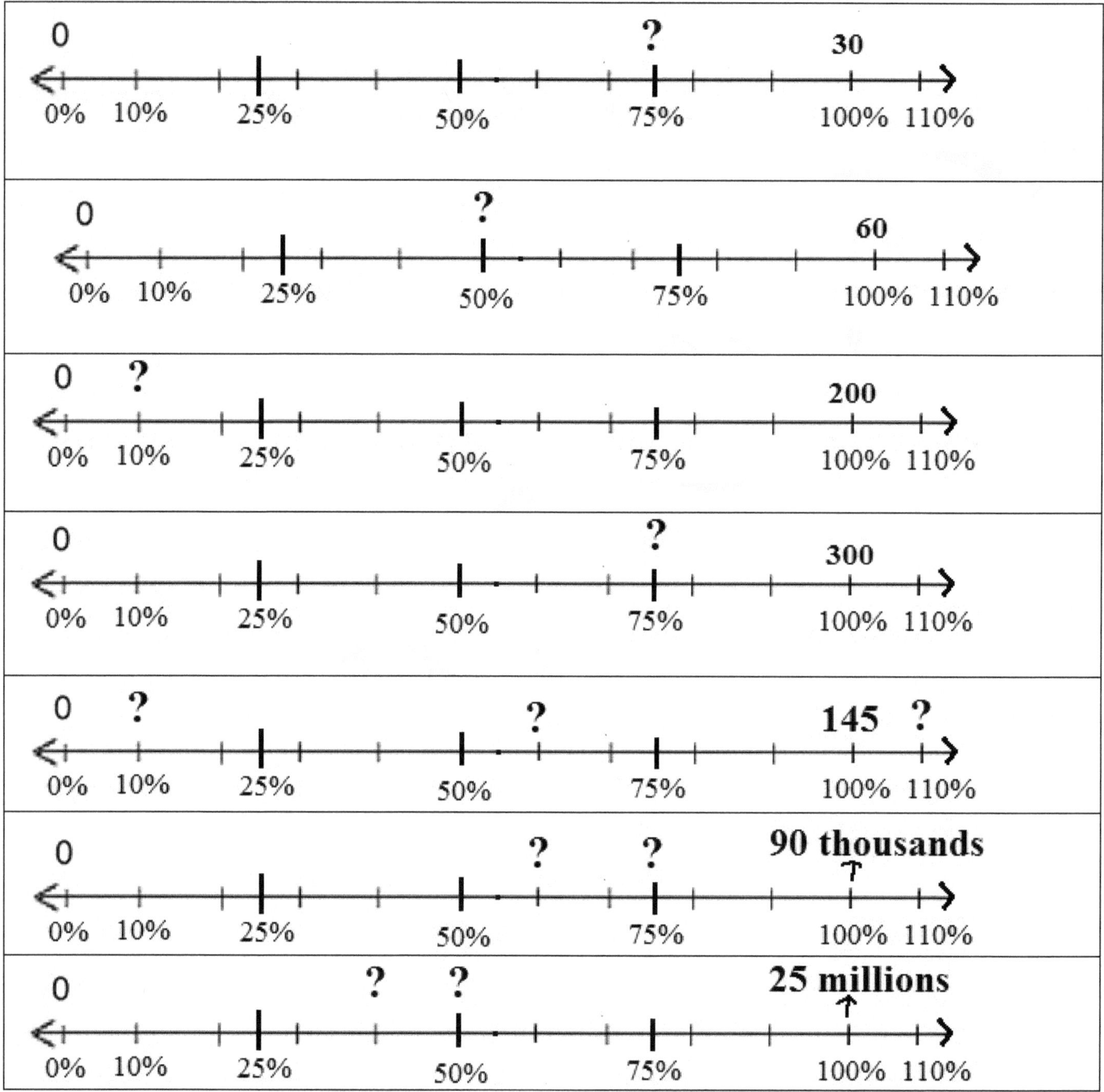

Student's name: ____________________ Assignment date: ________________

Test of percent word problems

Ten percent off is the same as $15 off what price?
Adam earns 10% interest in his savings every year. How much interest does he earn for every dollar after one year?

Student's name: ____________________ Assignment date: ________________

Conversion between fraction, percent, ratio

Original problems	fraction	percent	Alternate problems
3 out of 5 students wear white caps in Heather's class.	The fraction of students wearing white caps = ______. .	The percent of students wearing no-white caps = _____.	Suppose 9 students are wearing white caps in Heather's class. How many total students in Heather's class?

Student's name: ____________________ Assignment date: ________________

Ratio, proportion, rate

The ratio is a general term used to describe the relation of any two or more quantities (or variables). The way to compare two quantities is by a number of different techniques, and this is where the confusion starts. By definition, the ratio is used when 2 or more quantities are compared. Still, in practice, there are many different ways of writing the result of the comparison. For example, the ratio could be described in words, 2 out of 5 children are girls could be written as 2 out of 5 or 2 to 5 or ratio can also be expressed as a symbol such as 2:5. It can also be written as a fractional number$\frac{2}{5}$. Further, the ratio is not limited to just comparing 2 quantities. For example, the number of balls in red: black: white = 2: 3: 4 is a ratio to compare 3 quantities.

In order to make the comparison meaningful, the numbers compared normally have the same measuring unit but not necessarily so all the time. For example, the scale is one type of ratio but is normally expressed in different measuring units and only converted to the same unit when doing calculations. Rate is also one type of ratio but also expressed in different measuring units, but in a special case, that is when b is one.
Whenever any 2 (or more) quantities are compared either in words or in the form of $\frac{a}{b}$ where a and b are whole numbers and $b \neq 0$, the result could be called ratio. Ratio includes fraction, probability, scale, interest rate, rate, speed, or sides/angles ratio of similar triangle etc.

The ratio does not have to be a rational number. For example, the ratio of the circumference to its diameter is π, which is a non-terminating and non-repeating number (irrational number).

The ratio becomes more interesting when it is assumed to be a constant and thus can be used to predict either future a or b - this concept is called proportion.

The ratio is to compare two numbers in a simplified form without any unit. The ratio can be expressed in many ways but often the from $\frac{a}{b}$ is used for calculation. Without any further explanation of the meaning $\frac{a}{b}$, $\frac{a}{b}$ can be a ratio, fraction, division. Often a ratio is changed to or converted to $\frac{a}{b}$ and calculated as a fraction because we learn all 4 basic operations (+ , –, ×,÷) of fractions.

Because a ratio is reduced form so a ratio problem often could be solved by using the common factor idea.

There is a ratio $a : b$. The difference between the two ratios converted to original numbers could be expressed as follows:

$ax - bx = x(a - b)$

Student's name: ____________________ Assignment date: ________________

$\frac{ax-bx}{a-b} = x$ which is the common factor

Example

Two out of 5 students watched TV on the new year`s eve in Linda`s class. How many students did not watch TV if Lina`s class has 25 students?

Convert the wording Two out of 5`` into a fraction $\frac{2}{5}$.
Get the answer by using the concept of fraction. $25 \times \frac{3}{5} = 15$

Test of ratio word problems

Three times as many pens as erasers	P: E = 3:1	E: P = 1:3
	P = ___ E	E = _____ P

There are 3 boys for every 2 girls in Sarah's class. There are 24 children in her class. How many girls and boys in her class? There are 19 more boys than girls in Sarah's martial arts class. There are 41 children in her class. How many girls and boys in her class? There are many ways to solve this problem such as Sum and Difference, multiple methods (turning difference into multiples by subtracting 19, and ratio concept to make boy : girl = 1 : 1)

Student's name: ____________________ Assignment date: ________________

When writing ratio, remember the following points:

The numbers in a ratio should always be given in the same order as the statement stated.
The numbers in a ratio should always give in whole numbers.
The numbers in a ratio should always in simplest form.
The numbers in a ratio added together representing the LCM of a whole set (after reducing).

Proportion

Two equal ratios are called proportion.

Test of ratio, rate, and proportion

Emily collects coins. For every 5 coins, she collects 2 dimes. How many dimes does she have if she has 28 coins?
Kiko, the cat, brings home 3 leaves in 30 minutes. How many leaves will she bring in one and a half hours if she collects leaves at twice the speed of the given rate?

Student's name: ____________________ Assignment date: ________________

***** Part 18 Geometry *****

Lines

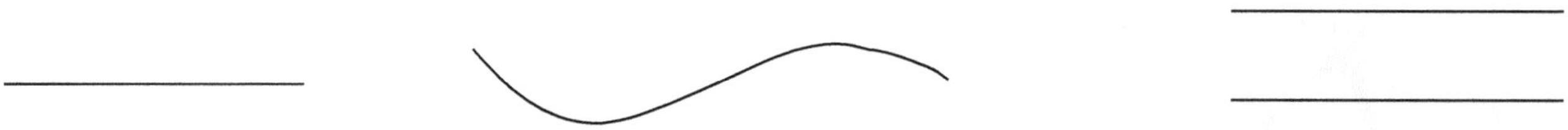

Straight-line	Curve	Parallel lines

1. Matching.

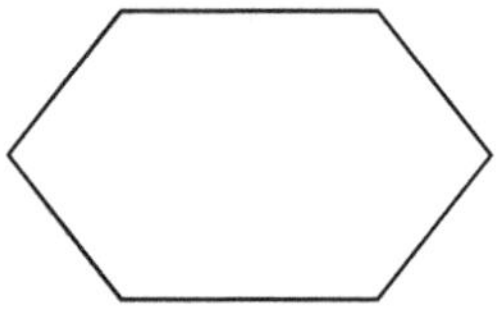

Straight lines

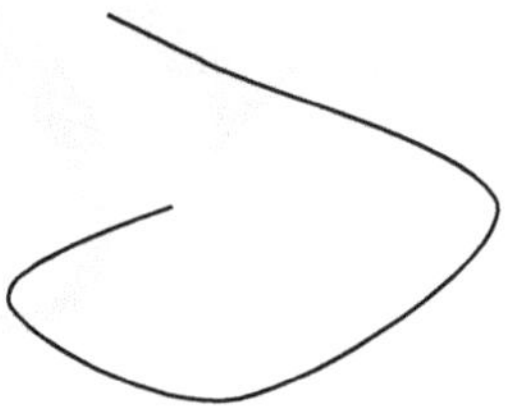

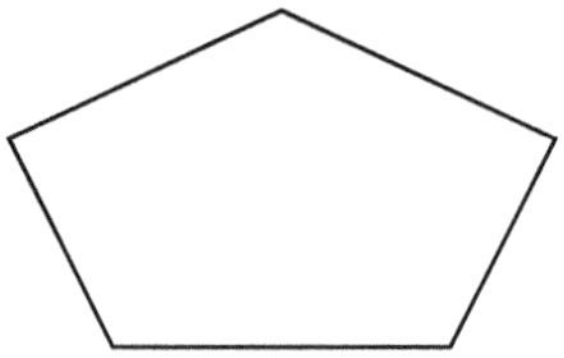

Parallel lines

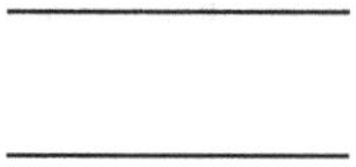

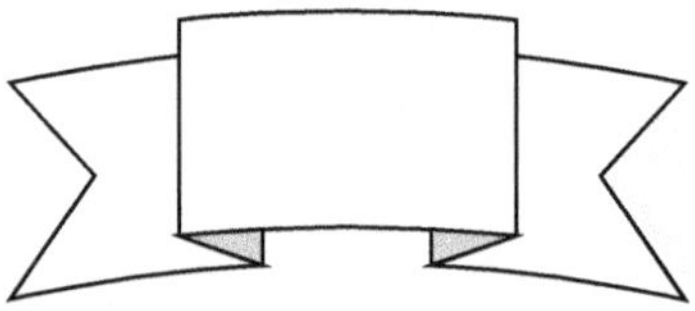

Curve

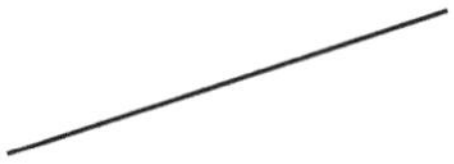

2. Write the name of the following lines.

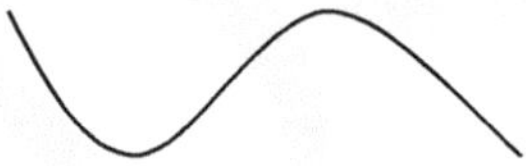

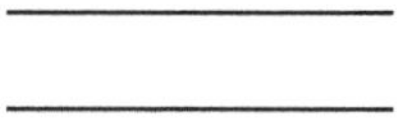

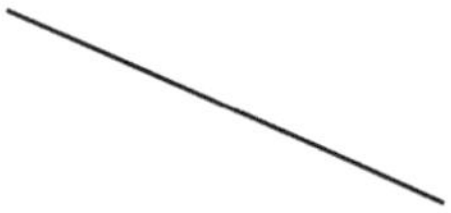

________________ ________________ ________________

Student's name: ____________________ Assignment date: ________________

3. What kind of lines does each picture have?

	Straight line	Curve	Parallel lines

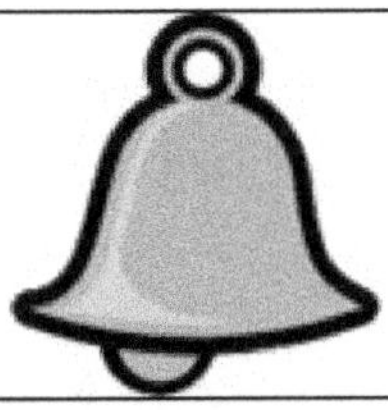

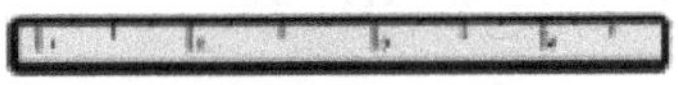

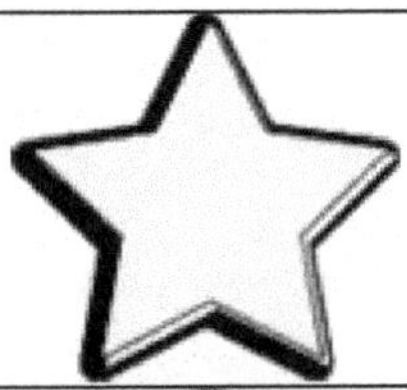

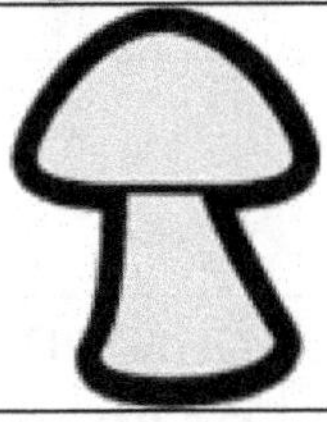

4. Draw line(s) through the following dots.

Straight line	Parallel lines	Curve
. B . A	. C . D	. E . F

Student's name: ____________________ Assignment date: ________________

Name of lines

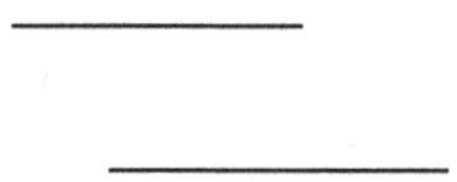 horizontal lines	 vertical lines	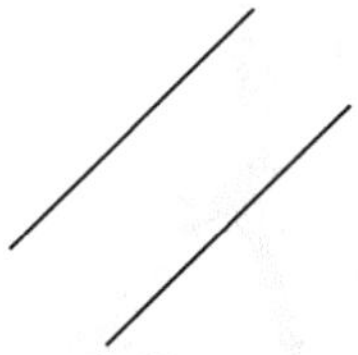 parallel lines
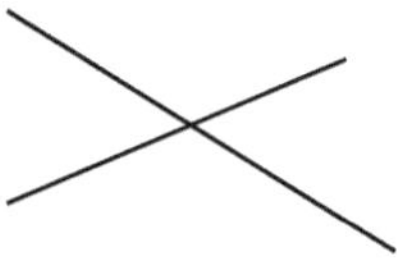 intersecting lines	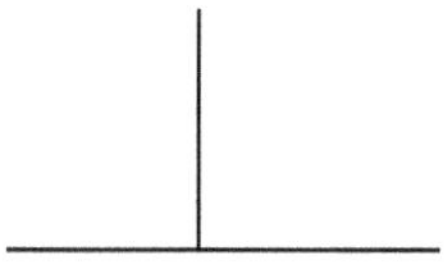 perpendicular lines	

What types of lines can you find in each figure?

	horizontal lines	vertical lines	parallel lines	intersecting lines	perpendicular lines
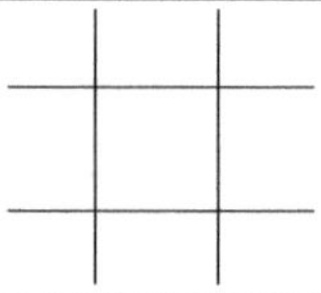					
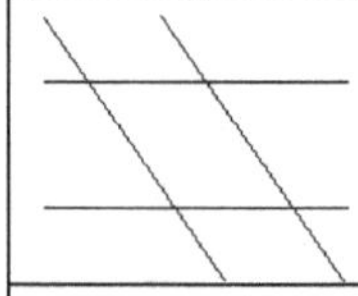					
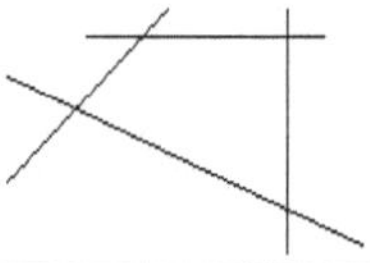					
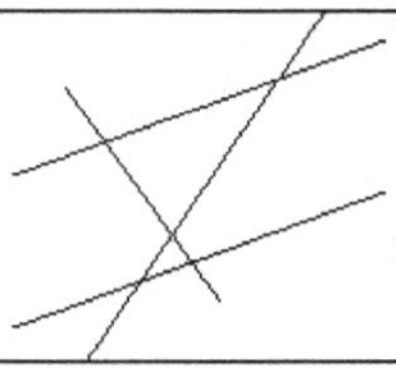					

Student's name: ____________________ Assignment date: ________________

Angles

An angle is formed by two rays intersected with a common endpoint.

An acute angle is an angle that is less than 90°.

A right angle is an angle that is 90°.

An obtuse angle is an angle that is greater than 90° but less than 180°.

A straight angle is an angle that is 180° exactly.

A reflex angle is an angle that is greater than 180° but less than 360°.

An angle such as B A 1 C can be expressed as ∠B, ∠1, ∠ABC, ∠CBA.

Student's name: ____________________ Assignment date: ________________

1. Arrange the angles in order of size from the largest to the smallest. Put in 1, 2, 3 to show.
   a.

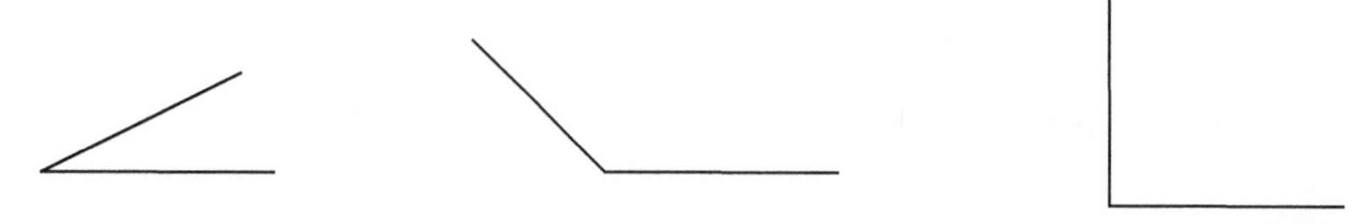

____ ____ ____

   b.

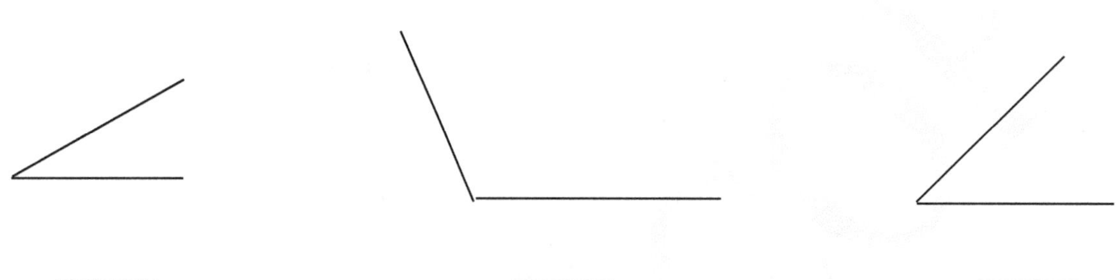

____ ____ ____

2. Find the number of right angles of the following figures.

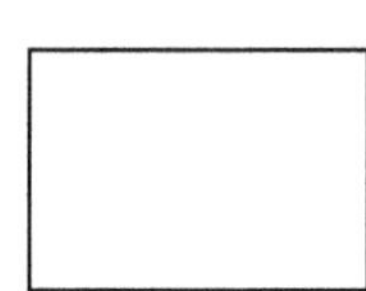 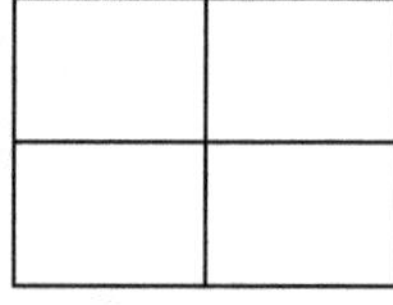 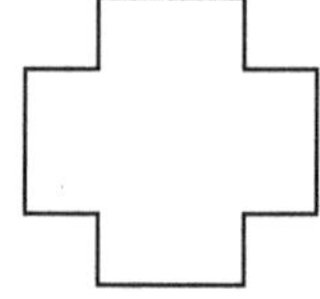

____ ____ ____

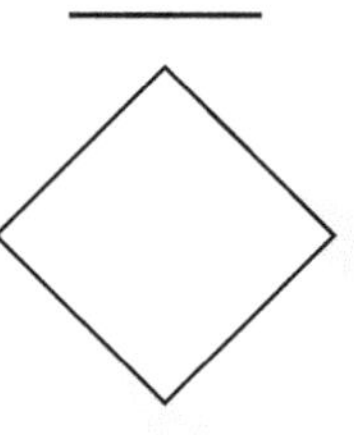 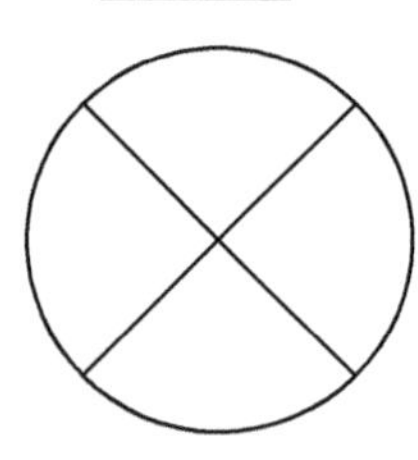

____ ____ ____

Student's name: ____________________ Assignment date: ________________

Measure the following angles.

1.

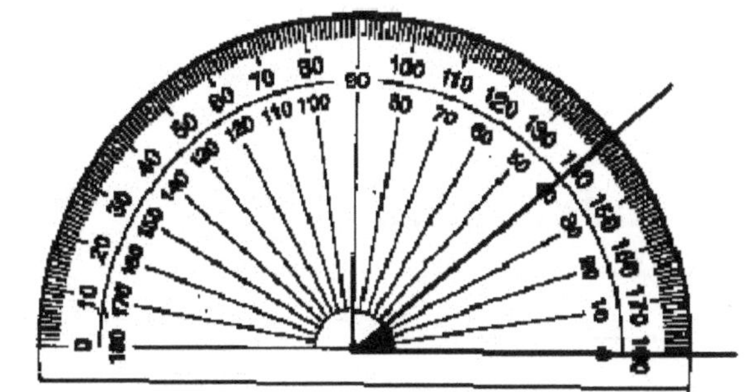

____

2.

____

3.

____

4.

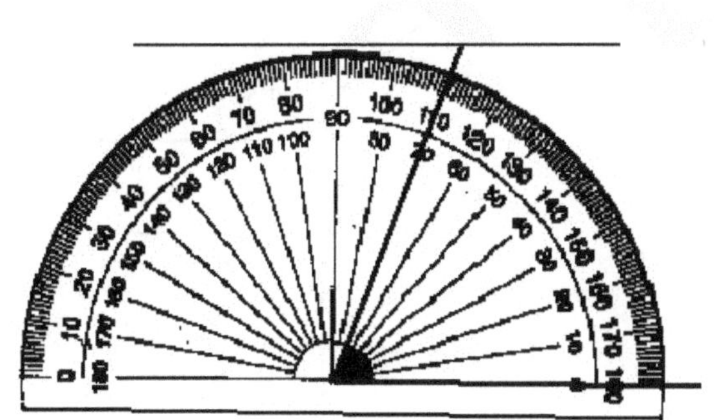

____

5.

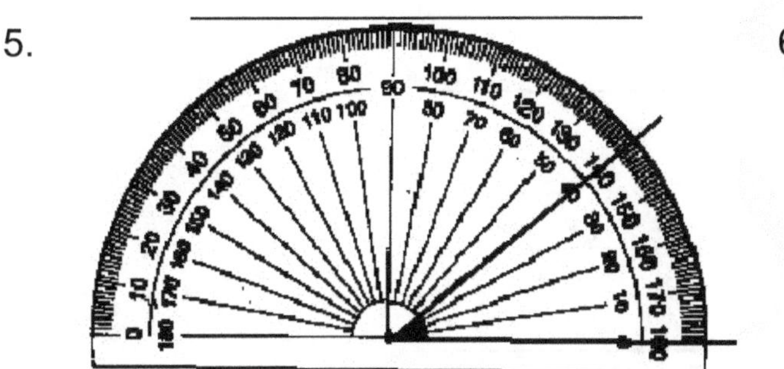

____

6.

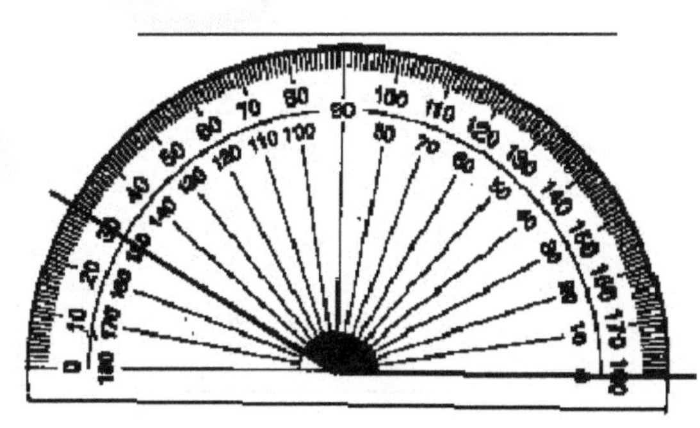

____

7.

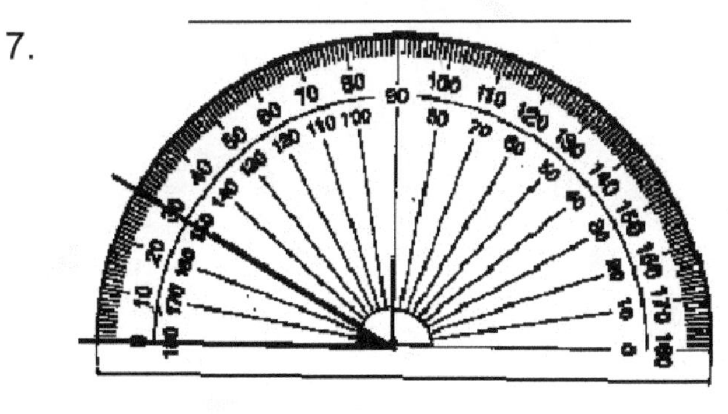

____

8.

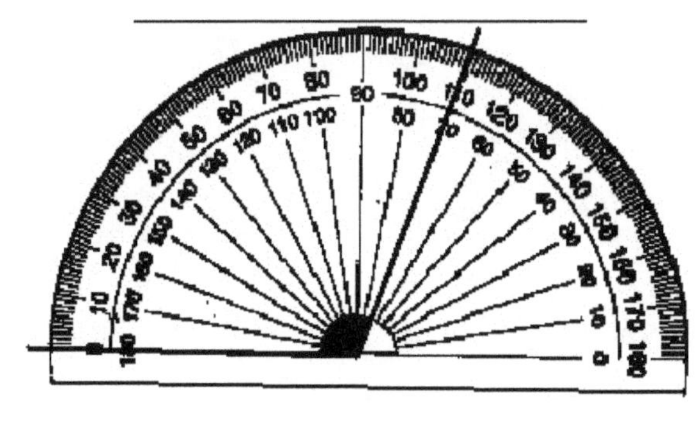

____

Student's name: ____________________ Assignment date: ________________

Measure the following angles.

1 ____________

2 ____________

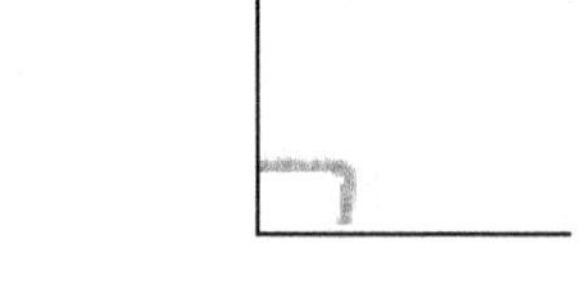

3 ____________

4 ____________

5 ____________

6 ____________

7 ____________

8 ____________

Student's name: ____________________ Assignment date: ________________

9.

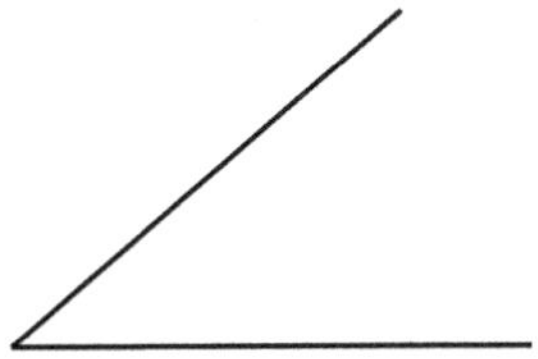

____

10.

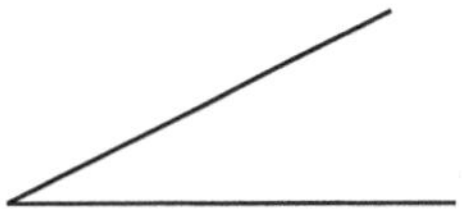

____

11.

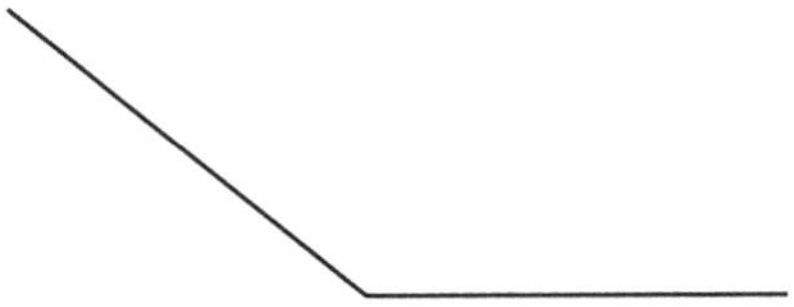

____

12.

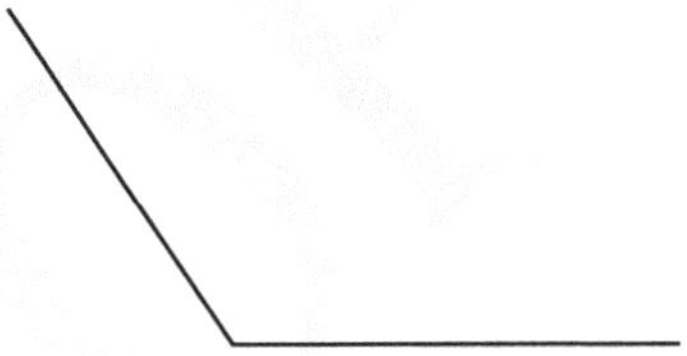

____

13.

____

14.

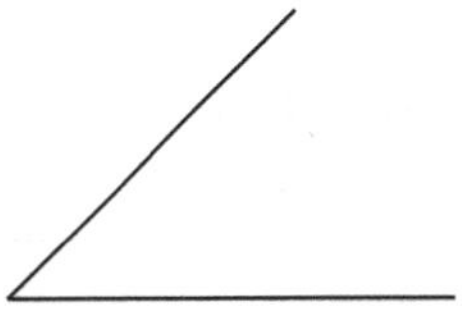

____

15.

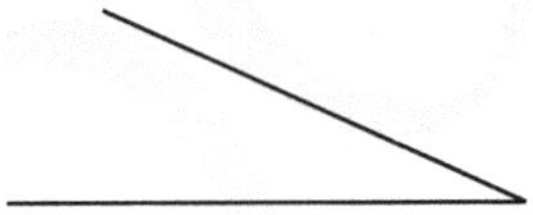

____

16.

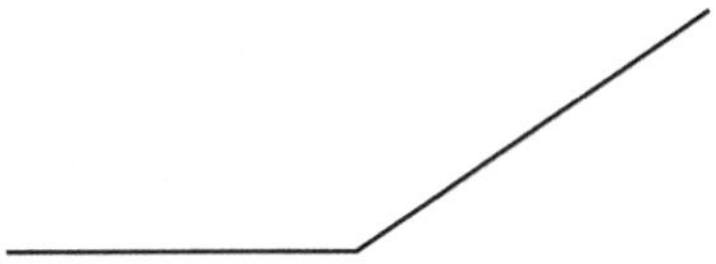

____

Student's name: ____________________ Assignment date: ________________

Shapes

Circle	Triangle	Rectangle
Circle The number of circle sides does not have a definite answer. It is not a polygon, so that the answer could be 0. If you think of the circle as a disk, then it has an up-side and a down-side. If you think of it as a curve, then it has an inside and an outside. If you think of it as the limit of an n-sided regular polygon, one can justify the answer that the circle has infinitely many infinitesimal sides.	Triangle (Three sides)	Rectangle (Four sides)
Pentagon (Five sides)	Hexagon (Six sides)	Octagon (Eight sides)

What types of shapes can you find in each figure?

	Circle	Triangle	Rectangle	Pentagon	Hexagon	Octagon
YOU ARE TODAY'S BIG WINNER!						
YOU ARE TODAY'S BIG WINNER!						

Student's name: ____________________ Assignment date: ________________

Triangle

Angles sum of a triangle is 180^0. This geometry is often not given in the problems, but students must know in advance.

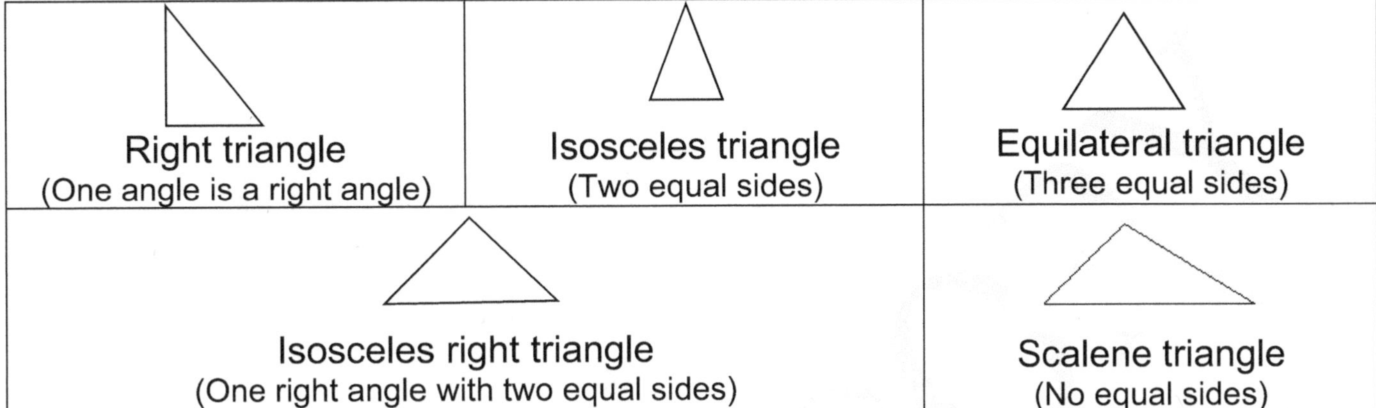

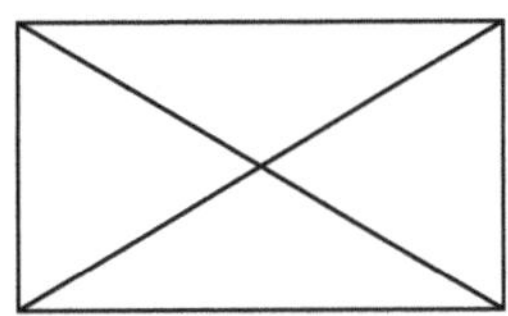

1. There are ________ right triangles in a rectangle.
2. There are ________ isosceles triangles in a rectangle.

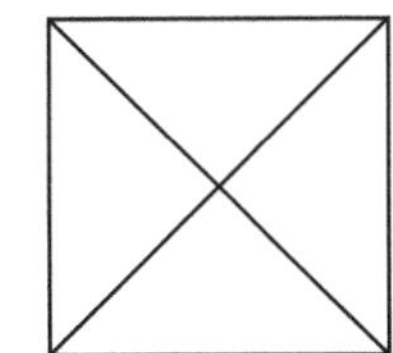

1. There are ________ isosceles right triangles in a square.

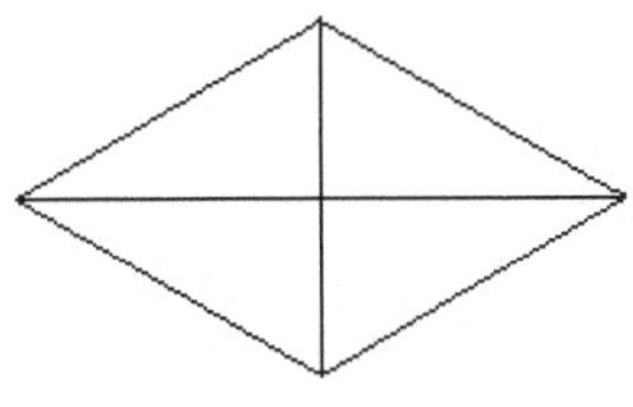

1. There are ________ right triangles in a rhombus.
2. There are ________ isosceles triangles in a rhombus.

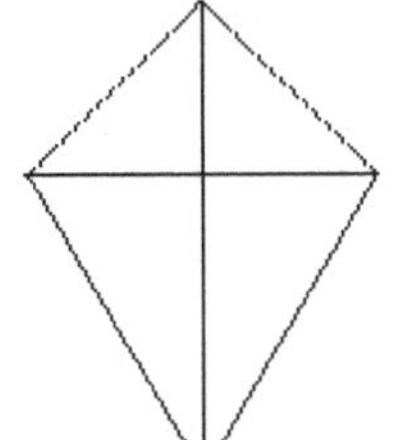

1. There are ________ right triangles in a kite.
2. There are ________ isosceles triangles in a kite.

Student's name: ____________________ Assignment date: ________________

Quadrilateral

The quadrilateral progressing diagram

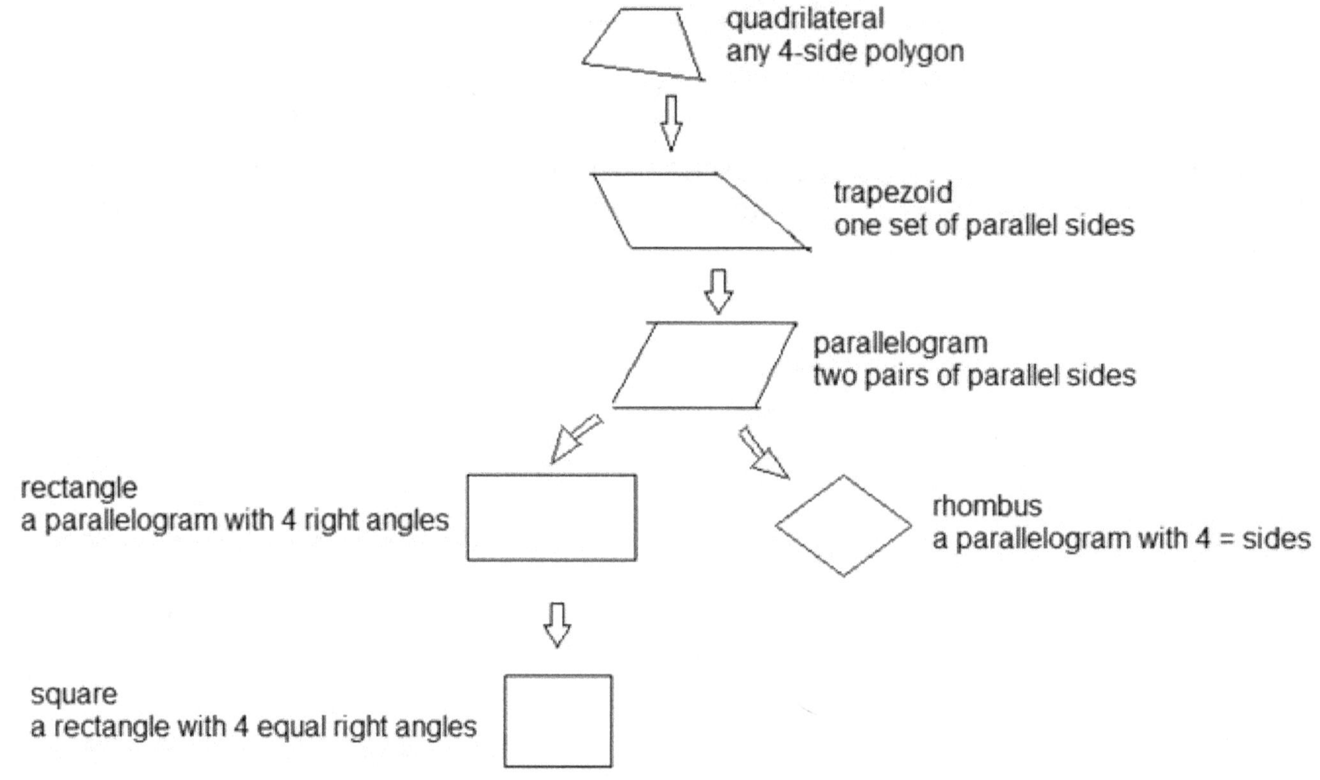

Student's name: ____________________ Assignment date: ________________

Quadrilaterals

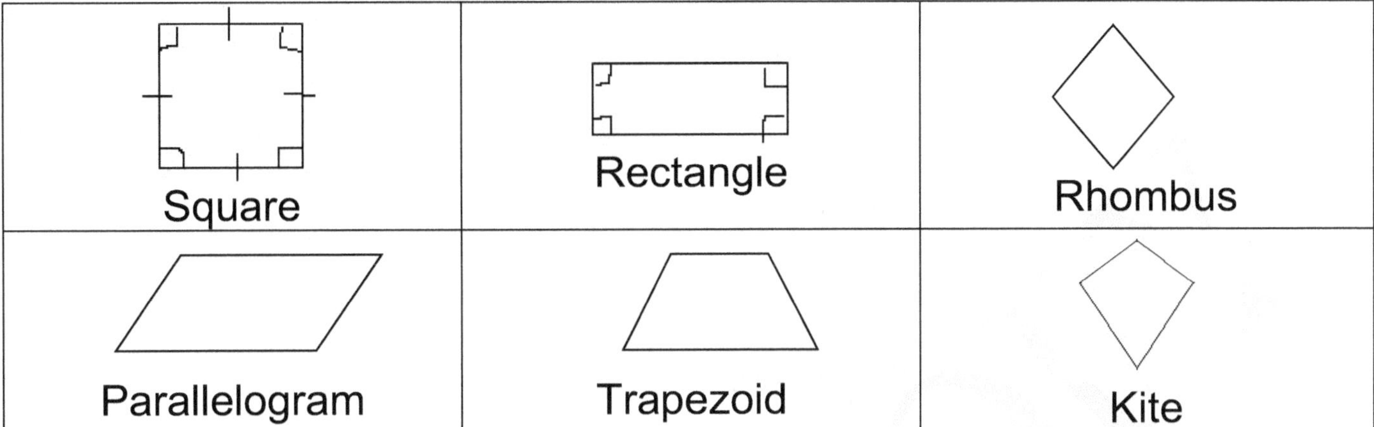

1. How many rectangles can you find?

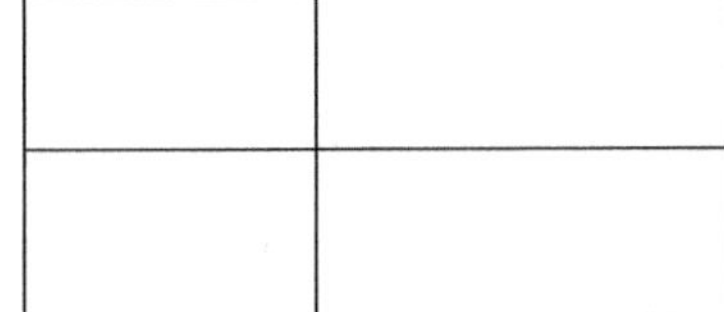

2. How many triangles can you find?

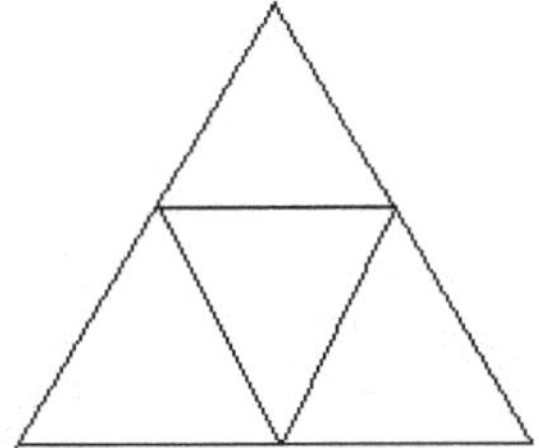

3. How many squares can you find?

Student's name: ____________________ Assignment date: ________________

4. Matching.

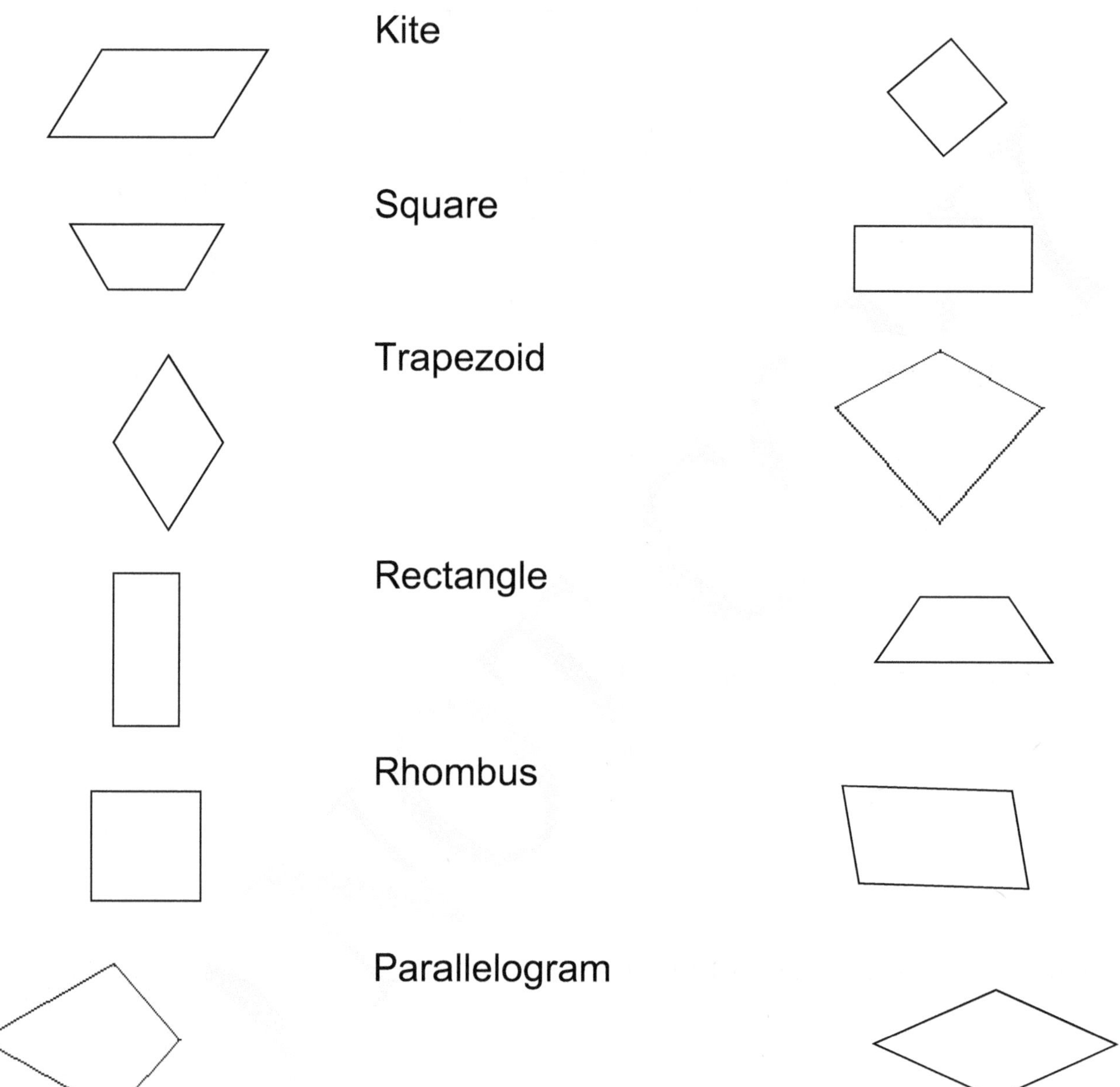

Student's name: ____________________ Assignment date: ________________

Shapes

The figure below is the Chinese Tangram. It is made up of seven pieces. Observe and fill in the blanks below.

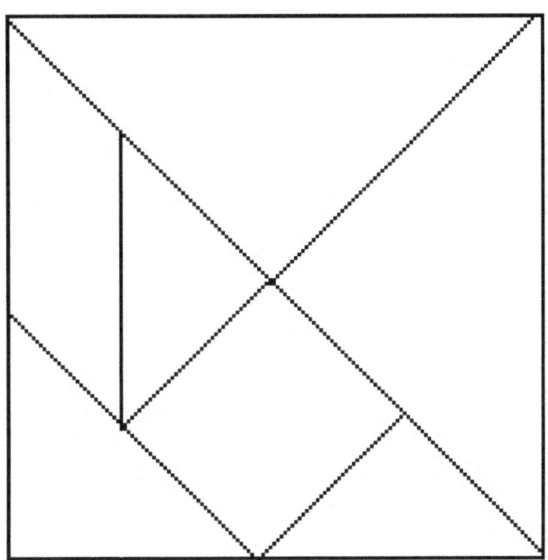

1. There are _____ triangles in the graph.
2. There are _____ squares in the graph.
3. There are _____ parallelograms in the graph.
4. There are _____ trapezoids in the graph.

Student's name: ____________________ Assignment date: ________________

Complete the following chart to show the property of each quadrilateral.

	Name	# of pairs of parallel sides	# of pairs of equal sides	# of equal angles
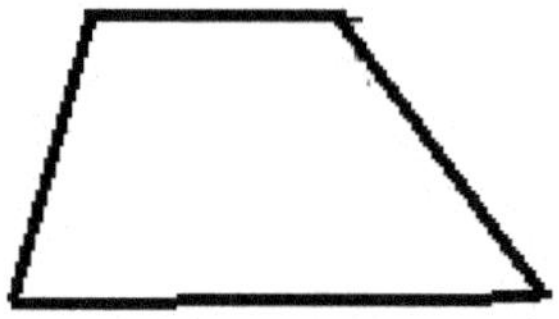				
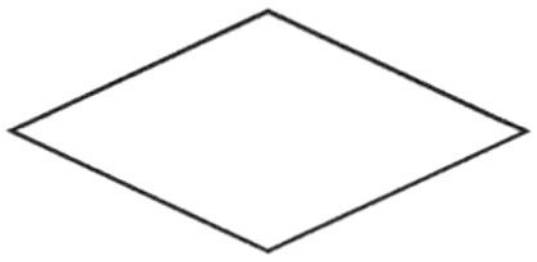				
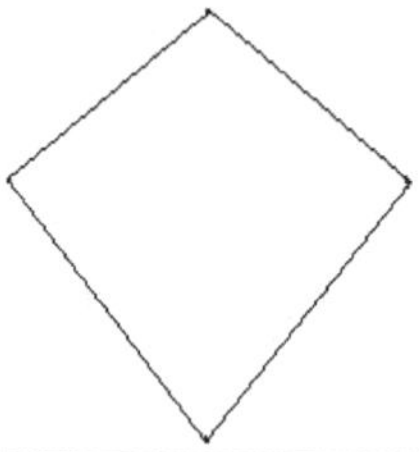				
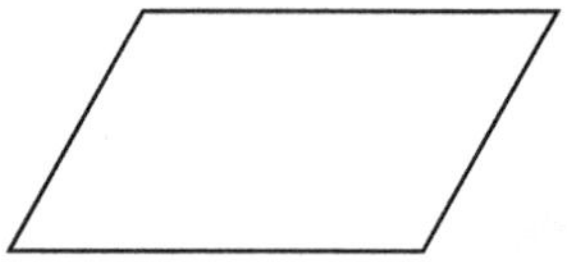				
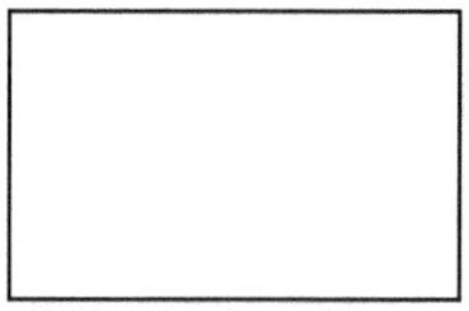				

Student's name: ____________________ Assignment date: ________________

Draw the quadrilateral according to each description.

2 pairs of parallel sides and 2 pairs of equal sides	2 pairs of parallel sides and 4 equal sides
4 right angles and 2 pairs of equal sides	4 right angles and 4 equal sides
2 pairs of opposite equal sides and 2 pairs of opposite equal angles	2 pairs of adjacent equal sides and 1 pairs of opposite equal angles
1 pair of parallel sides and no equal sides	2 pairs of opposite equal angles and 4 equal sides

Student's name: ____________________ Assignment date: ________________

Complementary and supplementary angles

Complementary angles add up to 90^0 $\angle a + \angle b = 90^0$ and each is a complementary angle. 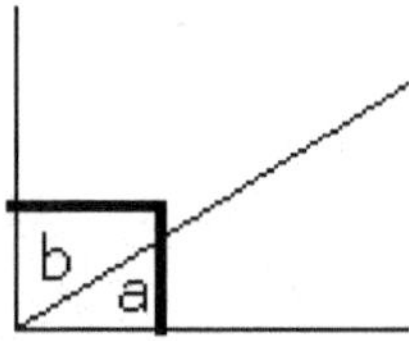	Supplementary angles add up to 180^0 $\angle a + \angle b = 180^0$, and each is a supplementary angle. 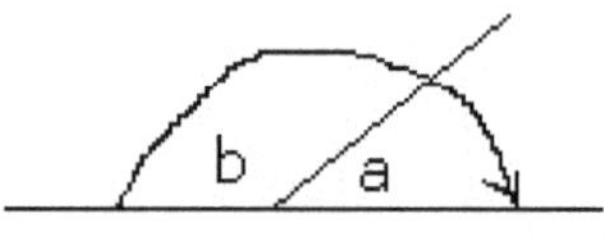

Find the missing angles and state the reason on how to find its size.

1.

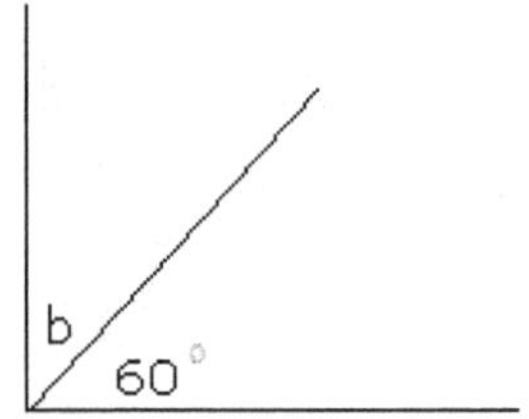

∠ b = __________

Reason: ____________________

2.

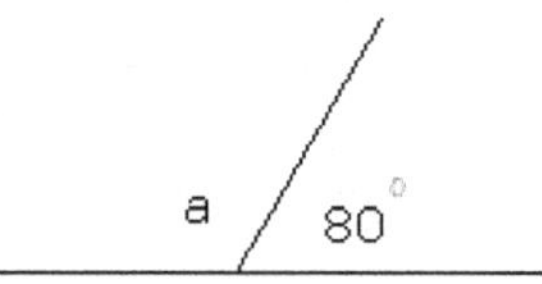

∠ a = __________

Reason: ____________________

3.

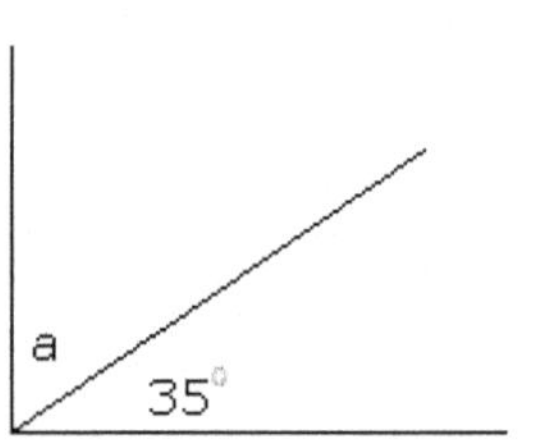

∠ a = __________

Reason: ____________________

4.

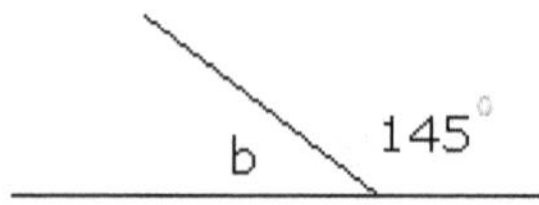

∠ b = __________

Reason: ____________________

5.

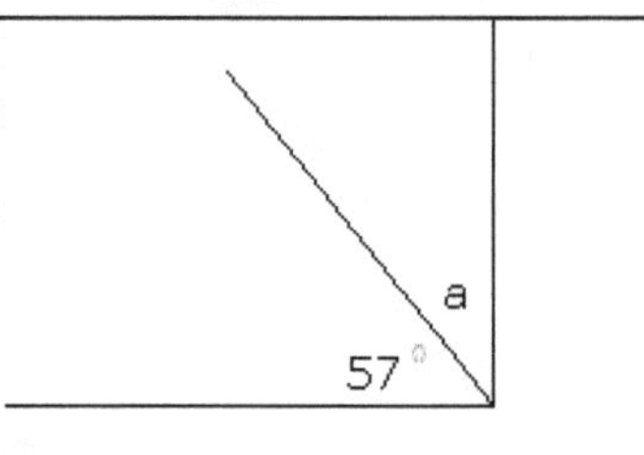

∠ a = __________

Reason: ____________________

6.

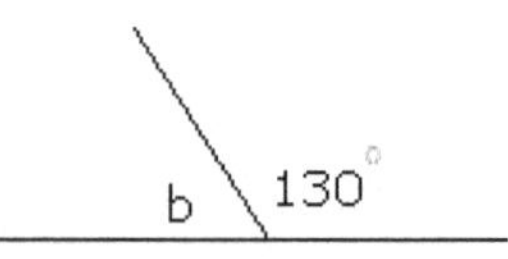

∠ b = __________

Reason: ____________________

Student's name: ____________________ Assignment date: ________________

Adjacent Angles and Angles at a Point

Adjacent angles on a line add up to 180^0 $\angle a + \angle b + \angle c = 180^0$ This is different from the supplementary angles in that this adjacent angles deal with 2 or more angles. All angles must be on the same line. 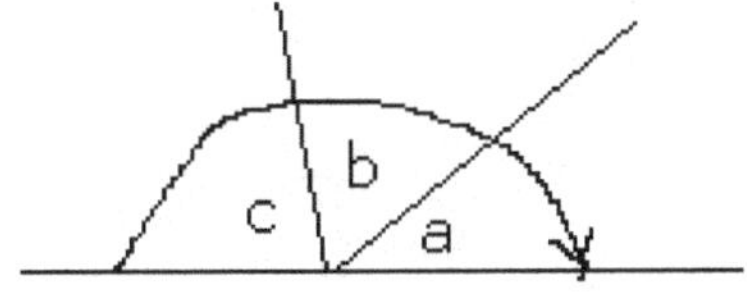	Angles at a point add up to 360^0 $\angle a + \angle b + \angle c + \angle d = 360^0$ 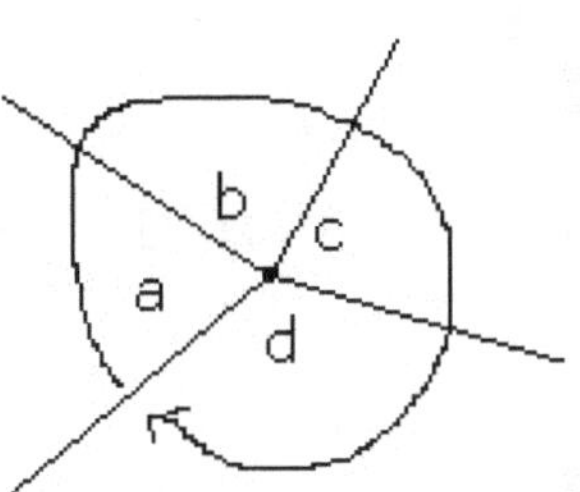

Find the missing angles and state the reason on how to find its size.

7.

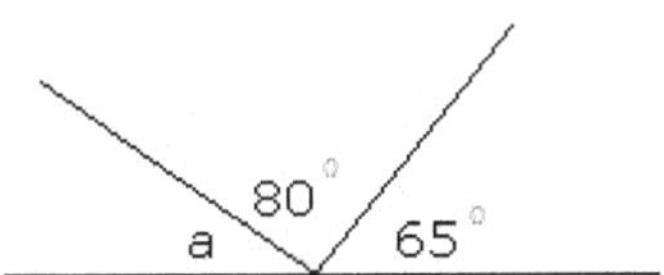

$\angle$ a = __________

Reason: ____________________

8.

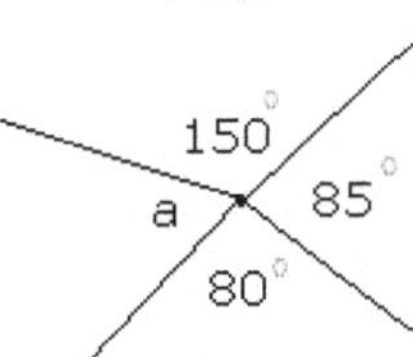

$\angle$ a = __________ Reason:

____

9.

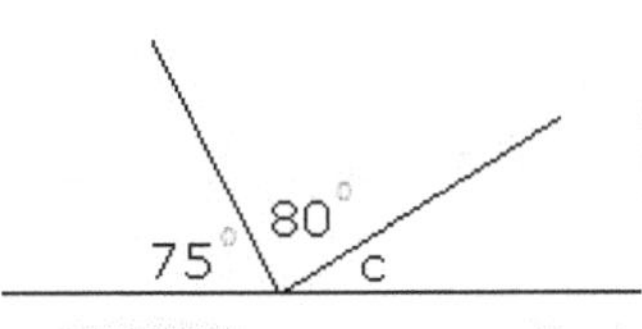

$\angle$ c = __________

Reason: ____________________

10.

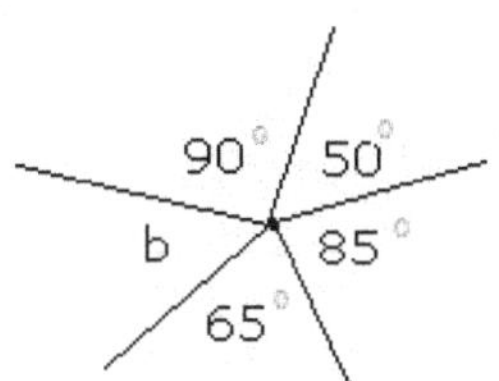

$\angle$ b = __________

Reason: ____________________

11.

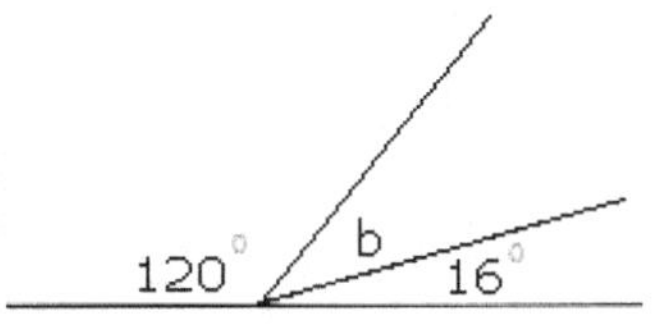

$\angle$ b = __________

Reason: ____________________

12.

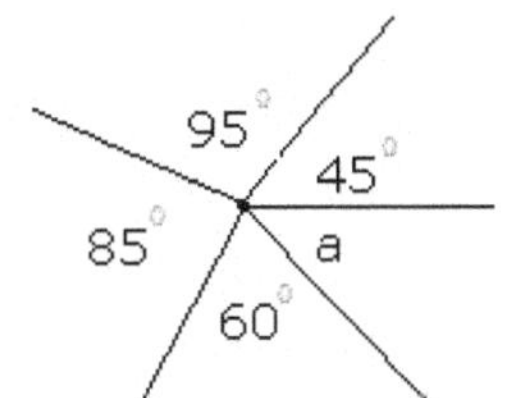

$\angle$ a = __________

Reason: ____________________

Student's name: ____________________ Assignment date: ________________

Opposite Angles

Opposite angles: are =. 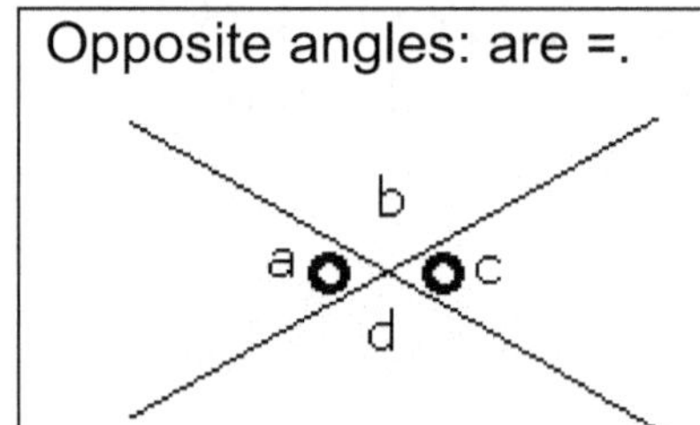	∠ a and ∠ c are opposite angles. ∠ b and ∠ d are opposite angles. We have: ∠ a = ∠ c, ∠ b = ∠ d

Find the missing angles and state the reason on how to find its size.

13.

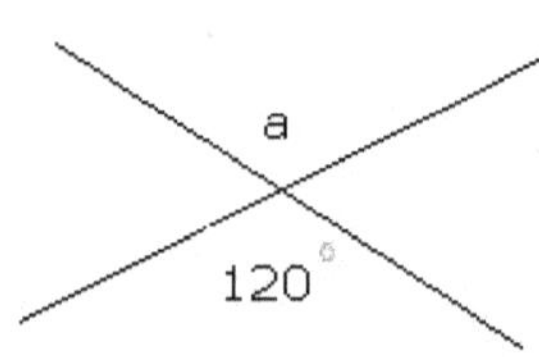

∠ a = __________

Reason: ____________________

14.

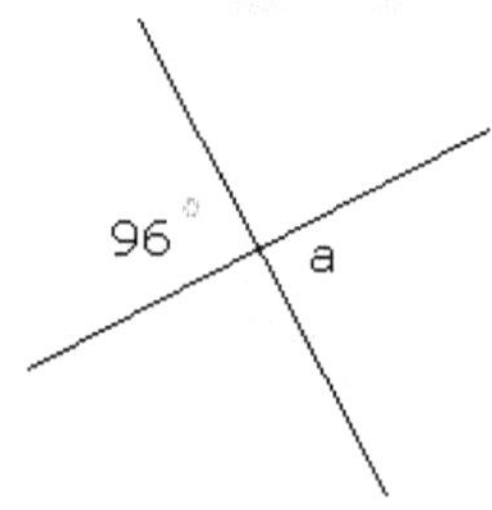

∠ a = __________

Reason: ____________________

15.

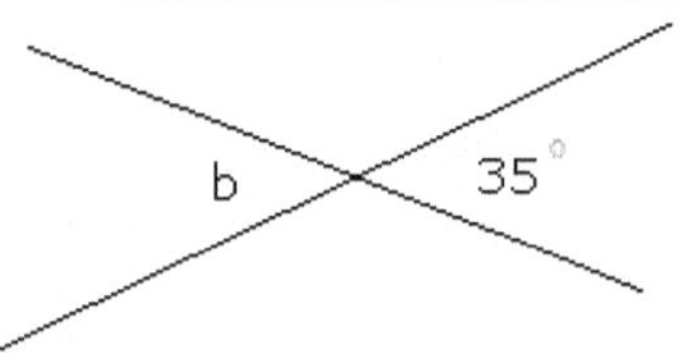

∠ b = __________

Reason: ____________________

16.

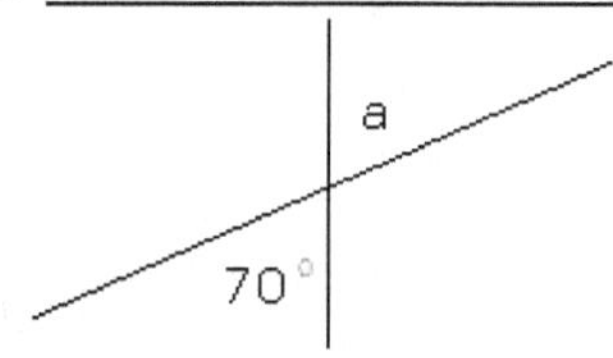

∠ a = __________

Reason: ____________________

17.

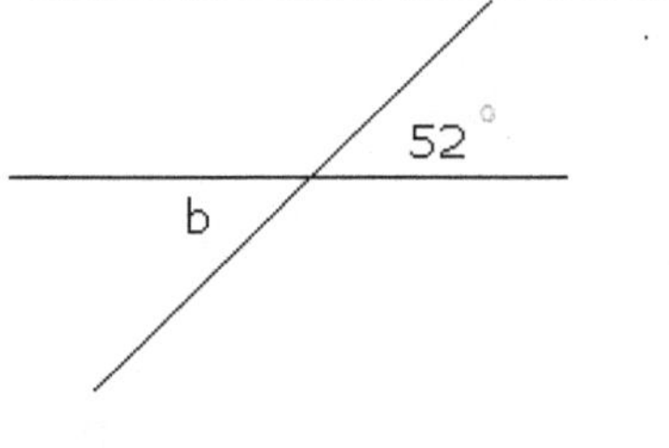

∠ b = __________

Reason: ____________________

18.

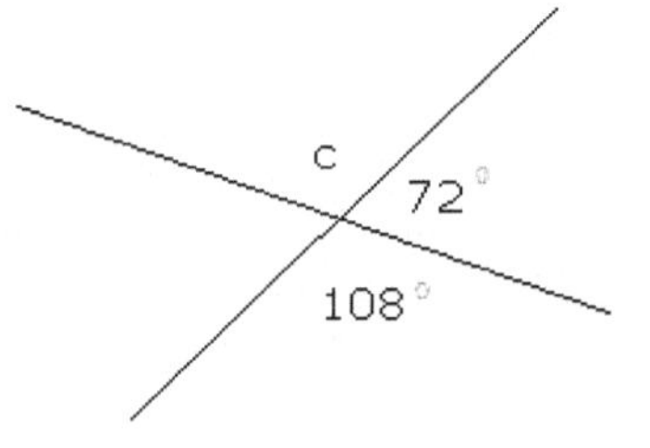

∠ c = __________

Reason: ____________________

Student's name: ____________________ Assignment date: ________________

Corresponding angles

Corresponding angles are =.	When AB // CD, then there are 4 pairs of corresponding angles. ∠ a and ∠ b are corresponding angles. ∠ c and ∠ d are corresponding angles. ∠ e and ∠ f are corresponding angles. ∠ g and ∠ h are corresponding angles. We have: ∠ a = ∠ b, ∠ c = ∠ d ∠ e = ∠ f, ∠ g = ∠ h
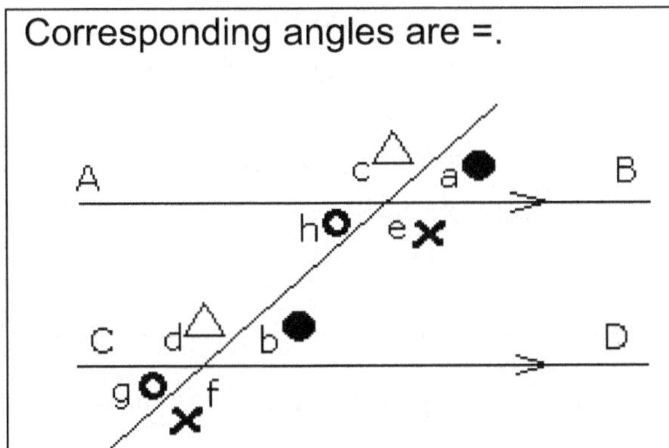	

Find the missing angles and state the reason on how to find its size.

19.

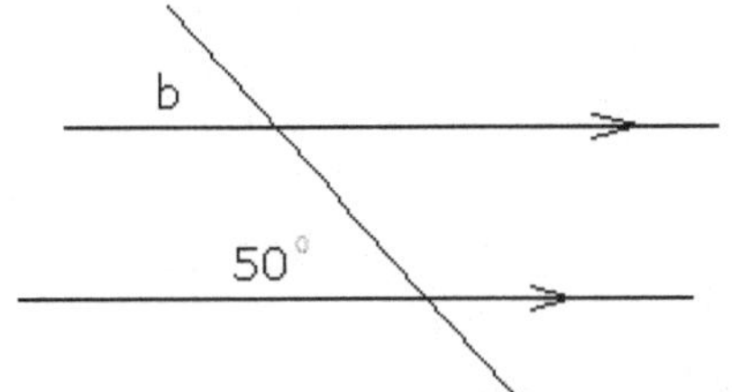

∠ b = __________

Reason: ____________________

20.

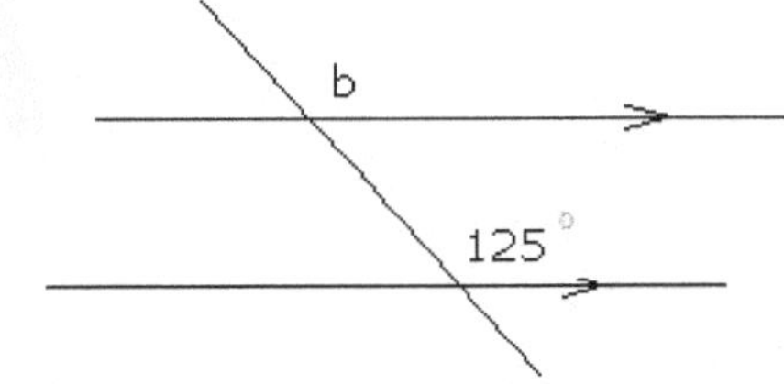

∠ b = __________

Reason: ____________________

21.

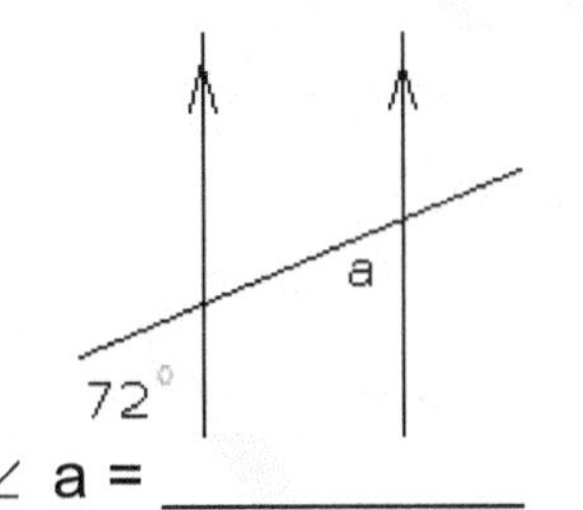

∠ a = __________

Reason: ____________________

22.

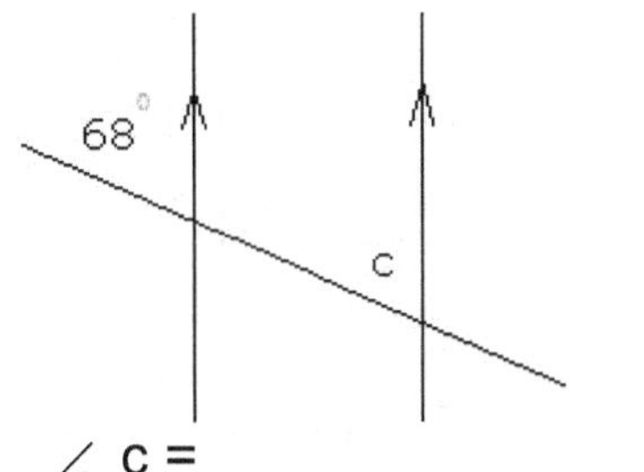

∠ c = __________

Reason: ____________________

23.

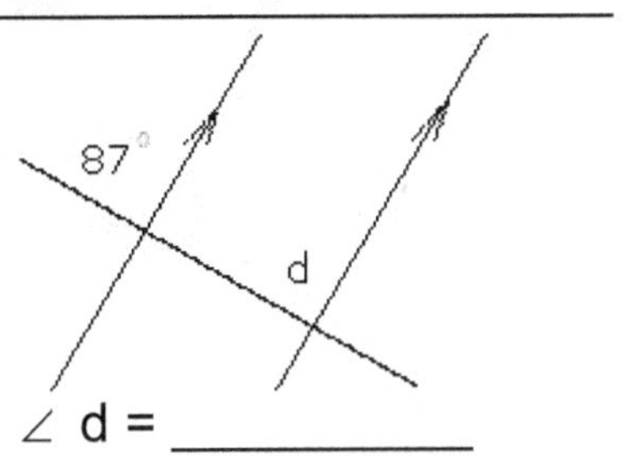

∠ d = __________

Reason: ____________________

24.

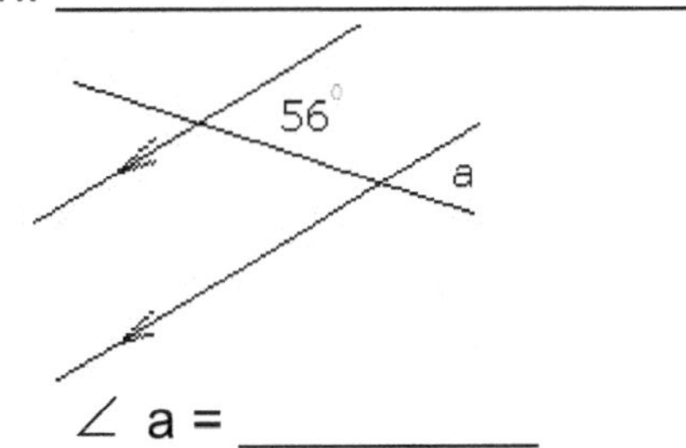

∠ a = __________

Reason: ____________________

Student's name: ____________________ Assignment date: ________________

Alternate Interior Angles

Alternate interior angles are =.	When AB // CD, then ∠a and ∠d are alternate interior angles. ∠b and ∠c are alternate interior angles. We have: ∠a = ∠d, ∠b = ∠c
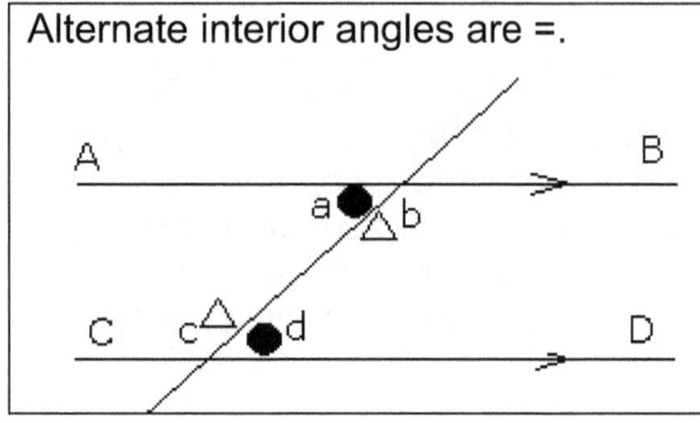	

Find the missing angles and state the reason on how to find its size.

25.

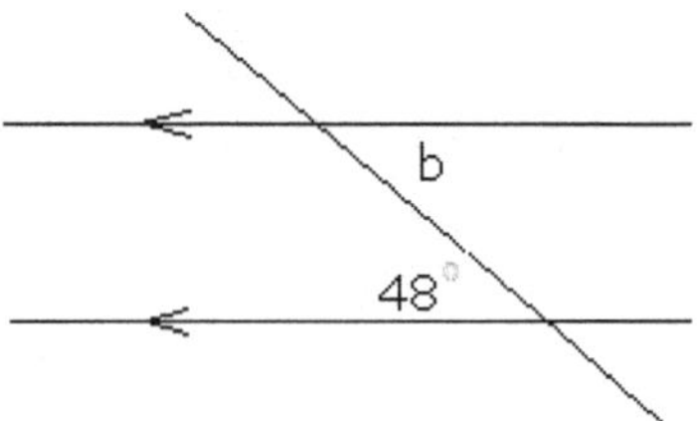

∠b = __________

Reason: ____________________

26.

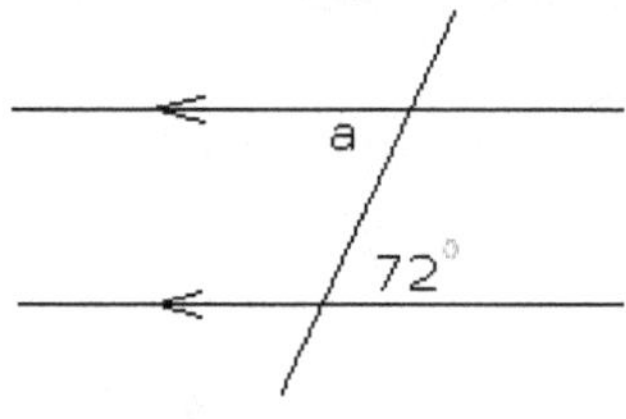

∠a = __________

Reason: ____________________

27.

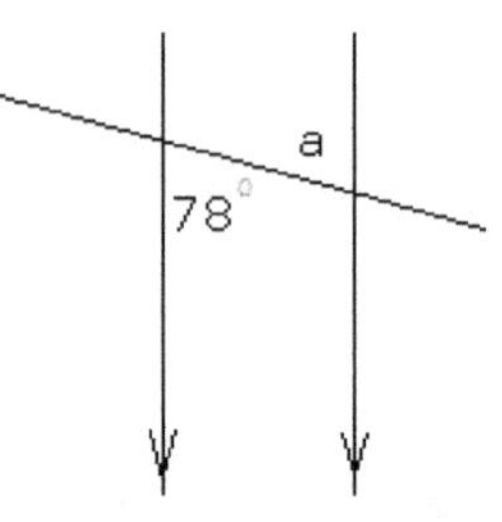

∠a = __________

Reason: ____________________

28.

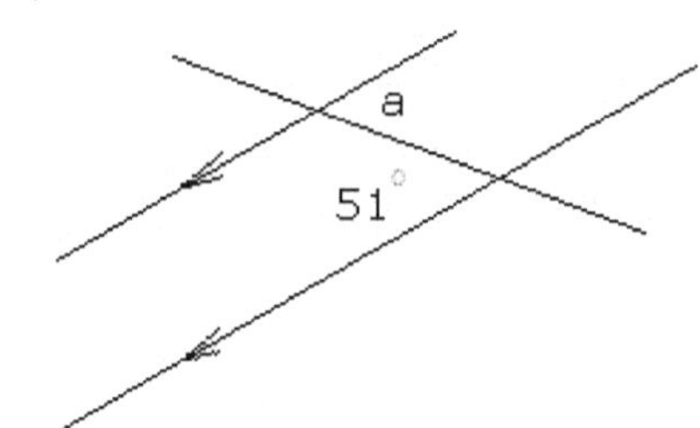

∠a = __________

Reason: ____________________

29.

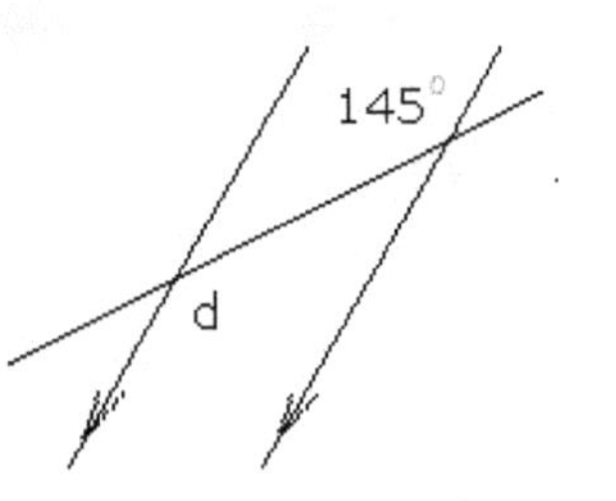

∠d = __________

Reason: ____________________

30.

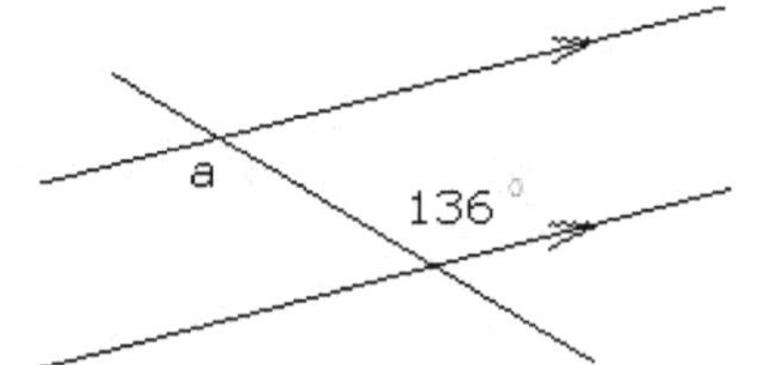

∠a = __________

Reason: ____________________

Student's name: ____________________ Assignment date: ________________

Co-interior Angles

Co-interior angles add up to 180^0.	When AB // CD, then
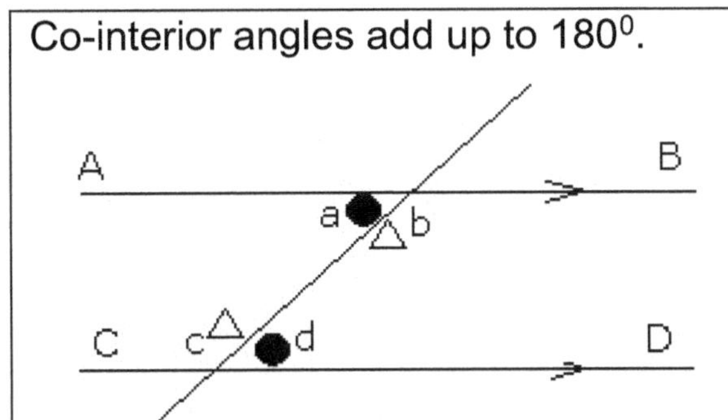	∠ a and ∠ c are co-interior angles. ∠ b and ∠ d are co-interior angles. We have: ∠ a + ∠ c = 180^0 ∠ b + ∠ d = 180^0

Find the missing angles and state the reason on how to find its size.

31.

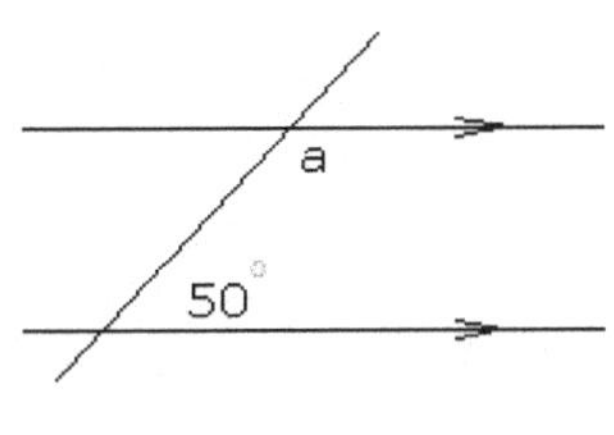

∠ a = __________

Reason: ____________________

32.

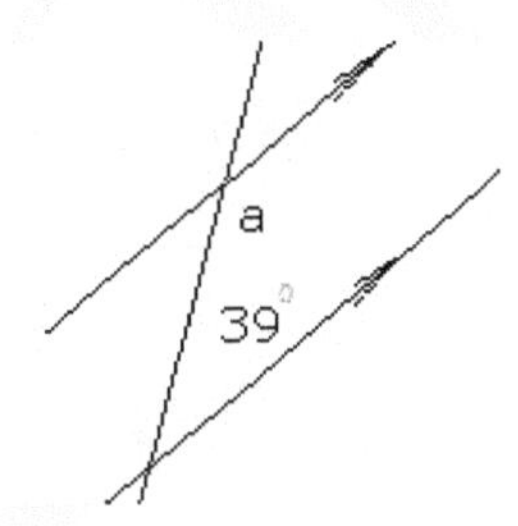

∠ a = __________

Reason: ____________________

33.

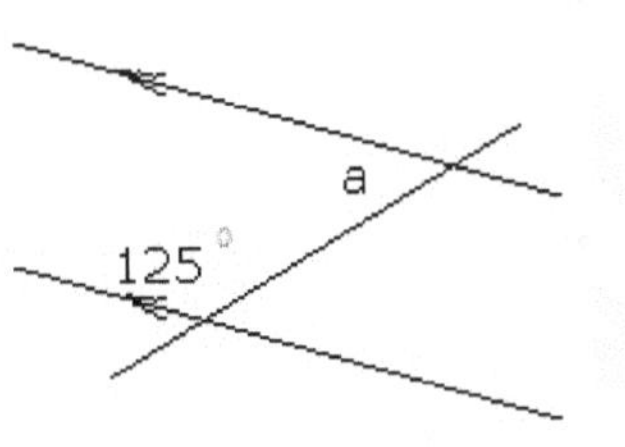

∠ a = __________

Reason: ____________________

34.

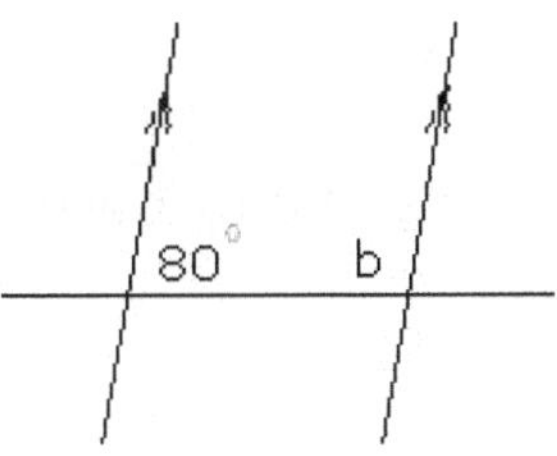

∠ b = __________

Reason: ____________________

35.

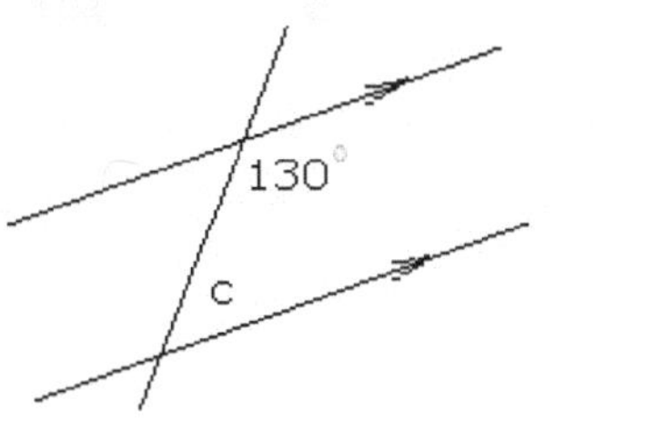

∠ c = __________

Reason: ____________________

36.

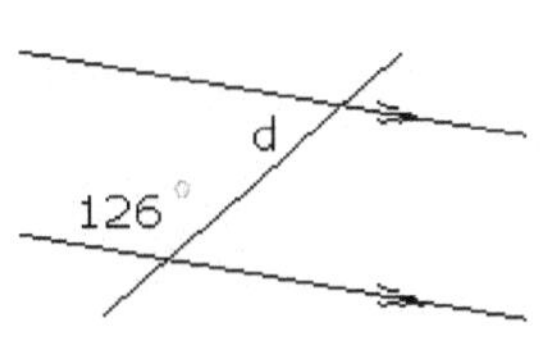

∠ d = __________

Reason: ____________________

Student's name: ____________________ Assignment date: ________________

Test of geometry

What is the perimeter of the following square? The diameter of the circle is 7 cm. 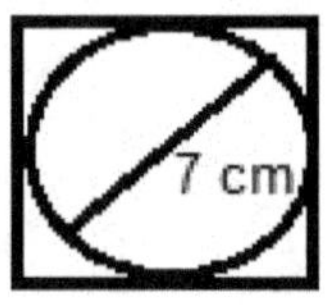
The perimeter of a rectangle is 48 cm, and its length is 14 cm. What is the length of its width?
Two sides of an equilateral triangle are $x - 1$ and $13 - x$, what is the value of x?
A rectangular shape has an area of 24 cm^2 with an odd number of width value. What could be its dimensions?
The two sides of an equilateral triangle have lengths of $x + 3$ and $19 - x$. What is the value of x?
Find the perimeter of the following figure. All measures are approximate and are in cm. 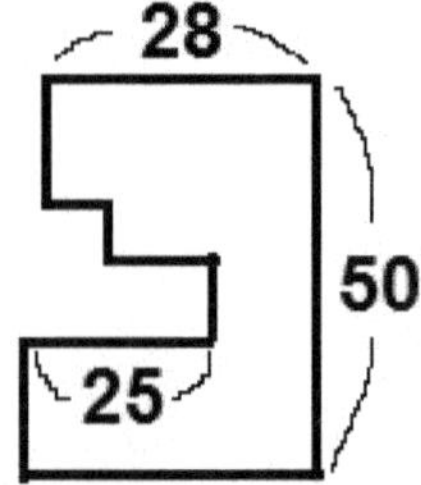

Student's name: ____________________ Assignment date: ________________

Calculate the perimeter of the following figures. 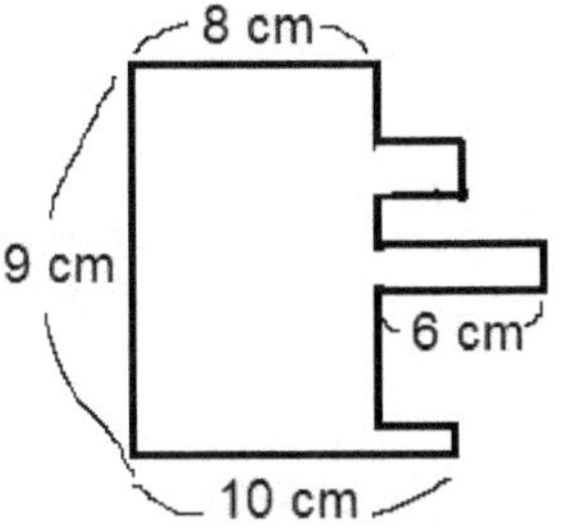
How many different rectangles can be made using exactly 24 square tiles placed side by side?

Student's name: ____________________ Assignment date: ________________

Transformation

Slide (translate)

Horizontal slide

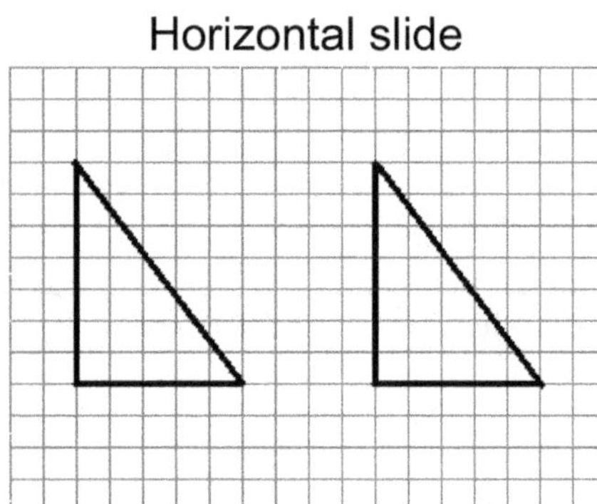

Vertical slide

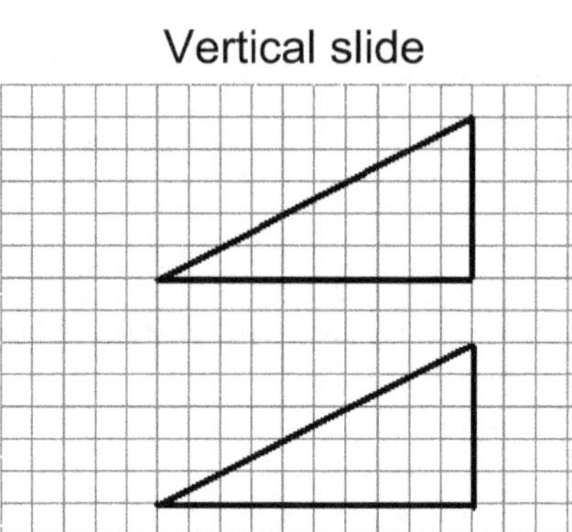

Diagonal slide

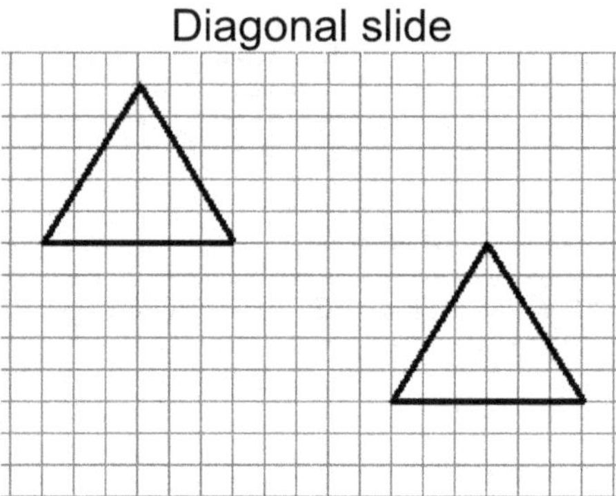

Indicate whether each slide a horizontal, a vertical, or a diagonal slide.

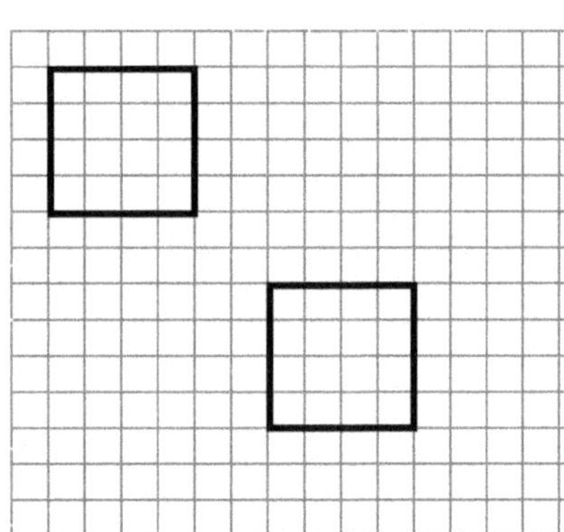

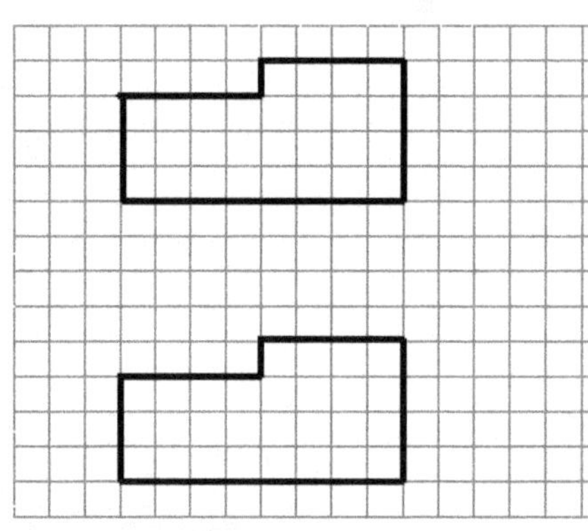

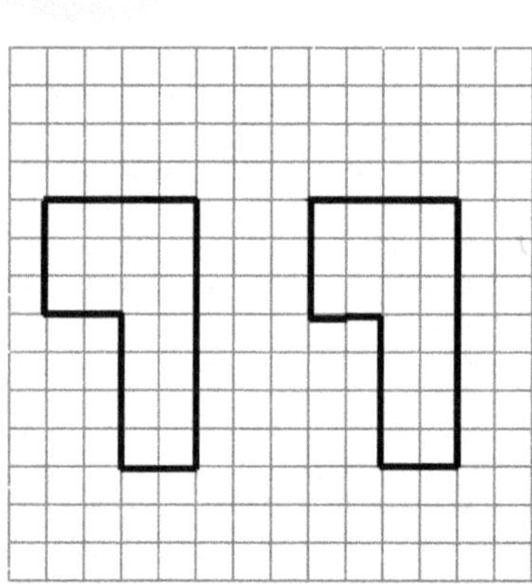

_________________ _________________ _________________

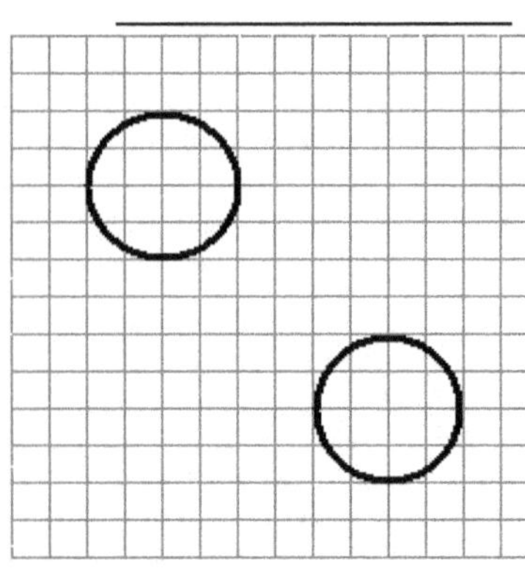

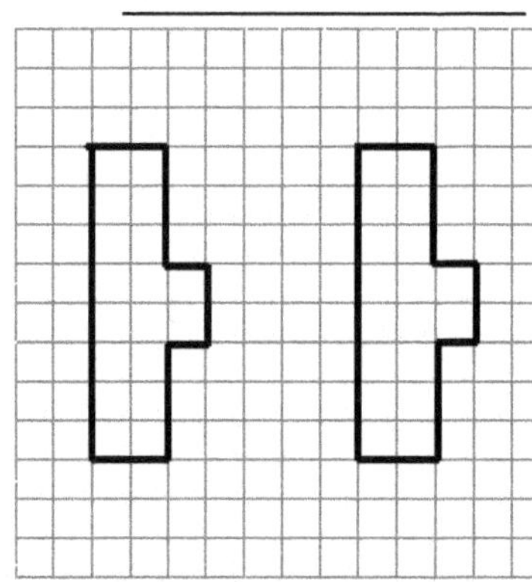

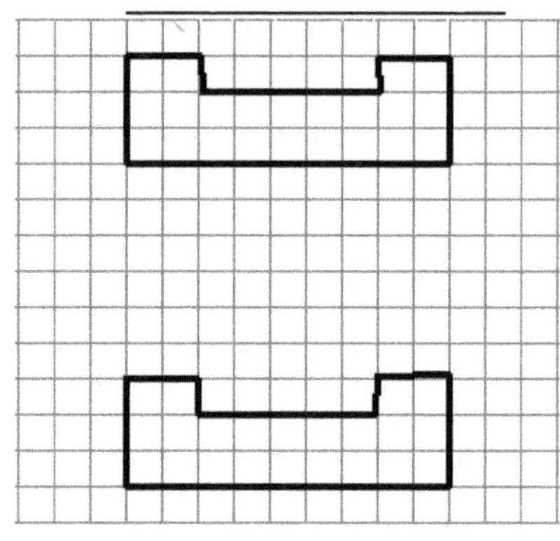

_________________ _________________ _________________

Student's name: ____________________ Assignment date: ________________

Turn (rotate)

Point C is the turn centre, figure A is turned from A to B,

A quarter-turn clockwise or a three-quarter turn counter clockwise	Half turn	Three-quarter turn clockwise or a quarter turn counter-clockwise

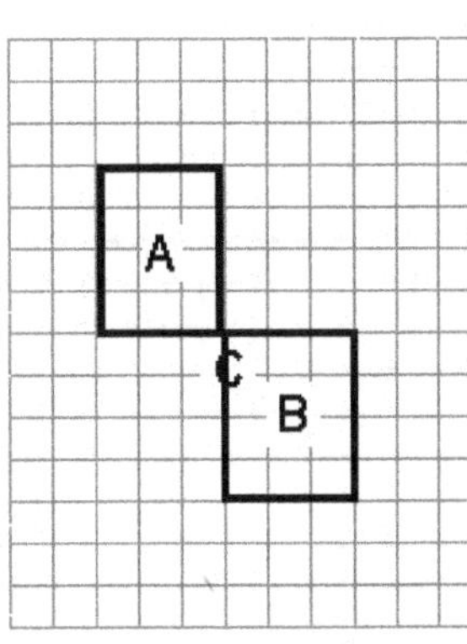

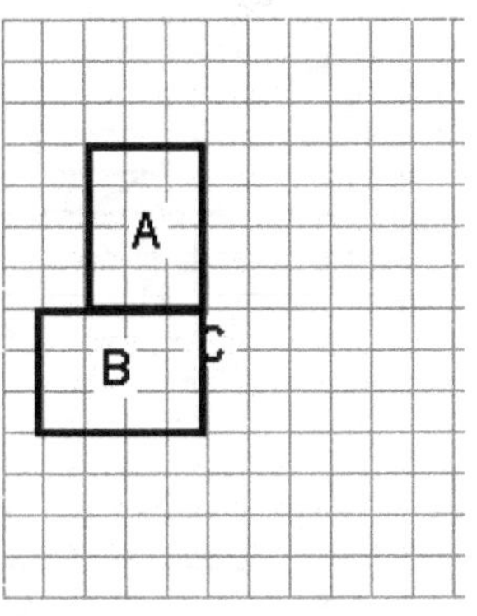

Each figure turned from A to B indicates whether each turn is a quarter-turn clockwise, half turn or a three quarter turn clockwise about point O.

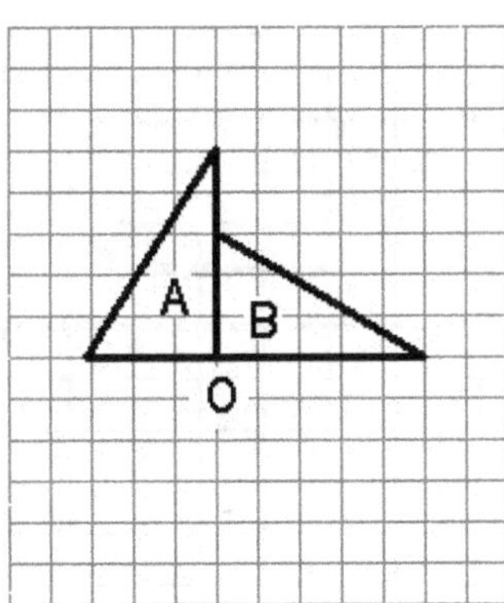

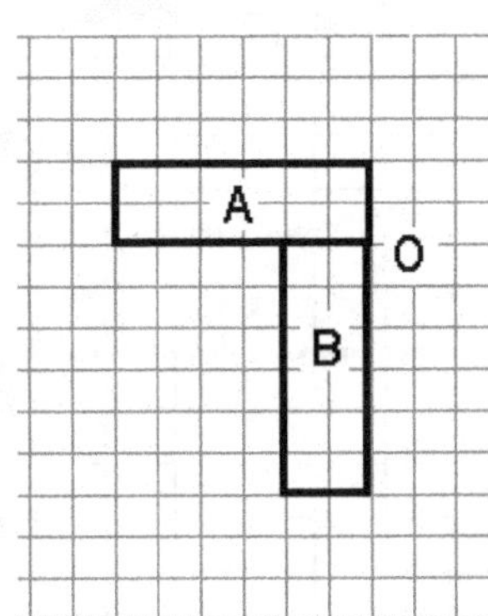

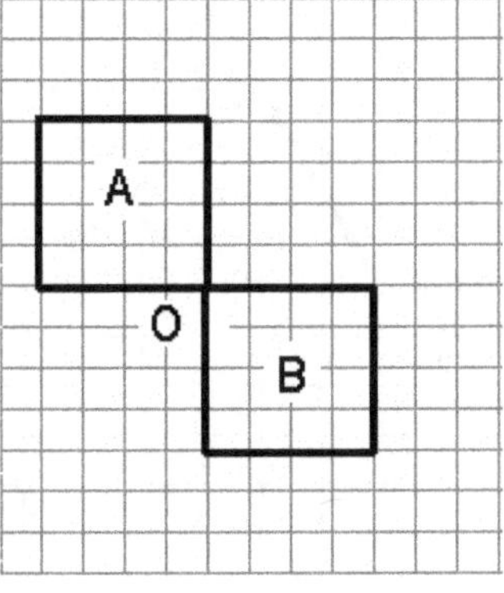

____________ ____________ ____________

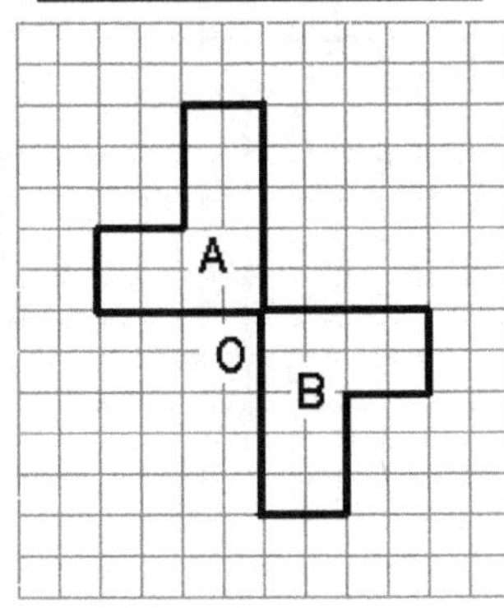

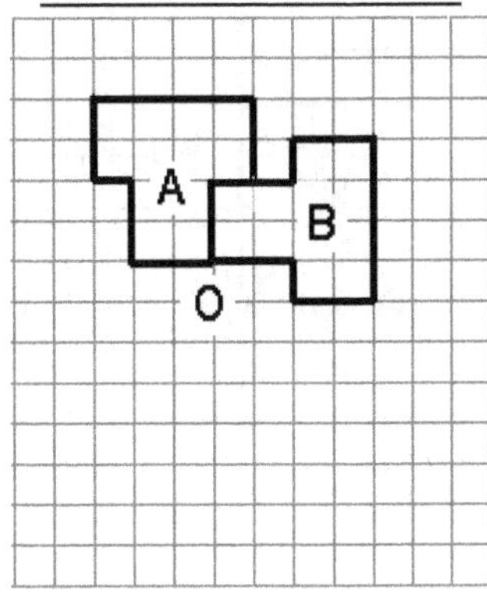

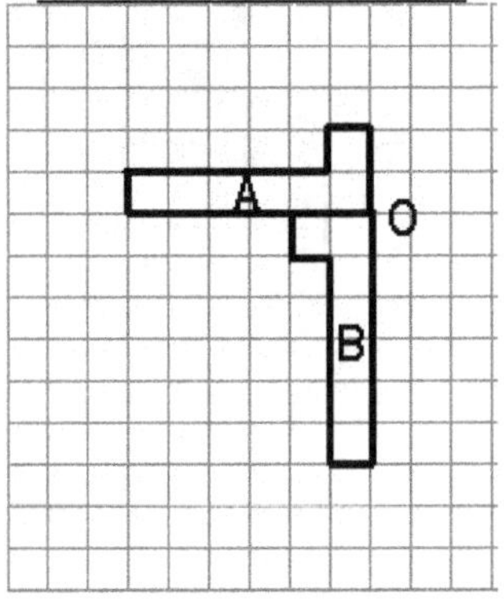

____________ ____________ ____________

Student's name: ____________________ Assignment date: ________________

Flip (reflect)

Finish the symmetric shapes below using the straight-line (mirror line) as lines of symmetry. Each vertex (corner) of the original figure flips to the opposite side with the same distance from the line to form an image.

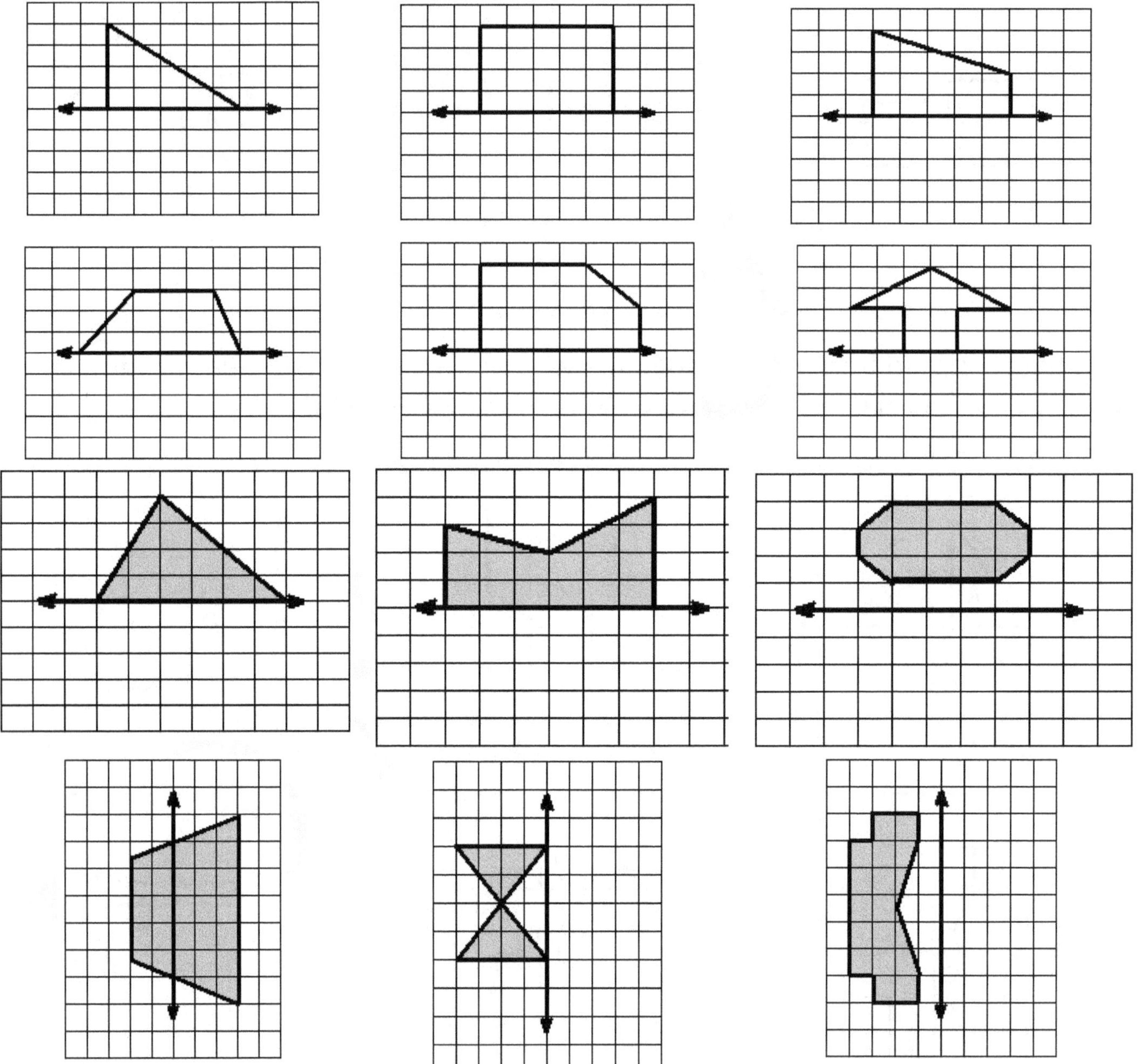

Student's name: ____________________ Assignment date: ________________

Symmetry line

Find the lines of symmetry for these drawings

Student's name: ____________________ Assignment date: ________________

Decide whether each figure is a slide, a turn, or a reflection of figure A.

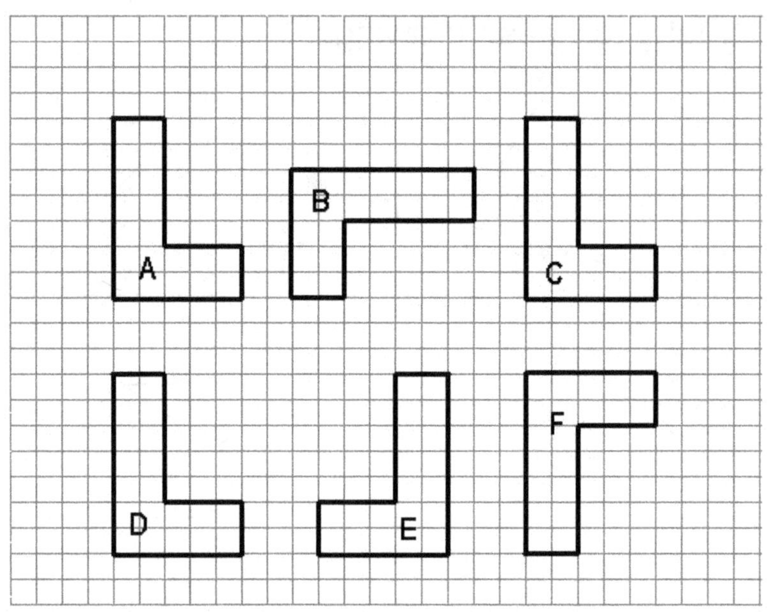

1. Figure B is a ____________________ of figure A.
2. Figure C is a ____________________ of figure A.
3. Figure D is a ____________________ of figure A.
4. Figure E is a ____________________ of figure A.
5. Figure F is a ____________________ of figure A.

Student's name: ____________________ Assignment date: ________________

Congruent Figures (figures with the same size and shape)

If figures have the same size and same shape, then these figures are congruent.
Example:

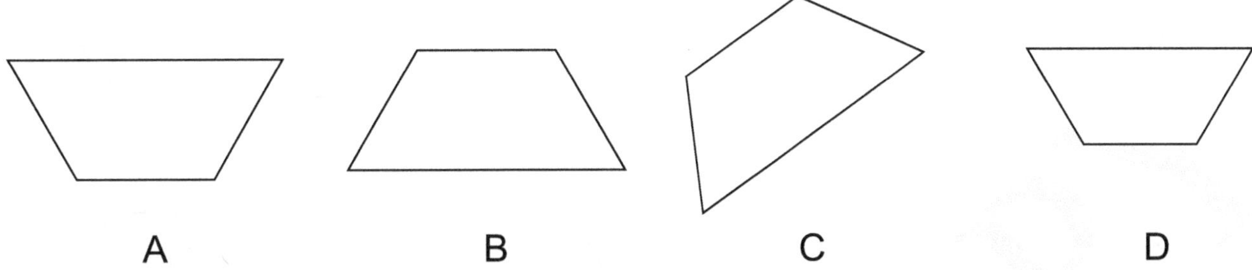

Figures A, B, and C are congruent because they have the same size and same shape.
Figure D is not congruent to A, B, or C, because they have different sizes.

Connect all the pairs of congruent figures.

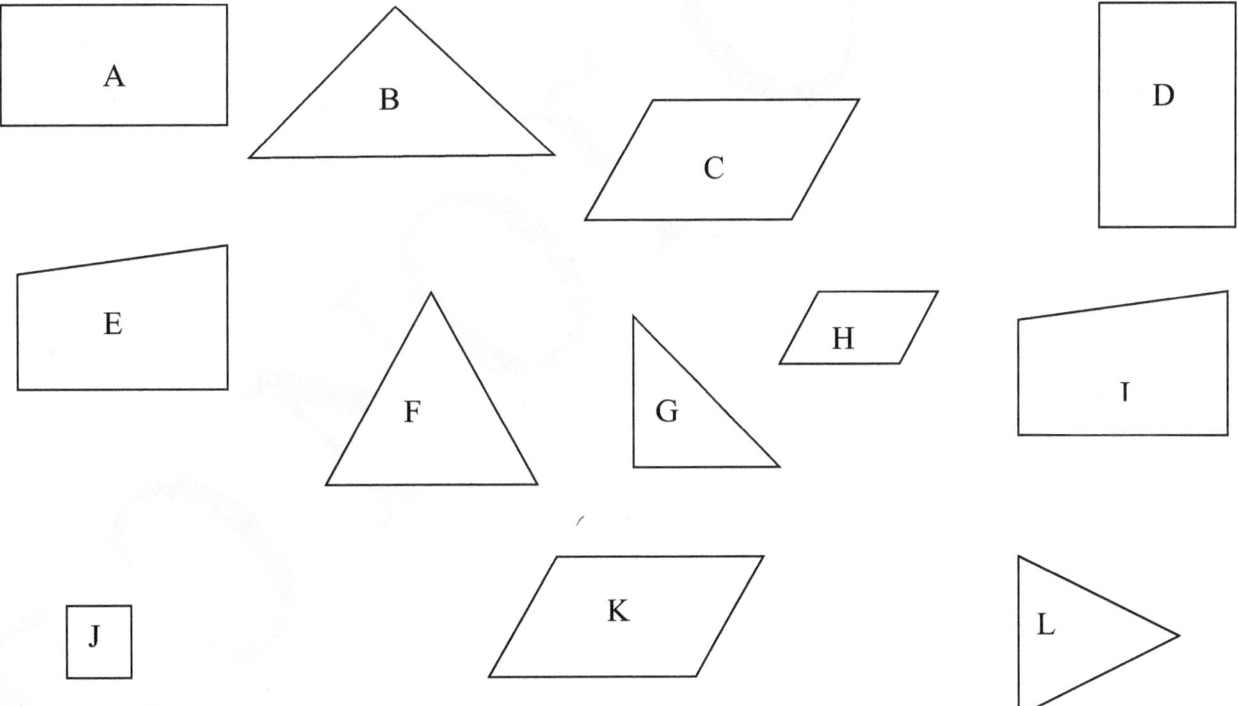

Student's name: ____________________ Assignment date: ________________

Divide the following figures into 2 congruent parts.

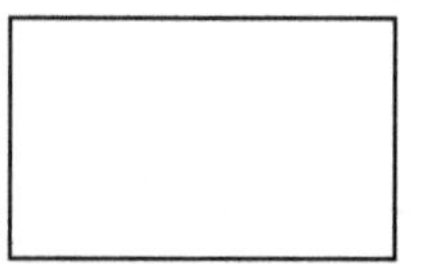
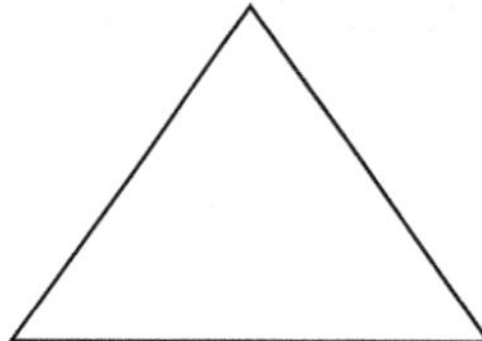
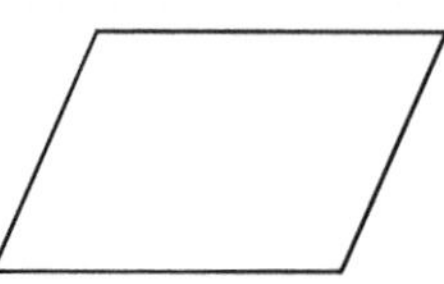
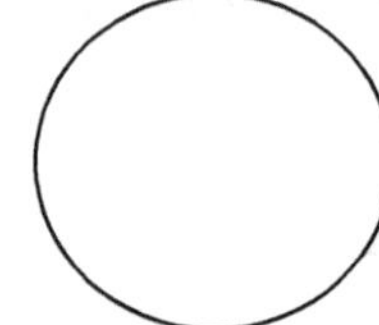

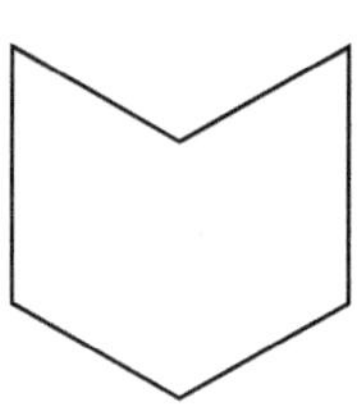
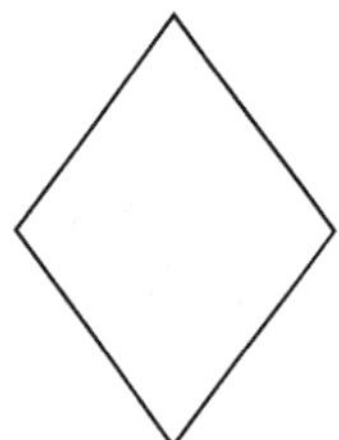
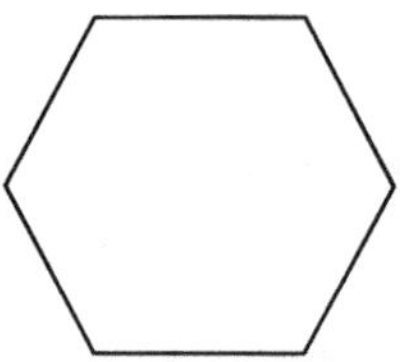
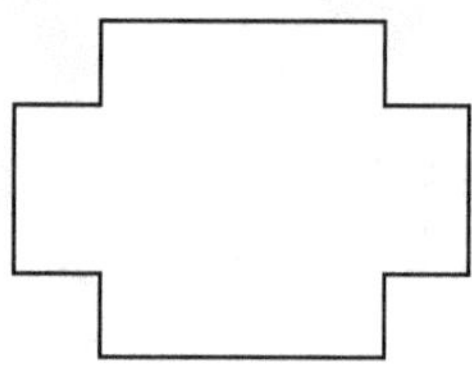

Divide the following figures into 4 congruent parts.

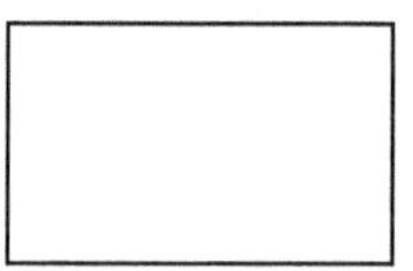
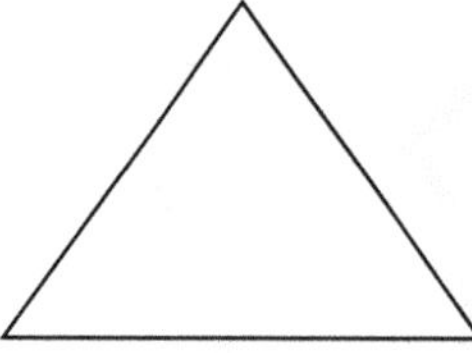
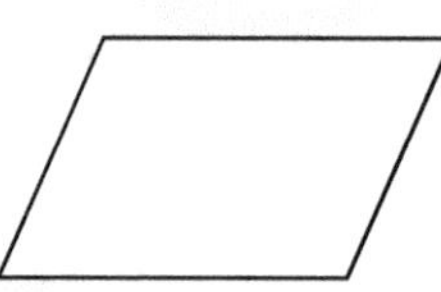
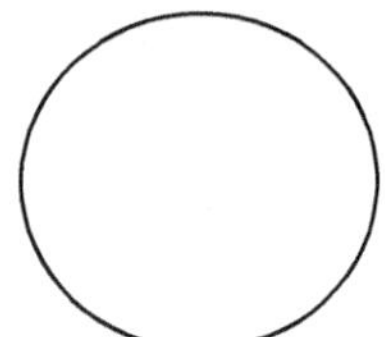

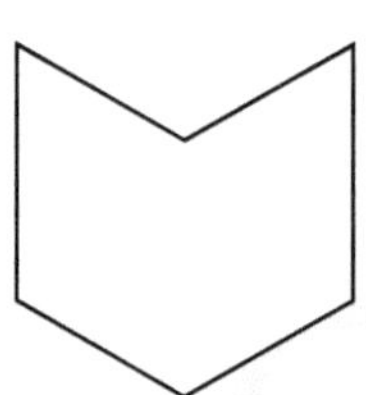
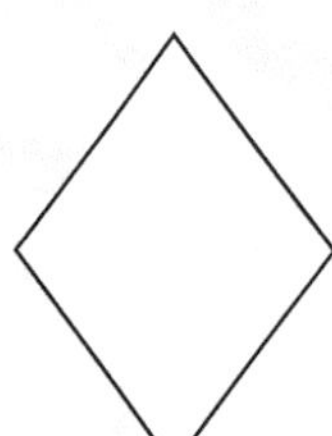
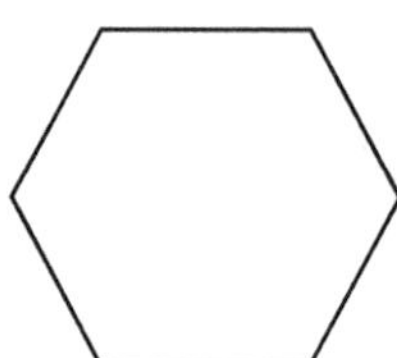
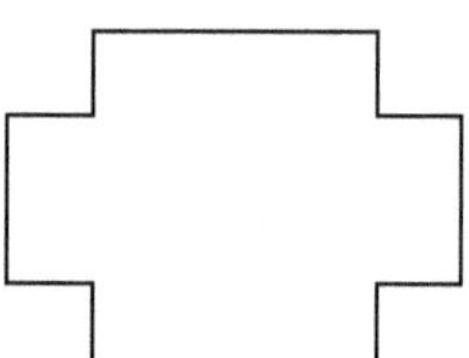

Student's name: ____________________ Assignment date: ________________

Find the figure that is congruent to the left.

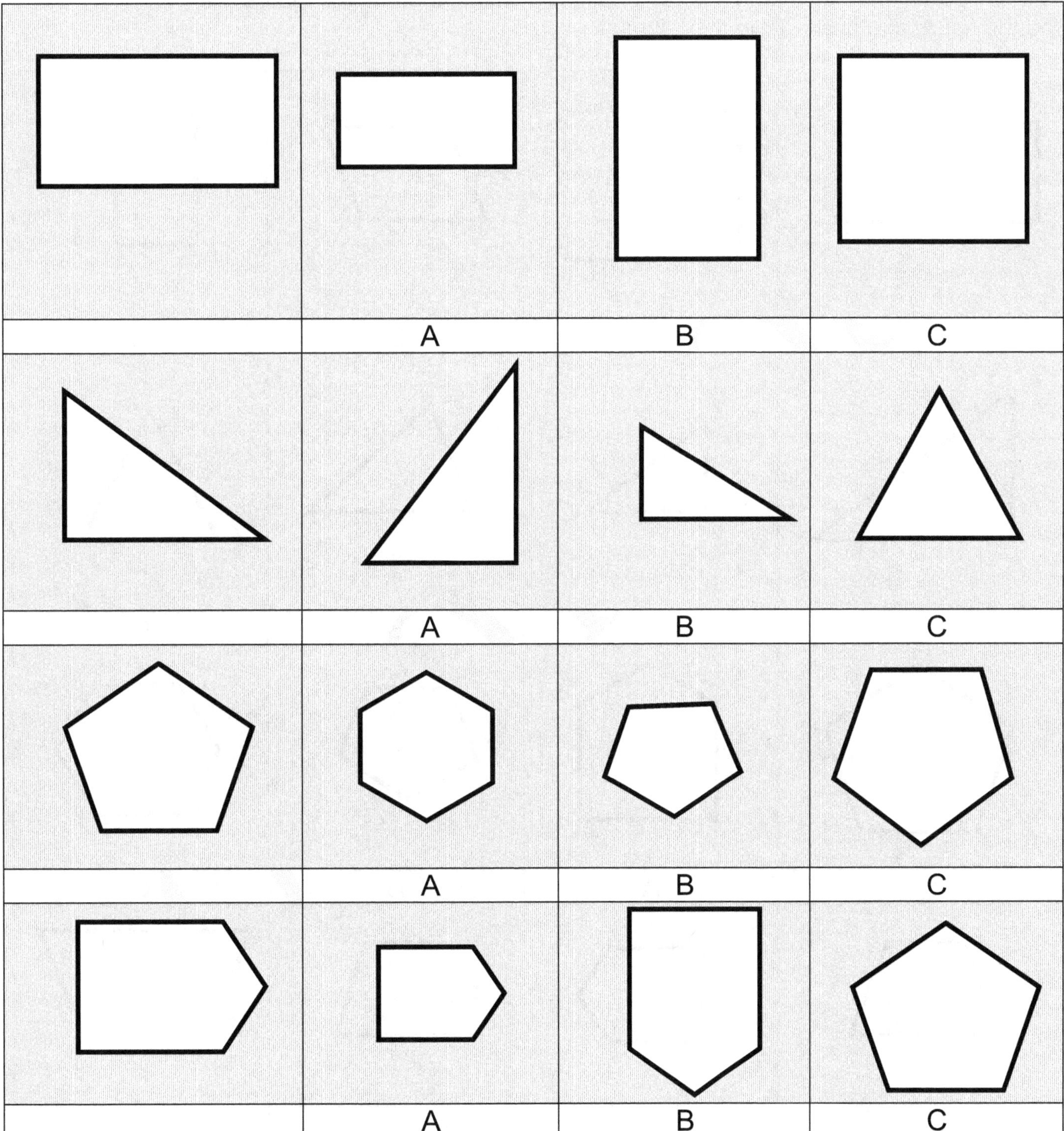

Student's name: ____________________ Assignment date: ________________

Similar Figures

If all the figures have the same shape but different sizes, then these figures are similar.
Find the figure that is similar to the leftmost.

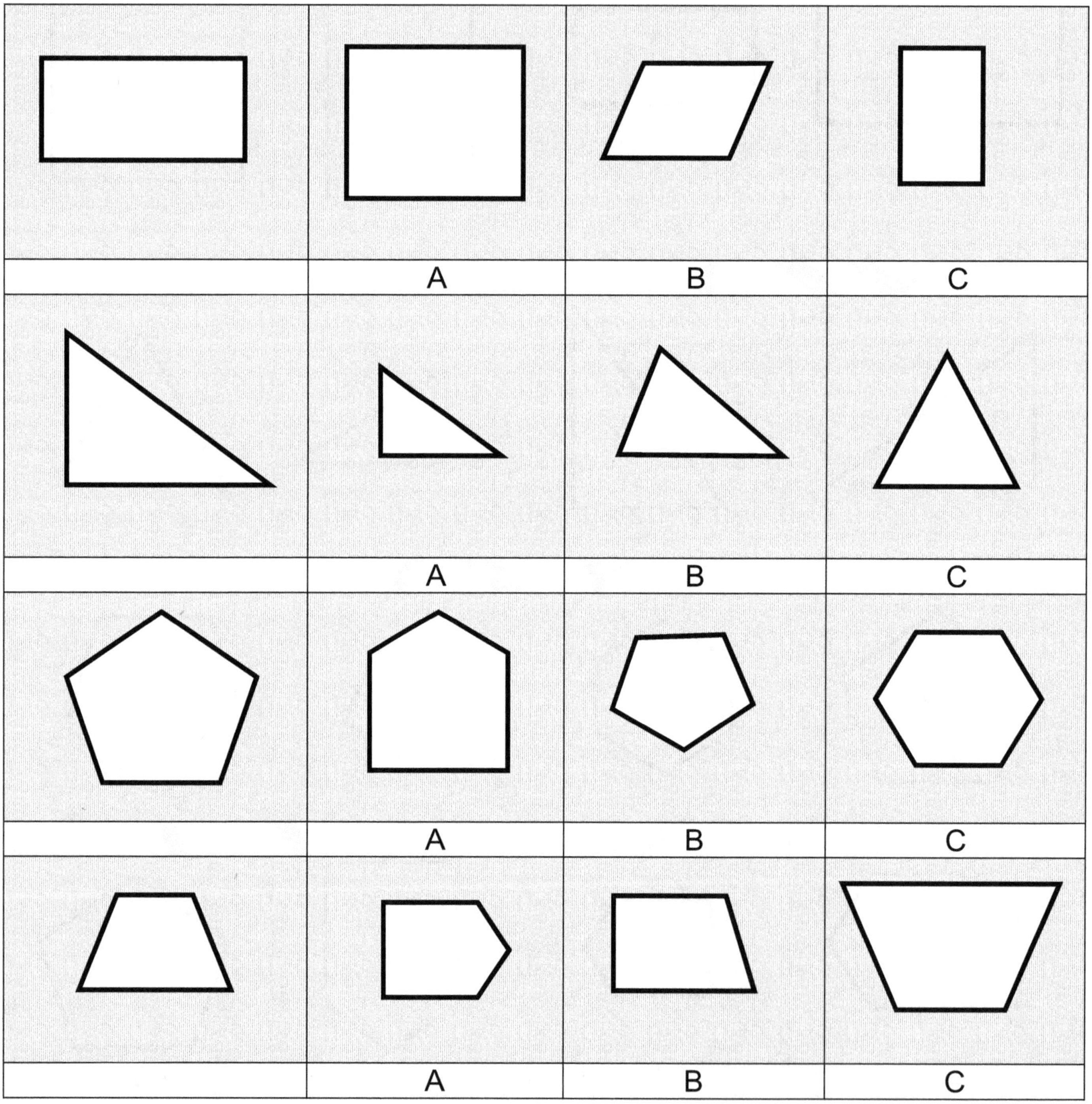

	A	B	C
	A	B	C
	A	B	C
	A	B	C

Student's name: ____________________ Assignment date: ________________

Identifying tessellations

A unit shape is a shape that can be repeated over and over to form a pattern. A unit shape can be a composite unit shape, which may consist of two or more basic shapes such as a triangle and a square.

When a unit shape is drawn repeatedly without any gaps between them or any overlaps between them, then the pattern is called tessellation.

Circle the unit shape of the following figures and then complete 3 more patterned unit shapes on the grid.

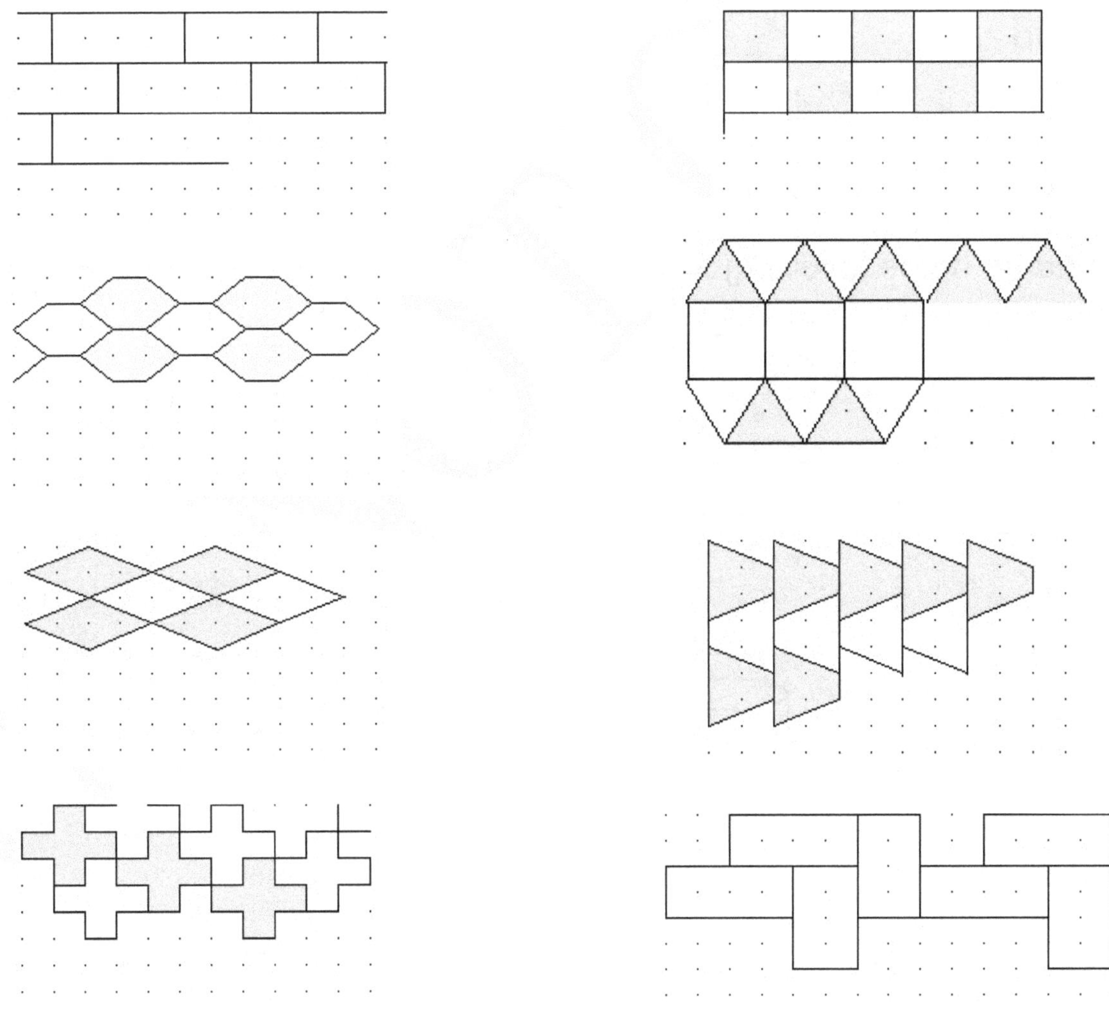

Student's name: ____________________ Assignment date: ________________

Solids

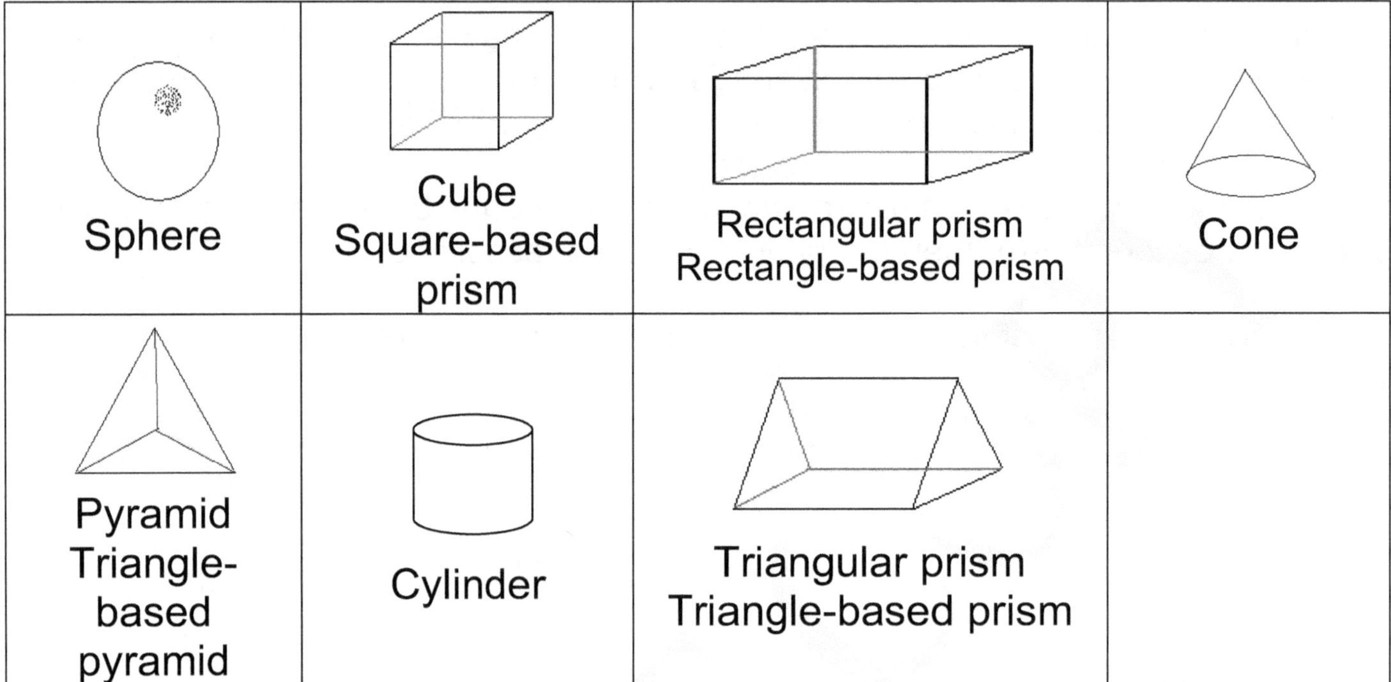

Write the name of the following solids.

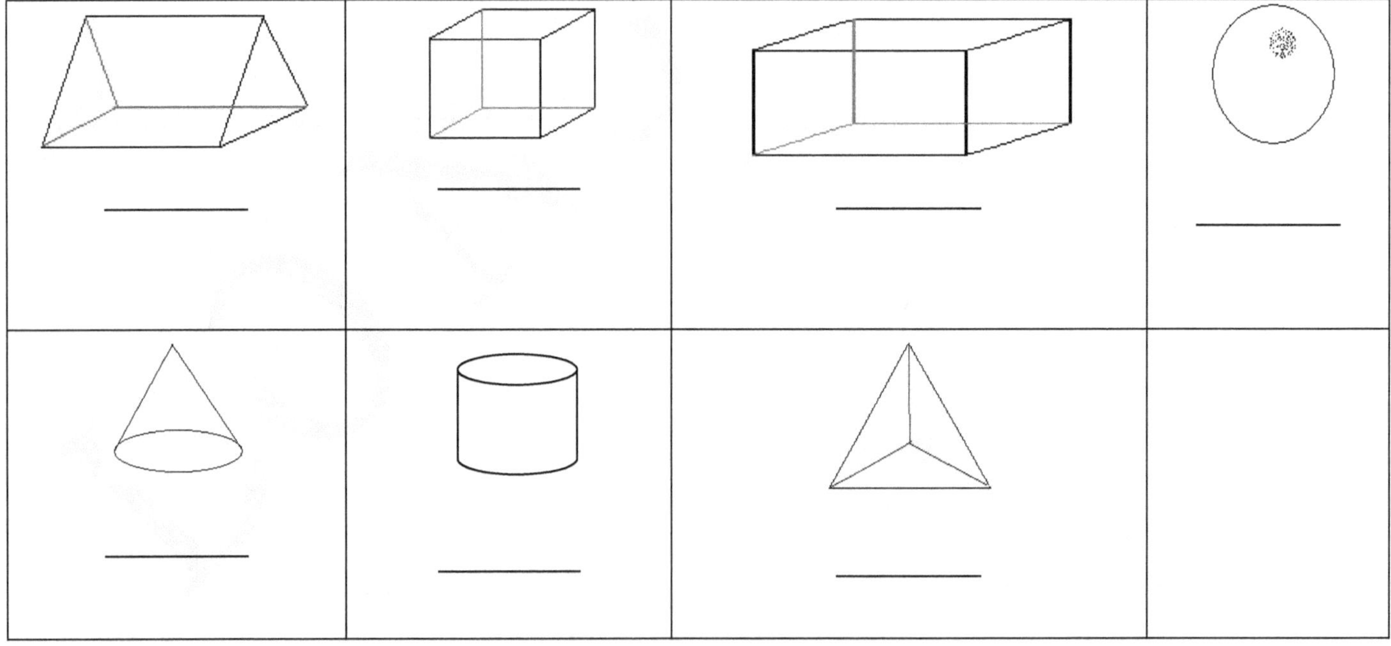

Ho Math Chess Primary Grades Math

Test Review assesssment 何数棋謎低年级数学测试複習考核

Student's name: ____________________ Assignment date: _______________

Pyramids or Prisms

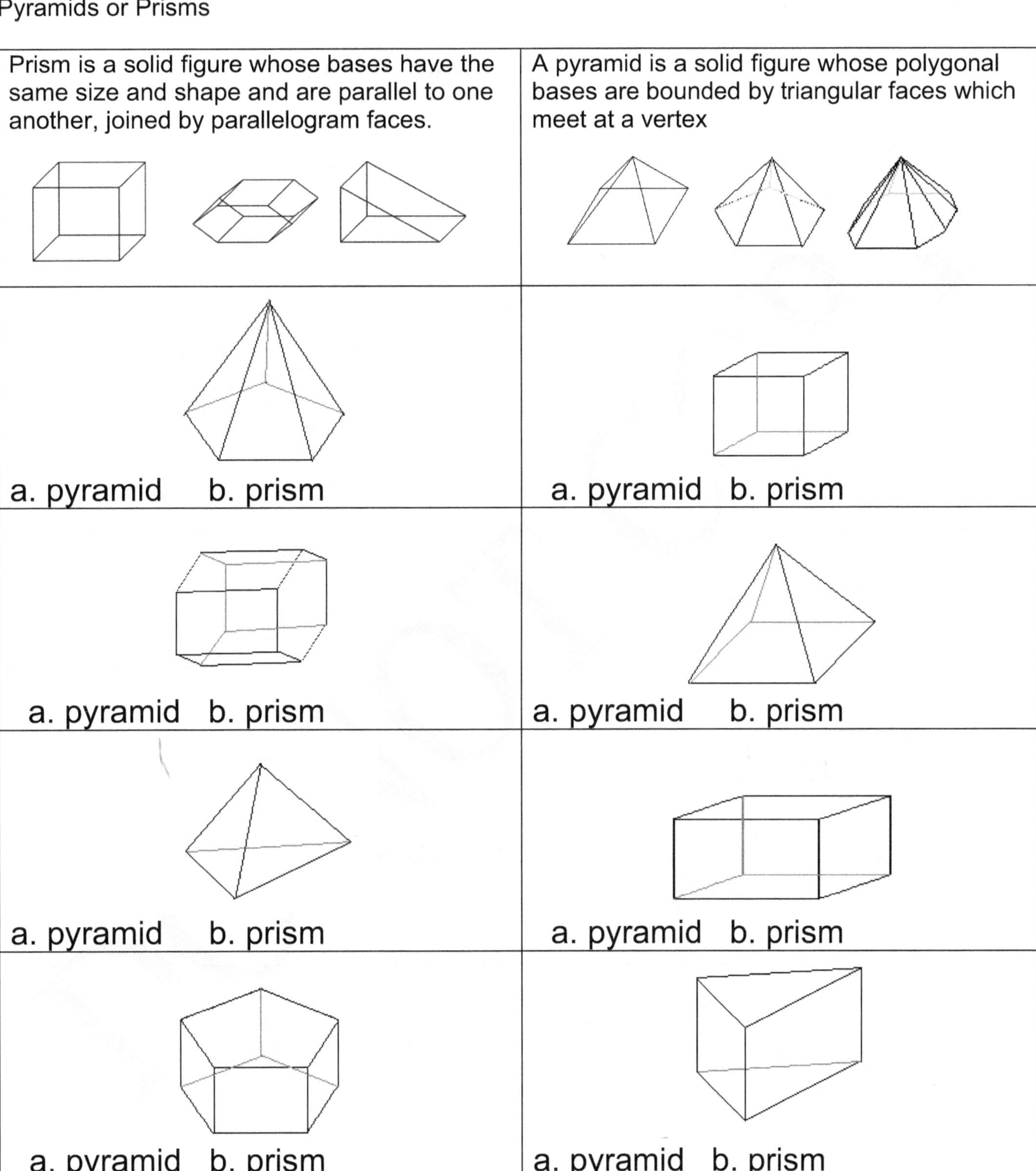

Student's name: ____________________ Assignment date: ________________

Matching left to the right

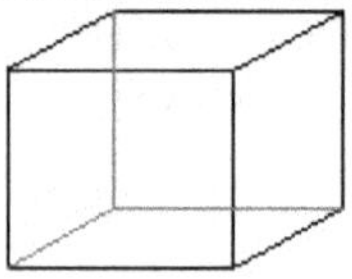	Triangular Prism
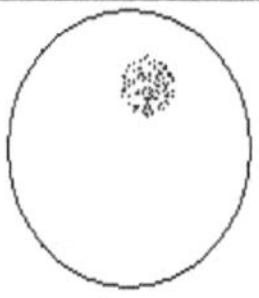	Pyramid
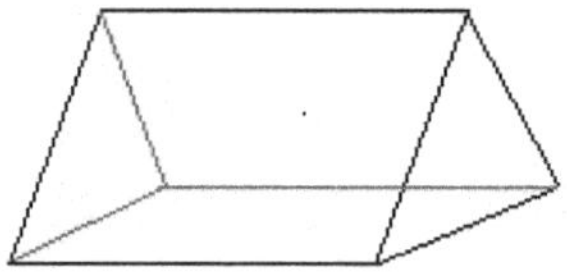	Cube
	Rectangular prism
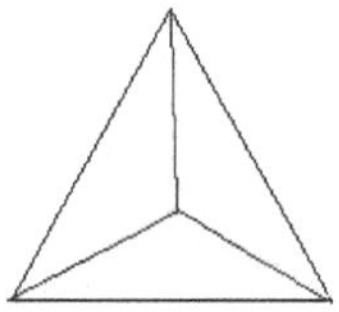	Cone
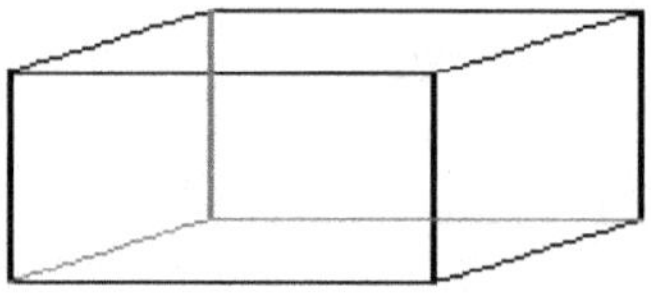	Sphere
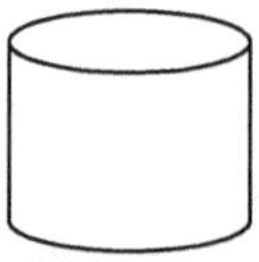	Cylinder

Student's name: ____________________ Assignment date: ________________

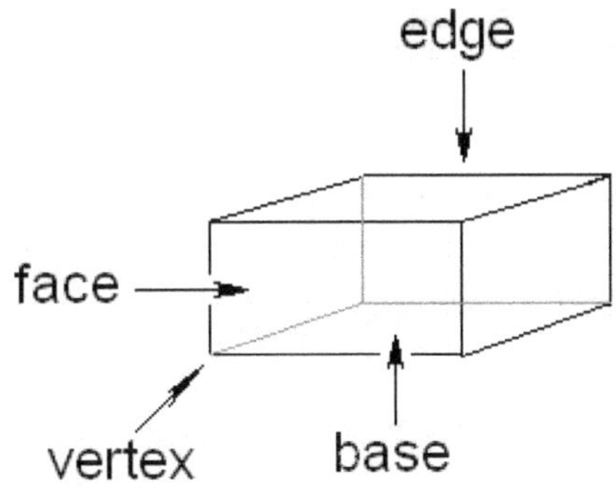

Complete the following chart.

Shape	Name	Number of faces	Number of edges	Number of vertices
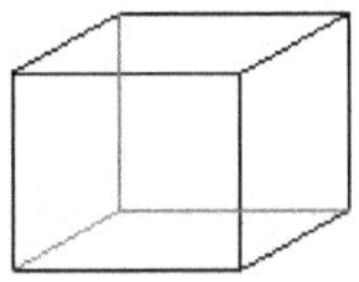				
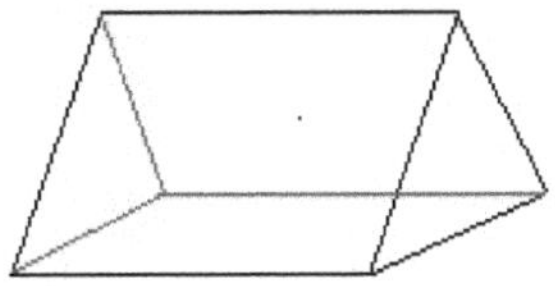				
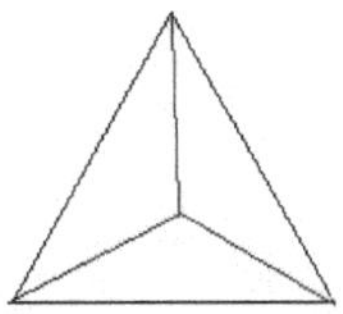				
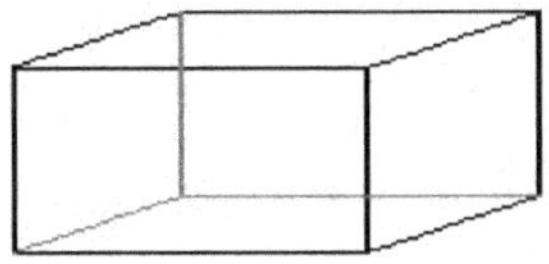				
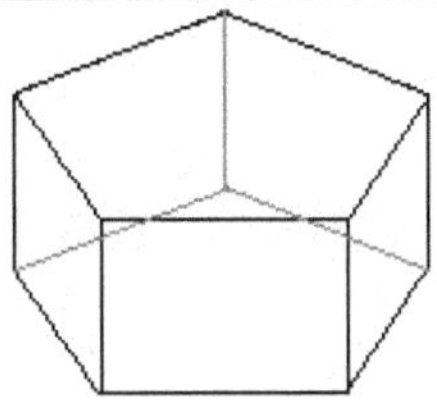				

Student's name: ____________________ Assignment date: ________________

Matching solids with their tracing faces.

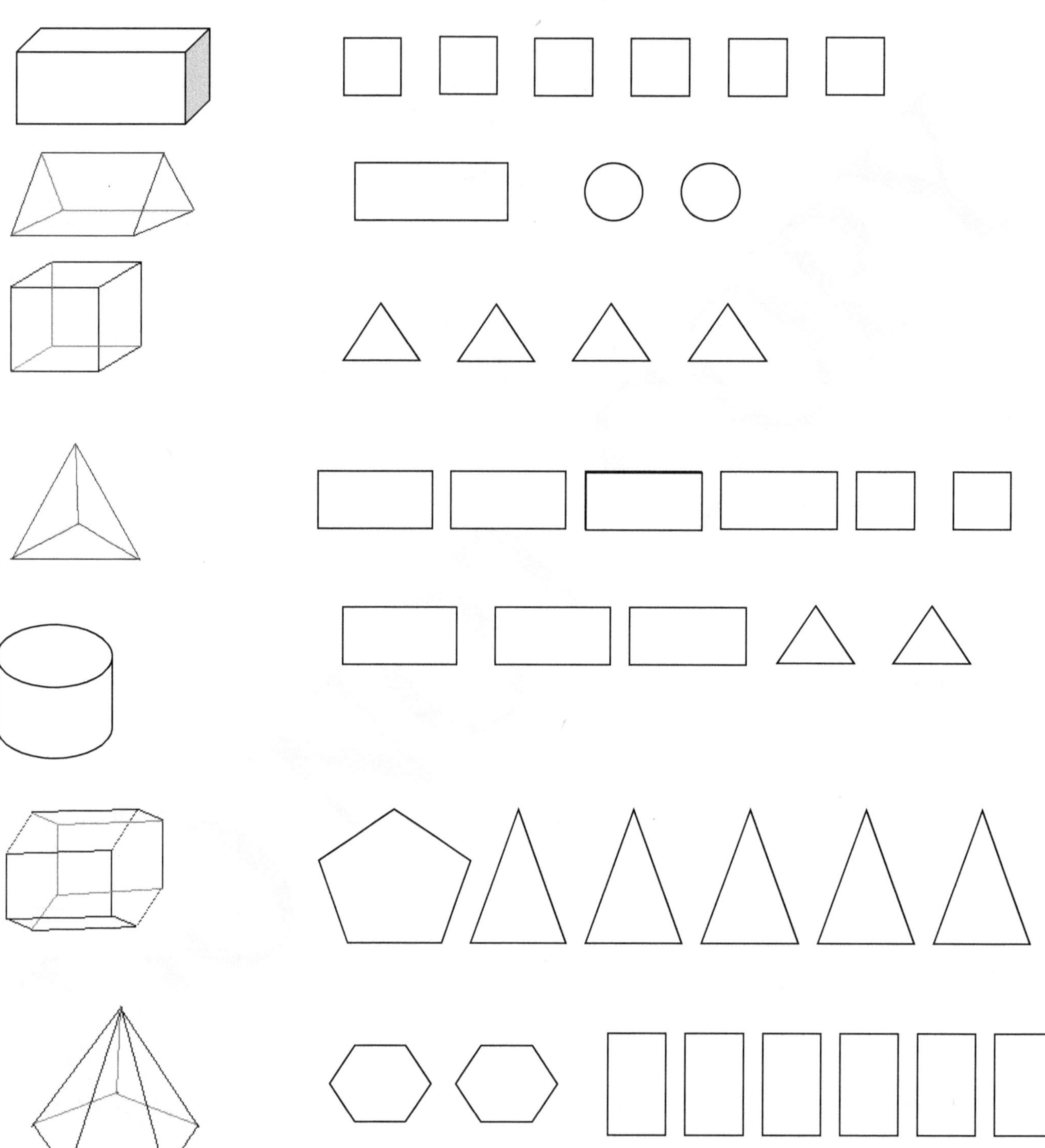

Student's name: ____________________ Assignment date: ________________

Faces of Solids

1. 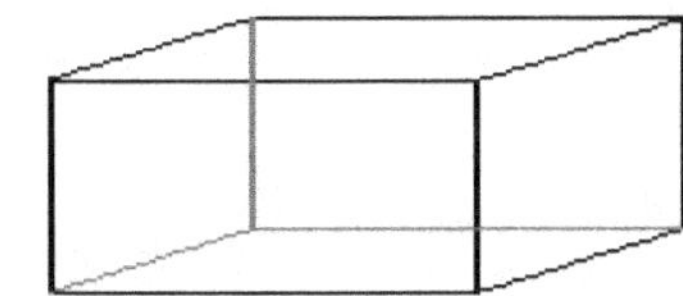

6 rectangular faces

2. 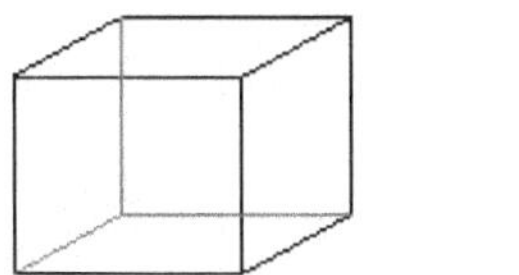

6 ______________ faces

3. 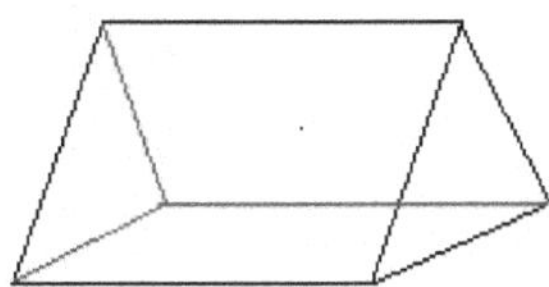

____ triangular faces and 3 ____________ faces

4. 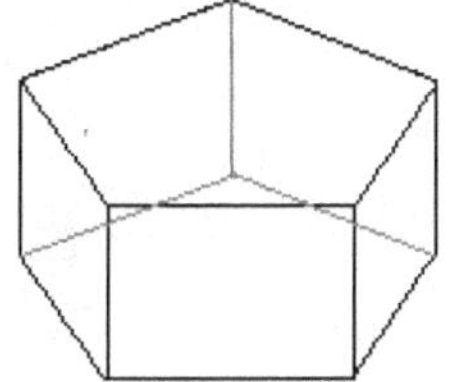

____ pentagonal faces and 5 ____________ faces

5. 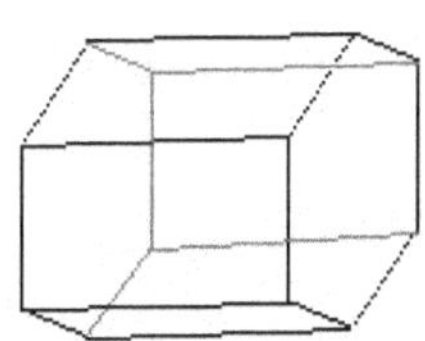

____ hexagonal faces and 6 ____________ faces

6. 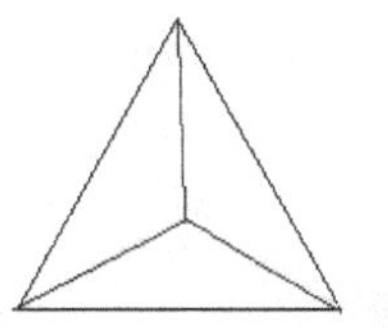

4 ____________ faces

7. 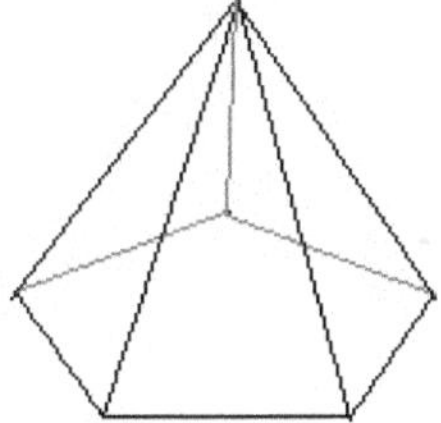

____ triangular faces and 1 ____________ face

8. 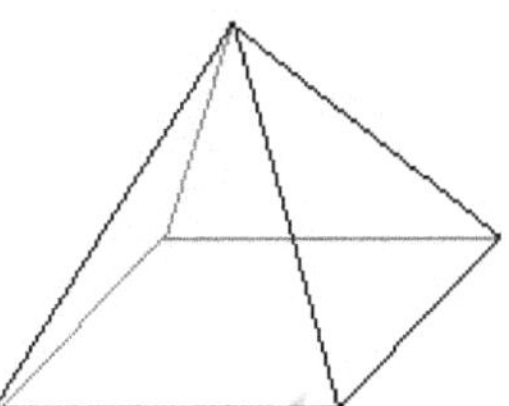

____ triangular faces and 1 ____________ face

Student's name: ____________________ Assignment date: ________________

Nets of Boxes a pattern for a solid

1. Circle the net, which can be folded to each solid?

1.

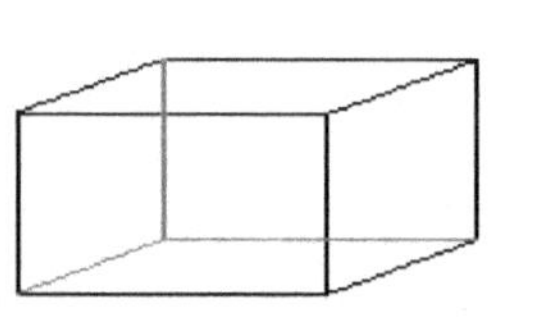
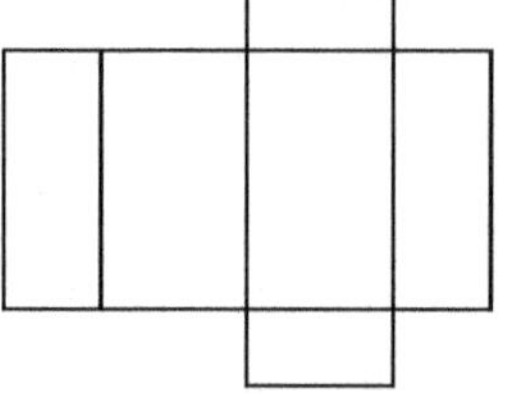
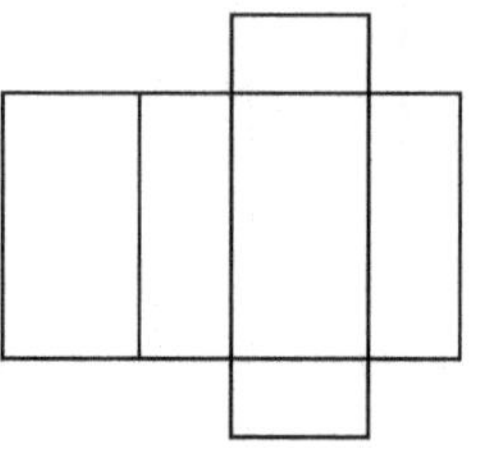
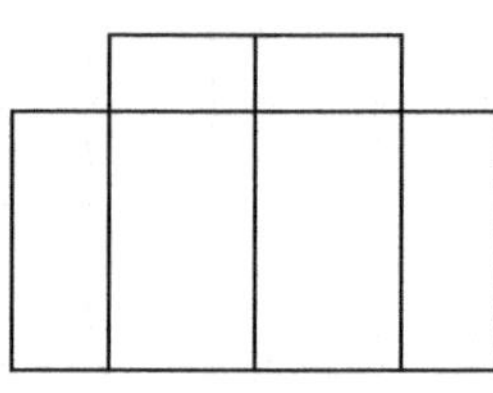

A B C

2.

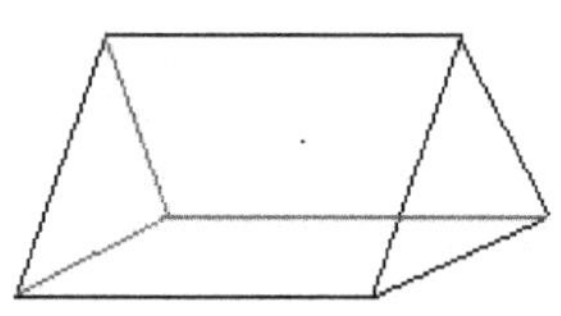
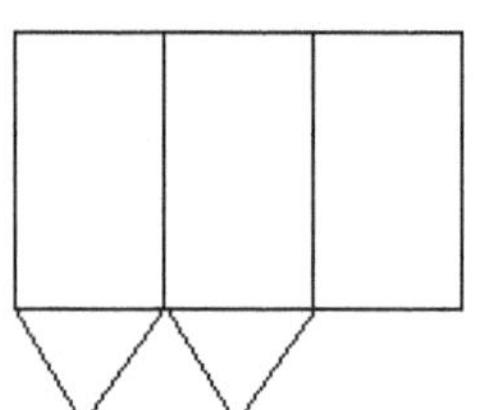
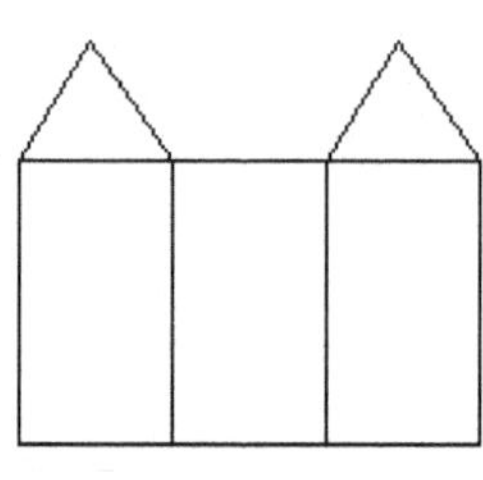
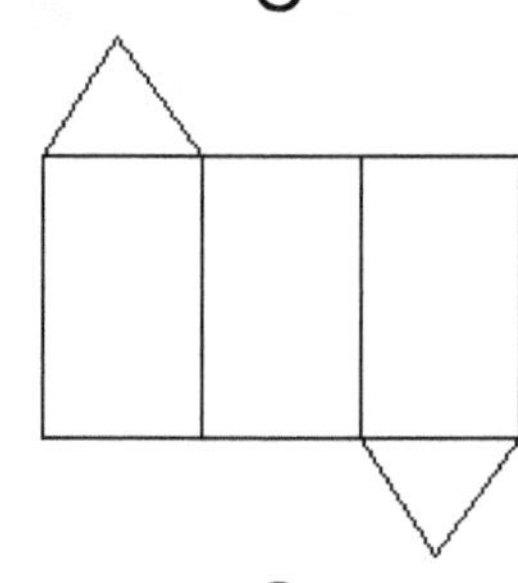

A B C

3.

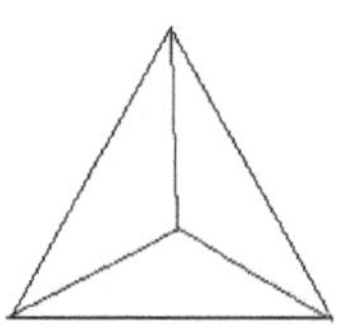
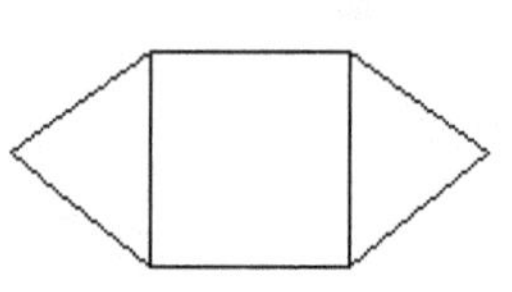
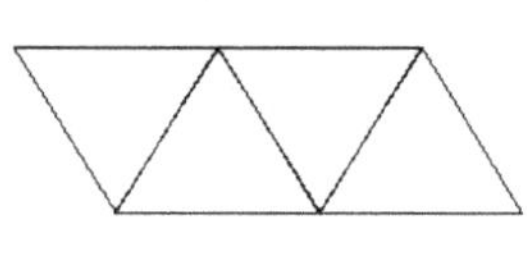
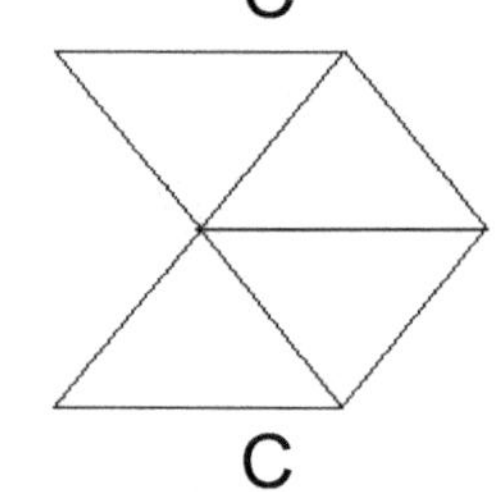

A B C

4.

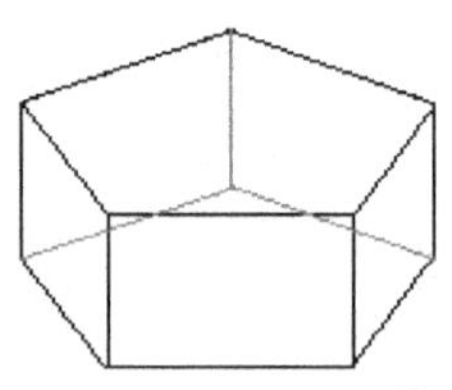
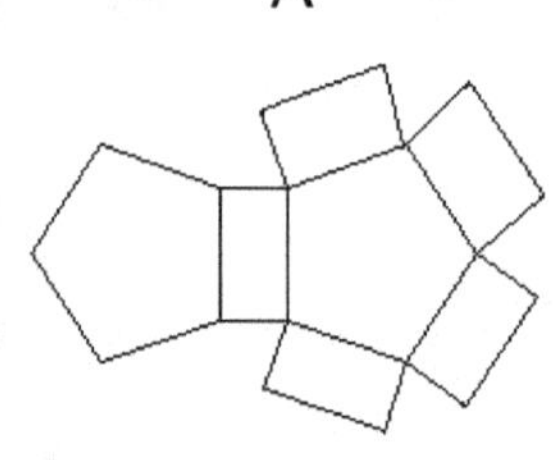
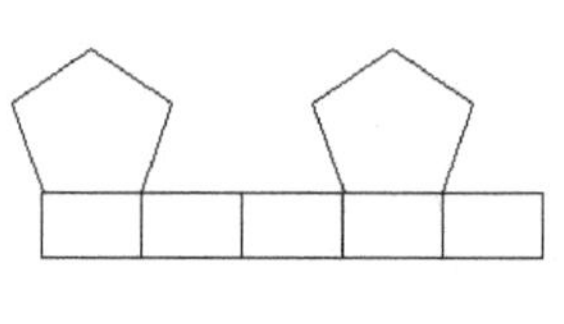
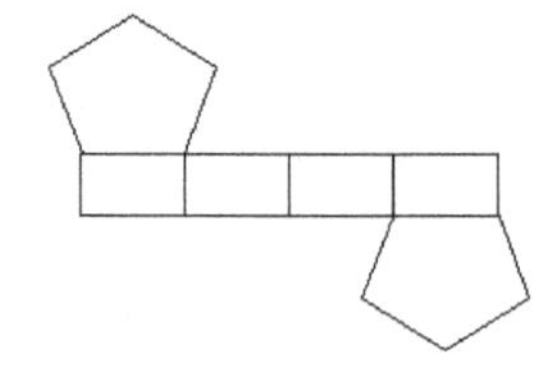

A B C

5.

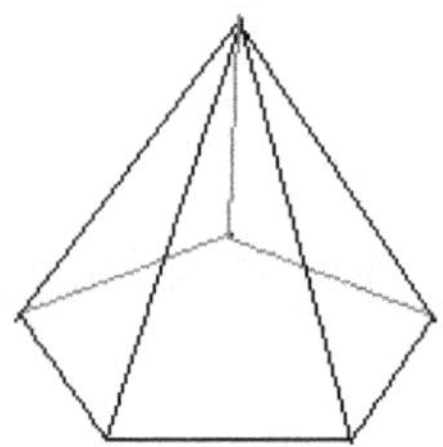
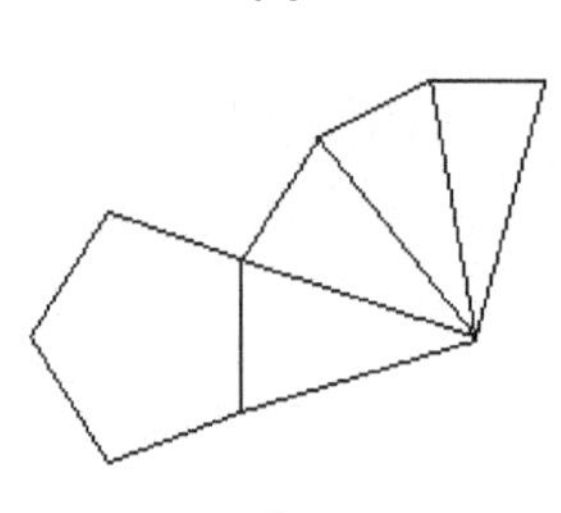
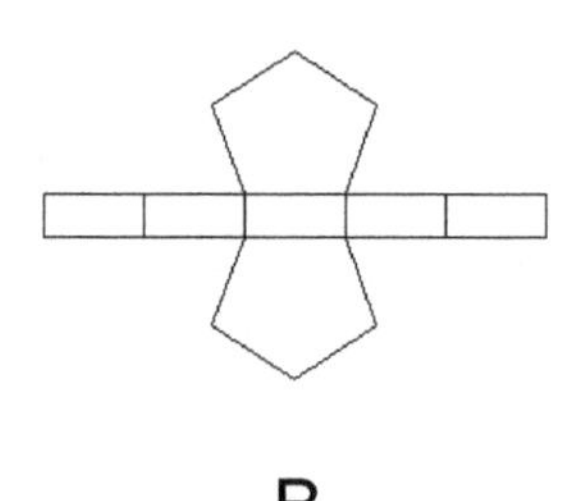
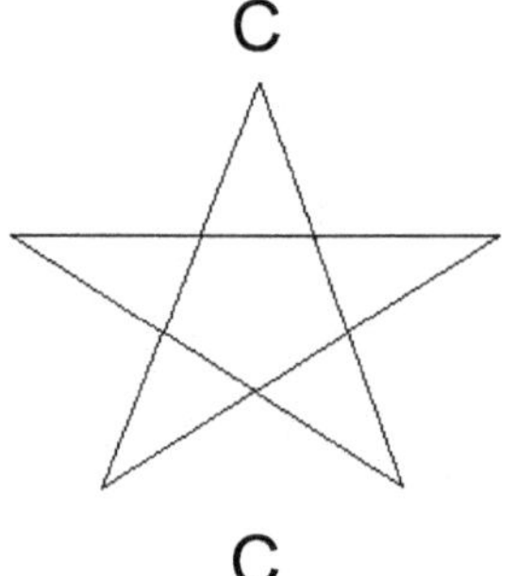

A B C

Student's name: ____________________ Assignment date: ________________

1. Circle the nets that can be folded into boxes.

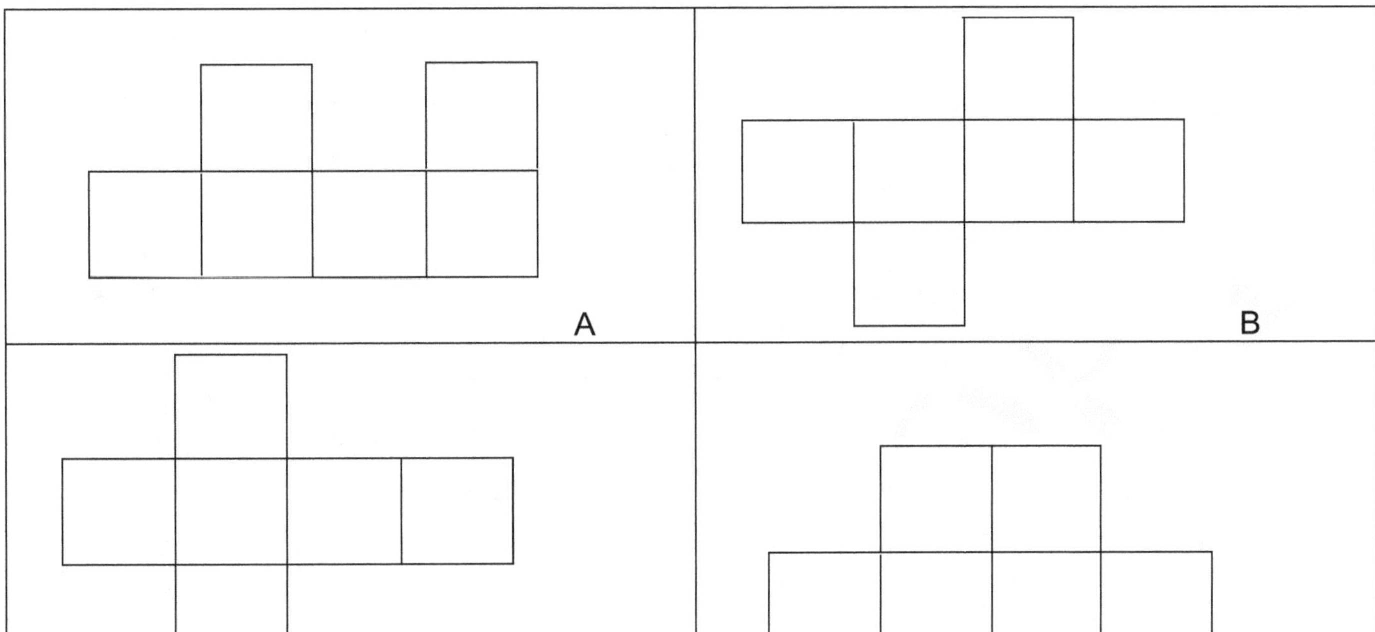

1. The following net makes up the cube.

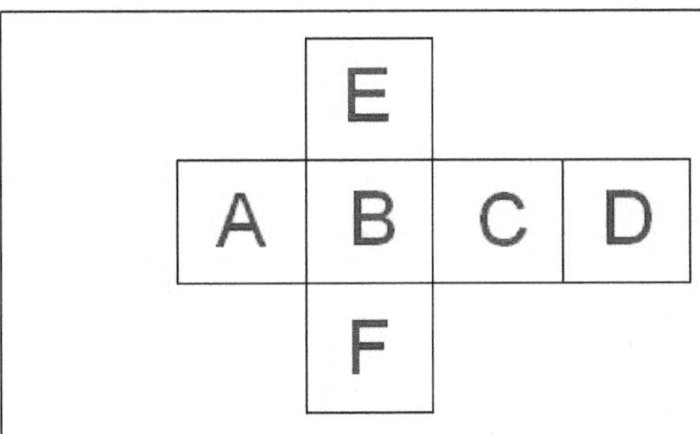

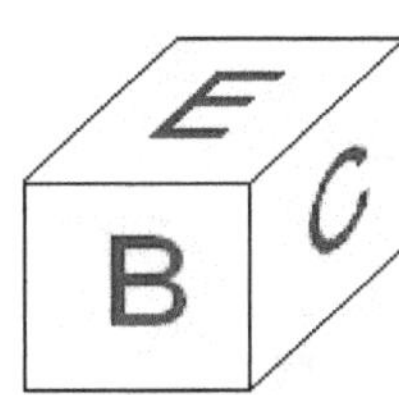

1. Which letter is on the base?
2. Which letter is opposite the letter "B"?
3. Which letter is opposite the letter "C"?

Student's name: ____________________ Assignment date: ________________

Skeletons
A model showing only edges and vertices

Skeleton	Name	Number of vertices	number of edges for each base	Number of edges for side
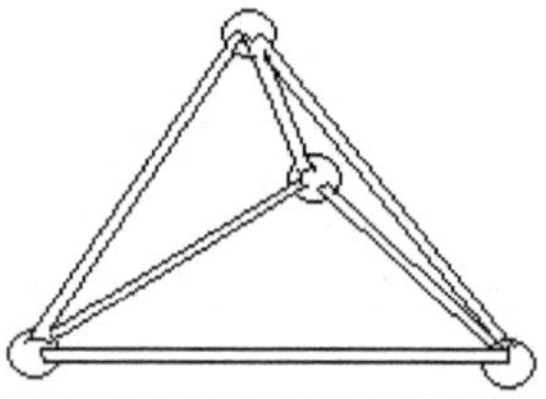	Triangular pyramid	4	3 equal edges	3 equal edges
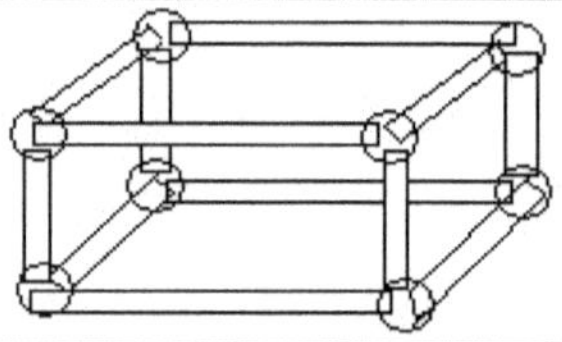	Rectangular prism	4	2 pairs of equal edges	4 equal edges
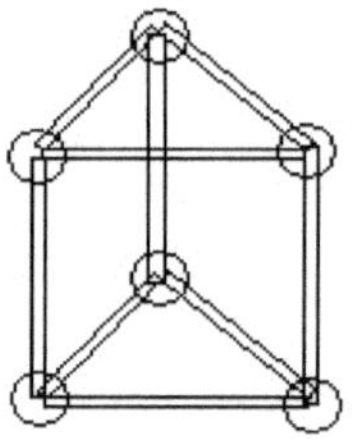				
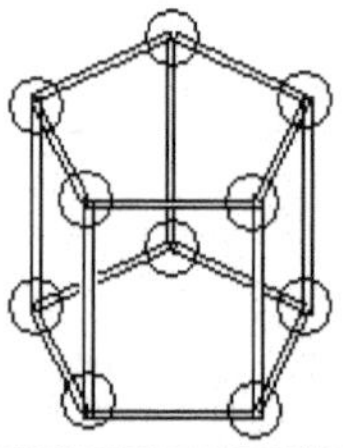				
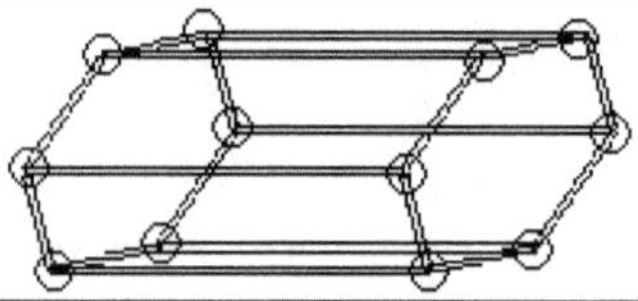				
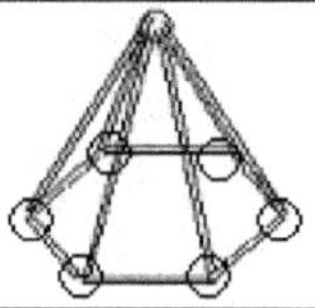				
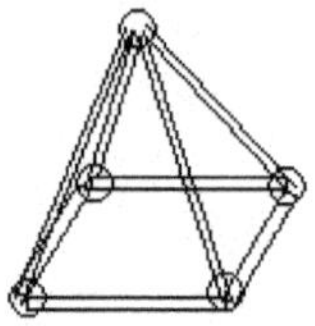				

Student's name: ____________________ Assignment date: ________________

***** Part **19** Graph and charts *****

Tally table

Complete the following chart and answer the questions.

1. Favourite Snack

Snack	Number	Tally
Cookie	7	卌 II
Chip	3	III
Fries	5	卌
Ice cream	9	
Popcorn	4	

1. How many people chose cookies as their favourite snack? ____________
2. How many people chose either chips or fries? ____________
3. How many people chose either fries or ice cream? ____________
4. How many people answered the survey? ____________

2. Favourite Colour

Colour	Number	Tally
Red		IIII
Blue		卌 III
Green		III
Yellow		卌 IIII
Purple		II

1. How many people chose blue as their favourite colour? ____________
2. How many people chose either green or red? ____________
3. How many more people chose yellow than chose purple? ____________
4. List the colour in the order of their popularity? ____________

Student's name: ____________________ Assignment date: ________________

3\. Favourite Food

Food	Number	Tally
Pizzas	15	
Hamburgers	8	
Sandwiches	13	
Pasta	7	
Sushi	6	

1. How many people chose pasta as their favourite food?

   ____

2. How many people chose either pizzas or Sandwiches?

   ____

3. How many fewer people choose sandwiches than chose sushi?

   ____

4. How many people were surveyed?

   ____

5. How many people didn't choose hamburgers as their favourite food?

   ____

4\. Favourite Drinks

Drinks	Number	Tally
Juice		卌 卌 IIII
Lemonade		卌 II
Punch		卌 卌
Tea		III
Coke		卌 II

1. How many people chose coke as their favourite drink?

   ____

2. How many people chose either punch or juice?

   ____

3. How many people answered the survey?

   ____

4. List the drink in order from least votes to most votes.

   ____

Student's name: ____________________ Assignment date: ________________

5. Clubs

Clubs	Number	Tally
Drawing	9	
Chess	15	
Dancing	8	
Skiing	6	
Swimming	11	

1. What club is the most popular?

   ____

2. If three more people chose the dancing club, how many people would have chosen the dancing club?

   ____

3. How many more people chose the swimming club than chose the skiing club?

   ____

4. How many people didn't choose the swimming club as their favourite club?

   ____

6. Sales

Sales	Number	Tally
Shirts	5	
Sweaters	2	
Jackets	7	
Coats	3	
Blouses	8	

1. How many shirts were sold?

   ____

2. How many were more blouses sold than sweaters?

   ____

3. If 3 more jackets were sold, how many jackets would have been sold?

   ____

4. How many items were sold totally?

   ____

5. List the sales from the most sold to the least sold.

   ____

Student's name: ____________________ Assignment date: ________________

Line plots

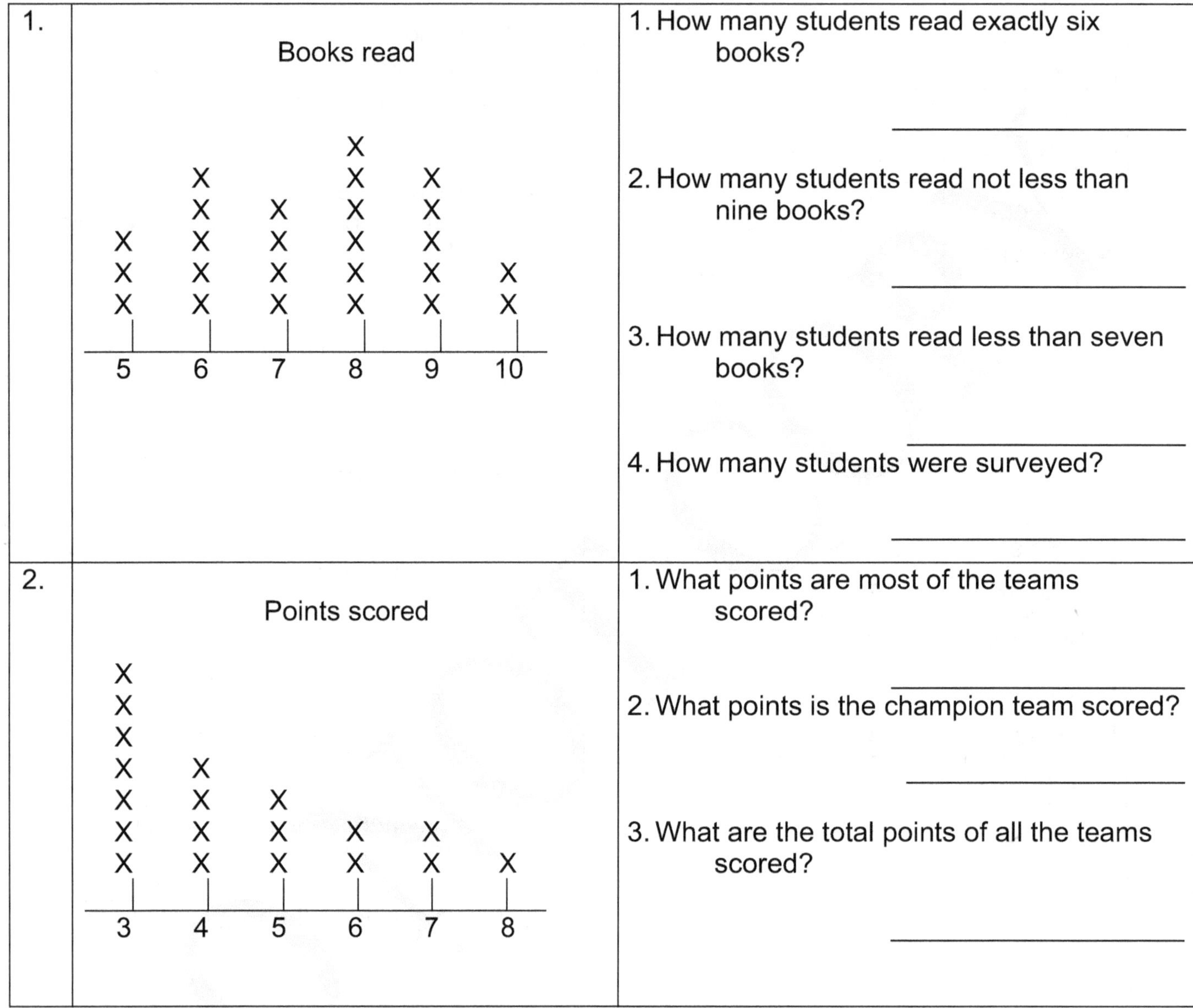

1.	Books read (line plot: 5 – 3 X, 6 – 5 X, 7 – 4 X, 8 – 6 X, 9 – 5 X, 10 – 2 X)	1. How many students read exactly six books? ________ 2. How many students read not less than nine books? ________ 3. How many students read less than seven books? ________ 4. How many students were surveyed? ________
2.	Points scored (line plot: 3 – 7 X, 4 – 4 X, 5 – 3 X, 6 – 2 X, 7 – 2 X, 8 – 1 X)	1. What points are most of the teams scored? ________ 2. What points is the champion team scored? ________ 3. What are the total points of all the teams scored? ________

Student's name: ____________________ Assignment date: ________________

3.

Games won

		X			
		X			
		X			
		X	X		
		X	X	X	
	X	X	X	X	
X	X	X	X	X	X
0	1	2	3	4	5

1. How many people joined the event? ____________
2. How many people won at least four games? ____________
3. How many people lost all the games? ____________
4. How many games did the champion win? ____________

4.

Days used to finish a project

		X			
		X			
		X	X		
	X	X	X		
	X	X	X	X	
X	X	X	X	X	X
2	3	4	5	6	7

1. How many students are there in the class? ____________
2. How many students use precisely 5 days to finish the project? ____________
3. How many students finished their projects in more than four days? ____________
4. How many students finished their projects within three days? ____________

Student's name: ____________________ Assignment date: ________________

5. This is a survey about the number of pets a student keeps. Draw a line plot according to the following information.

Family	Number of pets
Tom	2
James	4
John	3
Michael	6
Jimmy	3
Jenny	5
Laura	7
Cindy	3
Andy	5
Victor	4
David	3
Serena	6
Grace	3
Alex	5
Ann	3
Kelly	6
Christine	4
Jason	2

2 3 4 5 6 7

6. A dart competition was held. Draw a line plot according to the following information.
Three students scored five points.
Four students scored six points.
Eight students scored seven points.
Six students scored eight points.
Seven students scored nine points.
Two students scored ten points.

Student's name: ____________________ Assignment date: ________________

Stem-and-leaf plots

1. The following stem-and-leaf graph shows the heights of students in a class. (unit is in cm)

Stem	Leaves
11	8
12	2 4 5 5 9
13	0 8 4 6 6 0 9
14	5 7 3 6 4 6 2 8
15	1 3

1. How many students are 130 cm? ________________
2. How many students are between 130 and 139 cm (inclusive)? ________________
3. How many students are taller than 150 cm? ________________
4. How many students are there in the class? ________________

2. The following stem-and-leaf graph shows the score of the students got in a math test. (unit is in cm)

Stem	Leaves
5	1
6	2 8 3 6 9 4
7	0 4 7 2 9 5 3 8
8	1 6 3 0 7 9 5 3
9	2 7 4 1 8
10	0 0

1. How many students failed the test (below 60)? ________________
2. How many students got an "A"(at least 86)? ________________
3. How many students get full marks? ________________
4. How many students are there in the class? ________________
5. More students got the sixties or nineties? ________________

Student's name: ____________________ Assignment date: ________________

3. This is a record of the long-jump of a class. Make a stem-and-leaf graph according to the data. Unit is in cm.

104	125	117	121	136
138	107	116	129	109
115	117	125	136	124
109	112	114	126	132
117	127	119	137	125

Stem	Leaves

4. This is a record of sales in a different department of a store. Make a stem-and-leaf graph according to the data. Unit is in the dollar.

63	62	80	54	43
57	66	61	69	71
70	68	42	49	52
36	68	85	64	39
73	74	36	57	48

Stem	Leaves

5. This is a record of the weight of each apple in a basket. Make a stem-and-leaf graph according to the data. Unit is in gram.

75	81	68	90	108
82	95	79	112	79
98	83	86	105	103
116	86	78	67	102
79	92	95	86	103
98	107	113	104	107

Stem	Leaves

Student's name: ____________________ Assignment date: ________________

Mean and Range

Mean, or average, is the sum of all numbers divided by how many numbers there are.
The range is the difference between the greatest number and the least number.

Find mean and range for each set of numbers.

Example: Find mean and range of 4, 7, 2, 8, and 9.
Sum = 4 + 7 + 2 + 8 + 9 = 30
How many numbers? 5

Mean = $\frac{sum}{\#of\ numbers} = \frac{30}{5}$ = 6

Greatest number = 9
Least number = 2
Range = Greatest number – least number = 9 – 2 = 7

	Numbers	mean	range
1.	5, 16, 7, 10, 12	______	______
2.	6, 13, 9, 8	______	______
3.	3, 15, 8. 12, 9, 13	______	______
4.	5. 12, 3, 8	______	______
5.	10, 15, 16, 9, 5	______	______
6.	8, 11, 15, 12, 7, 13	______	______
7.	24, 18, 19, 16, 13	______	______
8.	18, 22, 25, 23	______	______
9.	11, 16, 9, 22, 12	______	______
10.	13, 16, 15, 18, 13	______	______

Student's name: ____________________ Assignment date: ________________

Find mean and range from line plot.

Example: Find mean and range from the line plot below.

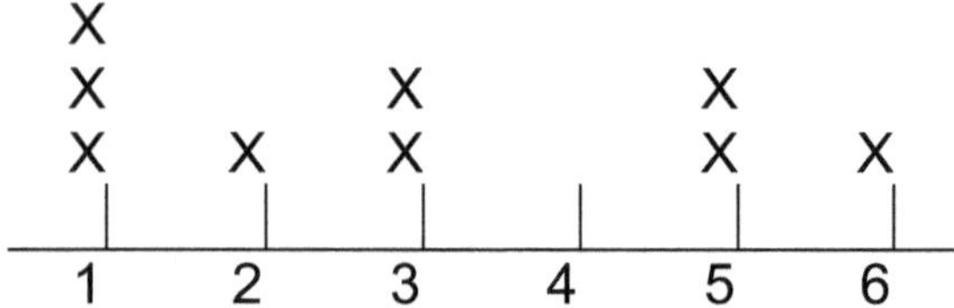

There are 3 of 1, 1 of 2, 2 of 3, 2 of 5 and 1 of 6. So,
Total = 3 × 1 + 1 × 2 + 2 × 3 + 2 × 5 + 1 × 6 = 27
# of numbers = 3 + 1 + 2 + 1 + 2 = 9

Mean = $\frac{sum}{\#of\ numbers} = \frac{27}{9} = 3$

Greatest number = 6
Least number = 1
Range = Greatest number – least number = 6 – 1 = 5

1.

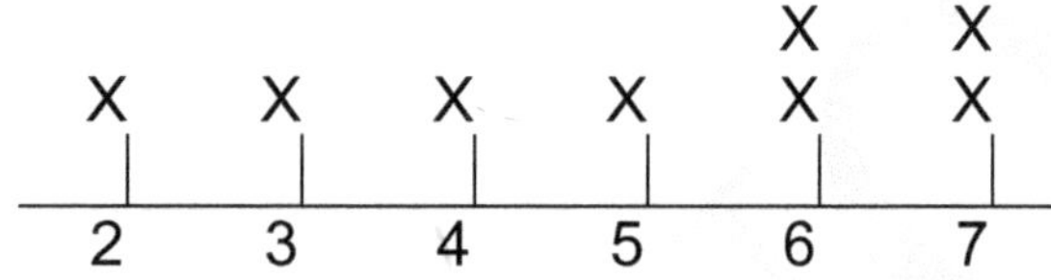

Mean =______ Range = ________

2.

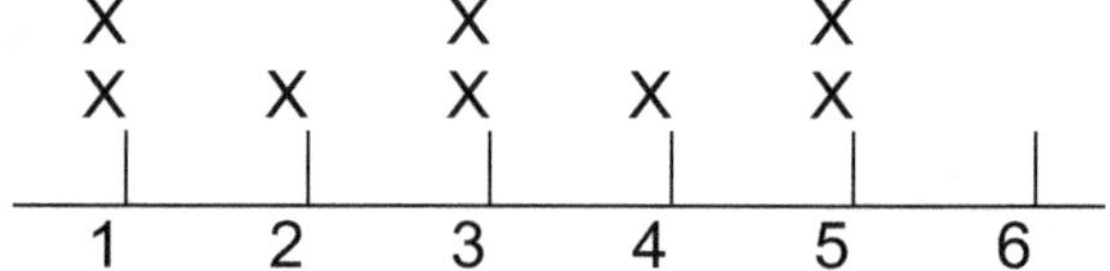

Mean =______ Range = ________

3.

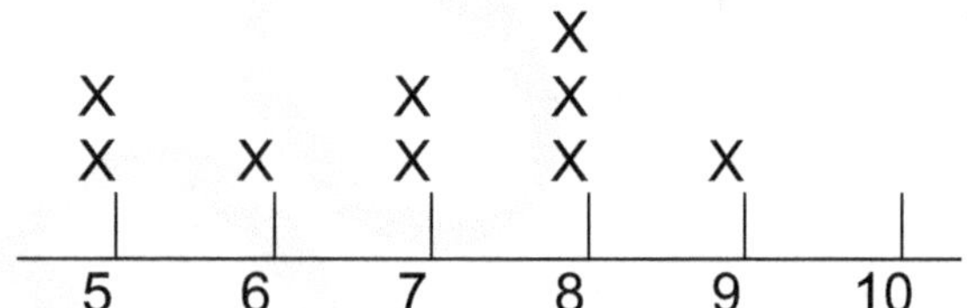

Mean =____ Range = ________

4.

Mean =______ Range = __________

Student's name: ____________________ Assignment date: ________________

Find mean and range from stem-and-leaf plot.

Example: Find mean and range from the stem-and-leaf plot below.

Stem	Leaves
1	1 4 7
2	0 2 5
3	1

There are 7 numbers in the plot above: 11, 14, 17, 20, 22, 25, and 31.
Total = 11 + 14 + 17 + 20 + 22 + 25 = 140
# of numbers = 7

Mean = $\frac{sum}{\#of\ numbers} = \frac{140}{7} = 20$

Greatest number = 31
Least number = 11
Range = Greatest number – least number = 31 – 11 = 20

1.

Stem	Leaves
2	0
3	3 3 8
4	5 1

Mean =_______ Range = _________

2.

Stem	Leaves
3	1 0 8
4	2 5
5	4

Mean =_____ Range = ________

3.

Stem	Leaves
1	4 2 6 2
2	0
3	3 5 4

Mean =______ Range = __________

4.

Stem	Leaves
11	2 6
12	3 7 5
13	2 0 7 2 6

Mean =______ Range = __________

Student's name: ____________________ Assignment date: ________________

Pictographs

A pictograph uses a pictorial symbol to represent a physical object.

1.

Favourite Colours

Red	▣ ▣
Blue	▣ ▣ ▣ ▣ ▣
Green	▣ ▣ ▣
Yellow	▣ ▣
black	▣

▣ = 10 votes

1. What colour is the most popular?

____

2. How many students take green as their favourite colour?

____

3. How many students answered the survey?

____

4. List the popularity from greatest to least.

____

5. What is the range?

____

2.

Favourite Games

Soccer	☼ ☼ ☼ ☼
Basketball	☼ ☼
Hockey	☼ ☼ ☼ ☼ ☼
Tennis	☼ ☼
Swimming	☼ ☼ ☼
Skiing	☼

☼ = 8 students

1. What game is the most popular?

____

2. How many more students take hockey as their favourite game than basketball?

____

3. How many students answered the survey?

____

4. List the popularity from least to greatest.

____

5. What is the range?

____

Student's name: ____________________ Assignment date: ________________

Making pictographs

1.

Favourite Food	# of students
Pizzas	15
Sandwiches	20
Pasta	5
Hamburger	10
Sushi	25

Use  to present 5 students

2.

Name of poultry	# of poultry
Chicken	32
Ducks	8
Goose	20
Turkey	12

Use 🕊 to present 4 poultry

3.

Favourite drink	# of students
Coke	9
Juice	12
Tea	3
Water	6
Punch	15

Use 🍸 to present 3 students.

Student's name: ____________________ Assignment date: ________________

Pictograph problem

1. The fish caught, in average of four years, from 2013 to 2016 is ____________.
2. The fish caught in 2013 is what fraction of the year 2016? ________

Fish caught from 2013 to 2016

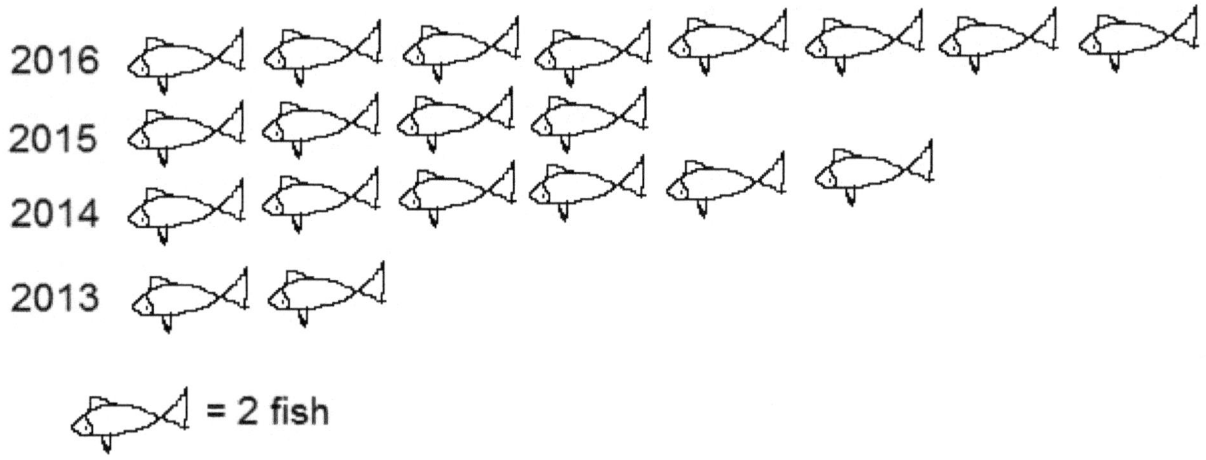

2016
2015
2014
2013

= 2 fish

Student's name: ____________________ Assignment date: ________________

Bar Graphs (Bar Charts)

There is a type of data that has no real numerical meaning of measurement; that is, you cannot use it to do any computation to have a meaningful result. For example, if assigning a numerical value to male = 1 and female = 3, then the average of these two items = 2, which is not meaningful. This type of data is categorical data.

A bar graph, also known as a bar chart, is a graphical display of categorical data using different heights of bars to correspond to the frequency (the number of occurrences) of the amount of data. The higher the bar, the higher the frequency of the data. The lower the bar, the lower the frequency of the data.

The purpose of using a bar chart is to use it to represent data so that it is easier for readers to understand. For example, after collecting the information of Vancouver rainfall by months in a year, we can show the monthly amount of rainfall by the different heights of bars that occurred in different months.

Bar graphs are most commonly drawn vertically, though they can also be depicted horizontally.

Double Bar graph

If there are two different types of categorical data, then a double bar graph can be drawn.

Histogram

If the data are not categorical (such as the scores of a test), then a type of graph called Histogram can be used.

Student's name: ____________________ Assignment date: ________________

How to draw a bar chart?

1. The title of the bar chart and two headings for the vertical axis and horizontal axis must be provided.
2. Decide the scale (number of points) of the vertical axis. Normally, the vertical axis shows the quantity, and the horizontal line shows the category. The origin should normally start with 0.

The size of intervals (the distance between any points) = $\frac{\textit{the maximum value}}{\textit{the number of interals (points or scales)}}$

Normally the lowest scale is below the lowest value in the data, and the largest scale is higher than the maximum value in the data.

3. The horizontal axis shows the number of categorical data, which in turn determines the number of bars.

Example,

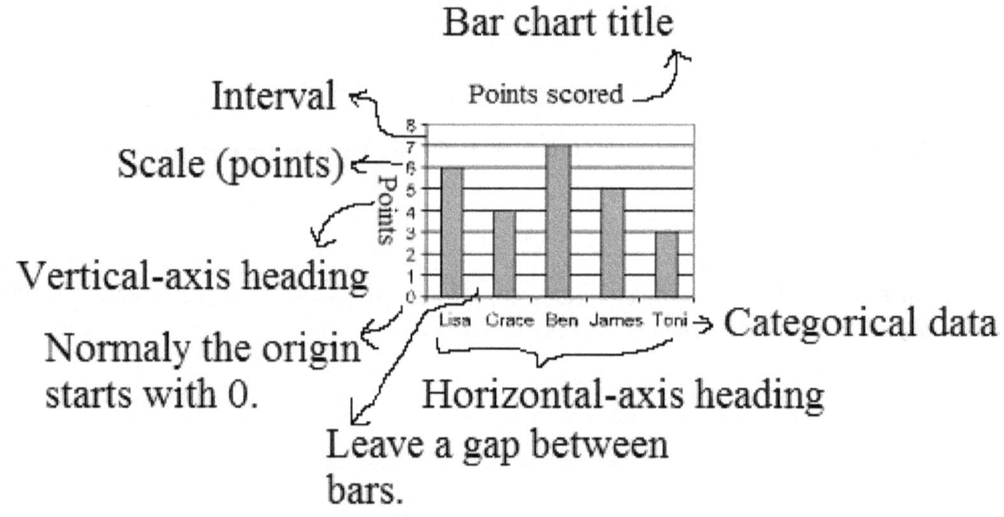

Student's name: ____________________ Assignment date: ________________

1. Vertical bar graph.

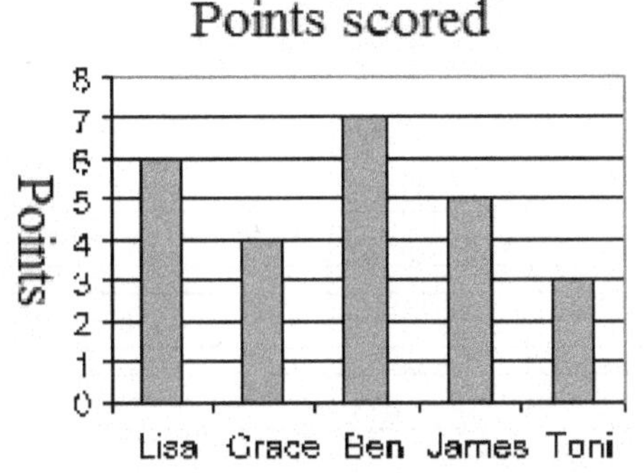

1. Who scored the most points?

____

2. What are the total points scored?

____

3. What are the mean points scored?

____

4. List the name of students according to their points from least to greatest.

____

5. What is the range?

____

2. Horizontal bar graph.

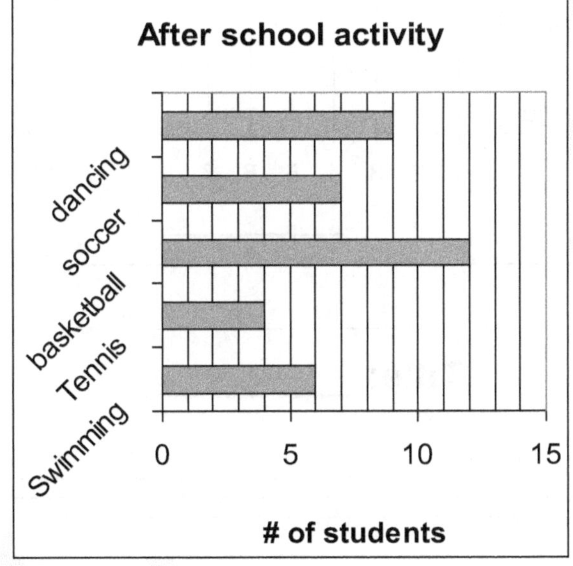

1. What is the most popular activity?

____

2. How many more students joined in soccer than tennis?

____

3. Which activities have at least 7 students joined in?

____

4. List the activities according to their popularity from greatest to least.

____

5. If the scale is 10 at the first grid, instead of 5, the graph would have to be shorter or longer to show the same data?
6. What is the range?

____

Student's name: ____________________ Assignment date: ________________

Make a bar graph from each below.

1.

Name	# of chin-ups
John	6
Tom	9
Sam	3
Justin	5
Ben	8

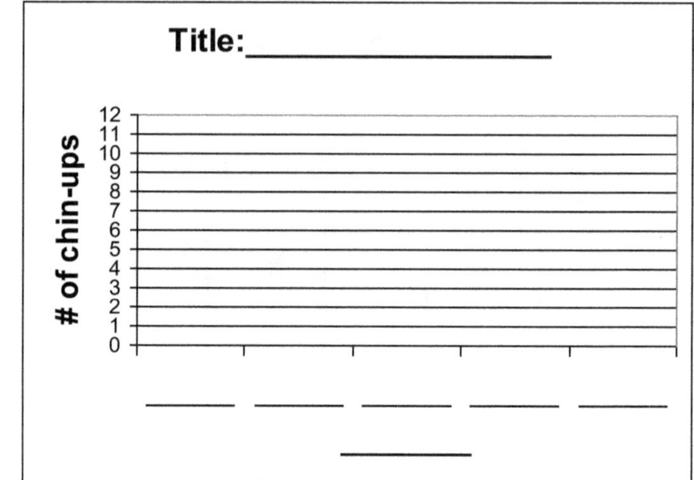

2.

Fruits in a basket	# of fruits
Orange	5
Apple	8
Pear	2
Peach	9
Plum	6

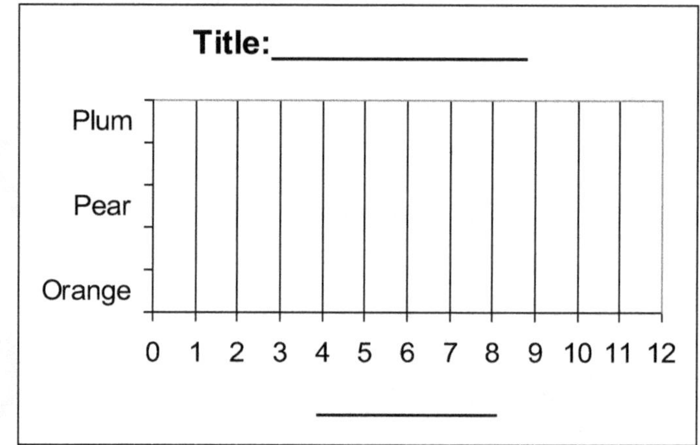

3.

Team	# of games won
Tiger	5
Hunter	8
Eagle	13
Giant	10
Hurricane	9

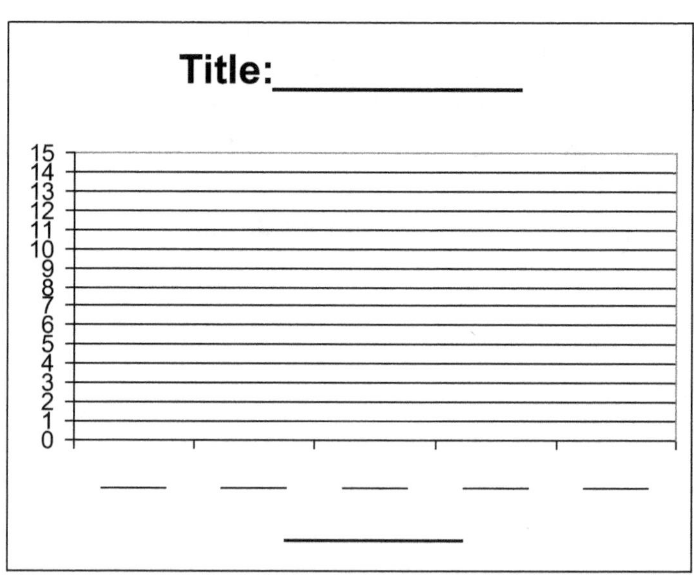

Student's name: ____________________ Assignment date: ________________

Line Graph

The following graph shows the sales of a store from 1998 to 2005.

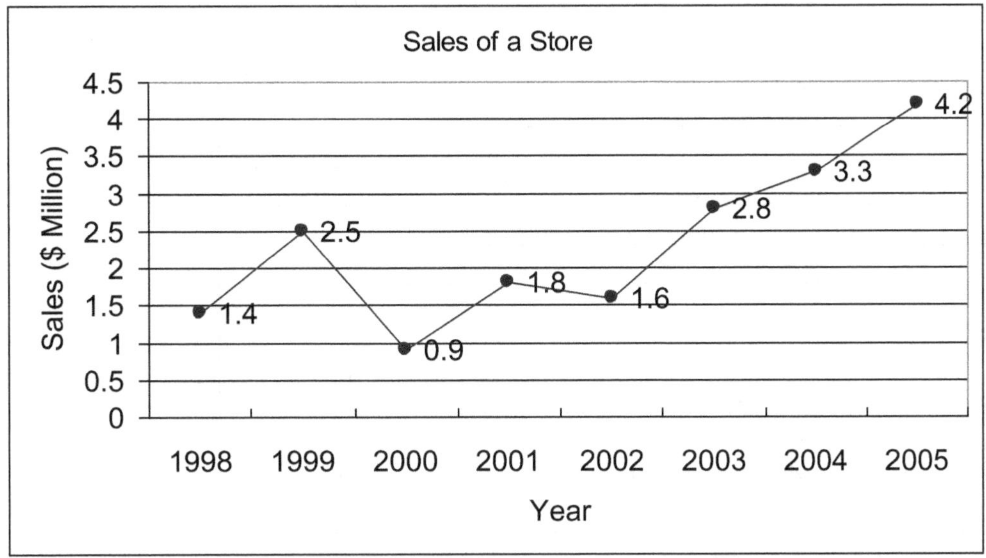

1. In which year did the store make the least amount of sale? 2000

   What was the sale? $0.9 million

2. In which year did the store make the greatest amount of sale? 2005

   What was the sale? $4.2 million

3. Between which two years did the sale of the store rise the most? 2002 & 2003

   How much did it rise? $1.2 million

4. Between which two years did the sale of the store drop the most? 1999 & 2000

   How much did it drop? $1.6 million

5. What can you predict for 2006, rise or drop? rise

Student's name: ____________________ Assignment date: ________________

The following graph shows the average price of a stock from 1995 to 2005. Draw a line graph to describe the change.

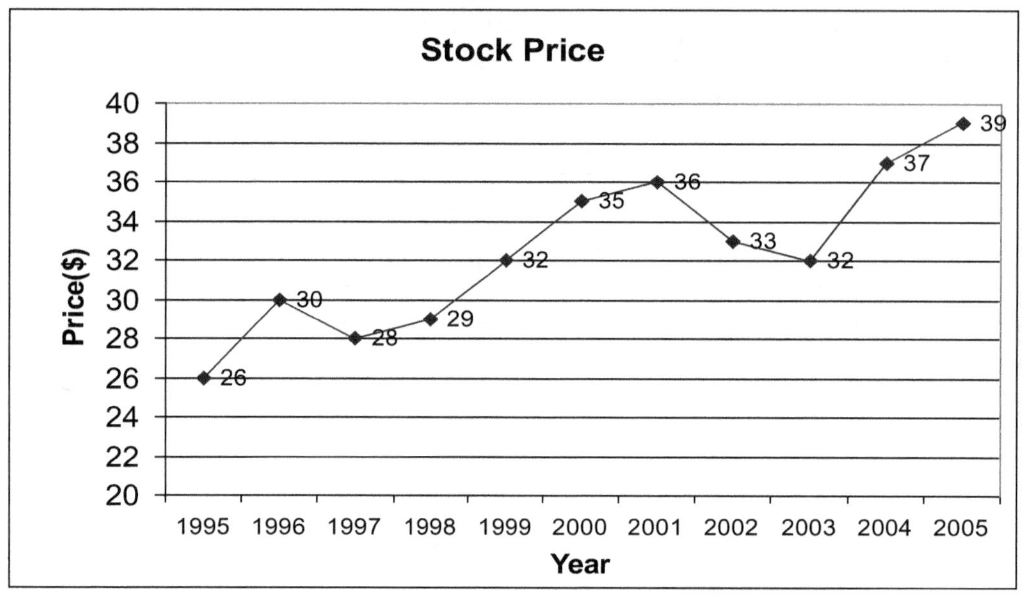

1. What is the highest price of the stock? $39

   In which year? 2005

2. What is the lowest price of the stock? $26

   In which year? 1995

3. Between which two years did the price of the stock rise the most? 2003 & 2004

   How much did it rise? $5

4. Between which, two years did the price of the stock drop the most? 2001 & 2002

   How much did it drop? $3

5. What is the mean (average price)? $32.45

6. What can you predict for 2006, rise or drop? rise

Student's name: ____________________ Assignment date: ________________

Circle Graphs

1. This circle graph shows the pets in a house.

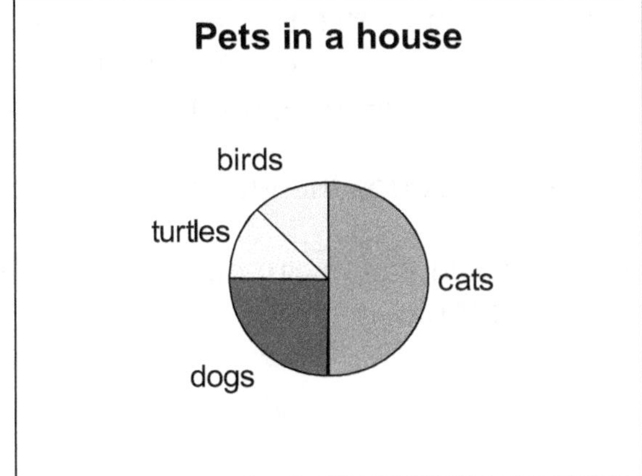

1. What fraction of the pets are cats? ____________
2. What fraction of the pets are dogs? ____________
3. Which two kinds of pets represent $\frac{1}{4}$ the pets? ____________
4. What is the greatest number of pets? ____________

2. This circle graph shows the votes of the students in a class on their favourite drinks.

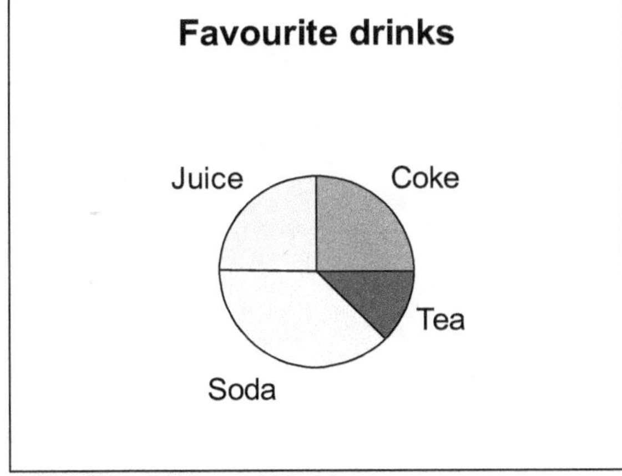

1. What fraction of the class chose juice as their favourite drink? ____________
2. What fraction of the class chose soda as their favourite drink? ____________
3. Do more students like coke or tea? ____________
4. What is the most popular drink? ____________
5. If there are 24 students in the class, how many students chose coke as their favourite drink? ____________

Student's name: ____________________ Assignment date: ________________

Comparing pictograph, bar chart, line graph, pie chart (circle graph)

1. It is easy to draw a pictograph because each pictorial symbol in the graph represents a value, but to get the actual value, the reader needs to calculate.
2. The bar chart provides a good visual so the reader can see the value of each category immediately, but we can not see the trend as clearly as the line chart, especially since the bar chart is awkward to compare multiple categories. Sometimes the double bar chart is drawn to show the subcategory, but if more categories are needed, then the line chart is better by using different line styles.
3. The pie chart shows something out of the total, and it provides the idea of fraction or % out of the whole.
4. The stem-and-leaf shows the branch data out of the main value. Suppose the details of each main category are needed, then the stem-and-leaf plot is good.

Student's name: ____________________ Assignment date: ________________

Venn diagram

A Venn diagram is a method to sort data using a circle.
For two sets: $n(A \cup B) = n(A) + n(B) - n(A \cap B)$

Part	Square	Black
A	Yes	No
B	Yes	Yes
C	No	Yes
D	No	No

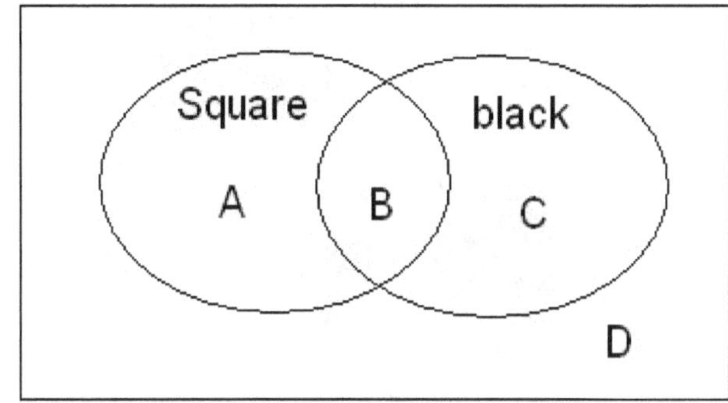

a. Below each object, write the part of the Venn diagram to which it belongs.

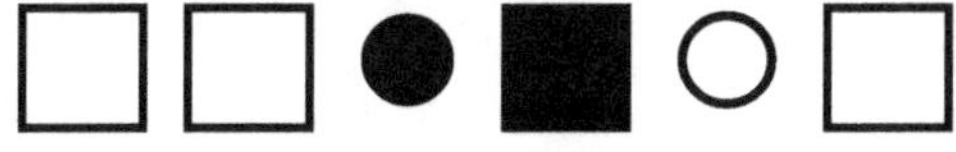

___ ___ ___ ___ ___ ___

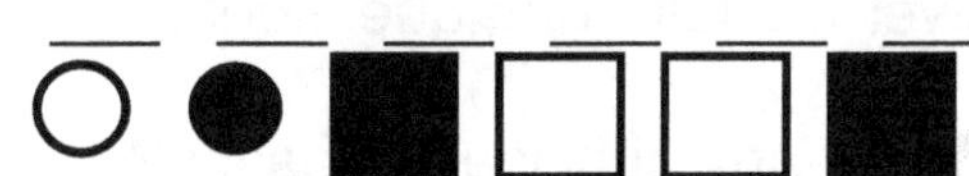

___ ___ ___ ___ ___ ___

___ ___ ___ ___ ___ ___

b. Write the number in each part.

A __________

B __________

C __________

D __________

Tina English French	James English	Melissa French	Isabel English French
______	______	______	______

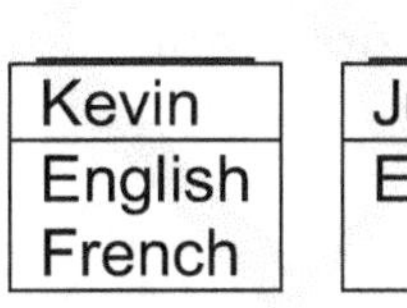

Justin English	Linda French	Steven English

______ ______ ______ ______

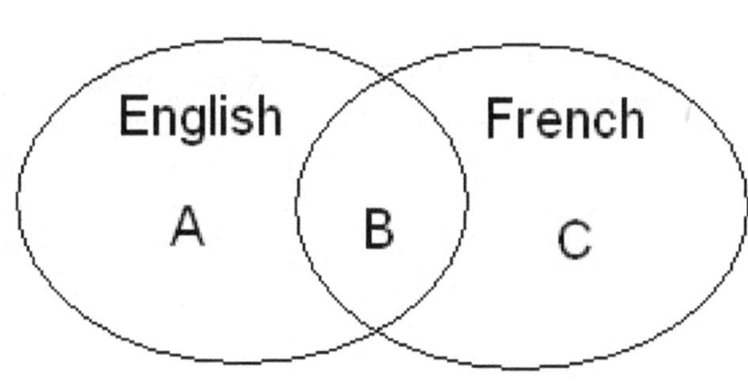

A ______ B ______ C ______

Student's name: ____________________ Assignment date: ________________

3.

Four sides A B C Black D

Write the number in each part.

A ___________

B ___________

C ___________

D ___________

4.

Tina	James	Melissa	Isabel
glasses		glasses	
____	____	____	____

Kevin	Justin	Linda	Steven
glasses		glasses	
____	____	____	____

Jasmine	Sarah	Tom	Mathew
	glasses		glasses
____	____	____	____

Girls A B C Glasses D

Answer the following questions.

1. How many girls wear glasses? ___________

2. How many students wear glasses? ___________

3. How many students are there? ___________

4. How many boys do not wear glasses? ___________

Student's name: ____________________ Assignment date: ________________

5.

There are 47 students in the Ho Math Chess Learning Centre summer program. 18 students took a math class. 12 students took chess class. 21 students did not take math or chess classes. How many students took both math and chess classes?

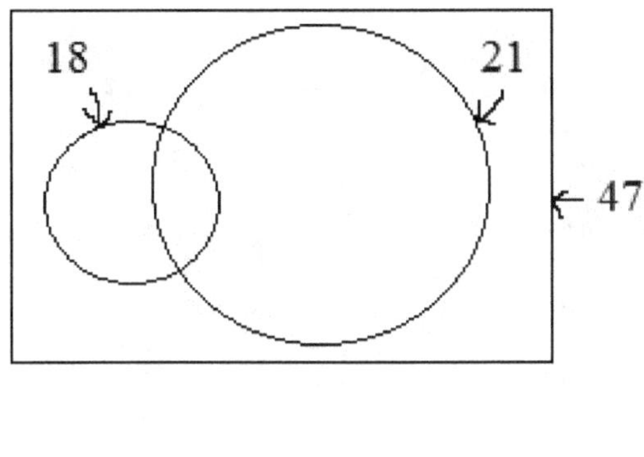

Carroll diagram

Sort and classify the following numbers using a Caroll diagram.

3, 50, 293, 98, 390, 879, 175, 46

	Odd	Even
Less than or equal to 100		
Greater than 100		

Student's name: ____________________ Assignment date: ______________

Temperature

Write the temperatures.

1. ____ °C

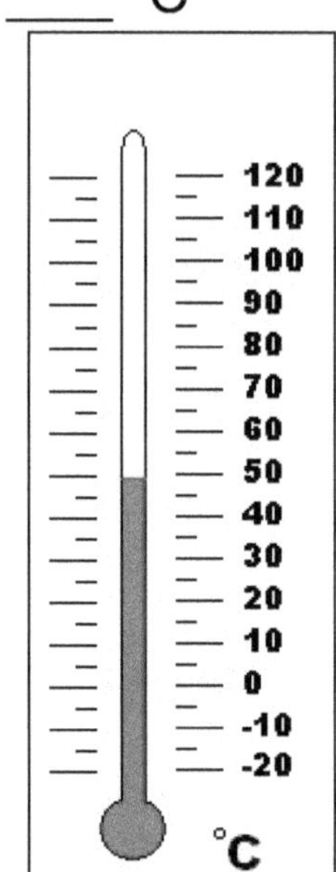

2. ____ °C

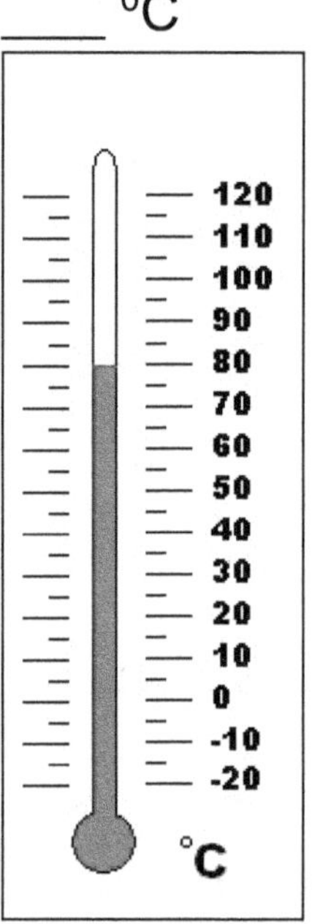

3. ____ °C

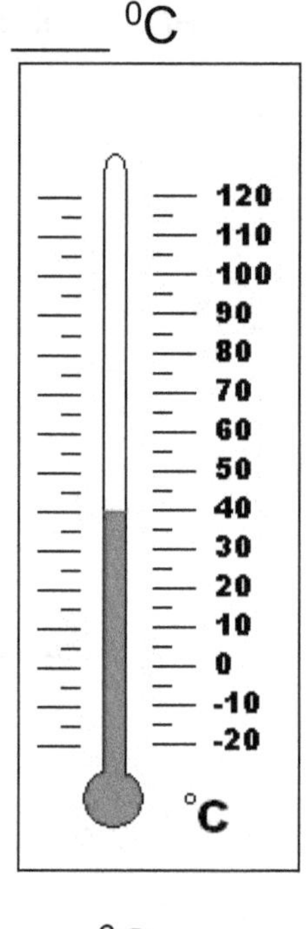

4. ____ °C

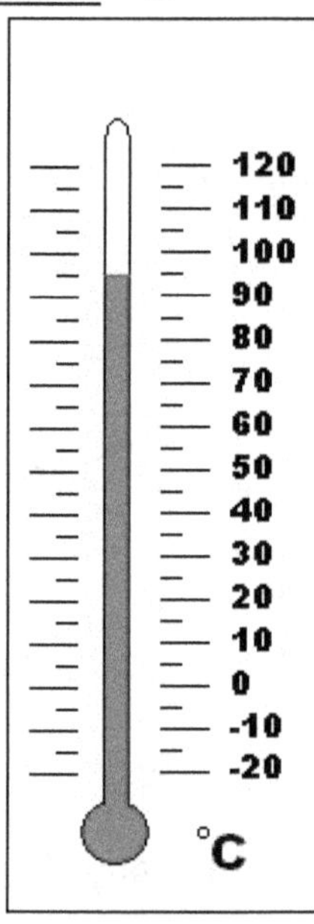

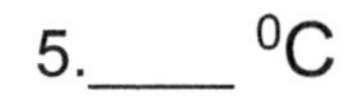

5.____ °C

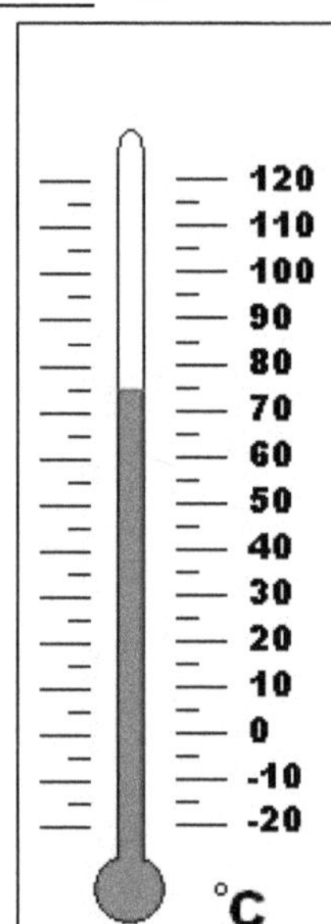

6. ____ °C

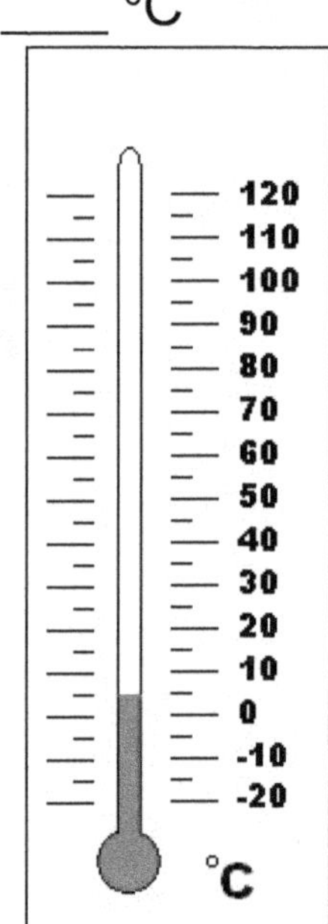

7.____ °C

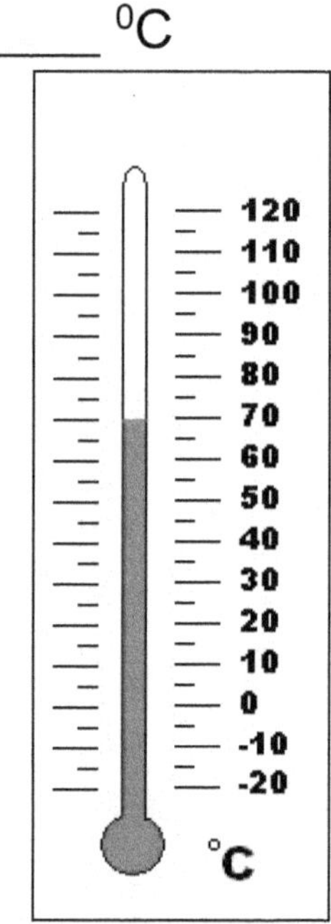

8. ____ °C

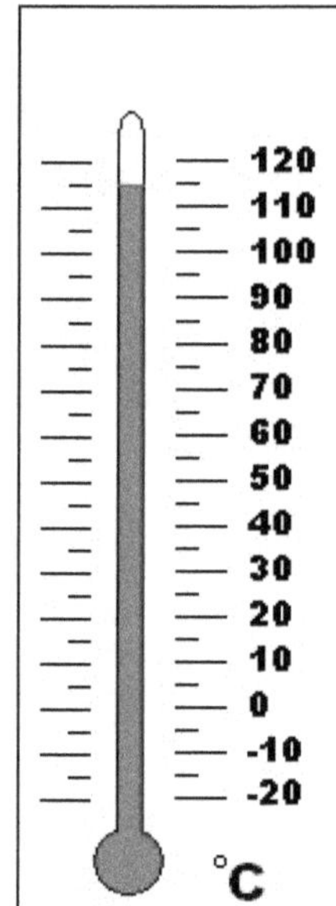

Ho Math Chess Primary Grades Math

Test Review assesssment 何数棋谜低年级数学测试複習考核

Frank Ho, Amanda Ho www.homathchess.com

Student's name: ____________________ Assignment date: ________________

Colour the thermometer to show the temperature.

1. 40 ^{0}C

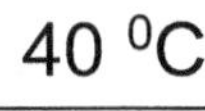

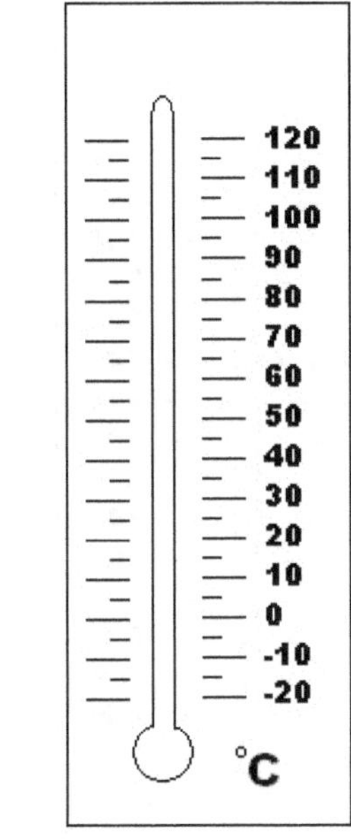

2. 80 ^{0}C

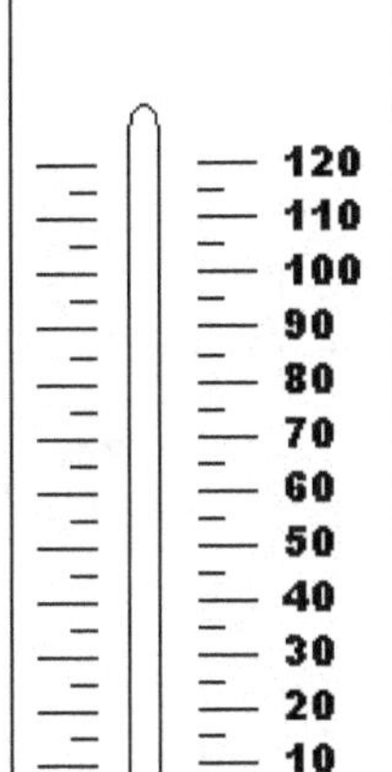

3. 55 ^{0}C

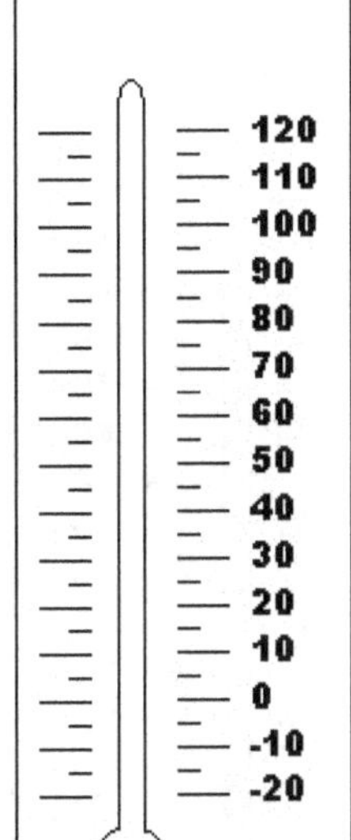

4. 75 ^{0}C

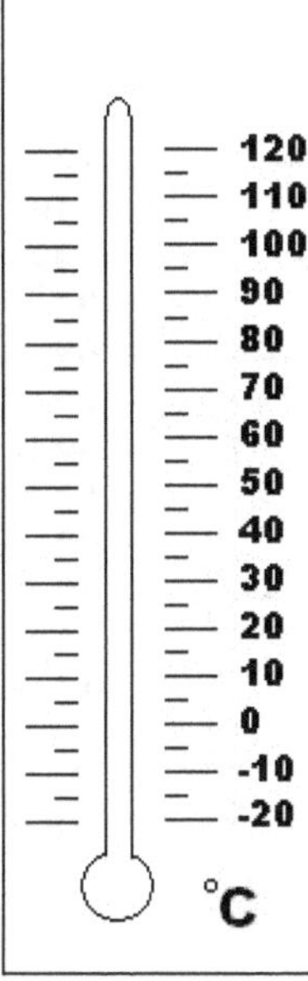

5. 5 ^{0}C

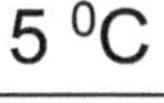

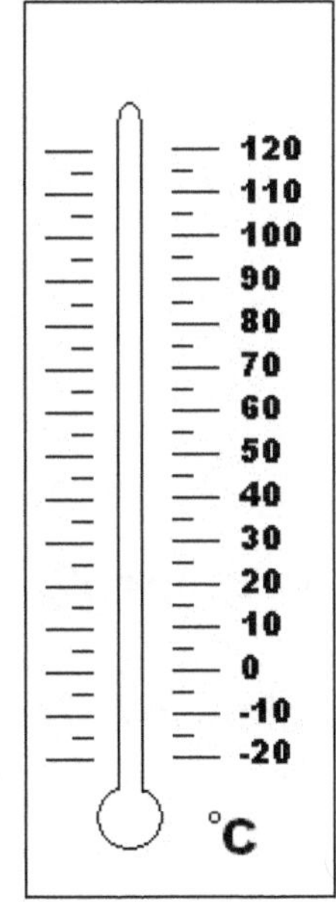

6. 60 ^{0}C

7. 95 ^{0}C

8. 100 ^{0}C

Student's name: ____________________ Assignment date: ________________

The following thermometers show midnight temperatures in four different cities: Vancouver, Winnipeg, Chicago, and San Carlos.

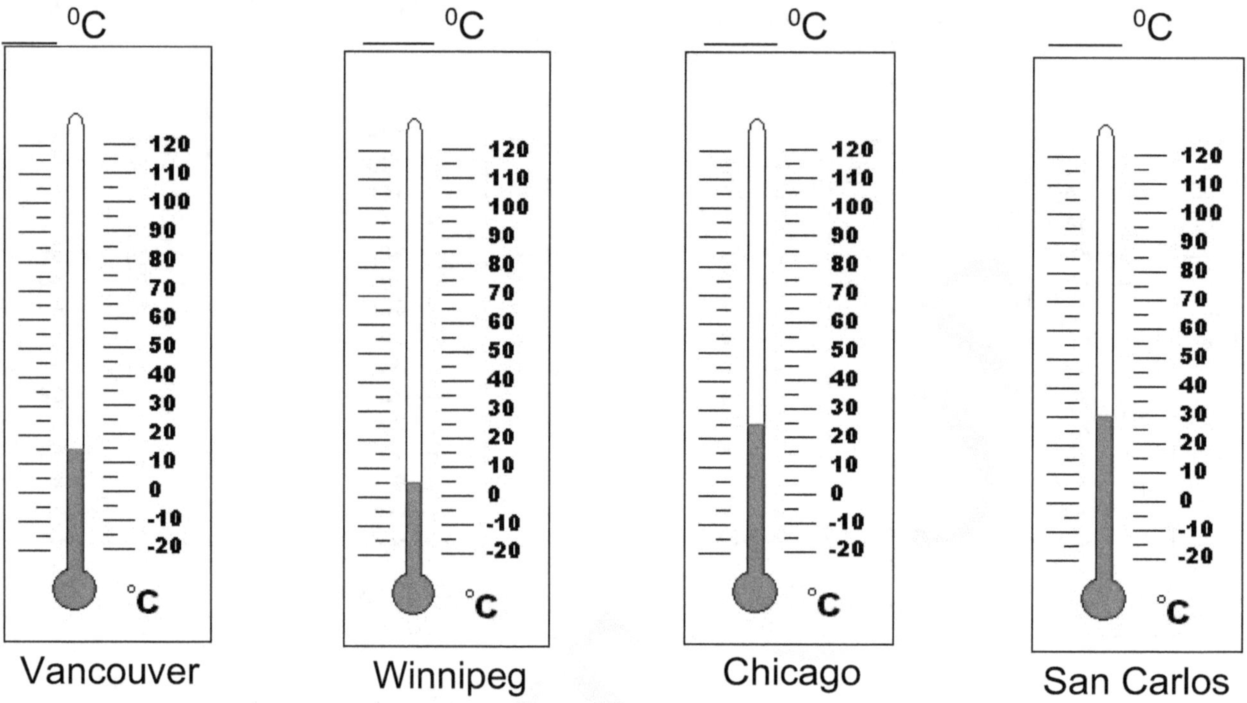

1. What is the temperature of Vancouver?

2. What is the temperature of Chicago?

3. What is the highest temperature? Which city?

4. What is the lowest temperature? Which city?

5. How many ^{0}C higher is the temperature of San Carlos than Winnipeg?

6. How many ^{0}C lower is the temperature of Vancouver than Chicago?

Student's name: ____________________ Assignment date: ________________

Cold or hot? Then estimate the temperature.

a. hot  b. cold

Temperature: ____________

a. hot b. cold

Temperature: ____________

a. hot b. cold

Temperature: ____________

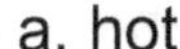

a. hot b. cold

Temperature: ____________

a. hot b. cold

Temperature: ____________

a. hot b. cold

Temperature: ____________

Student's name: ____________________ Assignment date: ________________

Directions

North

West East

So h

The little kitty got lost. Tell her where she should go.

1. If the kitty wants to find the shoe, she should go _________.
2. If she feels hungry, she should go ________ to buy a burger.
3. She can go ______ to the shopping mall to buy a cap for herself.
4. If she wants to go home, she should go _________.
5. The church is on the ________ of the shopping mall.
6. The shopping mall is on the ________ of the church.
7. The bus is on the ________ of the house.
8. The farm is on the ________ of the house.
9. The house is on the ________ of the farm.
10. The dog is on the ________ of the burger store.
11. If the bus drives to the church, it should go ________.
12. If the bus heads to the farm, it should go ________.
13. The dog misses his friends on the farm. He should go ________.
14. The dog goes east two blocks, then turn north one block, he can find a ________.

Ho Math Chess Primary Grades Math

Test Review assesssment 何数棋謎低年级数学测试複習考核

Student's name: ____________________ Assignment date: ________________

***** Part 20 Coordinates *****

An ordered pair (x, y) shows the position of a point on a grid. The value of x shows the horizontal distance from the origin. The value of y shows the vertical distance from the origin.

Example: Show the point P (4, 2) on a grid.

Start from the origin, move 4 units to the right and 2 units up.

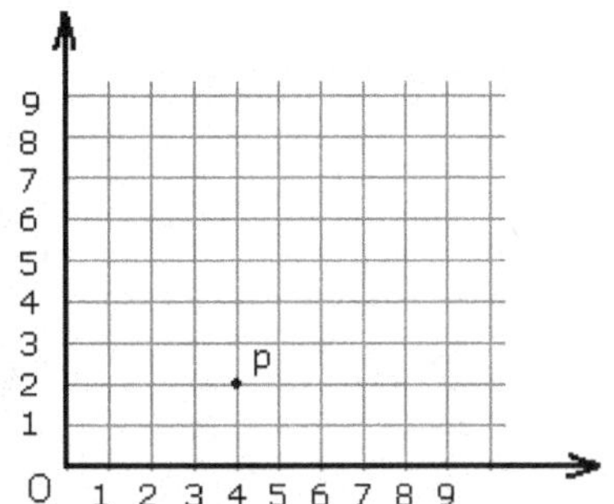

Write the ordered pair of each point on the grid.

1.

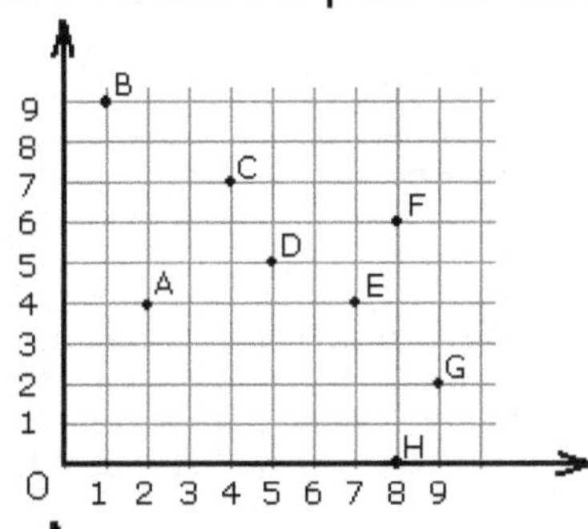

A ____________ B ____________

C ____________ D____________

E ____________ F ____________

G ____________ H ____________

2.

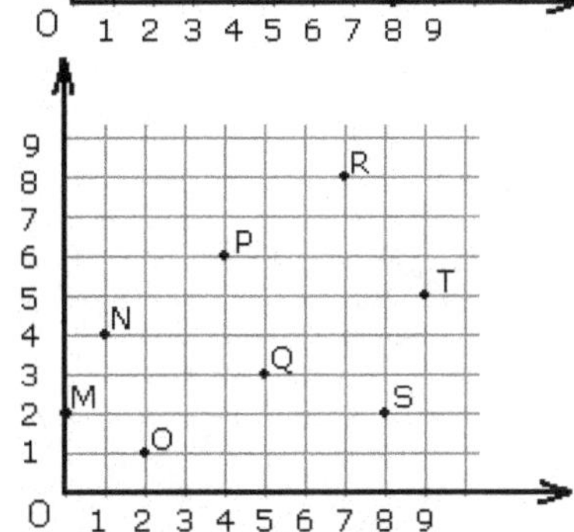

M ____________ N ____________

O ____________ P____________

Q ____________ R ____________

S ____________ T ____________

Plot each point on the grid and join these points in order.

3. A (2, 5) B (8, 5) C (3, 1)

D (5, 8) E (7, 1) F (2, 5)

Ho Math Chess Primary Grades Math

Test Review assesssment 何数棋谜低年级数学测试複習考核

Student's name: ____________________ Assignment date: ________________

4. A (1, 1) B (1, 6) C (4, 3)

   D (7, 6) E (7, 1)

5. A (7, 5) B (2, 5) C (2, 8)

   D (7, 8) E (7, 2) F (2, 2)

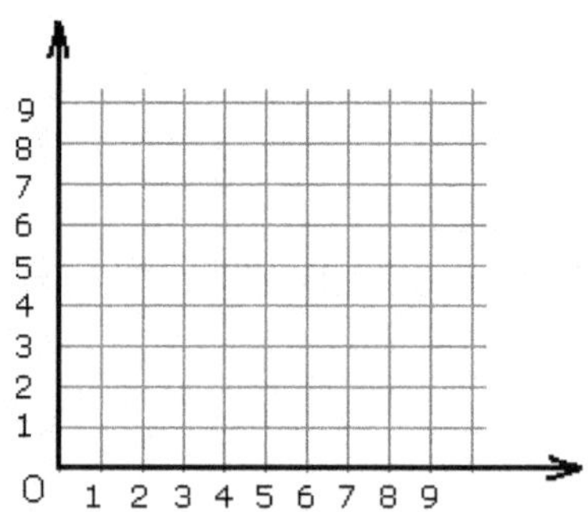

6. A (5, 2) B (3, 5) C (7, 5)

   D (5, 2) E (9, 2) F (5, 8)

   G (1, 2) H (5, 2)

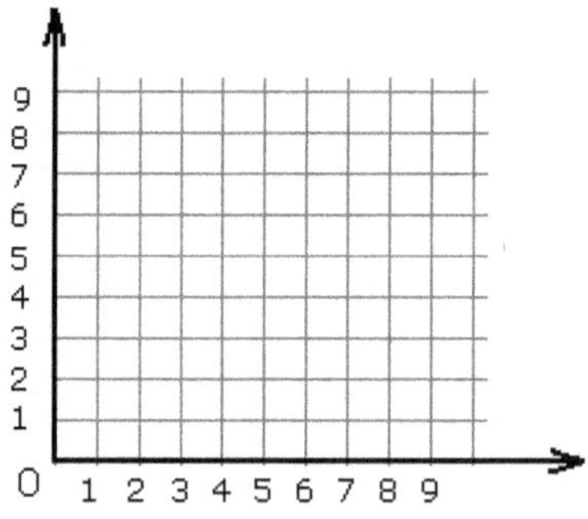

7. A (2, 8) B (3, 8) C (3, 7) D (4, 7)

   E (4, 8) F (5, 8) G (5, 7) H (6, 7)

   I (6, 8) J (7, 8) K (7, 6) L (6, 6)

   M (6, 2) N (7, 2) O (7, 1) P (2, 1)

   Q (2, 2) R (3, 2) S (3, 6) T (2, 6)

   U (2, 8)

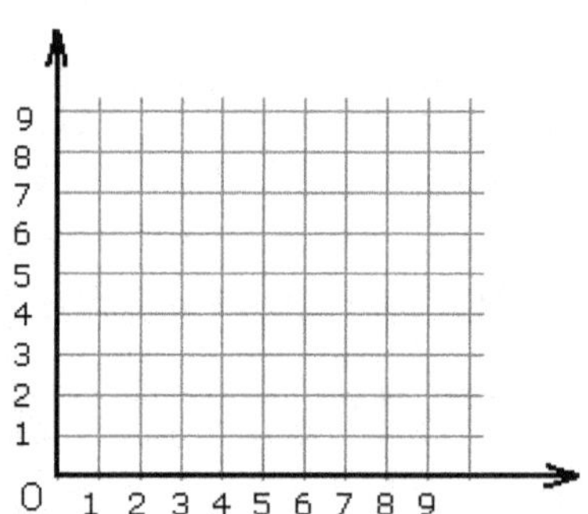

Ho Math Chess Primary Grades Math

Test Review assesssment 何数棋謎低年级数学测试複習考核

Student's name: ______________________ Assignment date: _________________

***** Part 21 Linear graph relationships *****

Example:

Input	Output	Ordered pairs
2	1	(2 , 1)
3	2	(3 , 2)
4	3	(4 , 3)
5	4	(5 , 4)
6	5	(6 , 5)
7	6	(7 , 6)
8	7	(8 , 7)

Graph ordered pairs.

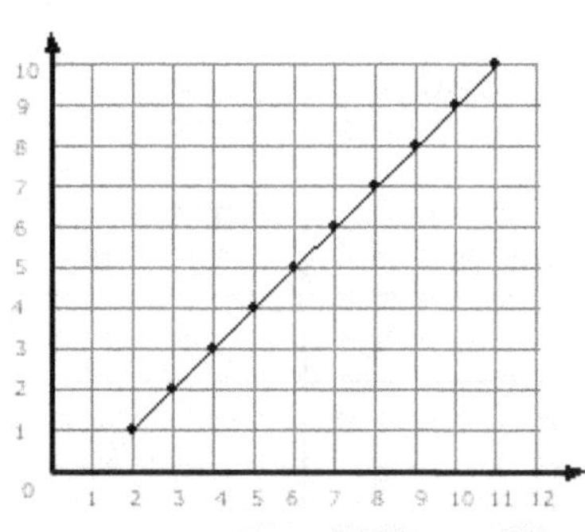

Find the pattern and complete the table. Then graph the relationship.

8.

Input	Output	Ordered pairs
2	1	(2 , 1)
4	2	(4 , 2)
6		
8		
10		
12		
14	7	(14 , 7)
16		

9.

Input	Output	Ordered pairs
1	1	(1 , 1)
2	3	(2 , 3)
3	5	(3 , 5)
4		
5		
6		
7		
8		

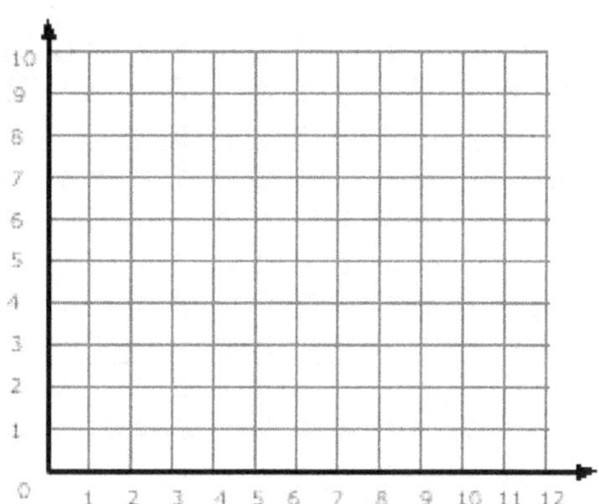

Student's name: ____________________ Assignment date: ________________

10.

Input	Output	Ordered pairs
1	10	(1 , 10)
2	20	(2 , 20)
3	30	
4		
5		
6		
7		
8		

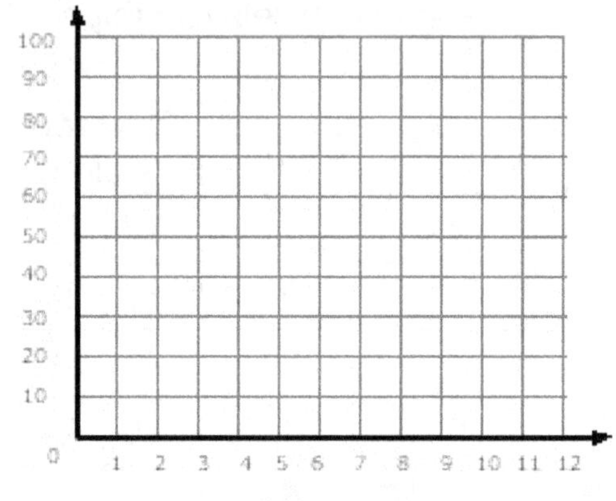

11.

Input	Output	Ordered pairs
1	5	(1 , 5)
2	10	(2 , 10)
3	15	
4		
5		
6		
10		
12		

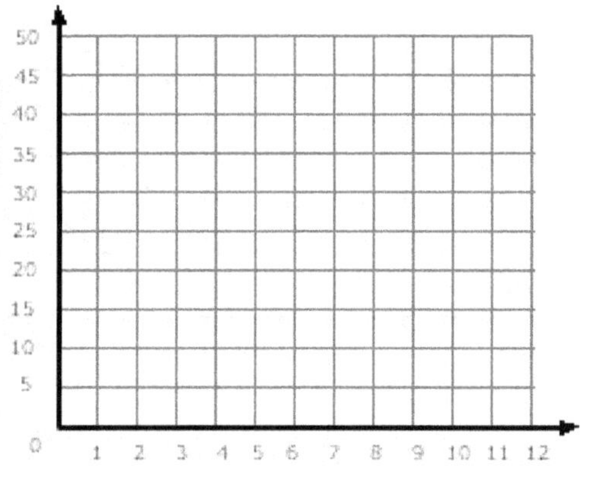

12.

Input	Output	Ordered pairs
1	1	(1 , 1)
2	4	(2 , 4)
3	9	
4		
5		
10		
20		
50		

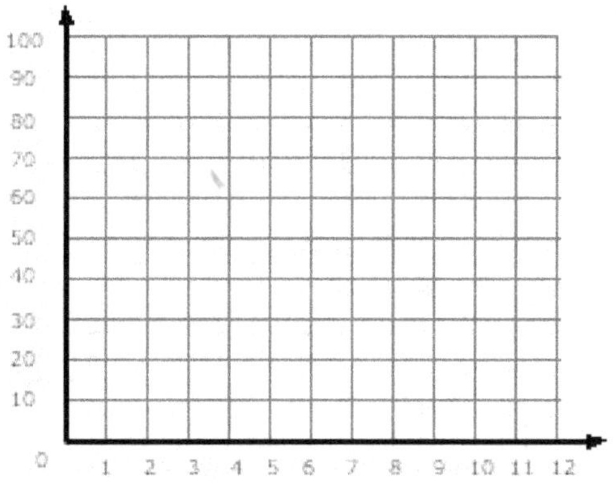

Student's name: ____________________ Assignment date: ________________

13.

Input	Output	Ordered pairs
1	4	(1 , 4)
2	7	(2 , 7)
3	10	
4		
5		
6		
10		
100		

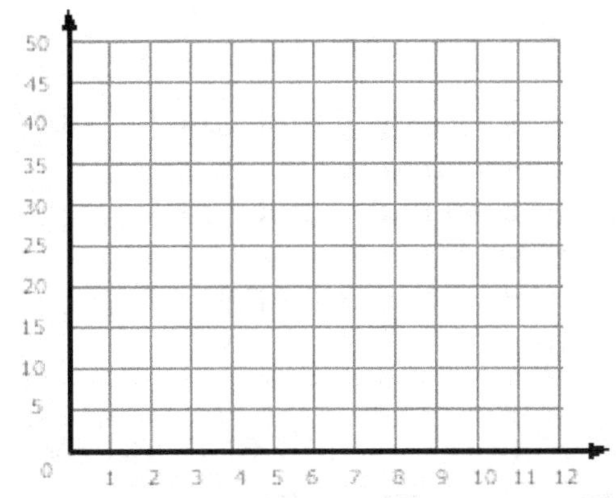

14.

Input	Output	Ordered pairs
1	3	
2	7	
3	11	
4		
5		
6		
10		
20		

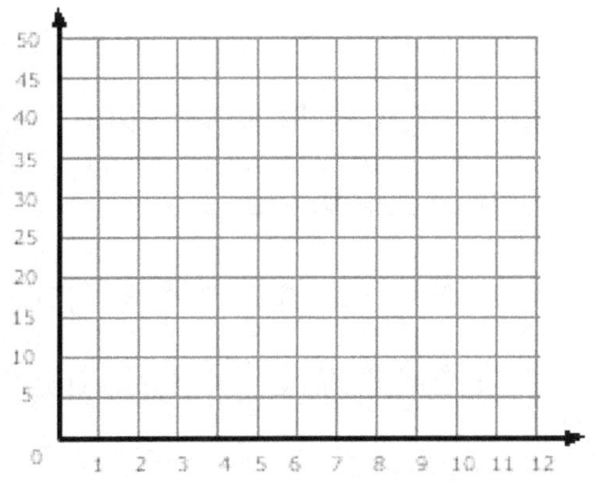

15.

Input	Output	Ordered pairs
5	1	
10	2	
15	3	
20		
25		
30		
50		
100		

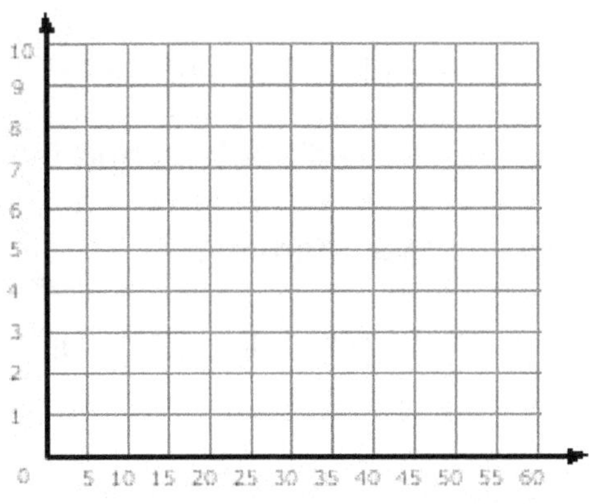

Student's name: ____________________ Assignment date: ________________

***** Part 22 Likelihood or possibility *****

The chance of an event that could happen is "unlikely" if the event is expected to happen less than half of the time.
The chance of an event that could happen is "likely" if the event is expected to happen more than half of the time.
The chance of an event that could happen is "even" if the event is expected to happen exactly half of the time.

Make predictions whether each event is impossible, unlikely, likely, even (exactly half of the time) or certain.

1. Throw a dice, the probability of getting an even number is __________
2. Draw a card from a deck. The probability of getting heart is __________
3. There are eight red marbles and one white marble. The probability of picking a white marble is __________
4. Throw a coin, the probability of getting a 'head' is __________
5. There are three dimes and five quarters. The probability of picking a dime or a quarter is __________
6. 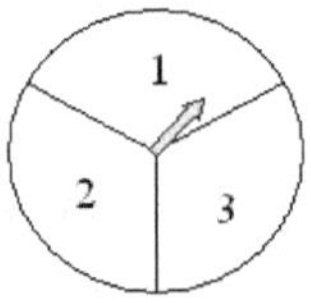 Spin a spinner, the probability of getting a '2' is __________
7. There are five red marbles and five white marbles. The probability of picking a black marble is __________
8. Draw a card from a deck. The probability of getting a King is __________

Student's name: ____________________ Assignment date: ________________

9. Denny played chess against Benny. Benny won six times and lost two times. The probability for Denny winning the next game is ____________

10. 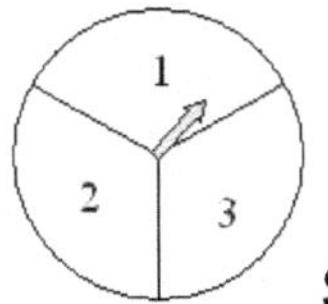

Spin a spinner, the probability of getting a '4' is ____________

11. Throw a dice, the probability of getting an odd number is ____________

12. Throw a dice, the probability of getting a number not less than 5 is ____________

Student's name: ____________________ Assignment date: ________________

Make predictions whether each event is impossible, unlikely, likely, or certain.

1. A train is faster than a car. __________
2. A dog is heavier than a cat. __________
3. A cow eats mice. __________
4. Steve can eat twenty eggs for each meal. __________
5. A tree turns green during spring. __________
6. The earth rotates around the sun. __________
7. Winter is warmer than in summer. __________
8. A cat will take a mouse. __________
9. A bird cannot fly. __________
10. A rabbit runs faster than a turtle. __________
11. You will go hiking during summer vacation. __________
12. You can write twenty words in a minute. __________
13. If Sam doesn't eat for a whole day, he will feel hungry. __________
14. If you run, your heart will beat slower. __________
15. A horse is heavier than an elephant. __________
16. A goldfish can live without water. __________
17. A snake has four legs. __________
18. A bicycle has two wheels. __________
19. A crow is white. __________
20. Stone is harder than mud. __________

Student's name: ____________________ Assignment date: ________________

Equal, likely, and unlikely by calculating their chances

1. There are four red marbles and four green marbles in a box. Pick up a marble randomly without looking. The probability of choosing green marble and the red marble is:

   a. equally likely b. unequally likely

2. There are three nickels, four dimes, and four quarters in a bag. Pick up a coin randomly without looking. The probability of choosing a dime and a quarter is:

   a. equally likely b. unequally likely

3. Throw a coin. The probability of getting a tail and getting a head is"

   a. equally likely b. unequally likely

4. 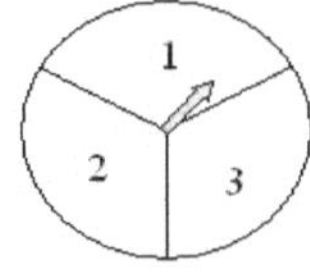

Spin a spinner. The probability of getting a '2' and getting a '3' is:

   a. equally likely b. unequally likely

5. 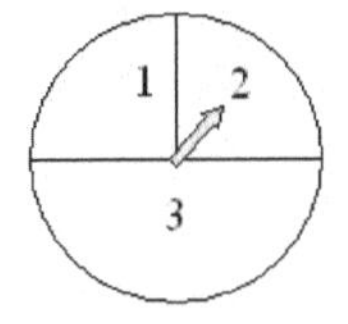

Spin a spinner. The probability of getting a '2' and getting a '3' is:

   a. equally likely b. unequally likely

6. From the box to the left, choosing a triangle and a square is:

   a. equally likely b. unequally likely

7. From the box to the left, choosing a circle and a square is:

   a. equally likely b. unequally likely

8. From the box to the left, choosing a triangle and a circle is:

Student's name: ____________________ Assignment date: ________________

a. equally likely b. unequally likely

7. Name an event that is (1) impossible, (2) likely, (3) unlikely, (4) certain.

____

Student's name: ____________________ Assignment date: ______________

Likelihood and comparisons on spinners

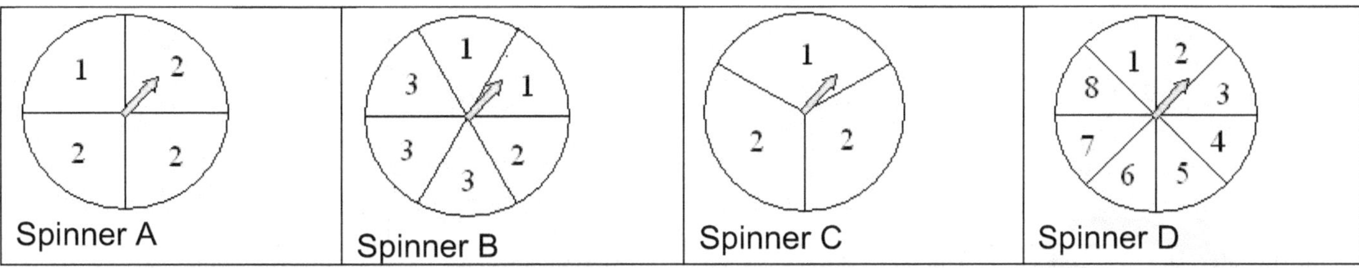

What could be the likely results of 24 spins for the Spinner A if the arrow lands on odd numbers? What could be the likely results of 24 spins for the Spinner B if the arrow lands on odd numbers? What could be the likely results of 24 spins for the Spinner C if the arrow lands on odd numbers? What could be the likely results of 24 spins for the Spinner D if the arrow lands on odd numbers?
What could be the likely results of 24 spins for the Spinner A if the arrow lands on the number 6? What could be the likely results of 24 spins for the Spinner B if the arrow lands on the number 6? What could be the likely results of 24 spins for the Spinner C if the arrow lands on the number 6? What could be the likely results of 24 spins for the Spinner D if the arrow lands on the number 6?
Which spinner would you choose if spinning an even number wins a prize?
What could be the likely results of 16 spins for the Spinner D if the arrow lands on even numbers?

Ho Math Chess Primary Grades Math

Test Review assessssment 何数棋謎低年级数学测试複習考核

Student's name: ____________________ Assignment date: ________________

***** Part 23 Probability *****

Write the probability of spinning each outcome.

1.	A, B, B, A, A, C	2.	1, 2, 3	3.	C, B, B, A, A, C	4.	1, 2, 2
	The letter B.		The number 1.		The letter B.		The number 2.
	2 out of 6.		___ out of ___.		___ out of ___.		___ out of ___.
5.	1, 3, 2, 4	6.	1, 3, 2, 3	7.	1, 1, 1	8.	A, B, B, A, A, B
	The number 3.		The number 3		The number 2		The letter B.
	___ out of ___.		___ out of ___.		___ out of ___.		___ out of ___.
9.	1, 2, 2, 2	10.	1, 1, 2	11.	1, 3, 1, 3, 2, 3	12.	1, 2, 8, 3, 7, 4, 6, 5
	The number 2.		The number 2.		The number 1.		The number 3.
	___ out of ___.		___ out of ___.		___ out of ___.		___ out of ___.
13.	1, 2, 3, 3, 3, 4, 4, 1	14.	C, B, B, A, A, A	15.	1, 2, 2, 3	16.	A, B, B, C, C, A, A, D
	The number 4.		The letter A.		The number 2.		The letter B.
	___ out of ___.		___ out of ___.		___ out of ___.		___ out of ___.

Student's name: ____________________ Assignment date: ________________

Write the probability of each outcome.

	Example: Toss a coin. What is the probability of getting a head?
	Total outcomes: head, tail
	The probability of getting a head is: 1 out of 2
1.	Throw a dice. What is the probability of getting '3'?
2.	One letter is randomly chosen from the word 'chess'. What is the probability of choosing the letter 's'?
3.	There are 12 boys and fifteen girls in the classroom. If one student is randomly chosen, what is the probability of choosing a boy?
4.	There are 5 red marbles, 3 white marbles, 4 green marbles, and 2 yellow marbles in a bag. Randomly choose a marble from the bag. What is the probability of choosing a white marble?
5.	Throw a dice. What is the probability of getting an even number?
6.	One letter is randomly chosen from the word 'butter' what is the probability of choosing the letter 't'?
7.	Throw a dice. What is the probability of getting a number not less than 5?

Student's name: ____________________ Assignment date: ________________

8.	There are 6 red marbles, 2 white marbles, 7 green marbles, and 5 yellow marbles in a bag. Randomly choose a marble from the bag. What is the probability of choosing a red marble?
9.	One letter is randomly chosen from the word 'singing'. What is the probability of choosing the letter 'i?
10.	A cube has 6 sides. The sides have the letters 'A', 'B', 'A', 'C', 'A', and 'B'. Throw the dice. What is the probability of getting the letter 'B'?
11.	There are 3 pennies, 5 nickels, 9 dimes, and 8 quarters. Pick a coin randomly. What is the probability of picking a quarter?
12.	There are 3 pennies, 6 nickels, 4 dimes, and 9 quarters. Pick a coin randomly. What is the probability of picking a penny or a dime?
13.	There are 4 red marbles, 5 white marbles, 8 green marbles, and 3 blue marbles in a bag. Choose a marble from the bag randomly. What is the probability of choosing a red or a green marble?
14.	One letter is randomly chosen from the word 'noon'. What is the probability of choosing the letter 'n' or 'o'?

Student's name: ____________________ Assignment date: ________________

Make predictions.

Example: There are 20 red marbles and blue marbles in a bag. Sam took out a marble, recorded the colour and put it back.

Red	Blue
卌	卌
	卌
	卌

The result shows that there are three times as many blue marbles as red marbles. So, Sam predicts 5 red marbles and 15 blue marbles.

1. There are 50 dimes and quarters in a bag. Linda took a coin, made a record, and put it back. The record is shown below. Predict the number of dimes and quarters.

Dimes	Quarters
卌	卌
卌	卌
卌	

2. There are 18 red and green tokens in a box. Linda took a token, made a record, and put it back. The record is shown below. Predict the number of red and green tokens.

Red	Green
卌	卌
卌	

Student's name: ____________________ Assignment date: ________________

3.		Spin the spinner 30 times. Prediction how many times the spinner will land on each number. 0 1: __________ 0 2: __________ 0 3: __________
4.		Spin the spinner 20 times. Prediction how many times the spinner will land on each number. 5 1: __________ 0 2: __________ 5 3: __________
5.		Spin the spinner 30 times. Prediction how many times the spinner will land on each letter. A: __________ 0 B: __________ 5 C: __________
6.	● ■ ▶ ▼ ■ ◆ ● ▼ ◀ ■	There are ten shapes in a box. Randomly pick a shape, make a record, and put it back. Repeat 50 times. Prediction how many times each shape will come up. 0 Circle: __________ Square: __________ 20 Triangle: __________
7.		There are 6 cards in a box. Choose a card randomly. Repeat 30 times. Prediction how many times each kind of card will show up. 5 : __________ 0 : __________ 5 : __________

Student's name: ____________________ Assignment date: ________________

According to the experiment result, draw a spinner that matches.

1.	Red	卌 卌		○
	Blue	卌 卌		
	Yellow	卌 卌		
2.	Red	卌		○
	Blue	卌		
	Yellow	卌 卌		
	Black	卌 卌		
3.	A	10		○
	B	20		
	C	30		
4.	1	卌 卌		○
	2	卌 卌 卌 卌		

Student's name: ____________________ Assignment date: ________________

5.

A	卌 卌
B	卌 卌
C	卌 卌 卌 卌

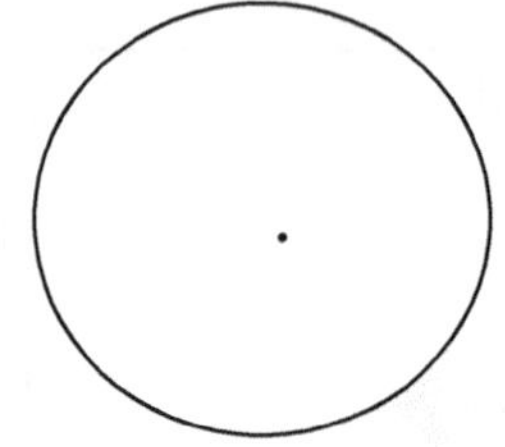

Student's name: ____________________ Assignment date: ________________

Analogue clock Time

Telling time

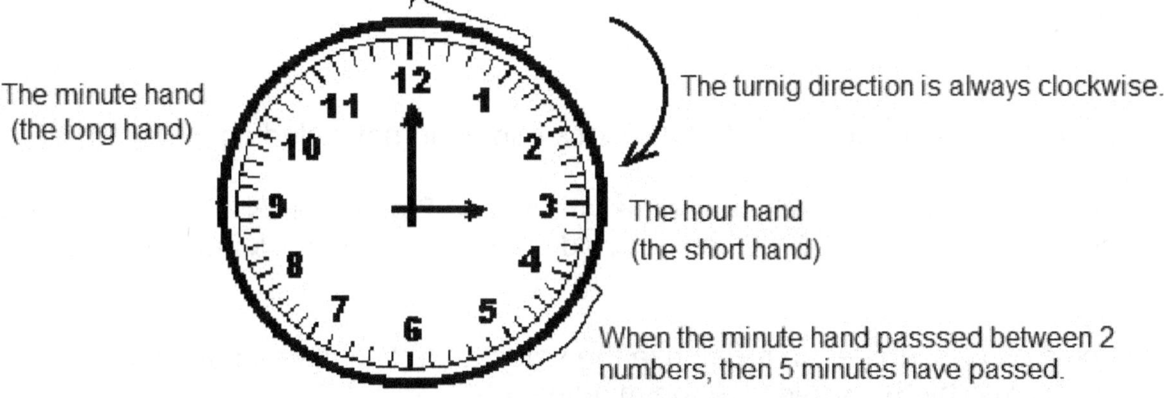

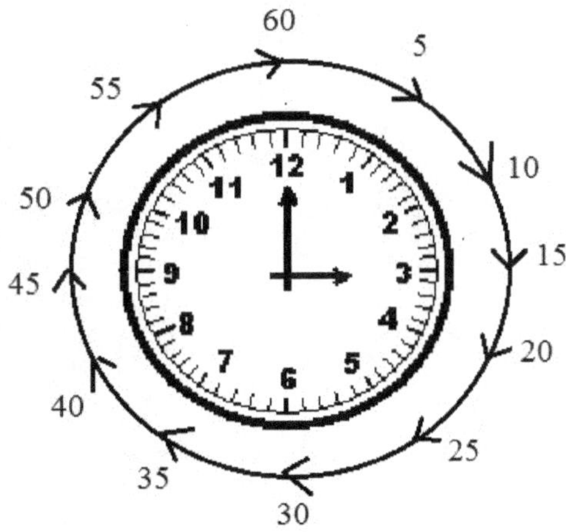

1. If the minute hand is pointing at 12, then the minute is 0 rather than 60 minutes. 12 is only on the clock for displaying to show 60 minutes = 1 hour.

2. By the time the minute hand travels back to the number 2 again, a total of 60 minutes have passed. In this case, the hour hand will increase by 1 hour, and the minute goes back to 0.

Student's name: ____________________ Assignment date: ________________

3. a.m. and p.m. is a 12-hour clock system. The 24 hours of a day are divided into two periods: a.m. (from the Latin ante meridiem, meaning "before midday") and p.m. (post meridiem, "after midday").

4. a.m. (before midday)
   The time from midnight to noon (not including noon) is called a.m.
   For the 12-hour expression, midnight is written as 12 a.m. For 24-hour expression, 12 o'clock midnight is written as 0:0. Often to avoid confusion, 12 o'clock midnight is often written as 12:00 midnight.

5. p.m.
   The time period from 12 o'clock noon to 12 o'clock midnight (not including midnight) is called p.m.
   For the 12-hour expression, 12 o'clock noon is written as 12 p.m. For 24-hour expression, 12 o'clock noon is written as 12:00. Often to avoid confusion, 12 o'clock noon is written as 12:00 noon

6. Students should be encouraged to memorize the times table of 5 instead of using the technique of counting by 5s to calculate the minutes.

Student's name: ____________________ Assignment date: ________________

5's multiples for telling time

5, ☐, 15, ☐, 25, ☐, 35, ☐, ☐, ☐, ☐, ☐, ☐
☐, ☐, 15, 20, ☐, 30, ☐, ☐, ☐, ☐, ☐, ☐
☐, ☐, ☐, 20, 25, 30, ☐, ☐, ☐, ☐, ☐, ☐
☐, ☐, ☐, ☐, ☐, ☐, ☐, ☐, ☐, 50, 55, 60
☐, ☐, ☐, ☐, ☐, ☐, 35, 40, 45, ☐, ☐, ☐, ☐

$5 \times 1 =$	$5 \times 3 =$
$5 \times 2 =$	$5 \times 4 =$
$5 \times 3 =$	$5 \times 5 =$
$5 \times 4 =$	$5 \times 6 =$
$5 \times 5 =$	$5 \times 7 =$
$5 \times 6 =$	$5 \times 8 =$
$5 \times 7 =$	$5 \times 9 =$
$5 \times 8 =$	$5 \times 1 =$
$5 \times 9 =$	$5 \times 2 =$
$5 \times 7 =$	$5 \times 6 =$
$5 \times 8 =$	$5 \times 8 =$
$5 \times 9 =$	$5 \times 9 =$
$5 \times 2 =$	$5 \times 3 =$
$5 \times 3 =$	$5 \times 4 =$
$5 \times 4 =$	$5 \times 6 =$
$5 \times 6 =$	$5 \times 5 =$
$5 \times 7 =$	$5 \times 9 =$
$5 \times 8 =$	$5 \times 3 =$
$5 \times 9 =$	$5 \times 4 =$
$5 \times 4 =$	$5 \times 8 =$
$5 \times 5 =$	$5 \times 5 =$
$5 \times 6 =$	$5 \times 2 =$
$5 \times 5 =$	$5 \times 3 =$
$5 \times 6 =$	$5 \times 4 =$
$5 \times 7 =$	$5 \times 7 =$
$5 \times 8 =$	$5 \times 8 =$
$5 \times 4 =$	$5 \times 9 =$

Student's name: ____________________ Assignment date: ________________

1.

____o'clock

_____ : _____

2.

____o'clock

_____ : _____

3.

____o'clock

_____ : _____

4.

____o'clock

_____ : _____

5.

____o'clock

_____ : _____

6.

____o'clock

_____ : _____

7.

____o'clock

_____ : _____

8.

____o'clock

_____ : _____

9.

____o'clock

_____ : _____

Student's name: ____________________ Assignment date: ________________

Telling time

1.

half past ____

____ : ____

2.

half past ____

____ : ____

3.

half past ____

____ : ____

4.

Quarter past ____

____ : ____

5.

Quarter past ____

____ : ____

6.

Quarter past ____

____ : ____

7.

Quarter to ____

____ : ____

8.

Quarter to ____

____ : ____

9.

Quarter to ____

____ : ____

Student's name: ____________________ Assignment date: ________________

What time is it to the nearest 5 minutes?

1. _____ :_____

2. _____ :_____

3. _____ :_____

4. _____ :_____

5. _____ :_____

6. _____ :_____

7. _____ :_____

8. _____ :_____

9. _____ :_____

Student's name: ____________________ Assignment date: ________________

Draw the hands on the clock to show the time.

1.

2:02

2.

4:04

3.

5:07

4.

8:24

5.

12:03

6.

3:12

7.

6:36

8.

9:59

9.

10:37

Student's name: ____________________ Assignment date: ________________

Draw the hands on the clock to show the time.

1.

2:31

2.

half past 5

3.

9:34

4.

quarter past 5

5.

3:11

6.

10:17

7.

1:47

8.

quarter to 4

9.

quarter to 12

Student's name: ____________________ Assignment date: ________________

Draw the hands on the clock to show the time.

1.

2: 07

2.

7:13

3.

12:11

4.

9:36

5.

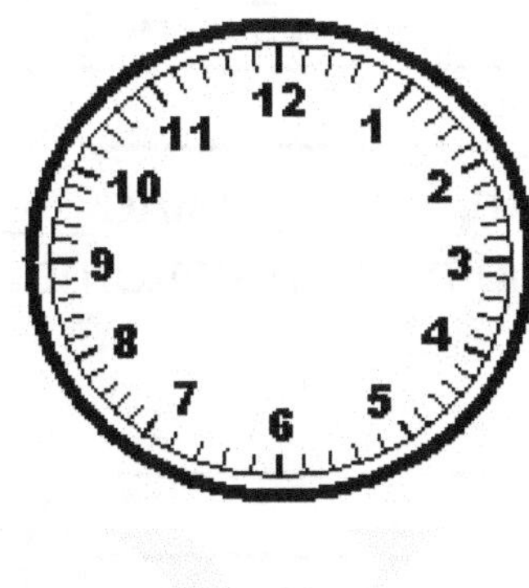

1:44

6.

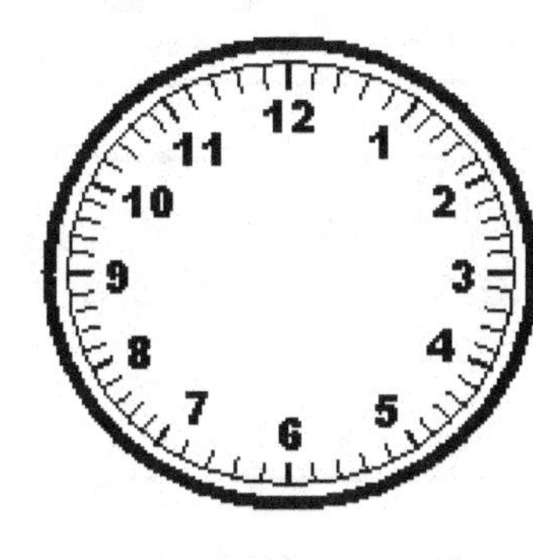

6:26

7.

15 minutes past 7

8.

20 minutes to 8

9.

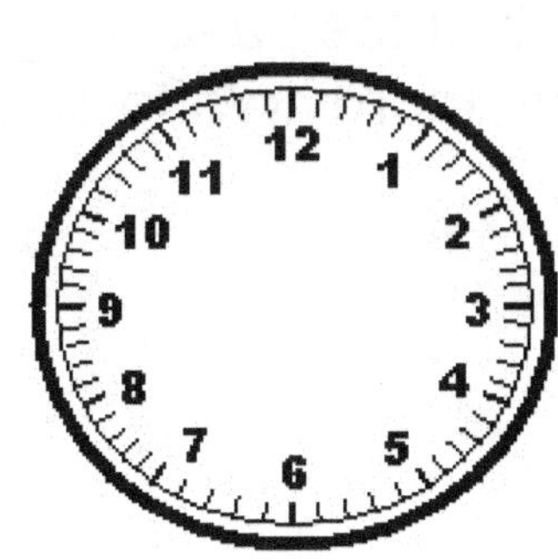

13 minutes after 5

Student's name: ____________________ Assignment date: ________________

Digital clock Time

01 : 25 am	09 : 55 am	03 : 40 pm
___ minutes past/to ___ in the morning/afternoon	___ minutes past/to ___ in the morning/afternoon	___ minutes past/to ___ in the morning/afternoon
10 : 50 pm	11 : 45 am	04 : 25 pm
___ minutes past/to ___ in the morning/afternoon	___ minutes past/to ___ in the morning/afternoon	___ minutes past/to ___ in the morning/afternoon
07 : 55 pm	06 : 10 am	08 : 40 am
___ minutes past/to ___ in the morning/afternoon	___ minutes past/to ___ in the morning/afternoon	___ minutes past/to ___ in the morning/afternoon

Student's name: ____________________ Assignment date: ________________

Time interval (Duration)

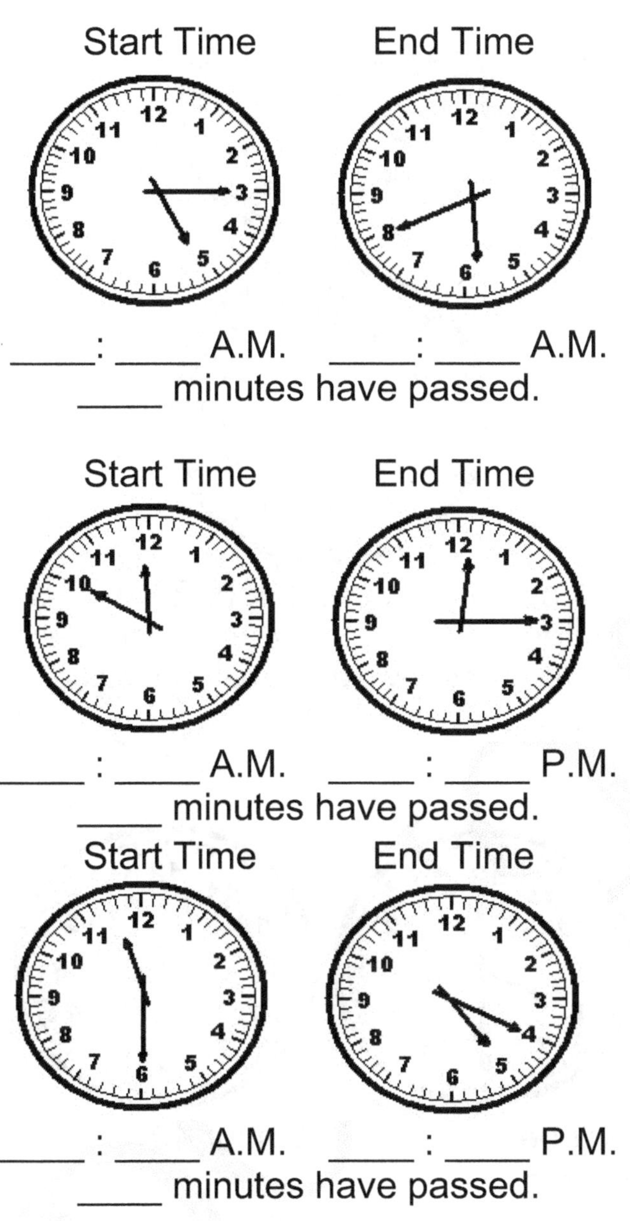

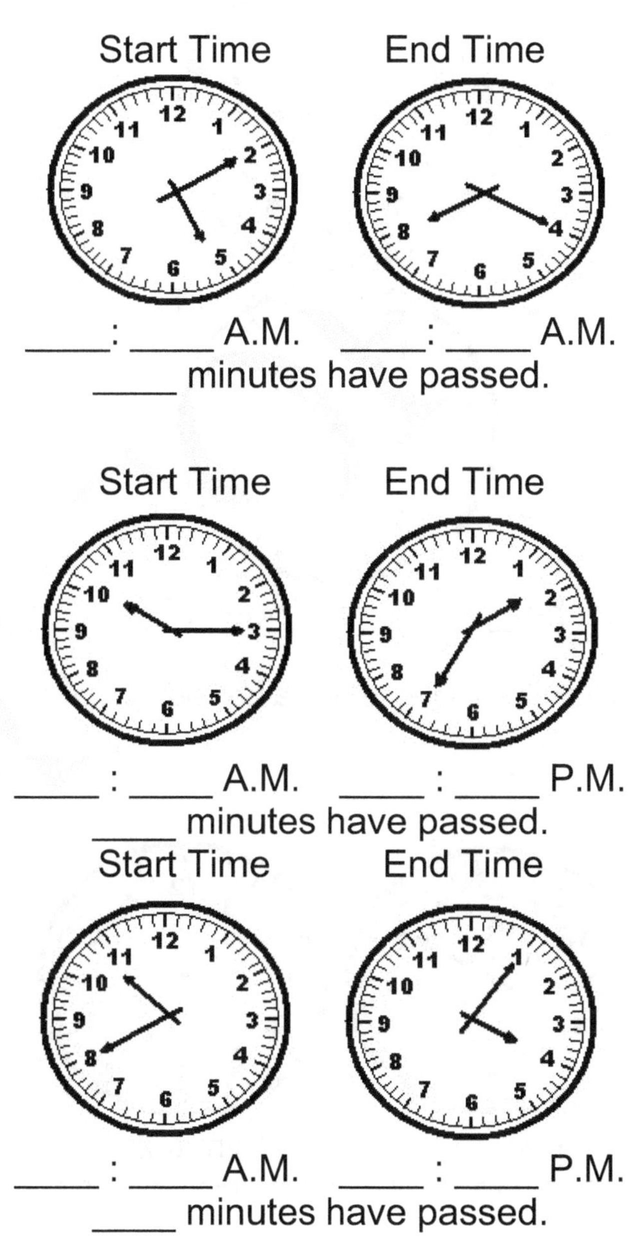

Student's name: ____________________ Assignment date: ________________

Time interval (Duration)

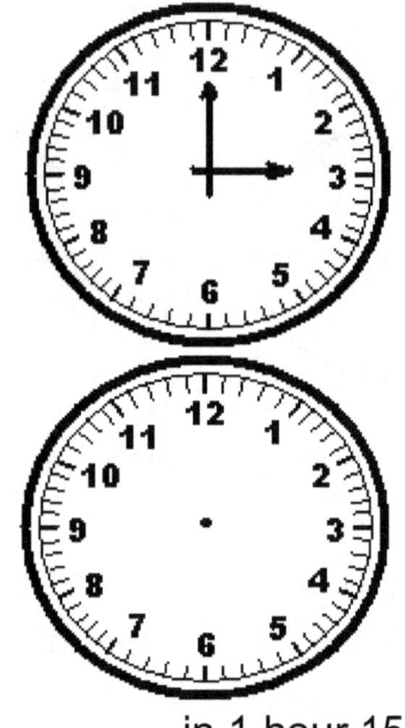

It will be _______ in 1 hour 15 minutes.
What time was it one and a half hours ago? _____

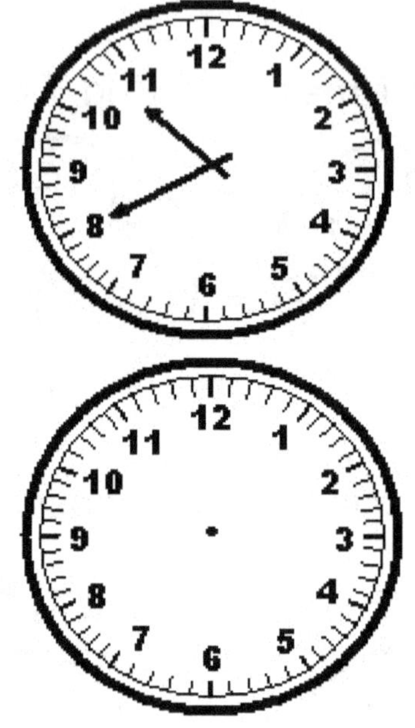

It will be _______ in 2 hour 20 minutes.
What time was it two and a half hours ago? _____

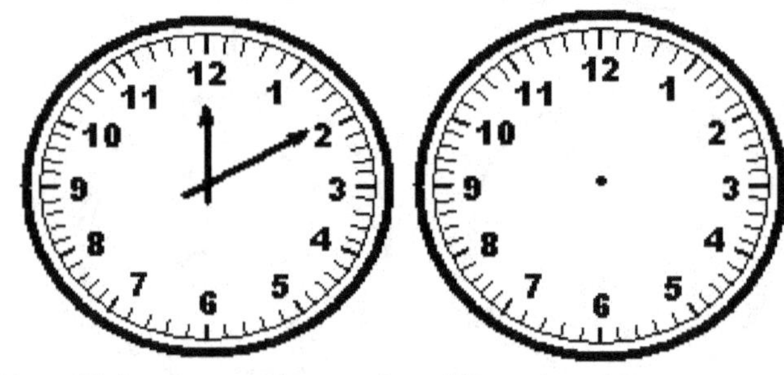

It will be _______ in 45 minutes.
What time was it two and 55 minutes ago? _____

It will be _______ in 1 hour 40 minutes.
What time was three hours and 20 minutes ago? _____

Student's name: ____________________ Assignment date: ________________

It will be _______ in 4 hour 25 minutes.

It will be _______ in 3 hour 50 minutes.

Student's name: ____________________ Assignment date: ________________

Pattern

Write the time and draw the clock hands on the clock.

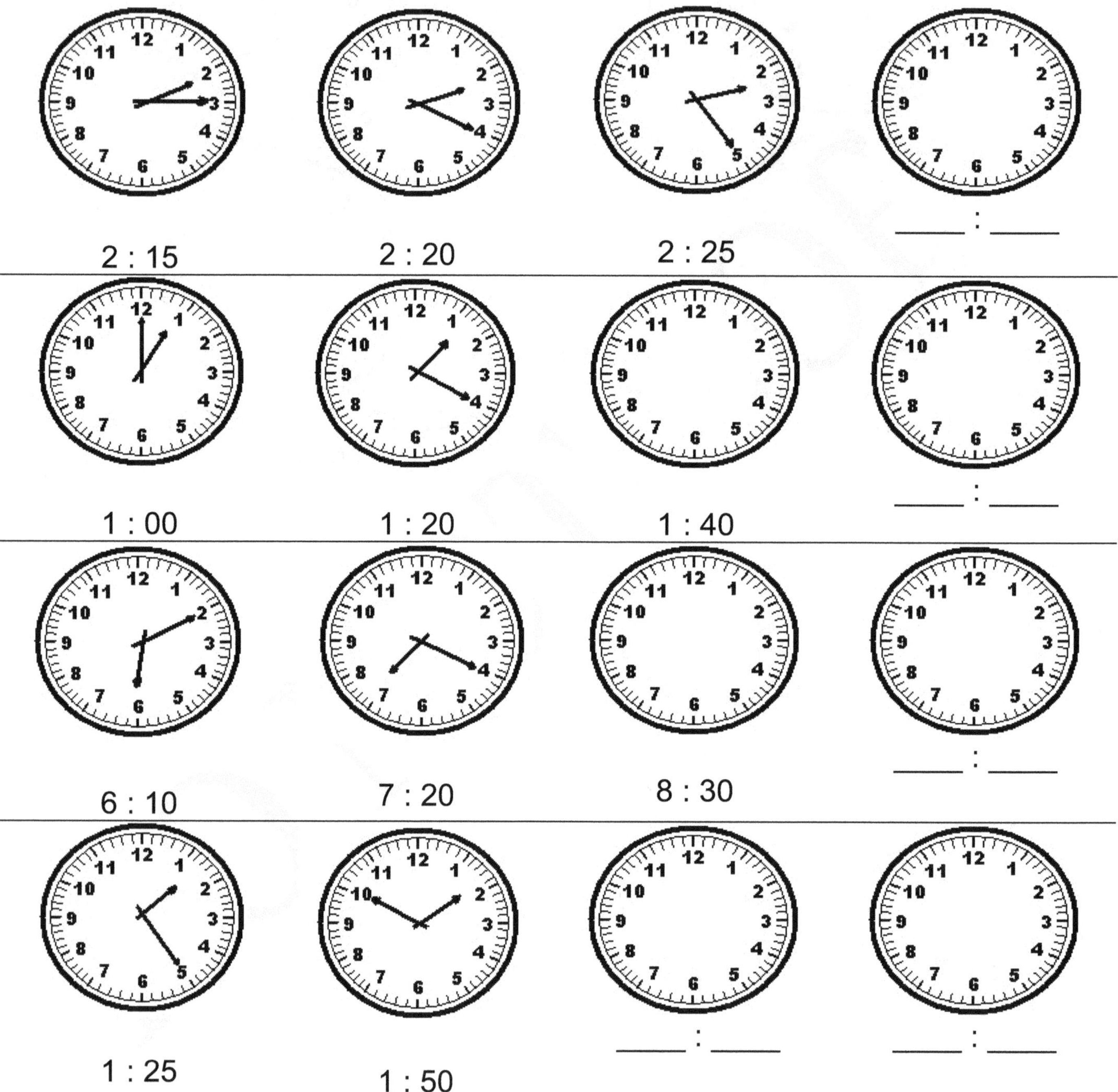

Ho Math Chess Primary Grades Math

Test Review assesssment 何数棋謎低年级数学测试複習考核

Student's name: ____________________ Assignment date: ________________

Pattern

Write the time and draw the clock hands on the clock.

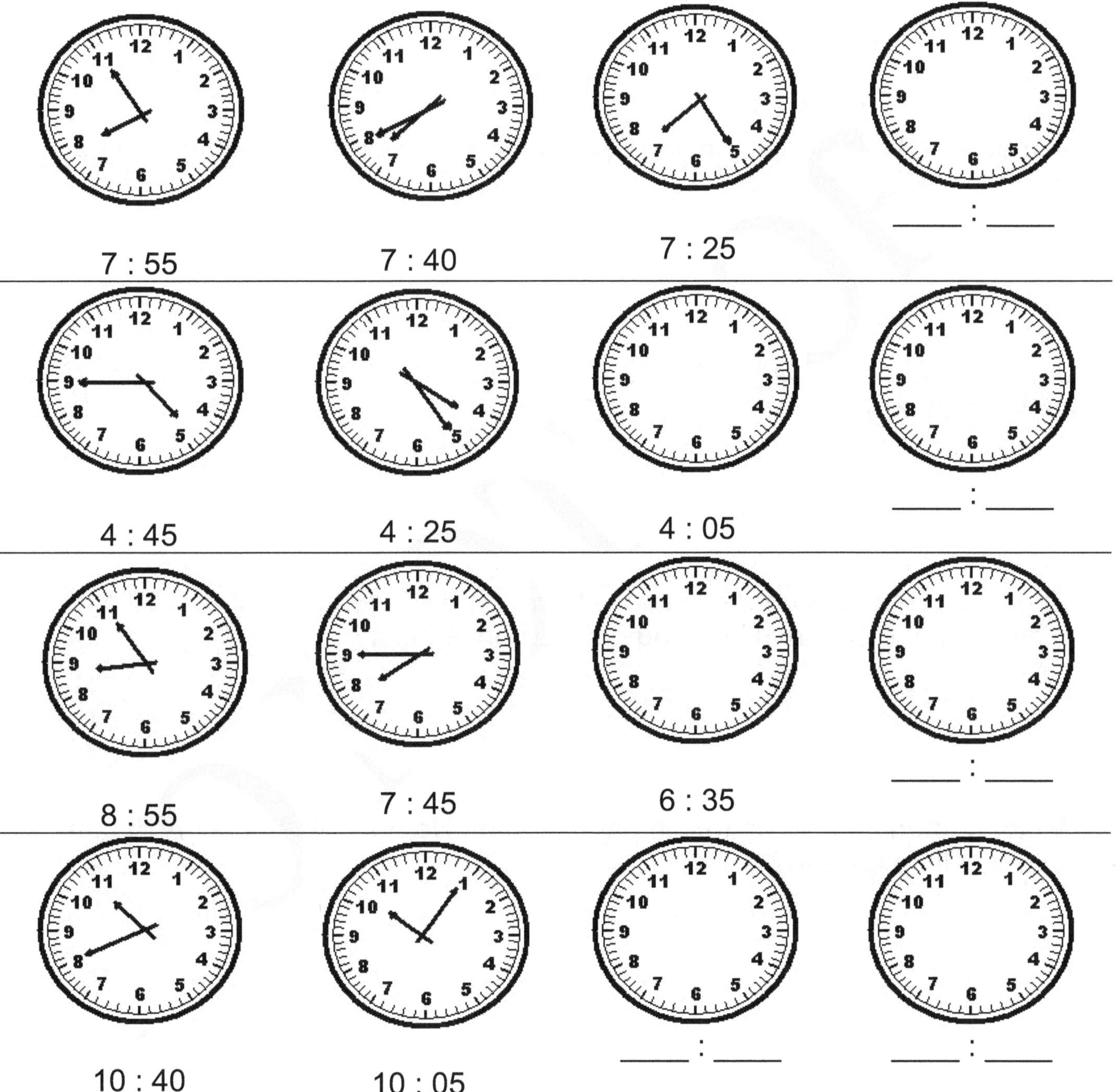

Student's name: ____________________ Assignment date: ________________

Time word problems

1. Adrian started playing piano at 4:00 p.m. He played until 5:30 p.m. How long did he play?

2. James and John started playing chess at 4:30 p.m. They played until 6:00 p.m. How long did they play?

3. Jennifer started drawing at 8:50 a.m. She finished at 9:10 p.m. How long did it take her to make?

4. The Joe's went to a concert in downtown. The concert started at 4:10 p.m. and finished at 6:30 p.m. How long did the concert last?

5. Victor started badminton training at 5:45 p.m. He got trained until 7:15 p.m. How much time passed?

Student's name: ____________________ Assignment date: ________________

Time word problems

1. Robbie plans to travel from Toronto to Seattle. The airplane will take off at 9:45 a.m. The trip will take him four hours and twenty minutes. When will he land on Seattle in Toronto time?

2. Shirley and Wendy went to a movie. The film started at 3:40 p.m. and would last two and a half hours. When would they get out of the cinema?

3. Betty went to school at 8:00 a.m. and went home at 2:30 p.m. How long did she stay at school?

4. Jonathan plans to go on a vacation in Hawaii from Vancouver. The airplane will take off at 10:00 a.m. He should arrive at the Vancouver international airport one and half an hour earlier before the departure time. It will take the bus for one hour to get to the airport. When should he arrive at the bus stop at the latest?

5. A Christmas party will start at 8:00 p.m. It will take the chef two and a half hours to prepare food. When should he start to work?

6. 1 hour 20 minutes multiplied by 4 = _______ hours _______ minutes

Student's name: ____________________ Assignment date: ________________

Calendar

Fill in the following blank.

1. There are ____ months in a year.

2. In a regular year, February has ____ days. A regular year has ____ days.

3. In a leap year, February has ____ days. A leap year has ____ days.

4. There are about ____ weeks in a year.

5. January, March, May, July, August, October, and December have ____ days each.

6. April, June, September, and November have ____ days each.

7. There are ____ days in a week. They are Monday, ________, ________, ________, ________, ________ and ________. I like _______ the best.

8. Today is January 6th . Tomorrow will be ________. The day after tomorrow will be ________.

9. Today is March 10th. Yesterday was ________. The day before yesterday was ________.

10. Today is Monday. Tomorrow will be ________. The day after tomorrow will be ________.

11. Today is Wednesday. Yesterday was ________. The day before yesterday was ________.

12. Today is July 25th. It will be ________ in 10 days.

Student's name: ____________________ Assignment date: ________________

13. Today is July 5th. 10 days earlier it was ________.

14. Today is Tuesday. It will be ________ in 10 days.

15. Today is Saturday. 10 days earlier it was ________.

16. Today is September 1st. It will be _____________ in one hundred days.

Student's name: ____________________ Assignment date: ________________

Use the calendar of February 2006 to answer the questions.

Sun	Mon	Tue	Wed	Thu	Fri	Sat
			1	2	3	4
5	6	7	8	9	10	11
12	13	14	15	16	17	18
19	20	21	22	23	24	25
26	27	28				

1. There are ____ Sundays in February 2006.
2. The date of the first Monday is ________.
3. The date of the second Wednesday is ________.
4. The date one week after February 4 is ________.
5. The date one week before February 4 is ________.
6. The date two weeks after February 23 is ________.
7. The date two weeks before February 23 is ________.
8. The date four weeks after February 23 is ________.
9. The date four weeks before February 23 is ________.
10. The day 5 days after February 10 is ________.
11. The day 5 days before February 10 is ________.
12. The day 10 days after February 10 is ________.
13. The day 10 days before February 10 is ________.
14. The day 20 days after February 10 is ________.
15. The day 20 days before February 10 is ________.
16. The day 30 days before February 10 is ________.
17. The day 30 days after February 10 is ________.
18. The day 100 days after February 6 is ________.

Student's name: ____________________ Assignment date: ________________

Multiple choices

1. There are ____ months with 31 days in one year.

a. 4 b. 5 c. 6 d. 7

2. There are ____ months with less than 31 days in one year.

a. 4 b. 5 c. 6 d. 7

3. There are ____ days in February 1978.

a. 28 b. 29 c. 30 d. 31

4. There are ____ days in February 1984.

a. 28 b. 29 c. 30 d. 31

5. There are ____ days in August 1991.

a. 28 b. 29 c. 30 d. 31

6. There are ____ days in September 1992.

a. 28 b. 29 c. 30 d. 31

7. ____ is a leap year.

a. 1836 b. 1537 c. 2562 d. 2006

8. ____ is a regular year.

a. 1636 b. 1996 c. 1984 d. 2005

9. ____ is a leap year.

a. 1998 b. 1999 c. 2000 d. 2001

10. ____ is a regular year.

a. 2004 b. 2008 c. 2010 d. 2012

11. There are ____ days from January 1, 2006, to March 31, 2006.

a. 89 b. 90 c. 91 d. 92

12. There are ____ days from January 1, 2004, to March 31, 2004.

a. 89 b. 90 c. 91 d. 92

Student's name: ____________________ Assignment date: ________________

Time word problems

1. The Lees will leave for California in 25 days. Today is April 2, 2015. What day will they leave?

2. Mark will go to a chess tournament held in Germany on June 24, 2016. He plans to get there 3 days ahead of time. The Journey will take him 2 days. What is the date he will go?

3. Grade 3 students plan to run 1 000 000 metres for Children Federation from June 22. They can run 20 000 metres every day. What date will the event end?

4. Emily planted a crop in her garden on March 25. If the crop grows 3 cm every day, and its full height is 63 cm. What date would the crop reach its full height?

5. A baby male kitten was born on October 18th and weighed 200 g. If he gains 4 g each day. In how many days will he reach 3 kg?

6. Grade 4 students will make 6000 paper airplanes for an airplane flying contest. They can make 150 airplanes every day after school. If they work on it from Monday to Friday every week and expect to complete the entire project by December 5th, should they start working on it at the latest?

Student's name: ____________________ Assignment date: ________________

Decades, Centuries and Millenniums

1 decade = 10 years 1 century = 100 years 1 millennium = 1000 years

1. It is 2007 this year. It was ________ one decade ago.
2. It is 2007 this year. It will be ________ in one decade.
3. It is 2007 this year. It was ________ one century ago.
4. It is 2007 this year. It will be ________ in one century.
5. It is 2007 this year. It was ________ one millennium ago.
6. It is 2007 this year. It will be ________ in one millennium.
7. 1 millennium =________ centuries =________ decades =________ years
8. 5 decades is ________ years.
9. 6 centuries are ________ years, _________ decades.
10. There are ________ millenniums in 2000 years.
11. There are 8 centuries in ________ decades.
12. The apple tree was planted 2 decades ago when it was 5 years old.

    It is ________ years old now.
13. That building celebrated its centennial year in 2005. It was established in ________.
14. The fossil was formed 3 millenniums ago. It is ________ years old.
15. The antique vase was made in the year 1500. It will have been ________ decades till 2020.
16. This clock was made 4 decades ago. If it is 2008 this year, then it was made in _______.

Student's name: ____________________ Assignment date: ________________

Test of time
Assume 1 month has 30 days.

5 weeks 3 days – 2 weeks 5 days =?
21 months 24 days ÷ 6 =?
20 hours 42 minutes ÷ 5 =?
21 hours 47 minutes ÷ 7 =?
18 days 13 hours – 8 days 14 hours =?

clock A

clock B

How many minutes have passed from clock A to clock B? ________________

Student's name: ____________________ Assignment date: ________________

Periodical data

Data appears to repeat the pattern core; then, it is called periodical data such as the calendar data.

Today is Wednesday. What day will it be 10 days after today?
Today is Wednesday. What day will it be 20 days before today?

Student's name: ____________________ Assignment date: ________________

Arrangement

Example

Kitty, Meghan, and Jordan are to sit in a row. How many different ways can they sit together? List all the ways.

Use the Box Method, then multiply all numbers.

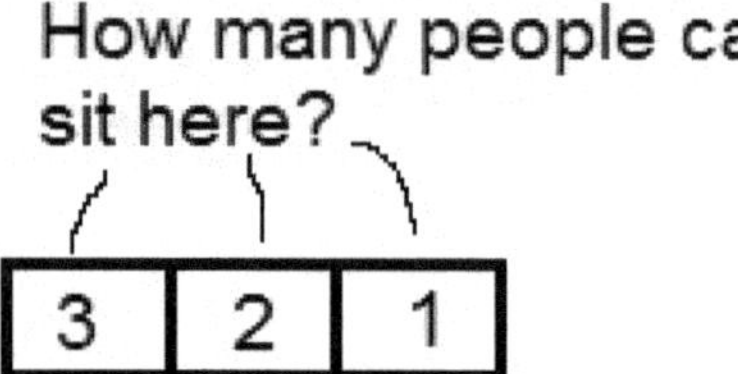

Heather has 2 shirts: red and blue. She also has a pair of pants and a skirt. How many different outfits that can she wear? Use the Multiplication method to get the answer.
Oscar has 3 digits: 3, 4 and 6. How many different numbers that he can create without using the same digit twice?
Oscar has 3 digits: 3, 4 and 6. How many different 3-digit numbers Oscar can create greater than 300 without using the same digit twice?
Oscar has 3 digits: 3, 4 and 6. How many different 3-digit numbers Oscar can create less than 400 without using the same digit twice?
Oscar has 3 digits: 3, 4 and 6. How many different even numbers that he can create without using the same digit twice? 6

Student's name: ____________________ Assignment date: ________________

Combinations using the T-table method

Example

A pencil costs 15 cents and an eraser costs 12 cents. Cindy has 50 cants. Show all the combinations of pencils and erasers that Cindy could buy. Cindy could buy only one item of both.

Use T-table to find four combinations.

How many different scores of using 2 darts? 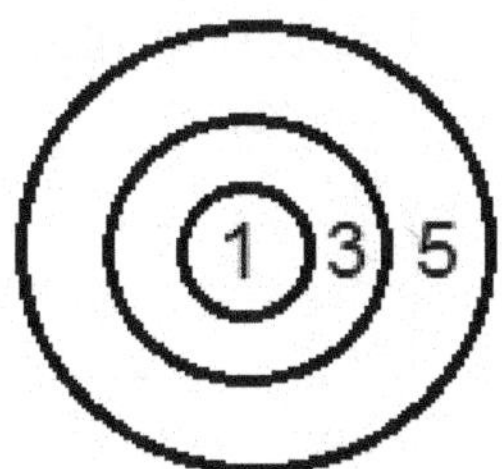
Jessica likes to choose 2 marbles out of a bag with three marbles, red, blue, and white. How many ways can she choose from?
Frank has two cats Kiko and Snow, and they like two kinds of cat food shredded or pate salmon. How many different ways can Frank feed his cats?
Kevin can choose one course in the morning out of two choices math or choose. He can also choose one activity out of three activities basketball, dance, or drama. How many choices that she can have? List all choices.

Student's name: ____________________ Assignment date: ________________

Brent has $0.37 consisting of 4 coins. How many nickels can he have?

Sarah got 9 points for throwing darts. There were 2-point and 3-point circles on the dart. How many 2-point darts did she get?

Alvin has $1.05 consists of quarters and dimes. Replace each ? with a number.

Dimes	Quarters	Total values	Total number of coins
?	?	$1.05	6
1	4	$1.05	5
3	3	$1.05	6

A chair can be purchased with the following choices:

Colours: red, blue, black
Sizes: small, medium, large
Material: metal, wood

How many different combinations are possible to choose from?

Student's name: ____________________ Assignment date: ________________

Model problems and strategies
Sum and difference

Some problems are classified as Model word problems in China, frequently appearing in lower grades. This kind of problem can be solved easily by using the algebraic method. Without using algebra, students could be taught with a story on how to solve it.

Example

A cell phone sells $15 more than a graphics calculator. Minnie buys a cell phone and a graphics calculator for a total of $395. How much does each item cost?

We can convert this kind of problem to a ``money dividing problem` that assumes two persons like to share a $395 pot of money and person C likes to have $15 more than person G.

$\frac{395-15}{2} = 190$ ……….. Cost of the graphics calculator
190 + 15 = 205 ……. Cost of the cell phone.

Students should check back the answer because if the cost of the graphics is calculated incorrectly, then the answer of cell phone depending on the cost of the calculator will also be wrong. There is an answer dependency problem here.

Student's name: ____________________ Assignment date: ________________

Floor and lineup problems

City Tower is 150 feet tall above ground and 75 feet below ground. How many feet is the tallest point higher than the lowest point?
Jocelyn is on the 6th steps of her school stairs. She walks down 3 steps, then up 2 steps. Finally, she walks up the remaining 3 steps to walk into her classroom. How many steps do the stairs have?
Kitty is on the ground floor of a condo. She walks up 7 floors, then down 5 floors, then up 3 floors, then down 2 floors. What floor does Kitty end up on?

Student's name: ____________________ Assignment date: ________________

Statistics

Austin scored 2 of 85% and 3 of 95% of his math tests. What was his average (mean) percent score for all five tests?
Three numbers are in a ratio of 1 to 2 to 3. The largest of these three numbers is 24. What is the average (mean) of these three numbers?
Fernando biked 62 miles to a park in 2 hours. What was his average speed?
Kathy bought 6 pencils at $0.75 each and 4 erasers. The average price of these 11 items was $0.66, what was the cost of one eraser?

Student's name: ____________________ Assignment date: ________________

Equation word problems

Five years ago, the sum of the ages of Jessica and her twin brother Kevin was 9. How old is Kevin now?
Brent is 10 years old. Two years less than two times his age is _______ years old.

Student's name: ____________________ Assignment date: ________________

Inequality

The way to sole inequality is the same as the equality equation other than the sign such as $-x >$ 3.

$-x > 3$
$x < -3$ (The inequality sign changes.)

Solve $\frac{x}{8} > \frac{1}{2}$
Four times of a whole number is less than 41 but greater than 32. What is the number?
If $\frac{3}{4} < x < 0.77$ then x could be ____ (Answer in 2 decimal places.).
Suppose N is a whole number and is divisible by 2 and is also a multiple of 5. What is N if it is between 10 and 30?

-

Student's name: ____________________ Assignment date: ________________

Work backwards

Arithmetic equation usually is working from left to right, so from the operation direction point of view, working backwards is to work from right to left and reverse its operators.

After Yi-yi spent \$9 on food and \$8 on a movie, she had \$29 left. How much money did she have at first?
If 150 × ☐ = 0.135, what is the value of ☐?
What is the smallest number that can be added to 50 to produce a number divisible by 8?

Student's name: ____________________ Assignment date: ________________

Scale - Making both sides balanced

1.

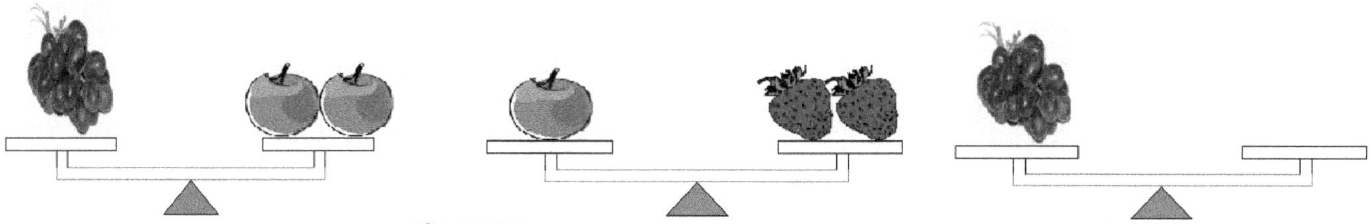

How many s can the balance? __________

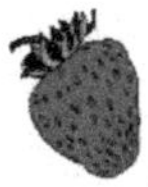

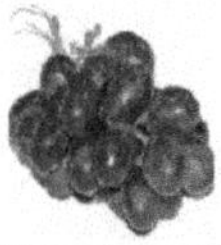

2.

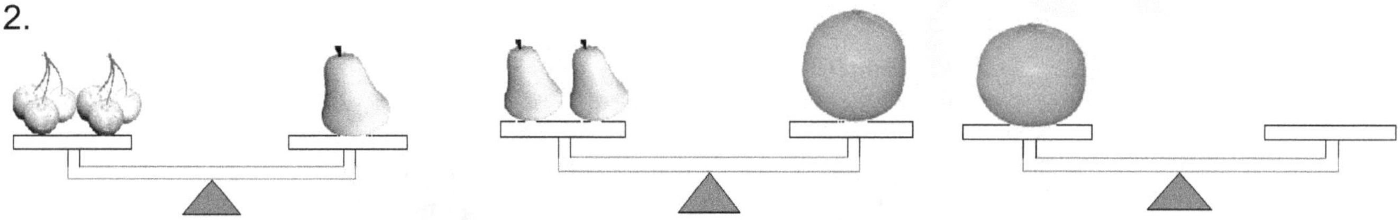

How many s can the balance? __________

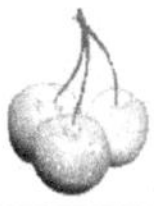

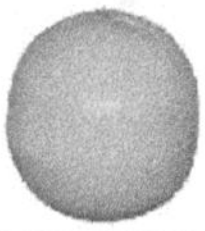

3.

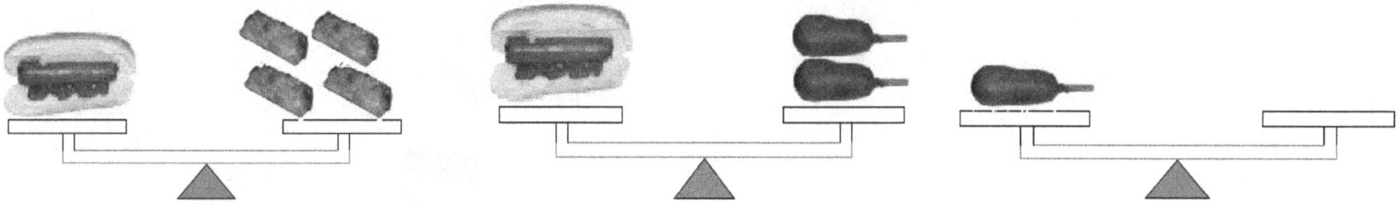

How many s can the balance? __________

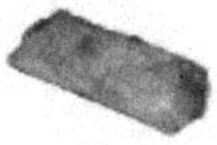

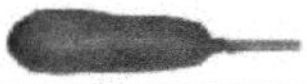

4.

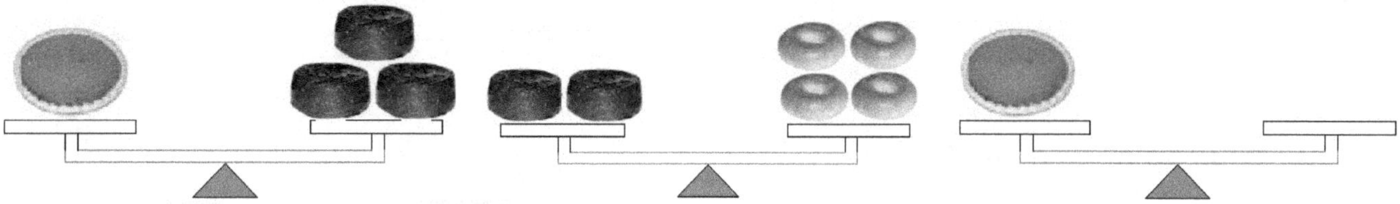

How many s can the balance? __________

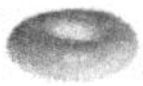

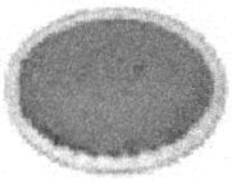

Ho Math Chess Primary Grades Math

Test Review assesssment 何数棋谜低年级数学测试複習考核

Student's name: ____________________ Assignment date: ________________

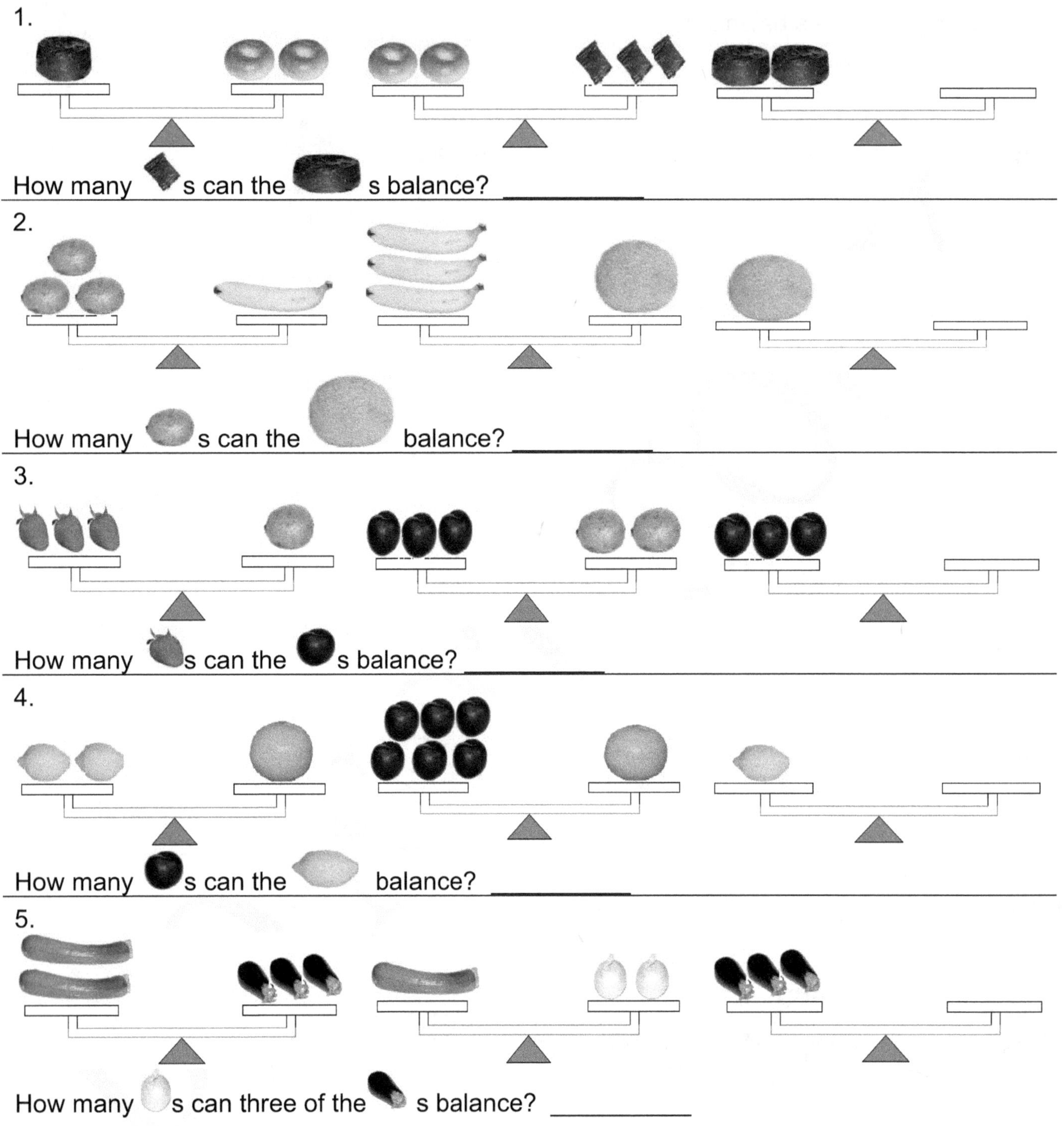

Student's name: ______________________ Assignment date: _________________

Number line

Number line

A number is drawn as follows to show 1 + 1 = 2.

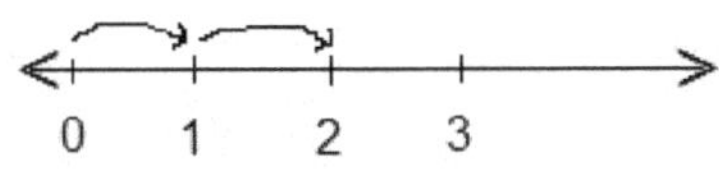

Look at the following diagram and come up with your equation.

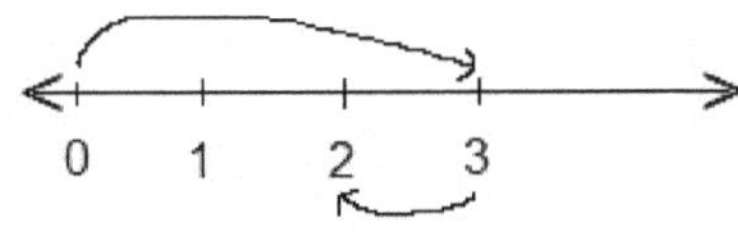

Write an equation for the following number line.

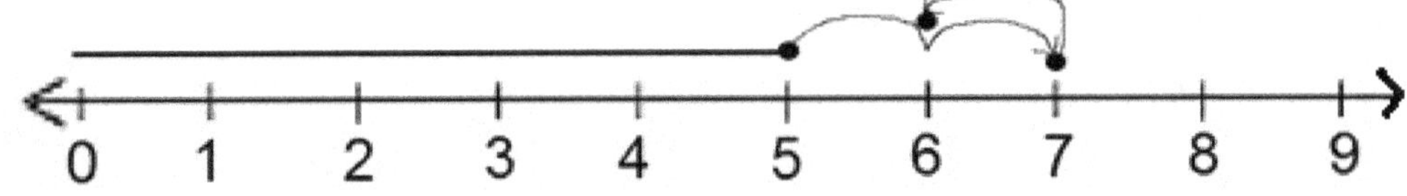

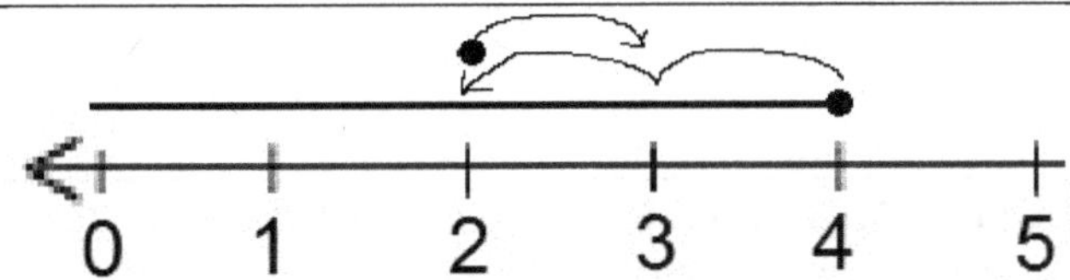

Write the equation for the above number line.

Student's name: ____________________ Assignment date: ________________

Do not always use 1 as an unknown quantity

Adding for less and subtracting for more

We often use "1" as a unit to solve the unknown quantity problem, for example, the work problem, but it is not convenient sometimes. The following example demonstrates the idea of not use "1" as the basic unit.

Example

In the following line segment diagram, the length of AB is 30 cm, the length of AC is equal to the length of DB, the length of the CD is $\frac{1}{2}$ of AC, what is the length of the CD?

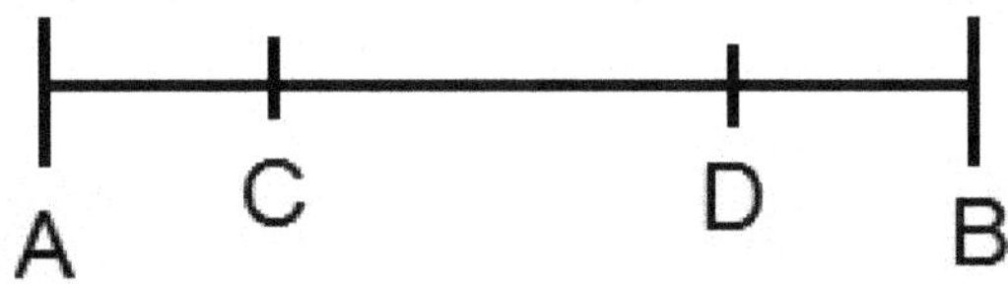

Assume AC = DB – 2
CD = 1
Ab is divided into 5 equal parts. Each pat is 6 cm.
CD = $6 \times 2 = 12\ cm.$

Pauline has half as many cat food cans as Elise. Jocelyn has half as many cat food cans as Pauline. Together they have 56 cans. How many cans does each one have?
Pauline has 2 less than twice as many cat food cans as Elise. Elise has 6 less than twice as many cat food cans as Jocelyn. Together they have 41 cans. How many cans does each one have?

Student's name: ____________________ Assignment date: ________________

Word problems

1. Harry Hiker saw 24 caterpillars when he was walking in the forest. When he stopped for lunch, he saw 5 more. How many caterpillars did he see altogether?

2. Wally Walker spotted and picked up 45 leaves on the grass. He then found 23 more in the park. What is the total number of leaves that Wally found?

3. Wendy Watcher saw 12 birds in her backyard today. Yesterday she saw 38 birds at the park. How many birds has she seen in all?

4. Tiffany owns 23 books. She received 2 more today for her birthday. What is the total number of books that Tiffany owns?

Student's name: ____________________ Assignment date: ________________

5. Tyler has 32 baseball cards. His friends give him 20 more. How many baseball cards does he have in all?

6. Christina counted 24 tulips in her garden. Her sister counted 15 roses. What is the sum number of flowers that they counted?

7. Anthony was on a Scouts trip and found 23 small twigs, 34 medium-sized twigs, and 25 large twigs for a campfire. How many twigs did he find altogether?

8. Tom, who was also on the camping trip, saw 10 squirrels climbing trees. He also saw 7 chipmunks scurrying to their homes. How many animals did Tom see in all?

Which two numbers have a sum of 22 and a difference of 12?

Student's name: ____________________ Assignment date: _______________

9. Jennifer went fishing with her dad, and she caught 3 fish. Her dad caught one. How many fish did Jennifer and her dad catch?

10. Larry, Curly, and Moe were playing a game of darts. Larry scored 10 points, Curly scored 12 points, and Moe scored 8 points. What is the total number of points that they scored?

11. Yumiko helped her mother make four rolls of sushi. Her younger sister helped make two. How many rolls of sushi did Yumiko and her sister help make?

12. Dave found 17 chocolates in the community Easter egg hunt. He also helped his little sister find seven. How many chocolates did he find altogether?

Student's name: ____________________ Assignment date: ________________

***** Part 24 Tests, reviews, and assessments *****

Kindergarten, grade 1 and above

If ◯ = 3, then ◯ + 1 = ______.
If ◯ = 4, then ◯ + 1 = ______.
If ● = 1, then ◯ = ●●● then ◯ + ● = ______.
If ◯ = ●●●, then ◯ + ●● = ______
If ◯ = ●●● and ● = 1, then ◯ – ● = _____
Match left to right by drawing lines. ● 4 ●●●● 2 ●● 3 ●●● 1
Out of 1, 2, and 3, what numbers added together will give answers of 3?

Student's name: ____________________ Assignment date: ________________

Number line
A number is drawn as follows to show 1 + 1 = 2.

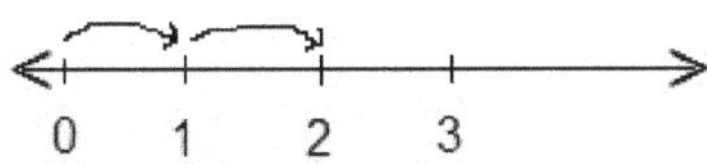

Look at the following diagram and come up with your equation.

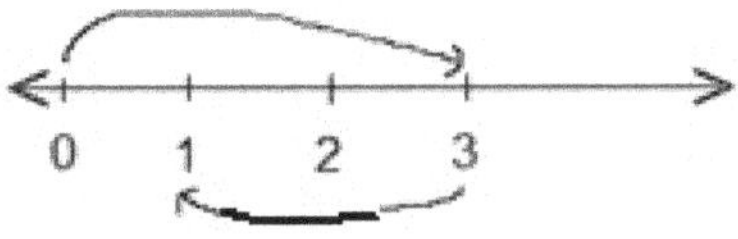

If the following diagram shows 3 - 1 = 2,

Then what is the value of the following diagram?

What is the value of the following diagram?

Write an equation for the following number line.

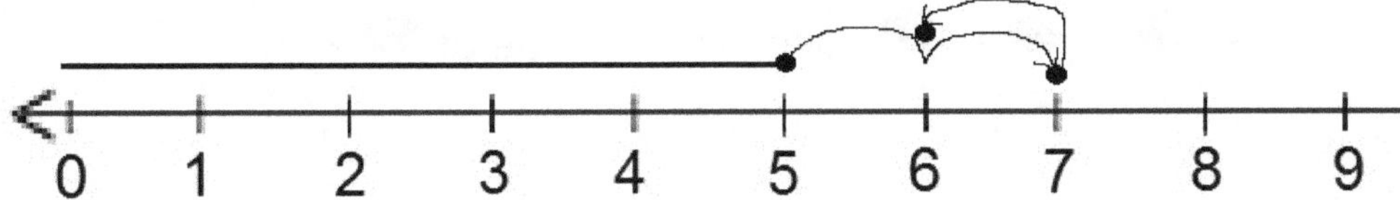

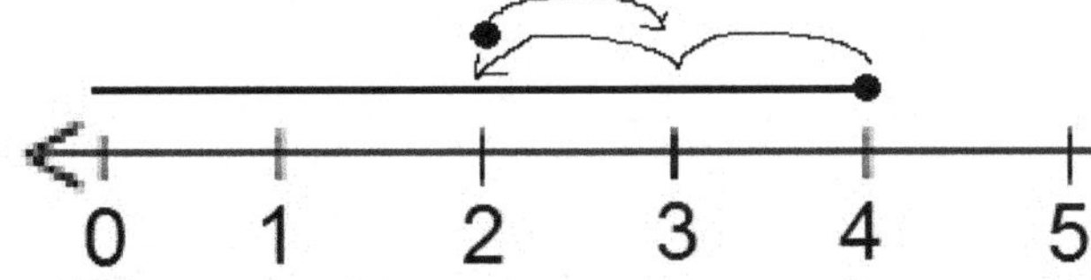

Write the equation for the above number line.

Student's name: ____________________ Assignment date: ________________

37 – 9 =
73 – 4 =
45 – 8 =
89 +7 =
36 – 17 =
What is the largest one-digit number?
What is the largest two-digit number?
What is the smallest two-digit number?
Circle the following even numbers. 177, 46, 8, 91, 32, 21

Insert >, <, or = in ☐.

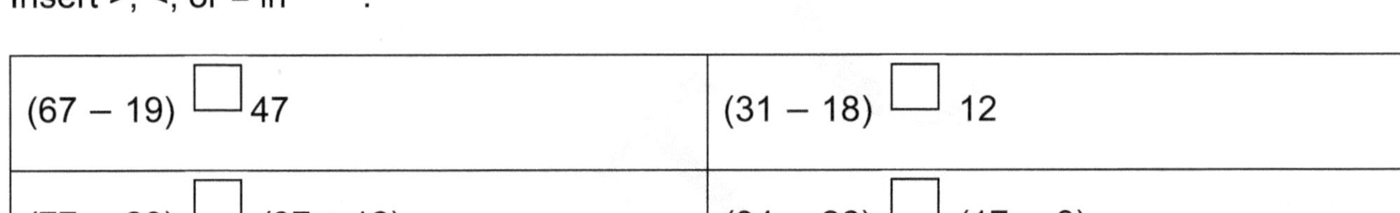

(67 – 19) ☐ 47	(31 – 18) ☐ 12
(77 – 28) ☐ (37 + 12)	(34 – 26) ☐ (17 – 8)

If ● + ● + ● + ● + 6 = 8 + ● + ● + ●, what is the value of ●?

Student's name: ______________________ Assignment date: _________________

Grade 1 and above

▲ – 7 = 16, ▲ + ● = 36 ▲ =? ● = ?
▲ + ▲ = 16, ▲ – ● = 8 ▲ =? ● = ?
▲ + ▲ = 24, ▲ – ● = 6 ▲ =? ● = ?
6+ ▲ = 13, ▲ + ● = 11 ▲ =? ● = ?
● – ▲ = 13, 15 – ▲ = 7 ▲ =? ● = ?
If ● + ■ + ▲ = 21, ● + ■ = 13, ■ + ▲ =12 What values are ●, ■, and ▲ each?
If ▲ + ▲ = 16, ▲ =? ▲ + ● =17, ● =? ● + ■ = 19, ■ =?

Ho Math Chess Primary Grades Math

Test Review assesssment 何数棋谜低年级数学测试複習考核

Student's name: ____________________ Assignment date: ________________

Grade 1 and above

■ + ▲ =12, ■ + ▲ + ▲ + ▲ + ▲ =24 ▲ =? ■ = ?
● – ▲ = 4 ● + ● – ▲ = 10 ● =? ▲ =?
▲ + ▲ + ▲ =44 ● + ● + ● =23 ▲ – ● =?
▲ – ● =10 ▲ + ● =12 ▲ = ? ● = ?
What are the odd numbers which are less than 15?

Student's name: ____________________ Assignment date: ________________

Grade 1 and above

How many squares are in the following figure?
What are the odd numbers which are less than 20?
Ethan is in a lineup for a concert. There are 3 people in front of Ethan and 5 people behind Ethan. How many people are in the lineup?
Adam is 2 years older than Bob now. How old will Adam be more than Bob next year?
Meghan had 17 apples, and she gave two of her friends every 4 apples then. How many apples does she have now?
Andrew has $13, and he wishes to buy applications software, which costs $29. How much more he has to save to buy the software he wants to?

Student's name: ____________________ Assignment date: ________________

Grade 2

Complete the pattern. 5, 51, 511, 5111, _____
Compute 17 + 15 + 13 + 11 + 9 + 7 - 16 - 14 - 12 - 10 - 8 - 6 =
Complete the pattern. 10, 101, 1011, 10111, ______
Circle the number which does not belong to the group. 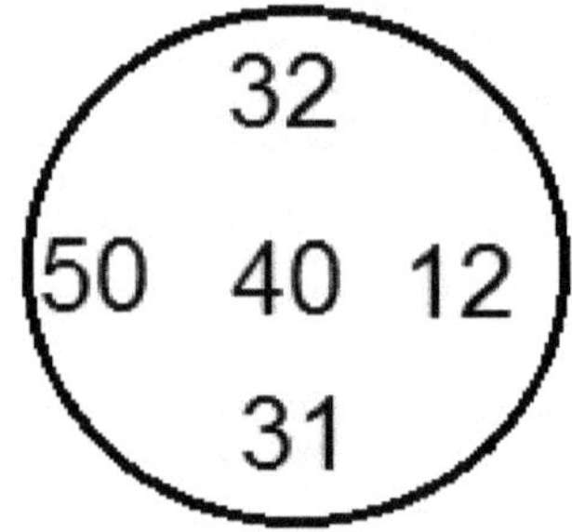
Find the next item.  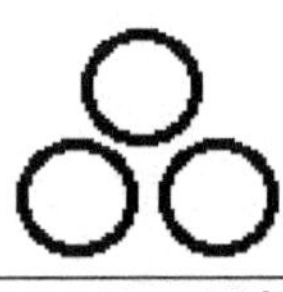 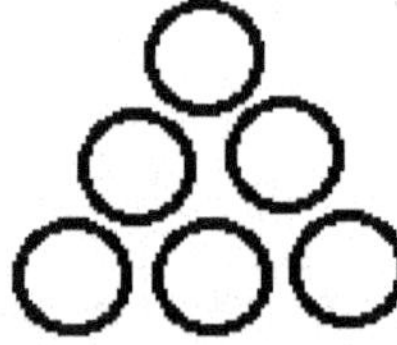
Complete the next number. 88, 96, 11, ______

Student's name: ____________________ Assignment date: ________________

Grade 2 and above

Questions	Solutions
Tammy has 15 books. Tina has 36 books. How many books do they have in all?	
Mike has 37 stickers. Aaron has 19 stickers. How many fewer stickers does Aaron have than Mike?	
Sandy Liang has 29 e-mail messages. Jeffrey Lai has 13 e-mail messages less than Sandy. How many messages do they have in all?	
Jun has 27 cookies, and Veronica has 16 cookies more than Jun. How many cookies they have in all?	
Shirley has finished reading 119 pages of a book, and there are 293 pages left. What is the total number of pages of the book in all?	
14 books were sold, and 29 books are left. How many books were there before selling?	

Student's name: ____________________ Assignment date: ________________

Grade 2 and above

10 people got on the bus, 8 people got off the bus, 5 people got off, and the bus was empty. How many people were on the bus initially (excluding the driver)?	
Jerry would have received as many e-mail messages as Julie if he had 16 more messages. Julie had 37 messages. How many messages did Jerry receive?	

Student's name: ____________________ Assignment date: ________________

Grade 2 and above

One chick has 2 legs. Three chicks, how many legs?
Circle the odd one.
Which figure should be in place of the "?"? ?
What number should replace ? to balance the weights on the scales? 8 + 3 4 + ?
I had 2 pairs of gloves. I lost one glove. How many gloves do I have now?
I am 8 years old, and my brother is 5 years older than me. How old will my brother be next year?
How many rectangles can you see in the following figure?

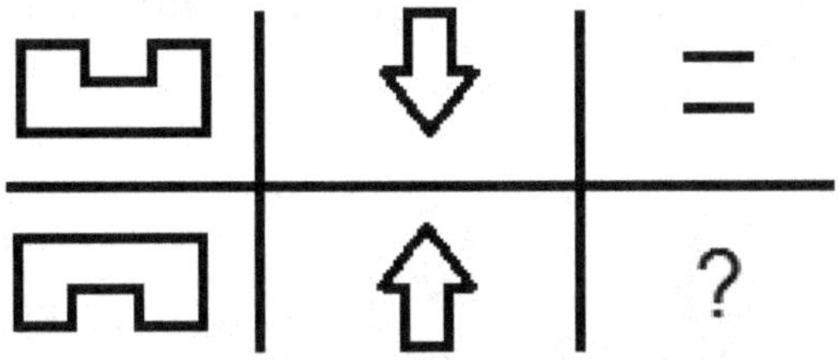

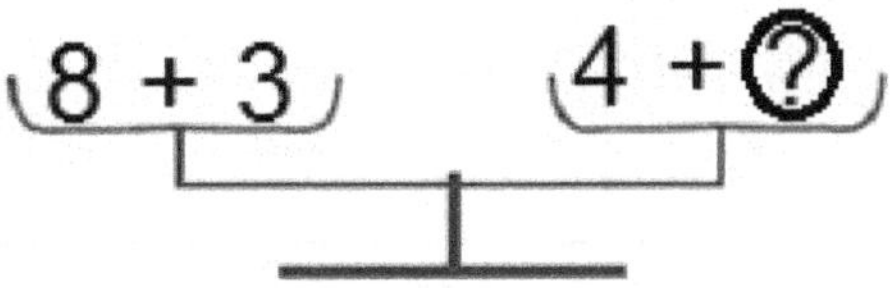

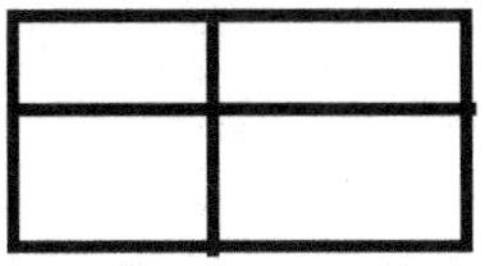

Student's name: ____________________ Assignment date: ________________

Grade 2 and above

After taking six plums from a basket, six were left in the basket. How many plums were in the basket at the beginning?
Bob has 14 oranges more than Adam, and Adam has six oranges. How many oranges do they have altogether?
Amy has nine more apples than Bryan. Bryan has 3 fewer apples than Cathy. Cathy has 13 apples. How many apples does each one of them have?
Bill has four more apples than Bob, and Bob has 8 more apples than Coco. Together, all three have 41 apples. How many apples does each one of them have?
Some birds were on the tree. Seventeen more birds flew back, and eight flew away. Now there are 24 birds on the tree. How many birds were on the tree originally?
Fill in each the same box with the same number. $6 + \square = 13$ $\square + \triangle = 12$

Student's name: ____________________ Assignment date: ________________

Grade 2 and above

If □ = 6 and ○ =3, then □ + ○ =?
5 = 7 – □
□ + 3 – 1 = □ + ?
6 + 4 + □ = 13
7 + 7 + □ = 15
8 + 2 + 5 + 5 + □ = 21
A half dozen is 6. How many is one dozen?
Mom gave me one-half of $4. How much was it?
□□□ – □□□□ + □□□ = ? □
If □ = 2 and ○ =3, then □ + ○ =?
4 + □ = 6
One dog has 4 legs. If there are 12 legs, then how many dogs are there?
One boy has 2 legs. Two boys have ____ legs.
One wagon has 4 wheels, ____ wagons have 8 wheels.
If □ = 7 and ○ = 5, then □ – ? = ○.

Student's name: ____________________ Assignment date: ________________

Grade 2 and above

If 13 + 7 + 6 + ? = 31, then what is ? ?
One boy has 2 legs, and one dog has 4 legs. How many legs are there for 2 boys and 2 dogs?
The following large square is made of 16 small squares, but some of them are missing. How many small squares are missing? 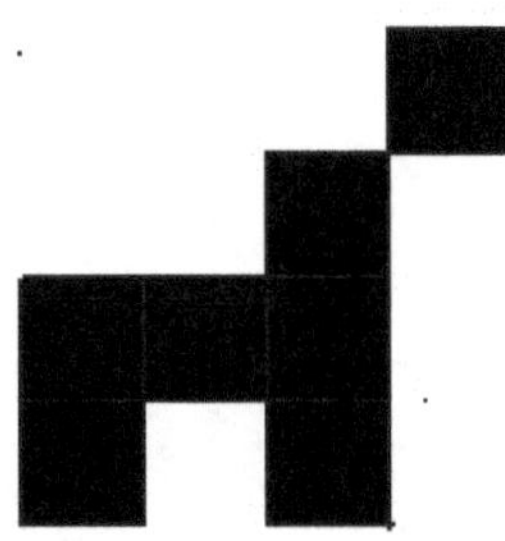
Each dot is two points. Find the value of one (5 dots) + (4 dots) = ○ ○ + □ =31
What number should replace ? to balance the weights on the scale 3. 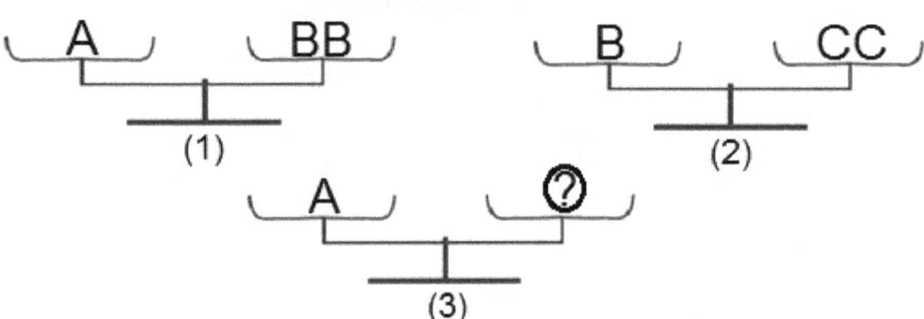 The first two scales are balanced. How many C's are needed to balance the scale 3?

Student's name: ____________________ Assignment date: ________________

Grade 2 and above

Which of the following figure has the longest line in the following figures?

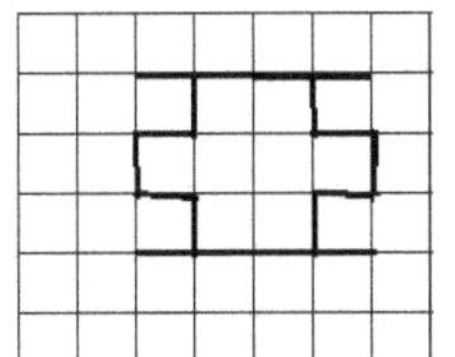 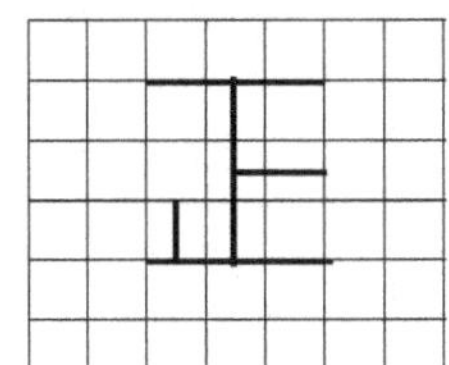 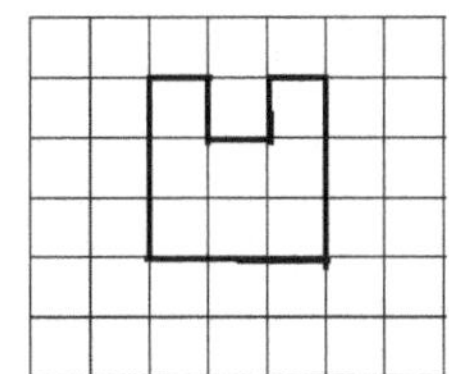 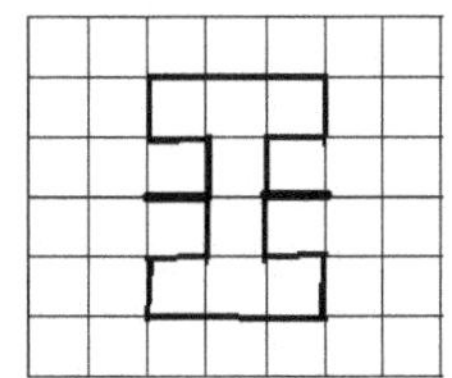

Last month, the cats Kiko and Snow together ate 12 cans of fish. This month they ate 5 more cans of fish than the last month. How many cans of fish did they eat in two months?

The cat Kiko likes to play with pom-pom balls, but often she lost them, and so far, she has lost 21 pom-pom balls in two months. This month she lost twice as many as the last month. How many pom-pom balls she lost last month?

The cat Snow likes to watch leaves falling from trees in the fall by turning his head up and down whenever he sees a leaf falling. This morning he saw 20 leaves falling, and in the afternoon, he saw one less than half of what he saw in the morning. How many leaves fell did Snow see in the morning and the afternoon?

The cat Snow likes to jump up to catch his toy. He jumped high 15 times in the morning, which was one more than twice as many times as he jumped in the afternoon. How many times did he jump in the morning and also in the afternoon altogether?

Student's name: ____________________ Assignment date: ________________

Find the values of the following figures.

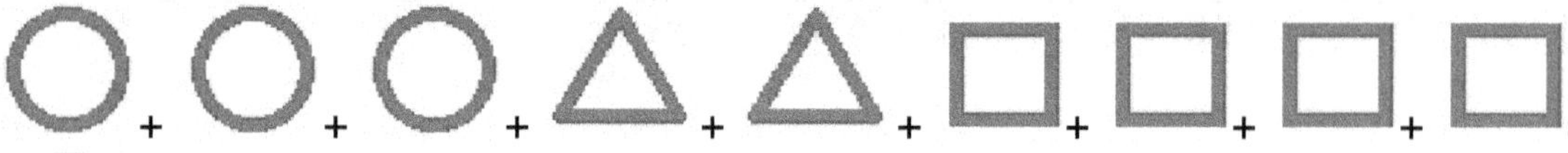

○ + ○ + ○ + △ + △ + □ + □ + □ + □ = 423

○ = ______

△ = ______

□ = ______

Fill in each square by a number from 1 to 6 such that the sum of each line is 9.

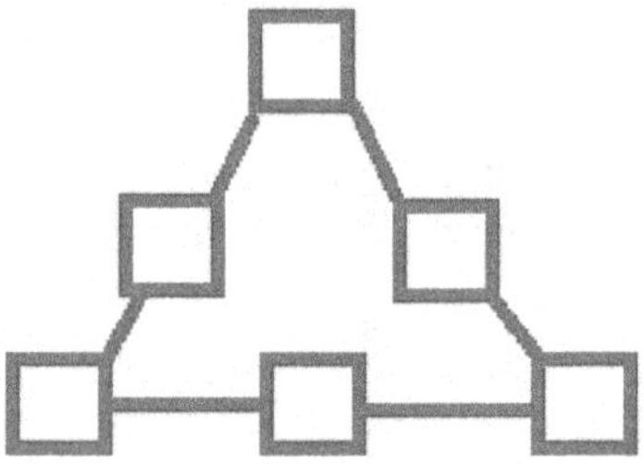

Place the numbers 1, 2, 3, 4, 5 and 6 in the circle so that each line's sum is the same.

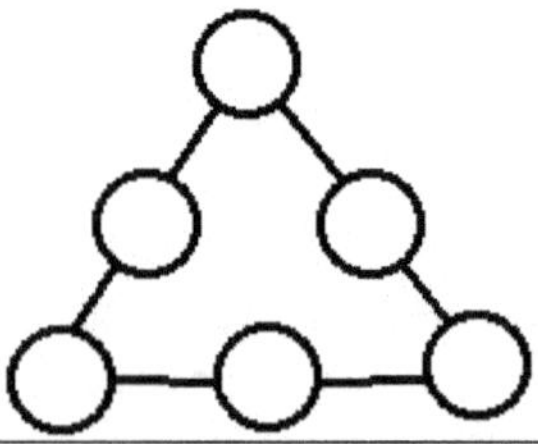

Student's name: ____________________ Assignment date: ________________

Grade 3 and above

Complete the pattern.

5, 51, 511, 5111, ______

Compute 17 + 15 + 13 + 11 + 9 + 7 - 16 - 14 - 12 - 10 - 8 - 6 =

Complete the pattern.

10, 101, 1001, 10001, ______

Circle the number which does not belong to the group.

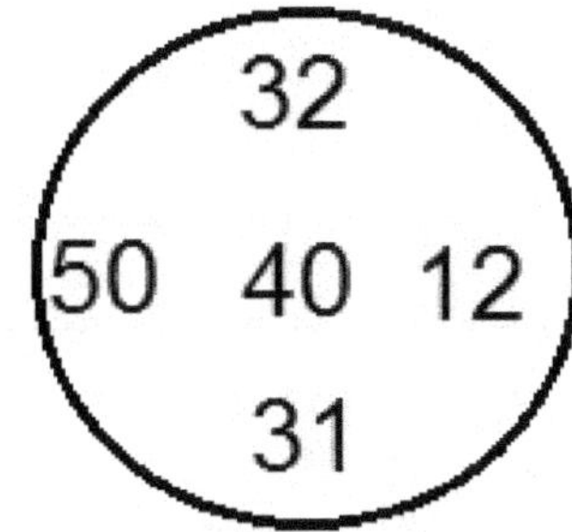

Find the next item.

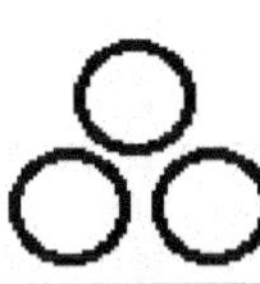

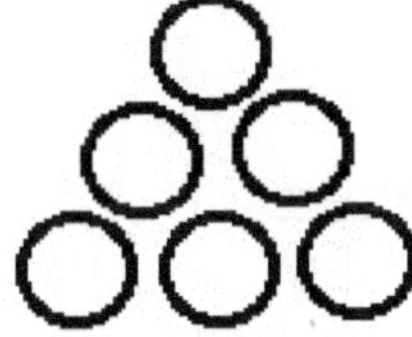

Complete the next number.

88, 96, 11, ______

Student's name: ____________________ Assignment date: ________________

Grade 3 and above

Questions	Solutions
Tammy has 15 books. Tina has 36 books. How many books do they have in all?	
Mike has 37 stickers. Aaron has 19 stickers. How many fewer stickers does Aaron have than Mike?	
Sandy Liang has 29 e-mail messages. Jeffrey Lai has 13 e-mail messages less than Sandy. How many messages do they have in all?	
Jun has 27 cookies, and Veronica has 16 cookies more than Jun. How many cookies they have in all?	
Shirley has finished reading 119 pages of a book, and there are 293 pages left. What is the total number of pages of the book in all?	
14 books were sold, and 29 books are left. How many books were there before selling?	

Student's name: ____________________ Assignment date: ________________

Grade 3 and above

10 people got on the bus, 8 people got off the bus, 5 people got off, and the bus was empty. How many people were on the bus originally (excluding the driver)?	
Jerry would have received as many e-mail messages as Julie if he had 16 more messages. Julie had 37 messages. How many messages did Jerry receive?	

Student's name: ____________________ Assignment date: ________________

Grade 3 and above

One chick has 2 legs. Three chicks, how many legs?
Circle the odd one.
Which figure should be in place of the "?"? ?
What number should replace ? to balance the weights on the scales? 8 + 3   4 + ?
I had 2 pairs of gloves. I lost one glove. How many gloves do I have now?
I am 8 years old, and my brother is 5 years older than me. How old will my brother be next year?
How many rectangles can you see in the following figure?

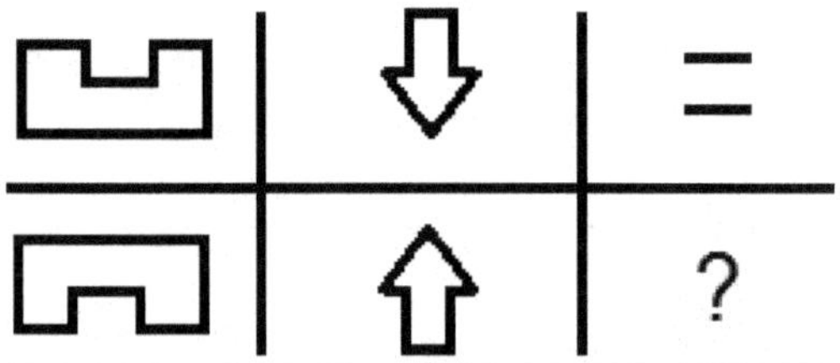

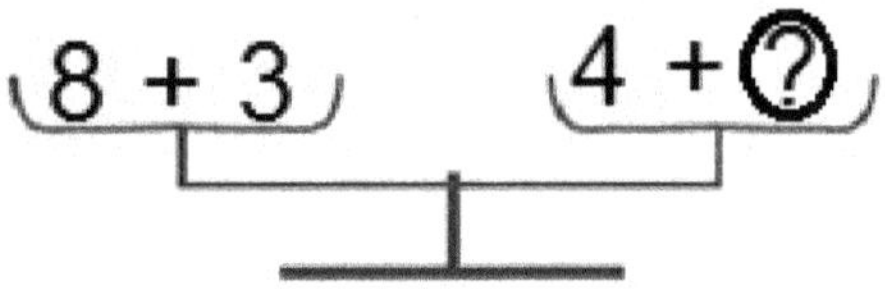

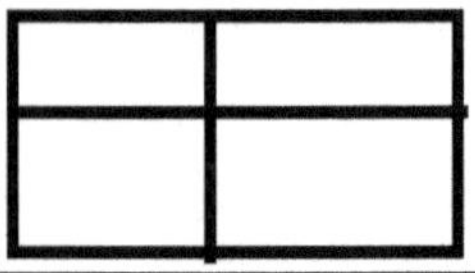

Student's name: ____________________ Assignment date: ________________

Grade 3 or 4

If □ = 6 and ○ =3, then □ + ○ =?
5 = 7 – □
□ + 3 – 1 = □ + ?
6 + 4 + □ = 13
7 + 7 + □ = 15
8 + 2 + 5 + 5 + □ = 21
A half dozen is 6. How many is one dozen?
Mom gave me one-half of $4. How much was it?
□ + □ + □ – □ – □ – □ – □ + □ + □ + □ = □ any number
If □ = 2 and ○ =3, then □ + ○ =?
4 + □ = 6
One dog has 4 legs. If there are 12 legs, then how many dogs are there?
One boy has 2 legs. Two boys have ____ legs.
One wagon has 4 wheels, ____ wagons have 8 wheels.
If □ = 7 and ○ = 5, then □ – ? = ○.

Student's name: ____________________ Assignment date: ________________

Grade 3 or 4

Tommy sent emails to a dozen of his friends. Half dozen of his friends received one page each, and the other half received two pages each. How many pages did his friends receive from Tommy altogether?
Alvin used matches to build square figures as follows. How many matches will he use for the 21st figure if the pattern continues?
Alvin drew squares as follows. How many squares will he draw for the 21st figure if the pattern continues? 2 squares 4 squares 6 squares
Circle the following odd fraction. $\frac{1}{2}$ $\frac{2}{8}$ $\frac{2}{4}$ $\frac{3}{6}$
Jason left Bapton by bike. He rode for one hour and reached the following sign. How long will take Jason to reach Apaton if he continues to ride at the same speed Bapton ⇦ 30 km 20 km ⇨ Apaton

Student's name: ____________________ Assignment date: ________________

Grade 3 or 4

Cathy ate $\frac{2}{3}$ of a pizza and later she ate $\frac{1}{6}$ of the same pizza. How much of the pizza did she eat altogether?
What are the factors of 16?
Paint sells in a 5-litre can. Taylor needs 39 litres. How many cans must he buy?
What is the value of the following underlined digit? 7$\underline{7}$77
Find the pattern rule of the following pattern and then use the pattern rule to find the next number. 3, 8, 18, 38, ______ The pattern rule is ____
The following shows that one apple is worth 2 pears and three pears are worth 4 oranges.  A. Meghan has 6 apples. Use the above information, how many pears could Meghan get? B. How many oranges could Meghan get?

Student's name: ____________________ Assignment date: ________________

Grade 3 or 4

Which of the following fractions is greater than $\frac{1}{2}$?

$\frac{3}{5}$ $\frac{3}{6}$ $\frac{4}{10}$ $\frac{3}{7}$

The scale on a map indicates that 1 cm represents 3 km on the land. If the distance between two towns is 9 cm, how many km are thee between two towns?

An egg pie recipe in the following is for 4 people.

Ingredients	
Eggs	4
Flour	10 cups
Milk	1 cup

Cathy uses the above recipe for 2 people. Find the amount for the ingredients.

Ingredients	
Eggs	?
Flour	?
Milk	?

Five thousand raffle tickets numbered 1 to 5000 were sold. The last three digits of 343 received prizes. What numbers had won the prizes? List all winning numbers.

Student's name: ____________________ Assignment date: ________________

Ho Math Chess Assessment Grade 1

1. Join dots by numbers starting from 1.

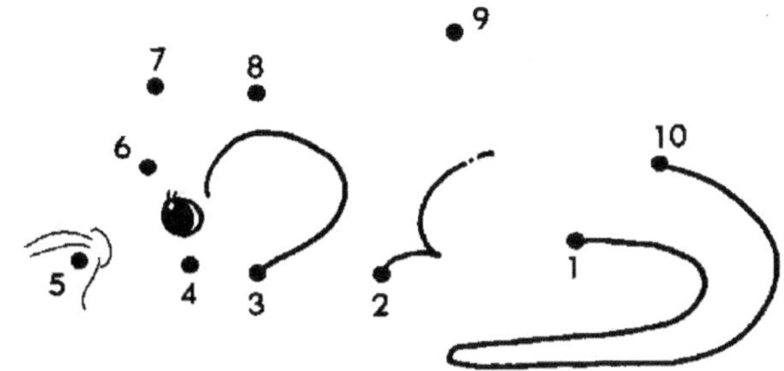

2. Complete each number sequence.
   0, 1, 2, 3, _____, _____, 6, _____
   8, 7, 6, _____, 4, _____, 2
   1, 3, 5, _____, 9
3. Add numbers.

$$\begin{array}{r} 4 \\ +\ 3 \\ \hline \end{array} \quad \begin{array}{r} 7 \\ +\ 9 \\ \hline \end{array} \quad \begin{array}{r} 15 \\ +\ 34 \\ \hline \end{array} \quad \begin{array}{r} 48 \\ +\ 39 \\ \hline \end{array} \quad \begin{array}{r} 64 \\ +\ 78 \\ \hline \end{array} \quad \begin{array}{r} 312 \\ +\ 254 \\ \hline \end{array} \quad \begin{array}{r} 674 \\ +\ 739 \\ \hline \end{array}$$

4. Subtract numbers.

$$\begin{array}{r} 8 \\ -\ 3 \\ \hline \end{array} \quad \begin{array}{r} 79 \\ -\ 47 \\ \hline \end{array} \quad \begin{array}{r} 46 \\ -\ 18 \\ \hline \end{array} \quad \begin{array}{r} 75 \\ -\ 49 \\ \hline \end{array} \quad \begin{array}{r} 638 \\ -\ 224 \\ \hline \end{array} \quad \begin{array}{r} 546 \\ -\ 228 \\ \hline \end{array}$$

5. Draw the correct sign (<, > or =) to make true sentences
   7 3   6 6   4 9   5 11

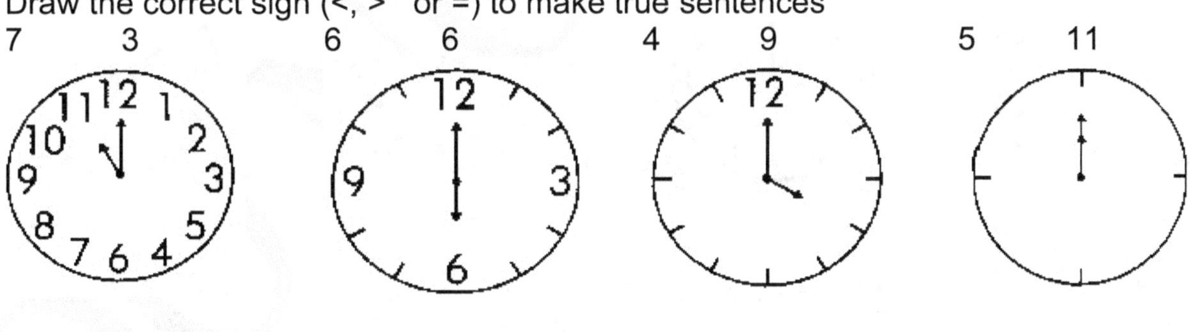

_____________ _____________ _____________ _____________

7. Copy a drawing along the symmetry line.

Ho Math Chess Primary Grades Math

Test Review assessssment 何数棋謎低年级数学测试複習考核

Student's name: ____________________ Assignment date: ________________

Ho Math Chess Assessment Grade 2

1. Fill in the blanks with the missing numbers.
   44 46 ______ 50 52
   996 997 998 999 ________

2. Add numbers.

47 + 32	38 + 84	36 + 28	699 + 248	1875 + 5726
$\begin{array}{r} 47 \\ +\ 32 \\ \hline \end{array}$	$\begin{array}{r} 38 \\ +\ 84 \\ \hline \end{array}$	$\begin{array}{r} 36 \\ +\ 28 \\ \hline \end{array}$	$\begin{array}{r} 699 \\ +\ 248 \\ \hline \end{array}$	$\begin{array}{r} 1875 \\ +\ 5726 \\ \hline \end{array}$

3. Subtract numbers.

57 – 24	71 – 26	84 – 59	468 – 219	906 – 578
$\begin{array}{r} 57 \\ -\ 24 \\ \hline \end{array}$	$\begin{array}{r} 71 \\ -\ 26 \\ \hline \end{array}$	$\begin{array}{r} 84 \\ -\ 59 \\ \hline \end{array}$	$\begin{array}{r} 468 \\ -\ 219 \\ \hline \end{array}$	$\begin{array}{r} 906 \\ -\ 578 \\ \hline \end{array}$

4. Write numbers in standard form.
   For example, Eight hundred thirty-five 835
   Four hundred twenty-one __________ Nine hundred nine
   ____

5. Connect the shapes with their names.

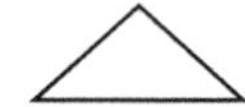

rectangle circle triangle parallelogram square

6. What time is it?

___________ ___________ ___________ ___________

. Multiply numbers.

$5 \times 4 =$ _______ $8 \times 6 =$ _______ $9 \times 7 =$ _______ $7 \times 6 =$ _______

$9 \times 5 =$ _______ $3 \times 7 =$ _______ $6 \times 4 =$ _______ $2 \times 9 =$ _______

$27 \times 6 =$ _______ $35 \times 4 =$ _______ $52 \times 7 =$ _______ $95 \times 6 =$ _______

8. Arrange the angles in order of size. Begin with the smallest one.

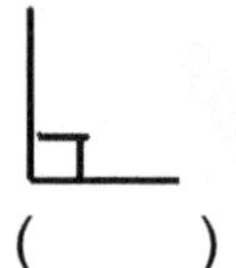

( ) (1)

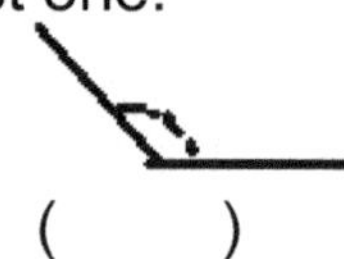

( )

9. Find the number

$7 + 3 - K - 2 = 1$ $9 - M - 1 = 8$ $A - 2 = 8 - A$

K = ________ M = _______ A = ______

Student's name: ____________________ Assignment date: ________________

Ho Math Chess Assessment Grade 3

1. Write the next three numbers in each sequence.
   14, 21, 28, ______, ______, ______
   0, 1, 3, 6, 10, 15, ______, ______, ______

2. Add and Subtract

$$\begin{array}{r} 74 \\ -\ 58 \\ \hline \end{array} \qquad \begin{array}{r} \\ -\ 15 \\ \hline 37 \end{array} \qquad \begin{array}{r} 75 \\ + \quad \\ \hline 123 \end{array} \qquad \begin{array}{r} 536 \\ + \quad \\ \hline 721 \end{array} \qquad \begin{array}{r} 840 \\ - \quad \\ \hline 578 \end{array}$$

3 Multiplication
   $8 \times 9 =$ _____ $5 \times 7 =$ _____ $9 \times 8 =$ _____ $3 \times 6 =$ _____ $7 \times 6 =$ _____

   $35 \times 7 =$ ______ $46 \times 8 =$ ______ $58 \times 26 =$ ______ $356 \times 58 =$ ______

4. Division
   $42 \div 6 =$ ______ $448 \div 7 =$ ______ $276 \div 12 =$ ______ $1344 \div 24 =$ ______

5. Write the numbers
   Five thousand, four hundred seven ________________
   One hundred twenty-two thousand, three hundred forty ________________

6. What fraction of the whole figure is shaded?

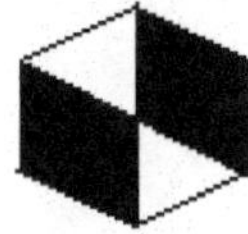   

________ ________ ________ ________

7. Shade the figures as the fractions show

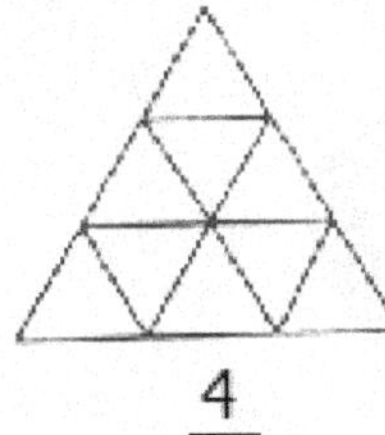

$\frac{4}{9}$

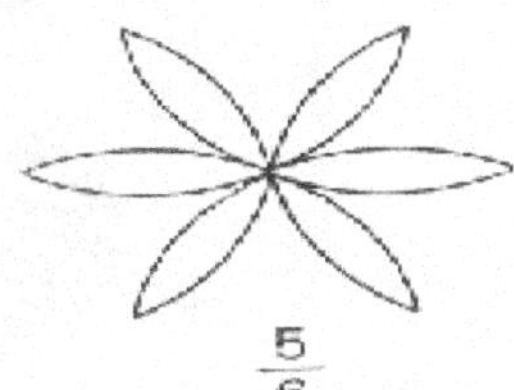

$\frac{5}{6}$

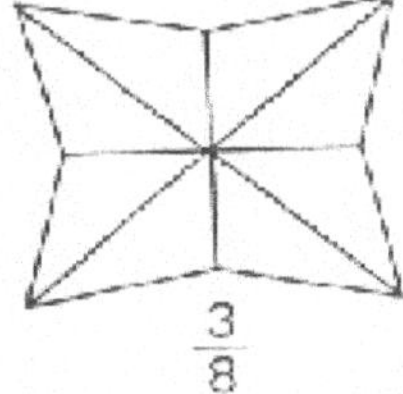

$\frac{3}{8}$

8. Area and Perimeter

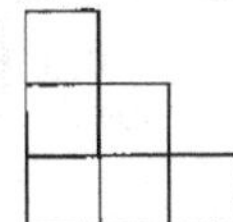

Area = _______ square units
Perimeter = _______ units

9. According to the calendar on the right, answer the following questions

The year 1902 began on what day of the week? ____________
What is the date of the second Tuesday in December 1901? ____________
What is the date of last Wednesday in November 1901? ____________

DECEMBER 1901

S	M	T	W	T	F	S
1	2	3	4	5	6	7
8	9	10	11	12	13	14
15	16	17	18	19	20	21
22	23	24	25	26	27	28
29	30	**31**				

Student's name: ____________________ Assignment date: ________________

Ho Math Chess Assessment Grade 4

1. Multiplication

$14 \times 53 =$ ________ $37 \times 68 =$ ________

$432 \times 26 =$ ________ $123 \times 456 =$ ________

2. Division

$186 \div 3 =$ ______ $4207 \div 7 =$ ________

$840 \div 24 =$ ______ $735 \div 42 =$ ______

3. Naming the face value of the digit 5

Example, 25.34 five ones

452.36 ________________

34.257 ________________

432.65 ________________

4. Write a name under each shape.
(rectangle, triangle, parallelogram, square)

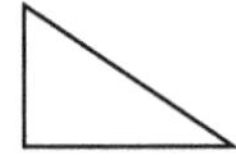

________ ________ ________ ________

5. Comparing decimal numbers
(Using >, <, or =)

(A) 5.0 5.00 (B) 0.4 0.04

(C) 0.2 0.20000 (D) 0.5 0.500

6. Adding and subtracting Fractions

$\frac{4}{6} + \frac{1}{6} =$ ______ $\frac{7}{10} - \frac{4}{10} =$ ______

$\frac{5}{6} - (\frac{5}{6} - \frac{1}{6}) =$ ______

$1\frac{1}{2} + \frac{1}{2} =$ ______

$\frac{2}{5} + \frac{3}{7} =$ ______ $\frac{6}{7} - \frac{4}{5} =$ ______

7. Adding and subtracting decimals

$3.4 + 6.5$ $4.63 + 2.59$ $0.7 - 0.136$

8. Multiplication and division of decimals

6.48×9 3.2×2.8 $2\overline{)4.32}$

9. Comparing fractions by using pictures
(Using >, < or =)

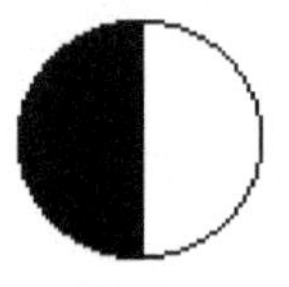

$\frac{1}{2}$ $\frac{2}{3}$

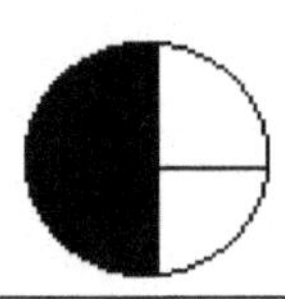

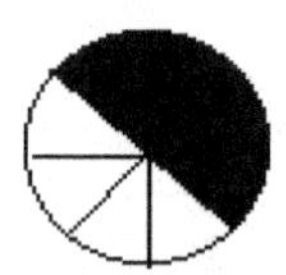

$\frac{2}{4}$ $\frac{4}{8}$

Word problems

1. I wrote 5 consecutive numbers on 5 cards. The sum of the numbers is 15. What numbers did I write on the cards?

2. Bob had 2 tickets for rides at the carnival. Each ride required 1 ticket. There were four rides available for him to take: merry-go-round, ferries wheel, airplane, and roller coaster. How many different ways could Bob use his 2 tickets if each ride needs one ticket?

3. May was arranging coins in the following manner: 1 penny, followed by 2 nickels, followed by 3 dimes, followed by 4 pennies, and then followed by 1 penny, 2 nickels and so on. If she continues in this manner, what coin will be in the thirteenth position?

4. I timed some children walking in the hallway. They walked 5 m in 8 seconds. How far will they walk in 72 seconds?

Student's name: ____________________ Assignment date: ________________

This sheet is for Teachers ONLY

Level 4 and Under Ho Math Chess Assessment
Preparation for Math Assessment

The purpose of Ho Math Chess assessment is not just to find out the potential student's math ability. The equally important purpose is to let the potential student work on a few sample Ho Math Chess problems to taste how Ho Math Chess worksheets are different from other traditional worksheets.

The most common problems that grade 4 and under students often encounter are:

If the student can do 11 – 2, 11 – 3, 36 borrowing subtractions and multiplication facts.

If the student already knows how to play chess, you can show the Ho Math Chess Teaching Set and play half-blind chess or even one-side half-blind chess.

If the student does not know how to play chess or is not interested in playing chess, there is no point in asking them to play chess other than show the Ho Math Chess Teaching Set.

The Assessment is designed to assess cumulative knowledge so you will find out the potential student's weakness and strength.

Students must discover the "fun' after working on Ho Math Chess worksheets, and the teacher should also point out to parents or students how Ho Math Chess worksheets are different from others.

This level 4 Assessment assesses the 4 basic operations of addition, subtraction, multiplication, and division. Not only 4 basic operations are evaluated; the math and chess integrated material is also included to let students understand how Ho Math Chess worksheets are different from others.`

Although level 4 can mean grade 4 in some countries, it is not absolute. Be careful not to dampen the student's enthusiasm if they are already a grade 5 student but are doing a level 4 assessment.

Student's name: ____________________ Assignment date: ________________

This sheet is for Teachers ONLY

Level 4 and Under
Ho Math Chess Assessment

Preparation for Chess Assessment

The teacher can play a short chess game against the potential student and gain a feeling, but to assess the knowledge of check, checkmate, stalemate, castling, or some basic tactics such as fork, pin, discovered check, skewer etc., some test sheets are required to give to the student, In this case, 2-hour assessment is not enough.

Use Ho Math Chess Teaching Set to play the game and introduce half-blind chess or blind chess.
If the student wants to learn chess only, then assign him or her to the chess class taught by the chess teacher.

Student's name: ____________________ Assignment date: ________________

For Students

Level 4 and Under

Ho Math Chess Assessment

www.homathchess.com

Frank Ho, Amanda Ho

Ho Math Chess Learning Centre

fho1928@gmail.com

Please skip any questions you cannot do. This assessment is not intended to evaluate your overall math ability but is specially designed to find out your working on basic math.

Student's name: ____________________ Assignment date: ________________

Assessment of math basics - addition
(♔ = 0, ♙ = 1, ♗ = 3, ♘ = 3, ♖ = 5, ♕ = 9)
(Explain the chess point system to students if they do not know.)

0123456789

(The above is the dotted Arabic numeration for children who like to use fingers. Count dots to replace counting fingers, and then finally, the student should be able to calculate intuitively without using fingers.)

170	123	103	613	23
– 6	– 15	– 18	– 19	– 16
167	100	15	24	33
– 19	– 8	– 7	– 6	– 14
– 19	– 114	– 12	– □□	– 17

Student's name: ____________________ Assignment date: ________________

- These sheets evaluate the addition of 1 digit + 1 digit and multi-digit addition and its reverse calculation with or without carrying over. Check carefully and see if the student can do carrying over or not.
- You can see how many digits of addition the student can do and if they can work backwards.
- This sheet also assesses whether the student can convert an abstract symbol to numbers (i.e., chess symbol to its corresponding point). Observe to see if the student knows how to add from the bigger number to the smaller number

Student's name: ____________________ Assignment date: ________________

Assessment of mental math from 1 to 10

Fill in each ____ by a number.

2 numbers	+	−	×	Larger number ÷smaller number. (use fraction if not divisible.)
__, __ 4, 2	6	2	______	______
______, ______	9	______	18	______
______, ______	3	______	______	2
______, ______	14	______	______	$\frac{9}{5}$
______, ______	15	1	______	_____
______, ______	______	5	24	______
______, ______	12	6	______	______
______, ______	______	4	12	______
______, ______	14	2	______	___

- Observe if the student can do math mentally. It will be helpful to the student to do word problems if the student can do math mentally
- If the student uses fingers to do the computation, these kinds of questions may present some difficulty for students.

Student's name: ______________________ Assignment date: _________________

Assessment of mental math from 11 to 18

Fill in each _____ by a number.

2 numbers	+	−	×	Larger number ÷ smaller number. (use fraction if not divisible.)
__14_, __5___	19	9	______ 70	______ $\frac{14}{5}$
______, ______	24	______	128	______
______, ______	______	______	48	3
______, ______	26	8	______	______
______, ______	______	9	______	2
______, ______	18	4	______	______
______, ______	18	8	______	______
______, ______	______	______	98	2
______, ______	______	9	______	2

- Observe if the student can do math mentally. It will be helpful to the student to do word problems if the student can do math mentally
- If the student uses fingers to do the computation, then these kinds of questions may present some difficulty for students.

Student's name: ____________________ Assignment date: ________________

Assessment of word problems – addition and subtraction

Ho gives 3 sheets of lined paper to Wendy, then each of them has an equal number of sheets. Altogether they have 28 sheets. How many sheets does each have originally?
If I add 4 and subtract 5, then add 7, I will get 22. What number am I?
If I subtract 5 and add 17, then subtract 6, I will get 39. What number am I?
If Coco gives Meghan 5 cookies and then Meghan gives 3 cookies to Coco, they have the same cookies. Together they have 24 cookies. How many cookies does each of them have in the beginning?
In 5 years, Andrew will be 12 years old, and 5 years ago, Meghan was 5 years old. What is the total age of both Meghan and Andrew now?

Student's name: ____________________ Assignment date: ________________

Spatial relation and logic

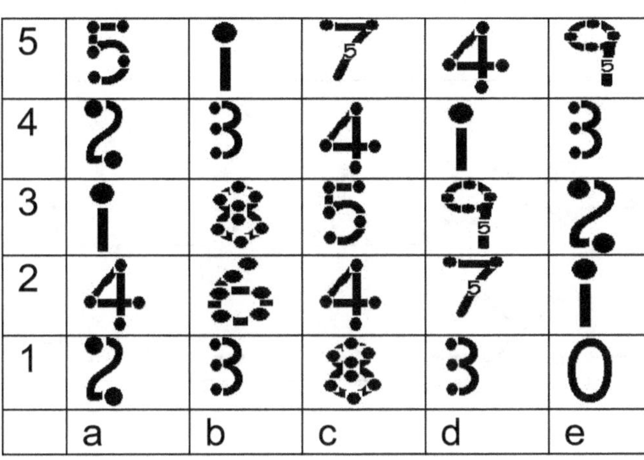

5 is the total of the following 2 numbers.

If you are at a3 and the symbol ✥ 3 indicates to move to the right 3 squares (to reach the square numbered 9), what number will ✥ 2 reach _______ .

If you are at a3 and the symbol ⤧ 2 indicates to move diagonally 2 squares (to reach the square numbered 7, what number will ⤧ 2 reach _______ .

This sheet is to let the student get a taste of what Ho Math and Chess integrated material is all about.

Student's name: ____________________ Assignment date: ________________

Assessment of multiplication

Fill in each ? by a number such that a1 × a2 = a3 and b1 × b2 = b3.

↘ = a1 × b2, ↙ = b1 × a2.

Example

3	6	1
2	? 2	? 1
1	? 3	? 1
	a	b

↘ + ↙ = __3__ + __2__ = 5

↘ − ↙ = __3__ − __2__ = 1

3	6	2
2	?	?
1	?	?
	a	b

↘ + ↙ = ____ + ____ = 13

↘ − ↙ = ____ − ____ = 11

3	6	2
2	?	?
1	?	?
	a	b

↘ + ↙ = ____ + ____ = 8

↘ − ↙ = ____ − ____ = 4

This is to see if the student can do the basics of multiplication and introduce math and chess-integrated problems.

This is the general multiplication. If the student has problems, then use the workbook of Multiplication or use the Test of Future Math Star workbook or High-Performance workbook.

Watch the speed when the student is working on this sheet.

Student's name: ____________________ Assignment date: ________________

Assessment of multiplication

Fill in each ? by a number such that a1 × a2 = a3 and b1 × b2 = b3.

╲ = a1 × b2, ╱ = b1 × a2.

<table><tr><td>3</td><td>6</td><td>2</td></tr><tr><td>2</td><td>?</td><td>?</td></tr><tr><td>1</td><td>?</td><td>?</td></tr><tr><td></td><td>a</td><td>b</td></tr></table>	╳ + ╳ = ____ + ____ = 7 ╳ − ╳ = ____ − ____ = 1
<table><tr><td>3</td><td>6</td><td>3</td></tr><tr><td>2</td><td>?</td><td>?</td></tr><tr><td>1</td><td>?</td><td>?</td></tr><tr><td></td><td>a</td><td>b</td></tr></table>	╳ + ╳ = ____ + ____ = 19 ╳ − ╳ = ____ − ____ = 17
<table><tr><td>3</td><td>6</td><td>3</td></tr><tr><td>2</td><td>?</td><td>?</td></tr><tr><td>1</td><td>?</td><td>?</td></tr><tr><td></td><td>a</td><td>b</td></tr></table>	╳ + ╳ = ____ + ____ = 11 ╳ − ╳ = ____ − ____ = 7

This is to see if the student can do the basics of multiplication and also to introduce the concept of math and chess integrated problems.

Watch the speed when the student is working on this sheet.

Ho Math Chess Primary Grades Math

Test Review assesssment 何数棋謎低年级数学测试複習考核

Frank Ho, Amanda Ho www.homathchess.com

Student's name: ____________________ Assignment date: ________________

Assessment of multiplication (order of operations)

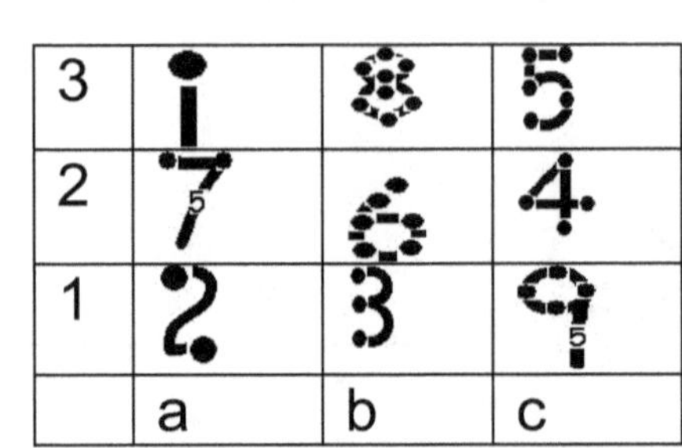

You are at b2 = ☐.

☐ + ✥ × (☐ – 1) = ____ + ____ × ____ = ____
☐ + ✥ × (☐ – 1) = ____ + ____ × ____ = ____
☐ + ✥ × (☐ – 1) = ____ + ____ × ____ = ____
☐ + ✥ × (☐ – 1) = ____ + ____ × ____ = ____
☐ + ╳ × (☐ – 1) = ____ + ____ × ____ = ____
☐ + ╳ × (☐ – 1) = ____ + ____ × ____ = ____
☐ + ╳ × (☐ – 1) = ____ + ____ × ____ = ____
☐ + ╳ × (☐ – 1) = ____ + ____ × ____ = ____

This is to see if the student can do the basics of multiplication and also to introduce the concept of math and chess integrated problems.

Watch the speed when the student is working on this sheet.

Student's name: ____________________ Assignment date: ________________

Whole number multiplying or dividing by a whole number

Horizontal division form	Fraction form	Work Area	Answer in decimal to tenth.	Answer in %
24 ÷ 2	$\frac{24}{2}=\frac{12}{1}$			1200%
2420 ÷ 11	220/1			22000%
14670 × 1000	$\frac{14670000}{1}$			1467000000%
170017 ÷ 17	10001/1			1000100%
90040523 ÷ 100	$900405\frac{23}{100}$			90040523%

This is the general division. If the student has a problem, use Division or use Test of Future Math Star workbooks or High-Performance Math.
Watch and see if the student can handle there are 0's in the middle of the dividend.
What happens when the divisor is 10's power. Does the student know the shortcut way of dividing by 10's power?
Does the student know the shortcut way of multiplying by 10's power?

Student's name: ____________________ Assignment date: ________________

Word problem for multiplication and division

What is the smallest 1-digit number if it divided by 2 the remainder is 1 and divided by 3 the remainder is 2? What is the smallest 2-digit number when it is divided by 2 the remainder is 1 and divided by 3, the remainder is 2?
,
How many different pairs of outfits can Melody have if she has 3 different kinds of skirts and 5 kinds of T-shirts?
The cost of each ticket for a child is $5 and for each adult is $7. What is the average cost per ticket if a family of 2 children and 2 adults bought tickets for every member of the family?

This is to evaluate the student's multiplication or division ability.

Student's name: ____________________ Assignment date: ________________

Introducing Ho Math Chess™

Ho Math Chess™= math + puzzles + chess

Frank Ho, a Canadian math teacher, intrigued by math and chess relationships after teaching his son chess, started Ho Math Chess™ in 1995. His long-term devotion to research has led his son to become a FIDE chess master and Frank's publications of over 20 math workbooks. Today Ho Math Chess™ is the world's largest and the only franchised scholastic math, chess and puzzles specialty learning center with worldwide locations. Ho Math Chess™ is a leading research organization in math, chess, and puzzles integrated teaching methodology.

There are hundreds of articles already published showing chess benefits children and that math puzzles are an excellent way of improving brainpower. So, by integrating chess and mathematical chess puzzles, the learning effect is more significant.

Parents send their children to Ho Math Chess™ because they like Ho Math Chess™ teaching philosophy – offering children problem-solving questions in a variety of formats. The questions could be pure chess, chess puzzles or mathematical chess puzzles in the nature of logic, pattern, tree structure, Venn diagram, probability and many more math concepts.

Ho Math Chess™ has developed a series of unique and high-quality math, chess, and puzzles integrated workbooks. Ho Math Chess™ produced the world's first workbook Learning Chess to Improve Math. This workbook is not only for learning chess but also for enriching math ability. This sets Ho Math Chess apart from other math learning centers, chess club, or chess classes.

The teaching method at Ho Math Chess™ is to use math, chess, and puzzles integrated workbooks to teach children fun math. The purposes of Ho Math Chess™ teaching method and workbooks are to:

- Improve math marks.
- Develop problem-solving and critical thinking skills.
- Improve logic thinking ability.
- Boost brainpower.

Testimonials, sample worksheets, reports, and franchise information can be found at www.homathchess.com.

More information about Ho Math Chess™ can also be found from the following publications:

1. Why Buy a Ho Math Chess™ Learning Centre Franchise: A Unique Learning Centre?
2. Ho Math Chess™ Sudoku Puzzles Sample Worksheets
3. Introduction to Ho Math Chess™ and its Founder Frank Ho

The above publications can be purchased from www.amazon.com.

www.ingramcontent.com/pod-product-compliance
Lightning Source LLC
LaVergne TN
LVHW081400110826
845149LV00010B/1624

* 9 7 8 1 9 8 8 3 0 0 3 4 4 *